Understanding North-West Indian Economy

Understanding North-West Indian Economy

Edited by

H. S. Shergill
Sucha Singh Gill
Gurmail Singh

SERIALS PUBLICATIONS
NEW DELHI (INDIA)

First Published - 2011

ISBN: 978-81-8387-453-3

Published by

SERIALS PUBLICATIONS
4830/24, Prahlad Street, Ansari Road
Darya Ganj, New Delhi-110002 (India)
Phone : 23245225 Fax : 91-11-23272135
E-mail: serials@sify.com

Contents

Acknowledgements

The inspiration to bring out this volume on North-western Region Economies came from Professor R.C. Sobti, Vice-Chancellor, Panjab University. We sincerely thank him for his continuous encouragement to complete this work in time. We are also grateful to Professor Sukhadeo Thorat, Chairman, UGC and President of Indian Economic Association, and Professor G.K. Chadha, C.E.O. South Asian University for encouragement and support in this venture. Our sincerest thanks also go to Dr. Anil Thakur, Organizing Secretary of Indian Economic Association for undertaking the task of getting it published in time. This volume includes 17 contributions made by 28 economists individually and jointly. We are grateful to them all for graciously acceding to our request to contribute their valuable research papers despite the short time given to them for this purpose. The colleagues in the Department of Economics, Panjab University have contributed to the completion of this volume in various ways; we are highly obliged them all.

Finally, we thank the publishers who made possible its publication in a record time.

List of Contributors

Deepty Bansal, Research Scholar, Department of Economics, Punjabi University, Patiala.

Reena Bhasin, Associate Professor of Economics, University School of Open Learning, Panjab University,Chandigarh.

Jaswinder Singh Brar, Reader, Centre for Research in Economic Change, Punjabi University, Patiala.

B.R.Garg, Department of Economics and Sociology, Punjab Agricultural University, Ludhiana.

Angrej Singh Gill, Lecturer in Economics, Government College of Commerce and Business Administration, Chandigarh.

Sucha Singh Gill, Director General, Centre for Research in rural and Industrial Development Chandigarh.

Ranjit Singh Ghuman, Professor and Head, Department of Economics, Punjabi University, Patiala..

Sanjay Gupta, Computer Programmer, Centre for Research in rural and Industrial Development, Chandigarh.

Shafali Jain, Research Scholar, Department of Economics, Punjabi University, Patiala.

Baljinder Kaur, Department of Economics and Sociology, Punjab Agricultural University, Ludhiana.

Manjeet Kaur,. Department of Economics and Sociology, Punjab Agricultural University, Ludhiana.

Parvinder Kaur, Department of Economics and Sociology, Punjab Agricultural University, Ludhiana.

H.S. Kingra, Department of Economics and Sociology, Punjab Agricultural University, Ludhiana.

M.R. Khurana, Professor of Economics, Department of Economics, Punjab University, Chandigarh.

Amrit Kaur Mahal, Department of Mathematics, Statistics and Physics, Punjab Agricultural University, Ludhiana.

Sangeeta, Department of Economics and Sociology, Punjab Agricultural University, Ludhiana.

M.K. Sekhon, Department of Economics and Sociology, Punjab Agricultural University, Ludhiana.

H.S. Shergill, Emeritus Professor of Economics, Department of Economics, Punjab University, Chandigarh

M.S. Sidhu, Professor and Head, Department of Economics and Sociology, Punjab Agricultural University, Ludhiana.

Jasdev Singh, Department of Economics and Sociology, Punjab Agricultural University, Ludhiana.

J.M. Singh, Department of Economics and Sociology, Punjab Agricultural University, Ludhiana.

Lakhwinder Singh Professor of Economics, Department of Economics, Punjabi University, Patiala.

Parminder Singh, Senior Research Investigator, Department of Economics and Sociology, Punjab Agricultural University, Ludhiana.

Sukhpal Singh, Centre for Management of Agriculture, Indian Institute of Management, Ahmedabad.

Sukhwinder Singh, Professor of Economics, Centre for Research in Economic Change, Punjabi University, Patiala.

Sukhpal Singh, Professor of Economics, Department of Economics and Sociology, Punjab Agricultural University, Ludhiana.

Varinder Pal Singh, Research Fellow, Department of Economics, and Sociology, Punjab Agricultural University, Ludhiana.

Madhu Tandon, Associate Professor, DAV PG College, Lucknow.

Biotechnology in Economic Development of India
(In Lieu of Foreword)

R. C. Sobti & Sanjeev Puri

Ever since a breakthrough discovery of double helical structure of DNA by Watson & Crick in 1953, last 58 years has seen some truly amazing developments. At present we are on the threshold of a new era where basic sciences powered with molecular, cellular, genetics, nano, and information technologies is fast revolutionizing the biotech sector in an unprecedented manner. Through this article an attempt has been made to showcase tremendous potential that biotechnology has for overall sustainable and economically viable development in a country like India which is multiethnic, multicultural with rich heritage and biodiversity. Today the biotech sector covers both the basic and the application based areas spanning pharma, agriculture, bioinstrumentation, bioinformatics, textile, biobased industry, medicine, environment and biodiversity. Focusing on these lines Indian Biotech sector has evolved tremendously and holds a promising future in the field of agriculture, pharma and molecular medicine, the three main pillars accounting for major chunk of sustainable economic development. Together, efforts are now targeted towards developing newer technologies for the overall maintenance of the ecosystem and biodiversity. Depleting biodiversity can lead to large financial risks for the economy. This has been demonstrated in a recent study called The Economics of Ecosystems and Biodiversity (TEEB) publically introduced for the first time in October at the COP 10 in Nagoya, Japan. The study has calculated the costs associated with diminishing biodiversity as exemplified by an epidemic among pollinating bees that led to significant crop shortfalls in fruits and vegetables. The annual economic loss due to this epidemic was found to be ~ 150 billion dollars. This exhibits that protecting biodiversity provides economies with many chances. Like this, there are numerous other examples where the biotech sector plays a significantly crucial role in paving a way for saving the biodiversity and thus stable and sustainable economy.

The economy of India is the eleventh largest economy in the world by nominal GDP and the fourth largest by purchasing power parity (PPP). Following strong economic reforms from the socialist inspired economy of a post-independence Indian nation, the country began to develop a fast-paced economic growth, as free market principles were initiated in 1990 for international competition and foreign investment. Since 1991, continuing economic liberalization has moved the country toward a market-based economy. A revival of economic reforms and better economic policy in first decade of the 21st century accelerated India's economic growth rate. In recent years, Indian cities have continued to liberalize business regulations, specifically in the biotech sector (Example of Karnatka government). In spite of the recession, compared to many other countries India is an emerging economic power with a very large pool of human and natural resources, and a growing large pool of skilled professionals. According to the book 'Contours of the World Economy, 1-2030AD' by Angus Maddison, India was the largest economy from the year 1 AD until the colonial period whereupon it was taken over by other countries such as China and the U.K. Economists predict that by 2020, India will be among the leading economies of the world.

The Biotech sector offers new opportunities for global partnerships to serve the needs of sustainable economic development. The vision document of department of biotechnology (DBT) on September 2001 laid down the clear and specific policies to channelize the public and private sectors efforts to make country a global leader in the biotechnology. There are almost 17 recombinant products, which have been approved for marketing in India as of today. It is expected that this number will move up to approximately 100 biotech products. (both domestic and imported) The industry has tremendous employment potential and about 50,000 scientists would be working in Indian biotechnology labs in 2010.

Agriculture is the backbone of Indian Economy. Agriculture and Allied sectors contribute nearly 25 per cent of Gross Domestic Production (GDP), while about 65-70 per cent of the population is dependent on agriculture for their livelihood. India has achieved a major breakthrough in agricultural production as a result of technology evolved by Indian scientists and its wide adoption by the farmers. However, India would need to increase the food production to 250 millions tones by the 2020. Therefore, there is a need for critical appraisal of the post-green revolution technology to draw up a balance sheet so that strategies are evolved for achieving sustainable agriculture. Realizing the need for the food grain and depleting solid fertility, policymakers have been emphasizing the need for new initiatives to boost agricultural outputs. This would not only be essential for ensuring healthy economic growth in the country but also for improving the livelihoods of the poor in rural India. This has been now made possible through cutting edge plant biotechnological advancement efforts that are inclined towards increasing the yield and improvising nutritional quality of food to meet the needs of average Indian citizen. The formulation of a comprehensive policy for agriculture biotechnology emphasizing on genomics, proteomics, trancriptomics, genetic engineering transgenesis, micro propagation, biofuels, biofertilizers, plant tissue culture and other molecular tools etc. has started giving fruit for the overall development in the country and saving lots of foreign revenue due to indigenized technology. Among many few examples are vitamin A enriched golden rice., insect/pest resistance varieties, with increased nutrional value and shelf life of rice, brinjal, tomato, banana, cabbage, mustard, mung bean and wheat etc. Thus Biotechnology in India has evolved from textbooks discipline in university/colleges/school to a level that is now yielding fruit in terms of profit-making business enterprises. In line with the success of the Biotechnology industry that led to sustained economic growth in the developed nations like US, European countries and Canada, India is also fast emerging as a key player in biotechnology related research activities and capital investments. This year only, i.e. 2010 the contribution of biotechnology in agriculture amounted to ~ 34% with a major thrust to the Indian economy.

Similarly the medical industry also got tremendous growth due to biotechnology. As per the CII estimate for the end of 2010 health care products may account for 40 % share of the market. Indian Biotech pharma/medicine sector has started newer initiatives including partnering and outsourcing activities in contract R&D, drug development and clinical trials with various countries. This would mean a stronger impact on building ties globally as well as the economic development in the country. As per one estimate the contract research and development alone could generate a revenue more than US $ 1 billion while the global requirement for the clinical trials can amount to about US $ 8 Billion, thus India is at a real advantage of reaping the best out of these through a focused biotechnological approach. Through out the world the pharma industry is under the pressure of developing new therapeutic molecules and presently focusing on bioifnformatics as a tool, of biotechnology, to achieve it. India is already on the benefit as bioinformatics requires the software capabilities together with biological information. In Software sector India has already a force to reckon with hence can provide credibility to major pharma players of the world to subcontract the bioinformatics skills and competence from India, certainly a win -win situation for the country.

Through Biotechnology, The costly lives saving drugs are now with in the reach of avergae person thus saving the life of millions who otherwise could not afford. The examples are fo various vaccines, Clot busters etc.

In India, The Department of Biotechnology (DBT) and various Centers of Excellence provide backbone of pushing research activities and laying foundation for generating knowledge and trained manpower to assist entrepreneurship programs and biotech private industry. Several industry houses from the "old industry" have already jumped in the Indian biotechnology market to take advantage of the opportunities this new and exciting field. The biotech industry, which currently boasts of ~600 biotech firms, will witness the doubling of these firms in next three-four years.

According to a report of Confederation of Indian Industries (CII) the expected growth of **biotechnology** sector in the country would go upto the tune of US $ US $ ~25 billion in the next four to five years. Equipped with the technologies like recombinant DNA Technology, cell and cell technologies, immunotechnologies, nanotechnology Stem Cell & tissue Engineering etc are increasingly being used to manufacture newer products and opened up newer avenues for the biotech industry both at national & international level.

The research & development in biotechnology has to be a global effort as this industry is both knowledge and capital intensive. The capital investment and international collaborations are mandatory for its future growth. The Govt of India under the headship of Mr. Kapil Sibal is thus spearheading a biotech program to involve foreign academic and research institutions with Indian counterparts with ultimate aim to strengthen the economic development for a stronger India.

R. C. Sobti

Vice Chancellor Panjab University, Chandigarh.

Sanjeev Puri

Professor, University Institute of Engineering and Technology,
Panjab University, Chandigarh.

1

Introduction

North-West India consists of states of Haryana, Punjab, Himachal Pradesh, Jammu and Kashmir, and Delhi and Union Territory of Chandigarh. Except for Jammu and Kashmir, all other four states have been largely part of Punjab state that came into existence in 1947 and after merger of PEPSU in it in 1956. Only small territory of Himachal Pradesh was not part of it. Thus, there are a large number of commonality among these states in terms of laws, rules and regulation of the old Punjab, applicable in them. Generally, pay scales, allowances and promotions to employees are given most of time on Punjab pattern. The North-West region constitutes about 11.33 per cent of the geographical area of the country, 6 per cent population (as per 2001 Census) and 8.01 per cent of the GDP of the country. But with their separation in 1966 into four states and union territory have allowed them to charter their own strategy of social and economic development. This has been reflected more vividly in the era of liberalized economy. In terms of rates of growth, the states of Haryana and Himachal Pradesh have achieved high growth rates matching all India average during Eighth (1992-97), Ninth (1997-2002) and Tenth (2002-07) Five Year Plans and have fixed target growth rates for the Eleventh Five Year Plan (2007-12) higher than the all India average of 9.0 per cent per annum (GOI, 2007). On the other hand, the

Punjab state having high growth rates and highest per capita income earlier has registered a slow growth rate ranging between 4.4 per cent to 4.7 per cent during three five year plans between 1992 to 2007 compared to all India average ranging between 5.5 per cent to 7.7 per cent. During the Eleventh Five Year Plan, the Punjab has fixed the target growth rate of 5.9 per cent (lowest among the states) against the all India target growth rate of 9.0 per cent per annum. The state of Jammu and Kashmir recorded a growth rate of 5.0 per cent to 5.2 per cent during the three plans between 1992-2007 and fixed a target growth rate for the Eleventh Plan at 6.4 per cent (second lowest in the country after Punjab). Thus, there are two fast growing states of Haryana and Himachal Pradesh and two are slow growth states of Punjab and Jammu and Kashmir. Consequently, Haryana has achieved highest per capita income of Rs.67,891 (at current prices) in 2007-08 compared all India per capita income of Rs.37,490/-. This is followed by Punjab (50,558/-), Himachal Pradesh and Jammu and Kashmir. The per capita income of Jammu and Kashmir is not only lowest (Rs.24,214/- during 2006-07) but is just 75 per cent of the all India average. The per capita income of all other states, including Delhi and UT Chandigarh, has been and continue to be higher than all India average (GOI, 2010).

The states in the North-West India differ not only in per capita income and growth rates, in their gross state domestic product (GSDP) but also in geographical features. The states of Himachal Pradesh and Jammu and Kashmir are Hill States located in ranges of Himalaya Mountains; the states of Punjab and Haryana are part of Indo-Gigantic plains. Both Punjab and Haryana states have been centres of green revolution and contribute a very high proportion of their grain production to the central pool of the grain procured in the country. The agriculture in both the states is dominated by wheat-paddy rotation and they produce surplus grains produced through irrigation system of perennial canals and electricity operated tube wells. In the hill states, agriculture is largely rain fed is dominated by horticulture crops supplemented by production of food grains. The state of Delhi and union territory of

Chandigarh are urban in nature and largely dependent on non-agricultural activities. These states are also differentiated in terms of industrial pattern of development and emergence of service sectors. The states of Haryana, Delhi and union territory of Chandigarh, have shown highest level of industrial development and are the centres in the country for modern service sector especially based on information computer technology (ICT). The geographic proximity to the National Capital Zone has provided considerable dynamism to modern industrial and commercial activities to Haryana.

Due to difference in geographical features the states in North-West India are categorized by Government of India for the purpose of statutory and non-statutory transfer of taxes and grants among the states in the country. The hill states of Himachal Pradesh and Jammu and Kashmir are included in the Special Category of the states, while Punjab, Haryana and Delhi are among the general category states. Besides, the Government of India in 2003 gave a special package of (central) tax concessions to the hill states for establishment of new industrial and commercial enterprises. This package was initially for five years, which was extended in 2008 for another five years benefiting the states of Himachal Pradesh and Jammu and Kashmir in this region.

Politically, the region has also shown differences among states. Punjab remained politically disturbed for more than a decade in 1980s and early years of 1990s. The state of Jammu and Kashmir has been politically in disturbed conditions since mid-1980s and remains in these conditions even now. On the other hand, the states of Himachal Pradesh, Delhi and Haryana did not experience such political turmoil since their existence. They have remained normal in their functioning and organization of their economy. In fact, the political turmoil in the neighbouring states benefited both Himachal Pradesh and Haryana in terms of shifting of some activities from the neighbouring states to them (tourism to Himachal Pradesh and some industry from Punjab to both Himachal Pradesh and Haryana. The papers in this book bring out different aspects of the economy of the North-West India.

M.S. Sidhu and Varinder Pal have provided a comprehensive treatment of the current State of Punjab agriculture. The saturation in area under cultivation, stagnation in yield rates of wheat and rice, falling water table and over use of fertilizers and insecticides have pushed up the cost of production and reduced the profitability of farming in Punjab in the post liberlisation era. This is resulting in a large number of small and marginal farmers becoming non-viable and consequently being forced out of agriculture. They recommend the creation of non-farm employment opportunities for rural youth, since farming is not able to provide adequate employment opportunities to growing number of rural youth.

M.R. Khurana in his paper argues that agrarian crisis in Punjab is multi-dimensional. The main problems are: unremunerativeness of farming, steep rise in input prices and slow increase in output prices, stagnation of yield rates, growing indebtedness of farmers, fall in water table, deterioration in rural infrastructure, adverse ecological effects of green revolution and deceleration in Public investment in agriculture. The other related dimensions of the problem are dominance of moneylender in farm credit market, lack of crop insurance cover and increasing corporatisation of agriculture. The roots of agrarian crisis are in green revolution technology and liberalization of the economy. To tackle the crisis he recommends creation of non-farm employment opportunities for farmers and rural based industrialization.

Sanjay Kumar and Parminder Singh examine in detail and depth the current state of Punjab agriculture and the main constraints facing it. They examine the land use pattern, irrigation status, changes in structure of holdings, changes in cropping pattern, growth of production and productivity of major crops, changes in input use and capital formation, changes in cost of production, prices of main crops and their profitability since the early 1970's. They are of the opinion that dominance of wheat and paddy monoculture has serious repercussions for soil health, water table and environment. Consequently, area under wheat and paddy monoculture be reduced by at least 10 per cent. They also recommend a sizeable increase in public investment and strengthening of the extension education set up in the state. They also recommend the rationalization of farm input subsidies.

Sukhpal Singh in his paper has discussed the role of various organs of the state in the development of small holder agriculture. After examining the nature of agrarian crisis in Punjab he highlights the importance of small farmers in Punjab. He is of the view that farm policy and practice in Punjab either ignored the small farmer or pays only lip service to their problems and concerns. This orientation of farm policy in the state is resulting in increasing corporatisation of the farm sector and exclusion of the small farmer. A fairly large number of corporate farms have already emerged that lease lot of land from the small farmers. Owing to the extreme fragmentation of farmer unions, the small farmer's interests do not get adequate protection. He advocates the diversification of cropping pattern by shifting area out of wheat and paddy to other crops. He also recommends the reforming of regulated markets in such a way that small farmers benefit adequately by marketing their crops at remunerative prices. He also advocates a general re-orientation of state farm policy in favour of the small farmer. He is of the opinion that New Generation Cooperatives and NGO's should be used to tackle the agrarian crisis in the state.

M.K. Sekhon et. al. in their paper emphasize the un-sustainability of small and marginal farmer's standard of living in Punjab due to continuous sub-division of land holdings and stagnation in farm production and yield rates. The stagnation of small farmer's income is resulting in a large number of small and marginal farmers to become non-viable and consequently are being forced out of agriculture by the distress faced by them. To make small and marginal farms sustainable they suggest provision of off-farm employment opportunities, subsidized education and health services, custom hiring services through cooperatives and the strengthening of the fair price shops. They also advocate that steps should be taken to keep the joint family system intact in rural areas and education of rural people for reducing their wasteful expenditure on social ceremonies.

Sukhpal et. al. in their paper have highlighted the agrarian crisis in Punjab state resulting in heavy indebtedness of the peasantry and increasing number of farmers suicides. The agrarian crisis is characterized by deceleration in agricultural growth rate, declining farm employment opportunities and squeeze in farm profitability. In recent years this has resulted in accelerated pace of pauperization of the peasantry, particularly of the small and marginal farmers. The growth of income of the farm sector has not been able to keep pace with growth of expenditure of farm families. This has resulted in a large number of farmers becoming heavily indebted and many of them committing suicides. They recommend a holistic solution to the agrarian crisis by adopting Chinese model of employment and cooperative farming in the state.

H.S. Shergill in his paper has traced the growth of farm debt in Punjab in the post – W.T.O. era due to liberlisation and globalization of the Indian economy. Between 1997 to 2008 total farm debt in Punjab more than doubled in real terms i.e. at constant prices, and outstanding loans amount quadrupled in real terms. The annual interest charge on farm debt now eats up almost one-third of the revenue surplus generated by Punjab agriculture. The heavy debt burden has pushed down about 17 per cent of Punjab farmers into a debt trap and they are not in a position to repay their debt out of their current farm incomes. These debt trapped farmers have to, sooner or latter, sell some of their land to extricate themselves out of accumulated debt.

Sucha Singh Gill and Sanjay Gupta in their paper have analysed the management of public finances in the North-Western region states. The analysis brings out that the states of North-Western region face inadequacy of resources to meet their constitutional obligations, and are accumulating debt. Only Haryana has escaped this fate by keeping its expenditure within its fiscal resources. They are of the view that Central Government should change the distribution of fiscal resources between Centre and states in a way that states do not experience chronic deficit in their budgets. The transfer of resources from Centre to states should be made more objective and transparent.

States like Punjab may be compensated in view of the adverse impact on their fiscal position of the special category status given to hill states like HP and JK. The North-Western states should also rationalize and reduce their expenditure without adversely affecting development and social welfare programmes. The fiscal management needs improvement by better tax compliance and innovative new taxes. These states should swap old high interest debt with low interest debt to reduce their debt burden.

A.S. Gill and J.S. Brar in their paper have analysed the pattern of public expenditure on education in the North-Western region. The proportion of budget allocated to education in the North-Western region has been smaller than the all India average during the post-reform period. The public spending on education in North-Western region has been less than even the constitutionally agreed norm of minimum six per cent of state income. Moreover, the proportion of budget allocated to education declined continuously during the reform period. They strongly recommend increase in the share of education in state budgets and its more rational allocation among elementary, secondary and higher education.

R.K. Mahajan and Deepty Bansal in their paper have analysed the condition of Micro finance in rural Punjab. They have found that development of micro finance in Punjab is very limited compared to southern states. Their analysis indicates that micro finance programme has increased the income of participants and benefited the poor people. The composite empowerment index shows that participant women are more empowered than the non-participants. The current micro finance programme is focused on regular savings, but provision of insurance services is inadequate. They recommend that micro finance programme should be so altered that it reaches more the poor people and provide insurance cover to the poor people.

Reena Bhasin in her paper has analysed the dynamics of human development in Punjab. She has found that districts in which secondary sector is dominant are having a higher level human development compared to districts in which primary sector is predominant. A very low index of GDI indicates a lower female work participation rate in the state. The share of SDP going to health and education has continuously declined in Punjab and this is resulting in negative repercussions by reducing the quality and quantity of these social services to the people. She suggests the widening of the resources base of the state economy so that expenditure on social sectors is expanded to the desirable level.

Madhu Tandon in her paper has discussed the question of gender difference in the most prosperous North-Western region of India. She used many parameters to test the hypothesis that gender gap is higher in the North-Western region despite its prosperity. The lowest sex ratio in the country and poor relative health of females in the region indicate a wide gender gap. However, she finds women empowerment in household decisions is rather high in North Western states. She recommends many measures to improve the status and role of women in the region.

Lakhwinder Singh in his paper has discussed the economic performance of Punjab in the post-reform period. Punjab economy has experienced deceleration in growth in the post-reform period. All the major sectors of the economy like agriculture, manufacturing, electricity etc. has experienced deceleration in growth rate. The factors responsible for deceleration are structural rigidities, macro economic policies, low investment rate, border state factor and many non-economic constraints. He suggests an alternative policy package that can again accelerate the growth process of Punjab economy. The main elements in this alternative policy package are diversification of cropping pattern, cooperatives on the pattern of Gujarat and increase in the investment rate in the state.

Sukhwinder Singh and Shifali Jain in their paper have analysed the utilisation of maternal and child health care facilities in the North-Western states. The antenatal care level seems to be almost same in the North-Western states; although Punjab and Haryana seem to have achieved significant improvement in this connection. The proportion of institution delivered child births has improved in all the four states, but the rural-urban gap in this service continues in all these states.

The postnatal care has also improved in all these states. In both antenatal as well as postnatal care Punjab has performed better than the other states of the region. They suggest that there should be universal registration of all pregnant women for antenatal care; and government should spread awareness among the public of the availability and benefits of antenatal and postnatal health care facilities.

Baljinder Kaur et. al. in their paper have analysed the causes and impact of out-migration from rural areas of Punjab. They have collected primary data from a sample of villages and households. They have found that the majority of migrants were in the age group of 25-50 years and having education upto secondary level. The main reasons for outmigration were lack of employment, small size of holding and indebtedness of the family. The outmigration of family members resulted in improvement in the income and social status of the family in the village and better education of the children. The outmigration also impacted positively investment in house building, repayment of old loans, improvement in farm buildings and increased leasing of land by households sending out migrants. The maximum impact on income and other aspects was seen in the case of households that have sent out permanent setters in foreign countries.

Parvinder Kaur and R.S. Ghuman in their paper analysed the enactment of the Mahatma Gandhi National Rural Employment Guarantee Act (MGNREGA) by the Indian Parliament in 2005. This would prove to be a historic landmark in the economic history of the Republic of India. The Act mandates 100 days of guaranteed employment to any rural household who holds the job card and demands for work under the Act. This paper has examined the performance of the National Rural Employment Guarantee Scheme (NREGS) in Punjab in general and in district Hoshiarpur in particular as this was the first district in Punjab where the NREGS was implemented in the first round in 2006.The analysis about Punjab is based on the secondary data and that of Hoshiarpur district is based both on secondary and primary data. The primary data pertains to randomly selected 300 beneficiary households selected out of 20 villages from all the ten development blocks of district Hoshiarpur. It has been found that the performance of the NREGS was far below the mandatory provision of 100 days employment under MGNREGA. Similarly there was no evidence of unemployment allowance to those job-card holders who were demanding employment. Again the awareness level of both the job-card holders and that of the Panchayats was also very low. The official machinery, too, was not very enthusiastic to implement the scheme. As such there is a long way to go for effective implementation of the NREGS.

The papers included in the volume focus on the diverse issues on the regional economy of North West India. They help to identify the strength and weakness in relative terms of economy of different states in the region. The analyses undertaken by different scholars help us to understand the present status of different facets of the economy of the region. The strength of the papers lies in their strong empirical foundation based analysis. The analysis by the contributors of the present status and past experience is followed by policy recommendations. Some of the suggestions are quite practical and need serious attention by the state governments in the region and they need to learn from the experience of each others. We take pride in bringing out this volume on the occasion of 93rd Annual Conference of the Indian Economic Association. It is hoped that the volume will generate further debate and research in regional economy of North-West India.

2

Problems and Prospects of Agriculture in Punjab

M. S. Sidhu and Varinder Pal Singh

Introduction

Punjab witnessed a major breakthrough in the farm production starting in the late 1960s. The increase in wheat and paddy production improved the economic status of the peasantry bringing about an all round change. A number of factors have made this possible. These include the introduction of high yielding varieties (HYVs) particularly of wheat and paddy, assured price policy and supporting infrastructure for supply of different inputs and dissemination of the technical know how. However, the prime movers in this growth process were the farmers themselves who were quick enough to exploit the new production possibilities. The result is that the state with 1.53 per cent of the geographical area of the country accounted for about 60-65 per cent of wheat and about 30-35 per cent of rice procured for the central pool of foodgrains during the last four decades or so.

The Punjab agriculture which was growing fast earlier has now reached a sort of plateau in terms of productivity and production. In the wake of a declining land-man ratio, it is not able to generate gainful employment and sufficient income for the growing population. Farm profitability has witnessed a decline in the recent years due to cost price squeeze. There is almost stagnation in farm income. Farming alone is not able to generate sufficient income for small and marginal farmers. Due to economic distress, 2116 farmers had committed suicides during the last 15 years in Punjab (Nibber, 2004).

However, some other organizations claim that actual figure is staggering, somewhere between 10000 and 13000 (HT Correspondent, 2006). At present, the rural indebtedness is to the extent of about Rs 35000 crore which work out to be about Rs 3.50 lakh per farming household. The Punjab farmers are in deep economic crisis. Keeping in view all this, the present study has been undertaken to examine various problems faced by the farm sector in the state and its prospects in future.

Data base

The secondary data used in this paper has been mainly taken from the published sources. Notable among these are Statistical Abstract of Punjab, Agricultural Statistics At A Glance, etc. The data published in reputed English newspapers have also been used. The information has also been taken from Department of Economics & Sociology, PAU, Ludhiana.

Results and discussion

Number of Operational Holdings

The information about number of operational holdings in Punjab is given in Table 1. There were 10.27 lakh operational holdings in 1980-81. Their number increased to 11.17 lakh in 1990-91 but marginally declined to 10.93 lakh in 1995-96 but in the year 2000-01, this number sharply declined to 9.97 lakh but marginally increased to 10.03 lakh in 2005-06. The maximum decline was observed in case of marginal and small farmers. Their number was 3.86 lakh in 1995-96 which plummeted to 3.17 lakh in 2005-06. These figures reveal that agriculture is becoming un-remunerative particularly for marginal and small farmers, therefore, they were forced to lease out their tiny holdings. In many cases, they also sold their land to clear their debts and to meet other social obligations.

Another phenomenon about the operational holdings in the state is regarding the number of large farmers. Although their number was just six to seven per cent during the last two decades but they operated about 27 to 29 per cent of the area during this period. Therefore, we can say that modern farming is more favourable to the large farmers as compared to their fellow marginal and small farmers. The average size of operational holding was 3.79, 3.61, 3.79, 4.03 and 3.95 hectares during the years 1980-81, 1990-91. 1995-96, 2000-01 and 2005-06 respectively. At the national level, it is just 1.32 hectares. Therefore, the Punjab scenario is better than other states.

It is worthwhile to mention here that in the pre-green revolution period in the state, the bachelor farmer used to donate their share of land to their nephews (bhatijas). This prevented the land from being further divided. It was known as the Draupati system after the wife shared by the pandavas princes in the Mahabharta and there was no stigma attached to it (Mishra, 1999). Due to spread of education and awareness among the farmers, this practice has almost disappeared from the rural Punjab during the post revolution period.

Increase in the Number of Workers

The information regarding the number of agricultural workers as cultivators and agricultural workers is given in Table 2. The number of cultivators has increased from about 16 lakh in 1961 to about 21 lakh in 2001 whereas the number of agricultural workers jumped from 3.35 lakh to 14.90 lakh in the corresponding period. The trend of sub-division of land holdings is reflected more evidently in the land operated per cultivator and agricultural worker (taken together) which has declined gradually form1.94 hectares of net area sown in 1961 to 1.20 hectares in 2001. In terms of gross cropped area, this figure has declined from 2.44 hectares to 2.23 hectares during the same period. The facts given above are not mere statistical figures but rather have wider social, economic and political implications for the state as well as the country.

Table 1
No. of Operational Holdings, Area Operated and Average Size of Operational Holdings in Punjab

Farm category	1980-81			1990-91			1995-96			2000-01			2005-06		
	No (Thousand ha)	*Area operated of (Thousand ha)*	*Av. Size operational holdings (ha)*	*No (Thousand ha)*	*Area (Thousand ha)*	*Av. Size of operated holdings (ha)*	*No (Thousand ha)*	*Area operated (Thousand ha)*	*Av. Size of operational holdings (ha)*	*No (Thousand ha)*	*Area operated (Thousand ha)*	*Av. Size of operational holdings (ha)*	*No (Thousand ha)*	*Area operated (Thousand ha)*	*Av. Size of operational holdings (ha)*
Marginal (Below 1 hect.)	197.32 (19.21)	118.33 (3.04)	0.60	295.67 (26.47)	164.13 (4.07)	0.56	203.88 (18.55)	122.00 (2.94)	0.60	123.00 (12.34)	77.00 (1.91)	0.63	134.00 (13.36)	83.00 (2.09)	0.62
Small (1-2 hect.)	199.37 (19.41)	281.04 (7.22)	1.41	203.84 (18.25)	328.26 (8.14)	1.61	183.45 (16.78)	240.00 (5.79)	1.31	173.00 (17.35)	242.00 (6.02)	1.40	183.00 (18.25)	258.00 (6.51)	1.41
Semi-medium (2-4 hect.)	287.42	79 (27.99)	0.952.75 (20.32)	288.78 (25.86)	841.62 (20.87)	2.91	320.34 (29.31)	833.00 (20.09)	2.60	328.00 (32.90)	876.00 (21.78)	2.67	319.00 (31.80)	855.00 (21.57)	2.68
Medium (4-10 hect.)	269.07 (26.20)	1565.55 (40.22)	5.82	261.48 (23.41)	1621.95 (40.22)	6.20	305.79 (27.98)	1754.00 (42.30)	5.74	301.00 (30.19)	1731.00 (43.04)	5.75	296.00 (29.51)	170.10 (42.91)	5.81
Large 10 hect. & above)	73.94 (7.19)	1136.60 (29.20)	15.37	67.17 (6.01)	1076.73 (26.70)	16.03	79.6 (7.28)	11198.00 (28.88)	15.05	72.00 (7.22)	1096.00 (27.25)	15.22	71.00 (7.08)	106.70 (26.92)	14.93
All holdings	1027.13 (100.00)	3892.46 (100.00)	3.79 (100.00)	1116.95 (100.00)	4032.69 (100.00)	3.61	1093.07 (100.00)	4147.00 (100.00)	3.79	997.00 (100.00)	4022.00 (100.00)	4.03	1003.00 (100)	396.40 (100)	3.95

Note: Figures in parentheses indicate percentages to the total

A perusal of Table 2 further revealed that net area sown per cultivator has declined from 2.34 hectares in 1961 to 2.06 hectares in 2001. This figure for the agricultural worker was 11.23 hectares and 2.85 hectares in the corresponding period. Due to increase in cropping intensity, the gross cropped area per cultivator has increased from 2.95 hectares in 1961 to 3.85 hectares in 2001. During the last one decade, i.e. 1991 to 2001, the gross cropped area per cultivator has declined from 3.91 hectares in 1991 to 3.85 hectares in 2001. As already discussed, there has been fast increase in the number of agricultural workers during the last four decades i.e. from 1961 to 2001. Their number was 3.35 lakh in 1961 which increased to 14.90 lakh in 2001. It had adverse impact on the gross cropped area available to each agricultural worker. The gross cropped area per agricultural worker declined from 14.14 hectares in 1961 to 5.33 hectares in 2001. The fast mechanism of agriculture in this state has also narrowed down the employment opportunities for the agricultural labourers. A recent study has shown that use of each harvest combine eroded an estimated 24000 person days of work in a year (Mander, 2004). Moreover, the increased use of weedicides for control of weeds in the major crops i.e. wheat and paddy, has obviated the need for human labour for inter-culture operations. The excessive use of weedicides has not only replaced the human labour but has adversely affected the soil health too.

Land Use Pattern

The information about land use pattern shows that the net area sown in the state was 4171 thousand hectares during the year 2008-09 out of a total reporting area of 5033 thousand hectares which means that about 83 per cent of the reporting area was already under cultivation which was the highest in the country. There was only negligible area available under current fallows and other uncultivated land. The net area sown increased from 3870 thousand hectares in 1966-67 to 4171 thousand hectares in 2008-09 which means on average increase of about seven thousand hectares per annum. On the other hand, the total cropped area increased by 2920 thousand hectares during this

Table 2
Net and Gross Cropped Area Available to the Cultivators and Agricultural Workers in Punjab, 1961 to 2001

Year	*As cultivators (No.)*	*As agri. workers (No)*	*Net sown area per cultivator (hect.)*	*Net area sown per agri. worker area (hect.)*	*Gross cropped sown per cultivator (hect.)*	*Gross cropped area sown per agri. worker (hect.)*
1961	1602666	334610	2.34	11.23	2.95	14.14
1971	1665153	786705	2.43	5.15	3.41	7.22
1981	1767286	1092225	2.37	3.84	3.82	6.19
1991	1917210	1452828	2.20	2.90	3.91	5.16
2001	2065067	1489861	2.06	2.85	3.85	5.33

Year	*Net area sown per cultivator and agri. worker (hect.)*	*Gross cropped area per cultivator and agri. worker (hect.)*
1961	1.94	2.44
1971	1.65	2.32
1981	1.47	2.36
1991	1.25	2.23
2001	1.20	2.23

Source: Statistical Abstract of Punjab, various issues.

period which gives an average increase of about 65 thousand hectares per year. It may be mentioned here that net area sown increased from 3870 thousand hectares in 1966-67 to about 4200 thousand hectares in 1980-81. After that, there has been no significant increase in net area sown in the state. It happened mainly because of the fact that size of the land is fixed and increase in area came mainly from increase in the total cropped area. Due to increase in the cropping intensity, the total cropped area increased from 5171 thousand hectares in 1966-67 to 7945 thousand hectares in 1998-99. After that, it has almost become constant because there is limit to increase the cropping intensity also. Therefore, there is little scope to increase cropping intensity in near future and the total cropped area will remain constant around 7900 thousand hectares. On the other hand, there is possibility of decline in net area sown in the state due to use of land for non-agricultural purposes. This will have adverse effect on the total cropped area also. Above all,the forest wealth of the state is very poor as is evident from Table 3.

Shifts in Cropping Pattern

The cropping pattern in the state is shown in Table 3. The figures show that during the year 2008-09, about 82 per cent of the total cropped area was under foodgrains, about nine per cent under cash crops, i.e. cotton, sugarcane, oilseeds and potatoes. It may be stated here that about nine per cent of the total cropped area was under rabi and kharif fodder crops and about two per cent under fruits and vegetables. Wheat is the principal crop of Punjab which alone had about a 45 per cent of the cropped area followed by rice which had about a 35 per cent area. In this way, these two crops taken together occupied about 79 per cent of the area.

Rice is not a traditional crop of Punjab. The area under rice was just 227 thousand hectares in 1960-61 which increased to 390 thousand hectares in 1970-71, 567 thousand hectares in 1980-81, 1183 thousand hectares in 1985-86 and 2015 thousand hectares in 1990-91. It reached to the level of 2612 thousand hectares in 2000-01 which further increased to 2735 thousand hectares in 2008-09. The major factors responsible for increase in its area are high and stable yield as compared to other kharif crops, assured price and public procurement. We can say that net returns to the farmers from paddy crop are high vis-à-vis other competing kharif crops. Paddy has replaced kharif pulses and oilseeds on a large scale in the last three decades. The area under wheat was 1400 thousand hectares in 1960-61 which increased to about 2300 thousand hectares in 1970-71, 2812 thousand hectares in 1980-81, 3273 thousand hectares in 1990-91, 3408 thousand hectares in 2000-01 which further increased to 3526 thousand hectares in 2008-09. Wheat crop has also replaced rabi pulses particularly gram and oilseed crops. This crop has also high and stable yield as compared to other rabi crops. Moreover, the Govt. of India procures it at the minimum support price (MSP). It is also a staple food of the Punjabis. Wheat bhusa, the by-product of wheat is also used on a very large scale by the farmers to feed dairy animals. Therefore, we

Table 3
Shifts in cropping pattern in Punjab, 1960-61 to 2002-03

(Area 000'hect.)

Years/crop	Wheat	Rice	Maize	Total cereals	Total pulses	Rapeseed & mustard	Total oilseeds	Cotton	Sugarcane	Potato
1960-61	1400	227	327	2160	903	107	185	447	133	9
	-29.58	-4.8	-6.91	-45.65	-19.08	-2.26	-3.91	-9.45	-2.81	-0.19
1970-71	2299	390	555	3514	414	103	295	397	128	17
	-40.48	-6.87	-9.77	-61.89	-7.29	-1.81	-5.19	(6.99))	-2.25	-0.29
1975-76	2439	567	577	3891	441	122	315	580	114	27
	-38.99	-9.06	-9.22	-62.21	-7.05	-1.95	-5.03	-9.27	-1.82	-0.43
1980-81	2812	1183	382	4513	341	136	238	649	71	40
	-41.58	-17.49	-5.65	-66.73	-5.04	-2.01	-3.52	-9.59	-1.05	-0.59
1985-86	3112	1714	260	5169	225	151	211	559	78	43
	-43.47	-23.95	-3.63	-72.21	-3.14	-2.11	-2.95	-7.81	-1.09	-0.6
1990-91	3273	2015	188	5525	143	69	104	701	101	23
	-43.63	-26.86	-2.51	-73.65	-1.91	-0.92	-1.39	-9.34	-1.35	-0.31
1995-96	3221	2185	171	5625	95	101	237	742	136	39
	-41.77	-28.33	-2.22	-72.94	-1.23	-1.31	-3.07	-9.62	-1.76	-0.51
2000-01	3408	2612	164	6222	55	55	86	473	121	64
	-42.95	-32.92	-2.07	-78.41	-0.69	-0.69	-1.08	-5.96	-1.52	-0.81
2005-06	3464	2647	149	6290	29	47	80	557	85	71
	-44.03	-33.64	-1.89	-79.94	-0.37	-0.6	-1.02	-7.08	-1.08	-0.9
2006-07	3467	2621	154	6268	29	41	70	607	99	76
2007-08	3487	2609	154	6271	27	30	60	605	108	90
	-44.31	-33.15	-1.96	-79.68	-0.34	-0.38	-0.76	-7.69	-1.37	-1.14
2008-09	3526	2735	151	6433	22	29	60	527	81	82
	-44.57	-34.57	-1.91	-81.31	-0.28	-0.37	-0.76	-6.66	-1.02	-1.04

Note: Figures in parentheses indicate percentages to the total cropped area

can say that wheat is a natural crop of Punjab. Moreover, its irrigation requirements are not high as in case of paddy.

Maize was an important crop of the state in the pre-green revolution period. The area under maize was 327 thousand hectares in 1960-61 which declined to 188 thousand hectares in 1990-91, 164 thousand hectares in 2000-01. Further, it plummeted to 151 thousand hectares in 2008-09. In percentage terms, the maize area declined from about seven per cent of the cropped area in 1960-61 to about two in 2008-09. As already discussed, with the fast increase in paddy area, the maize area declined significantly. Although MSP is announced for maize crop every year but there is no effective public procurement. Therefore, to avoid price risk, the Punjab farmers particularly in the central zone has shifted from maize to paddy on a large scale in the kharif season.

The area under potato crop has also increased during the last three decades. Its area was 17 thousand hectares in 1970-71 which increased to 90 thousand hectares in 2006-07 but due to price fluctuation, its area has also declined to 82 thousand hectares in 2008-09. Price of potato is a major factor for the increase or decrease of potato area. Generally, its market price is fixed according to the forces of demand and supply. This crop is also not covered effectively under the public procurement programme.

All this reveals that cereals particularly wheat and paddy have come to dominate the cropping pattern in the state in the wake of new farm technology and axe has fallen mainly on pulses and oilseeds. As already discussed, this outcome is the consequence of higher profitability of wheat and paddy cropping system. There is another dimension of this problem. Pulses and oilseeds are legumes and their cultivation was an important natural source of restoring the soil fertility. The decline in their area has resulted in reduced availability of natural sources of fertilization of soils.

There is also concern over the long range effect of cereals dominated cropping pattern particularly the rice cultivation and also overall exploitative agriculture which could have deleterious effect on the soil health. The indiscriminate and uncontrolled use of underground water may not also be desirable in several areas of the state from the long-run point of view of sustained use of this scarce and precious resource.

Over-exploitation of Ground Water

In the post-green revolution period, the number of tube-wells for irrigation purpose has increased very fast. There were only 1973 tube-wells in the state in 1950-51.This number increased to about 12000 in 1960-61, 1.92 lakh in 1970-71, 6.00 lakh in 1980-81, 7.73 lakh in 1990-91, 10.73 lakh in 2000-01 and 11.68 lakh in 2004-05. At present, about 75 per cent of the irrigation is through tube-wells and the rest about 25 per cent by canals. This phenomenon resulted in over-exploitation of ground water. Paddy is a water intensive crop. The over-exploitation of ground water is also linked mainly with the paddy crop. During the year 1984, there were only about 45 per cent over developed blocks in the state (Table 4). This number increased to about 76 per cent during the year 2004. The number of white blocks was about 31 per cent in 1984 which declined to about 12 per cent in 2004. Similarly, the share of grey blocks declined from about 19 per cent in 1984 to about six per cent in 2004.

Already due to decline in water table, more than one lakh tube-wells have been replaced with submersible pumps and around 3.9 lakh centrifugal pumps will have to be replaced by submersible pumps in the next few years, costing crores of rupees and increasing the energy requirements three-fold to pump out the same quantity of water (Aulakh, 2004). The PAU experts always advise the farmers not to transplant paddy before 15th June because transplantation of paddy before PAU recommendation results in fall of water table. It may be stated here that paddy transplanted on May 1 result in 70 cms decline in water table, 60 cms in case of May 10, 50 cms on May 20, 28 cms on May 30 and 10 cms on June 10. For the last two decades, the PAU advice to the farmers did not have significant impact in this regard. According to the press reports, some farmers of Moonak block (Sangrur district) transplanted paddy as early as on April 20, 2006 (Sharma, 2006). In the central Punjab, the water table is declining very fast which would have wide implications in the years to come. From the years 1982-87, the water table in the central Punjab declined by 18 cms per year. This figure increased to 25 cms in the years 1992-97, 42 cms in 1997-2002, 69 cms in 2003-04 and 74 cms in 2004-05 (Govt. of Punjab, 2006). Keeping in view these facts, the State Government has put a ban on transplantation of paddy before 10th June every year.

The district-wise categorization of water table in Punjab for the year 2004 is given in Table 5. The cent percent blocks of Amritsar, Faridkot, Fatehgarh Sahib, Jalandahr, Kapurthala, Mansa, Moga and Sangrur were over developed where the withdrawal of ground water was more than 100 per cent of the recharge. This figure was about 91 per cent for Ludhiana district, 89 per cent for Patiala district, 70 per cent for Ferozepur district, 57 per cent each for Bathinda and Gurdaspur districts, 29 per cent for Ropar district and 20 per cent for Hoshiarpur district. As far as the state as a whole was concerned, about 76

Table 4
Groundwater Exploitation in Punjab, 1984 to 2004

Water blocks/year	*1984*	*1989*	*1991*	*1997*	*2004*
Overdeveloped	53	62	62	73	104
	(44.92)	(52.54)	(52.54)	(52.90)	(75.91)
Developed	7	7	8	11	9
	(5.93)	(5.93)	(6.78)	(7.97)	(6.57)
Grey	22	20	15	16	8
	(18.64)	(16.95)	(12.71)	(11.59)	(5.84)
White	36	29	33	38	16
	(30.51)	(24.58)	(27.97)	(27.54)	(11.68)
Total number of water blocks	118	118	118	138	137
	(100.00)	(100.00)	(100.00)	(100.00)	(100.00)

Note: (i) Figures in parentheses indicate percentages to the total number of water blocks

(ii) Overdeveloped blocks are those where withdrawal of groundwater was more than 100 per cent of the recharge of water. In dark blocks, the withdrawal of groundwater was between 85 per cent and 100 per cent of the recharge of water. In grey block, the withdrawal of Groundwater was between 60 and 85 per cent of recharge of water. In whole blocks, the withdrawal of groundwater was less than 60 per cent of the recharge of water.

Source: Water Resources Directorate, Punjab, Chandigarh.

per cent of the water blocks were over developed. The share of dark blocks was about seven per cent, grey blocks about six per cent and white blocks about 12 per cent.

Table 5
District-wise Categorization of Water Blocks in Punjab 2004

District	*Over-developed (OD)*	*Dark (D)*	*Grey (G)*	*White (W)*	*Total number of water blocks*
Amritsar	16 (100.00)	-	-	-	16 (100.00)
Bathinda	4 (57.14)	-	1 (14.29)	2 (28.57)	7 (100.00)
Faridkot	2 (100.00)	-	-	-	2 (100.00)
Fatehgarh Sahib	5 (100.00)	-	-	-	5 (100.00)
Ferozepur	7 (70.00)	1 (10.00)	-	2 (20.00)	10 (100.00)
Gurdaspur	8 (57.14)	2 (14.29)	2 (14.29)	2 (14.28)	14 (100.00)
Hoshiarpur	2 (20.00)	2 (20.00)	3 (30.00)	3 (30.00)	10 (100.00)
Jalandhar	10 (100.00)	-	-	-	10 (100.00)
Kapurthala	5 (100.00)	-	-	-	5 (100.00)
Ludhiana	10 (90.91)	1 (9.09)	-	-	11 (100.00)
Mansa	5 (100.00)	-	-	-	5 (100.00)
Moga	5 (100.00)	-	-	-	5 (100.00)
Muktsar	-	-	1 (25.00)	3 (75.00)	4 (100.00)
Nawan Shahr	3 (60.00)	-	-	2 (40.00)	5 (100.00)
Patiala	8 (88.89)	-	1 (11.11)	-	9 (100.00)
Ropar	2 (28.57)	3 (42.86)	-	2 (28.57)	7 (100.00)
Sangrur	12 (100.00)	-	-	-	12 (100.00)
Punjab	104 (75.91)	9 (6.57)	8 (5.84)	16 (11.68)	137 (100.00)

Source: Water Resources Directorate, Punjab, Chandigarh
Note: Figures in parentheses indicate percentages to the total number of water blocks

Keeping in view the problem of declining water table and other related issues, the Punjab Government constituted the Committee under the Chairmanship of Dr S.S.Johl an eminent agricultural economist to suggest various measures for the diversification of agriculture in Punjab. The Committee suggested that one million hectares area each under paddy and wheat may be replaced with other crops particularly oilseeds and pulses. According to the existing water resources of the state, we can sustain paddy in about 16 lakh hectares only. But due to various reasons, the recommendations of this Committee have not been implemented as such by the Government of India. The severe drought in the year 2002-03 resulted in fall of foodgrain production by about 38 million tones in a year. The buffer stocks also declined considerably. Rather, India has been forced to import about seven million tonnes of wheat in the year 2006 to 2008. Since food security of the country is in the hands of the Punjab farmers, therefore, shifting of 10 lakh hectares of paddy area to other crops in near future will be a very difficult task. The policy framework and market infrastructure are in favour of wheat and paddy crops.

Compound Growth Rates of Area, Production and Yield

The compound growth rates of area, production and yield for important crops of the state are shown in Table 6. A perusal of the figures shows that rice production recorded the higher growth, i.e. 18.41 per cent per annum from the years 1966-67 to 1980-81. The contribution of area and yield was 11.00 per cent and 6.67 per cent respectively. Among the cereals, wheat was the next crop to record a high production growth rate (6.48 per cent per annum) during this period. The contribution of area in this was 3.34 per cent and yield contributed 3.05 per cent. Potato and American cotton also recorded significant production growth rates of 13.30 per cent and 8.09 per cent respectively in this period. In case of potatoes, the contribution of area was 9.38 per cent and that of yield 3.66 per cent. In case of cotton (A), the increase in production mainly occurred as a result of increase in area (7.37 per cent) and contribution of yield was (-) 0.11 per cent. Sugarcane witnessed a negligible growth rate of 0.23 per cent. The other crops like maize, barley, bajra, pulses, oilseeds and cotton (D) had negative growth rates for production during this period. This happened primarily on account of decrease in area. Area released from maize crop in kharif season was largely replaced by the paddy crop and that from pulses and oilseeds to wheat in the rabi season. The area under cotton (D) has mainly been replaced by cotton (A).

The compound growth rates of area, production and yield of important crops in the state for the period 1981-82 to

1990-91 revealed that rice crop again recorded the highest production growth rate. It was 5.61 per cent per annum. The contribution of area was 4.85 per cent and that of yield 0.72 per cent. Among the cereals, wheat was the next crop to record 3.70 per cent per annum production growth rate. The contribution of area was 0.97 per cent and that of yield 2.70 per cent. The cotton (A) recorded 11.16 per cent production growth rate. In this, the contribution of area and yield was 2.79 per cent and 8.15 per cent respectively. The sugarcane also did not show a high growth rate in this period. The crops like maize, barley, bajra, pulses, oilseeds, potato and cotton (A) showed the negative production growth rates. It happened mainly due to decrease in area under these crops.

Table 6

Compound Growth Rate of Area, Production and Yield of Important Crops in Punjab

Sl.No.	*Crop*	*Area*	*Production*	*Yield*
1966-67 to 1980-81				
1	Rice	11.00***	18.41***	6.67***
2	Wheat	3.34***	6.48***	3.05***
3	Maize	-1.33*	-0.90NS	0.42NS
4	Barley	-4.44*	-0.30NS	4.21***
5	Bajra	-7.92***	-7.27***	0.71NS
6	Pulses	-3.36***	-4.05***	-0.72NS
7	Oilseeds	-2.91***	-2.91***	-0.0009NS
8	Sugarcane	-4.15***	0.23NS	4.55***
9	Potato	9.38***	13.30***	3.66***
10	Cotton (A)	7.37***	8.09***	-0.11NS
11	Cotton (D)	-1.77*	-2.91**	-1.65***
1981-82 to 1990-91				
1	Rice	4.85***	5.61***	0.72NS
2	Wheat	0.97***	3.70***	2.70***
3	Maize	-5.72***	-7.08***	-1.40NS
4	Barley	-8.79***	-3.32NS	6.08***
5	Bajra	-18.46***	-19.66***	-1.63NS
6	Pulses	-7.15***	-4.39*	2.97*
7	Oilseeds	-6.01***	-4.16NS	2.21*
8	Sugarcane	0.95NS	0.77NS	-0.80NS
9	Potato	-2.77NS	-2.01NS	-0.08NS
10	Cotton (A)	2.79NS	11.16***	8.15**
11	Cotton (D)	-9.07***	-3.52NS	6.09*

Contd...

Sl.No.	Crop	Area	Production	Yield
1991-92 to 2000-01				
1	Rice	2.72***	2.86***	0.12NS
2	Wheat	0.36*	2.48***	2.13***
3	Maize	8.23 NS	1.54NS	3.42**
4	Barley	-4.60***	-2.36*	2.48***
5	Bajra	-7.92**	-5.80NS	-2.80*
6	Pulses	-5.62***	-7.97***	-2.50**
7	Oilseeds	-7.41**	-9.64***	-2.40***
8	Sugarcane	2.29 NS	2.07NS	0.23NS
9	Potato	14.59***	14.56***	0.18NS
10	Cotton (A)	-5.21***	-13.29***	-8.53**
11	Cotton (D)	6.23 NS	5.57NS	-0.62NS
2001-02 to 2008-09				
1	Rice	0.98***	3.02***	2.02***
2	Wheat	0.46***	0.74NS	0.28NS
3	Maize	-0.16NS	4.44*	5.21**
4	Barley	-6.49***	-5.91***	0.62NS
5	Bajra	-5.32**	-4.44*	1.99*
6	Pulses	-10.33***	-7.95***	2.88*
7	Oilseeds	-6.35***	-2.87NS	3.29NS
8	Sugarcane	-7.30**	-4.39*	-0.44NS
9	Potato	5.49***	5.65**	0.92NS
10	Cotton (A)	4.33*	14.36***	9.61***
11	Cotton (D)	-21.92***	-14.18***	10.06***
1966-67 to 2008-09				
1	Rice	5.56***	7.86***	2.17***
2	Wheat	1.39***	3.62***	2.20***
3	Maize	-3.37***	-1.97***	1.85***
4	Barley	-3.89***	-0.27NS	3.77***
5	Bajra	-10.02***	-10.27***	-0.16NS
6	Pulses	-7.31***	-7.35***	0.01NS
7	Oilseeds	-3.80***	-2.65***	1.11***
8	Sugarcane	-0.33NS	0.69**	0.99***
9	Potato	3.58***	4.54***	0.87***
10	Cotton (A)	1.85***	3.00***	1.08***
11	Cotton (D)	-4.12***	-3.02***	1.06***

Note: NS, ***, **, * indicate non-significant and significant at 1 per cent, 5 per cent and 10 per cent respectively.

During the period 1991 92 to 2000 01, the production growth rates of rice and wheat were low as compared to the earlier periods, i.e. 1966-67 to 1980-81 and 1981-82 to 1990-91. Among the cereals crops, the production growth rate of rice was 2.86 per cent per annum from the years 1991-92 to 2000-

01. The increase in production was mainly due to increase in area, i.e. 2.72 per cent per annum. The contribution of yield was non-significant, i.e. 0.12 per cent per annum. The major reason for increase in rice area during this period was replacement of cotton (A) by the farmers with rice. Due to attack of American bollworm on the cotton (A) crop on a large scale during this period, the farmers had no option but to shift to paddy crop in the kharif season. In the cotton belt, the ground water is brackish and unfit for water intensive crop like paddy. But economic hardships faced by the farmers due to failure of cotton (A) crop forced them to shift to rice cultivation.

Wheat crop recorded the production growth rate of 2.48 per cent per annum during the period 1991-92 to 2000-01. The contribution of area and yield was 0.36 per cent and 2.13 per cent respectively. Potato crop witnessed significant production growth rate, i.e. 14.56 per cent per annum during this period. The contribution of area and yield was 14.59 per cent and 0.18 per cent respectively. Sugarcane production also witnessed the growth rate of 2.07 per cent per annum but it was not significant. The cotton (D) showed 5.57 per cent production growth rate which was not found to be significant whereas cotton (A) production declined by 13.29 per cent per annum. The other crops like barley, bajra, pulses and oilseeds showed negative production growth rates. Maize crop witnessed non-significant 1.54 per cent production growth rate.

During the period 2001-02 to 2008-09, among the cereals crops, the production growth rate of rice was 3.02 per cent per annum. The increase in production was due to increase in area, i.e. 0.98 per cent per annum and yield i.e. 2.02 per cent per annum. Wheat crop recorded the non significant production growth rate of 0.74 per cent per annum during the period 2001-02 to 2008-09. The contribution of area and yield was 0.46 per cent and 0.28 per cent respectively. Maize crop witnessed 4.44 per cent production growth rate which was mainly due to increase in yield i.e. 5.21 per cent per annum. Potato crop witnessed significant production growth rate, i.e. 5.65 per cent per annum during this period. The contribution of area and yield was 5.49 per cent and 0.92 per cent respectively. The cotton

(A) showed 14.36 per cent production growth rate whereas cotton (A) production declined by 14.18 per cent per annum. The other crops like barley, bajra, pulses, oilseeds and sugarcane showed negative production growth rates.

The overall growth rate of area, production and yield of important crops for the period 1966-67 to 2008-09 indicated that rice crop was at number one having the highest production growth rate, i.e. 7.86 per cent per annum. The contribution of area and yield was 5.56 per cent and 2.17 per cent respectively for the increase in rice production. Among the cereal crops, wheat was next important crop having 3.62 per cent growth rate in production. The contribution of area was 1.39 per cent and yield 2.20 per cent. The growth rate of production of cotton (A) was 3.00. The contribution of area was 1.85 per cent and that of yield was 1.08 per cent. Potato was another important crop which showed the growth rate of production, i.e. 4.54 per cent per annum. The contribution of area and yield was 3.58 per cent and 0.87 per cent respectively. Sugarcane recorded the production growth rate of 0.69 per cent per annum. This increase was mainly due to increase in productivity. The other crops like maize, bajra, pulses, oilseeds and cotton (D) recorded negative growth rates in production.

The overall comparison of growth rates of different periods show that Punjab agriculture is facing the problem of stagnation in production particularly in the last one decade. The slow down in the growth rates of different crops had negative impact on the income and employment of the farmers as well as agricultural labourers. The area under different crops has almost reached to the maximum possible level. Any increase in area of particular crop will result in decline of another crop. In this way, the overall picture of Punjab agriculture may not change significantly.

Trends in Production and Productivity

The rice and wheat crops have shown remarkable increase in production in the state during the last 44 years. But during the last few years, the production of wheat has declined form 159 lakh tones in 1999-2000 to about 142 lakh tones in 2002-03. The production of wheat crop is almost stagnant since 2000-01. It was 155.51 lakh tonnes in 2000-01 and increased marginally to 157.33 lakh tonnes during 2008-09. Similarly, the rice production has declined from about 92 lakh tones in 2000-01 to about 89 lakh tones in 2002-03. It may be mentioned here that weather also played an important role in production of various crops. Sometimes, it is favourable to the crops. On the other hand, it is unfavourable also in many years. The floods in Punjab during the month of September, 1988 damaged the rice crop on a large scale and consequently, the rice production declined to about 49 lakh tones during 1988-89 compared to about 54 lakh tones in 1987-88 and about 59 lakh tones in 1986-87. The severe drought condition in 1987-88 also adversely affected the rice production of the state. As already discussed, the production of cotton (A) has declined during the last ten years due to attack of American bollworm. The production of other crops except sugarcane and potato has declined through time.

Productivity

The yield per unit of area is a good indication of the efficiency in production. The yield figures for important crops show that in case of wheat, the productivity after showing an increase during the initial years (during the period 1966-67 through 1971-72) showed no improvement during the period, i.e. 1972-73 to 1976-77 and stagnated around 24 quintals per hectare. In the later years, however, there was an improvement in productivity although it was marked by inter-year fluctuation. In the recent years, the maximum yield of wheat was 4696 kgs per hectare in 1999-2000. After that peak yield, it had started declining. As already discussed, the weather also played an important role in this regard.

In case of rice, the productivity increased form 1185 kgs per hectare in 1966-67 to 3507 kgs per hectare in 1993-94. This meant about three times increase in productivity during the period. After that, the yield witnessed decline up to the year 1999-2000 but again showed increase in 2000-01. It was 3506 kgs per hectare in this year. It went to the level of 3545 kgs per hectare in 2001-02 but marginally declined to 3510 kgs per hectare in 2002-03 and increased to 4022 kgs in 2008-09. There were inter-year fluctuations in yield. This happened due to floods, drought, and diseases to the crops, etc. There is need for technological breakthrough in case of rice particularly hybrids.

The productivity of cotton (A) increased from 335 kgs per hectare in 1966-67 to 636 kgs in 1992-93. During this period also, there were inter-year fluctuations in productivity due to various factors. After 1992-93, the yield of cotton (A) started declining due to attack of American bollworm and it reached to the lowest level of 179 kgs per hectare in 1998-99. In the subsequent years, it picked up. The yield of cotton (A) was 743 kgs per hectare in 2008-09.

The productivity analysis of other crops reveal that yield of maize, sugarcane, potato, oilseeds and barley crops has increased overtime although there were inter-year fluctuations due to various reasons. The productivity of pulses and cotton (D) did not show any remarkable improvement. To increase the production of various crops, there is need for technological breakthrough in productivity.

A Case of Stagnation

The productivity analysis reveals that breakthrough in productivity has been achieved mainly in few crops like rice, wheat, sugarcane, potato, maize and barley. Except wheat and rice, the area under other crops is not quite large. There are marketing constraints for other crops because public procurement is effective only in case of wheat and paddy. In case of pulses, desi cotton and bajra, the productivity has almost stagnated. Overall also, the Punjab agriculture is facing the problem of stagnation in production and productivity.

Extent of Exploitation of Potential Yield

Table 7 shows the information regarding the extent of exploitation of potential yield of various kharif and rabi crops. A perusal of the table reveals that among the kharif crops, the extent of the exploitation of potential yield was highest in Bt cotton i.e. 84.95 per cent followed by paddy (83.21 per cent), moong (79.77 per cent), basmati (75.00 per cent), desi cotton (71.22 per cent), sugarcane (71.08 per cent), maize (68.85 per cent) etc. The lowest exploitation of the potential yield is in the case of bajra (30.42 per cent) followed by groundnut (42.00 per cent), mash (49.75 per cent), soyabean (60.83 per cent) etc. In case of the rabi crops, the extent of the exploitation of potential yield was highest in sunflower i.e. 90.90 per cent followed by wheat (90.30 per cent), barley (88.23 per cent), gobhi sarson (69.57 per cent) etc. The lowest exploitation of the potential yield is in the case of lentil (54.58 per cent) followed by field pea (63.60 per cent), gram (67.28 per cent), etc. Hence there is

Table 7
Extent of Exploitation of Potential Yield

Sl. No.	*Crop*	*Potential yield (q)*	*State average yield (q)*	*% potential exploited*
Kharif crops				
1	Paddy	29	24.13	83.21
2	Bt cotton	10.5	8.92	84.95
3	Moong	4.5	3.59	79.77
4	Basmati	14	10.50	75.00
5	Desi cotton	9	6.41	71.22
6	Sugarcane	325	231	71.08
7	Maize	20	13.77	68.85
8	Arhar	6	3.92	65.33
9	Sesamum	2.1	1.36	64.76
10	Soybean	6	3.65	60.83
11	Mash	4	1.99	49.75
12	Groundnut	9	3.78	42.00
13	Bajra	14	4.26	30.42
Rabi Crops				
1	Wheat	20	18.06	90.30
2	Sunflower	7.8	7.09	90.90
3	Barley	15.8	13.94	88.23
7	Gobhi Sarson	7	4.87	69.57
4	Gram	7	4.71	67.28
6	Field Pea	7.5	4.77	63.60
5	Lentil	4.8	2.62	54.58
8	Toria	5	-	-
9	Linseed	4.7	-	-
10	Winter maize	28	-	-

Source: Deptt. of Economics & Sociology, PAU, Ludhiana

an ample scope of further exploitation of potential yield of the crops where the exploitation is less which calls for the need of adequate extension services and providing the technical knowhow to the farmers. There are sizeable productivity differentials among districts which are otherwise more or less homogenous with respect to availability of irrigation facilities and soil type. It should be possible to increase the productivity levels in these districts by giving due attention to the limiting factors in these districts.

Comparative Economics of Different Crops

The information regarding economics of various rabi and kharif crops is shown in Table 8. A perusal of the table reveals that among the kharif crops, gross returns were highest from the sugarcane planted crop (Rs 60750) followed by sugarcane ratoon (Rs 56600), Bt cotton (Rs 30600), paddy (Rs 29870), basmati (Rs 27650) and cotton desi (Rs 25220). The respective variable costs of th ese crops were Rs 35088, Rs 22777, Rs 13900, Rs 10044, Rs 10947 and Rs 10951 per acre. The returns over variable cost were the maximum (Rs 28823) for sugarcane ratoon followed by sugarcane planted (Rs 26662), paddy (Rs 19826), basmati (Rs 16703), Bt cotton (Rs 16700) and cotton desi (Rs 14269). Although the returns over variable cost were the highest in sugarcane ratoon and sugarcane planted but being an annual crop, the actual returns were lower in comparison to the lesser duration crops like paddy, basmati, cotton etc.

In case of the rabi crops, gross returns were the highest from the winter maize (Rs. 27040) followed by wheat (Rs. 25000), celery (Rs. 20625), gram (Rs 18375), fennel (Rs. 17550) and field pea (Rs. 16875). The respective variable costs of these crops were Rs. 12281, Rs. 10126, Rs. 20625, Rs. 8550, Rs 6522 and Rs 8553 per acre. The returns over variable cost were the maximum (Rs 17874) for wheat followed by winter maize (Rs. 14759), celery (Rs. 11354), fennel and gram (Rs. 9825).

Future Possibilities

It is often talked that Punjab may not be able to add much to its agricultural production since it is already near the saturation point so far as exploitation of new areas is concerned. Besides water is going to become the most limiting resource in further intensification of agriculture. We are of the view that unless the states make rational use of its irrigation resource, it would

Table 8
Comparative Economics of Different Crops, 2010-11
(Based on PAU Recommendations)

(Rs/acre)

Sl. No.	*Crop*	*Yield (q/acre)*	*GR*	*TVC*	*ROVC*
Kharif crops					
1	Paddy	29	29870	10044	19826
2	Basmati	14	27650	10947	16703
3	Maize	20	18000	10864	7136
4	Bt cotton	10.5	30600	13900	16700
5	Cotton (Desi)	9	25220	10951	14269
6	Sugarcane planted	325	60750	35088	26662
	Sugarcane Ratoon	275	56600	22777	28823
7	Mash	4	10150	4668	5482
8	Moong	4.5	13145	6816	6329
9	Arhar	6	16300	6111	10889
10	Bajra	14	13740	6968	6772
11	Groundnut	9	19600	10440	9160
12	Sesamum	2.1	6685	6265	420
13	Soybean	6	9180	6593	2587
Rabi crops					
1	Wheat	20	25000	10126	14874
2	Barley	15.8	16470	7151	9319
3	Winter maize	28	27040	12281	14759
4	Gram	7	18375	8550	9825
5	Lentil	4.75	14412	7114	7298
6	Field Pea	7.5	16875	8553	8322
7	Gobhi Sarson	7	16590	8024	8566
8	Toria	5	11350	7327	4023
9	Linseed	4.7	12640	11276	1364
10	Sunflower	7.8	16380	8840	7540
11	Celery	5.5	20625	9271	11354
12	Fennel	4.5	17550	6522	11028
13	Coriander	2.75	12375	7194	5181
14	Summer moong	4.5	16275	6842	9433
15	Summer mash	4.25	13500	7325	6175

GR = Gross returns, TVC = Total variable costs, ROVC = Returns over variable costs

Source: Deptt. of Economics & Sociology, PAU, Ludhiana

be difficult to maintain even the present type of cropping pattern in the long run. Already the state is facing the problem of felling water level our vast areas in the central Punjab. This is coupled with water logging problem in some parts of south western districts where underground water is brackish. This does not, however, mean that there is no scope to increase agricultural production. Even with the known level of technology, it is possible to enhance agricultural production by bridging the adoption gaps.

There are sizeable productivity differentials among districts which are otherwise more or less homogenous with respect to availability of irrigation facilities and soil type. It should be possible to increase the productivity levels in these districts by giving due attention to the limiting factors in these districts. As far as diversification of crops is concerned, we are of the view that alternative crops should provide net returns almost equal to wheat and paddy crops. Only then, the farmers will shift to those crops. In this regard, production technology and marketing will have to play a crucial role. At present, the farmers face problems related with these issues.

Summary and Conclusions

Wheat is the principal crop of Punjab which has about 45 per cent of the cropped area followed by rice which has about 35 per cent area. In this way, these two crops taken together occupy about 79 per cent of the area. Rice is not a traditional crop of Punjab. The area under rice was just 227 thousand hectares in 1960-61 which increased to 390 thousand hectares in 1970-71, 567 thousand hectares in 1980-81, 1183 thousand hectares in 1985-86 and 2015 thousand hectares in 1990-91. It reached to the level of 2612 thousand hectares in 2000-01 which further increased to 2735 thousand hectares in 2008-09. In the post-green revolution period, the number of tube-wells for irrigation purpose has increased very fast. There were only 1973 tube-wells in the state in 1950-51. This number increased to about 12000 in 1960-61, 1.92 lakh in 1970-71, 6.00 lakh in 1980-81, 7.73 lakh in 1990-91, 10.73 lakh in 2000-01 and 11.68 lakh in 2004-05. At present, about 72 per cent of the irrigation is through tube-wells and the rest about 28 per cent by canals. This phenomenon resulted in over-exploitation of ground water.

The overall comparison of growth rates of different periods show that Punjab agriculture is facing the problem of stagnation in production particularly in the last one decade or so. The slow down in the growth rates of different crops has negative impact on the employment and income of the farmers as well as agricultural labourers. The area under different crops has almost reached to the maximum possible level. Any increase in area of particular crop will result in decline of another crop. In this way, the overall picture of Punjab agriculture may not change significantly. The productivity analysis reveals that breakthrough in productivity has been achieved mainly in few crops like rice, wheat, sugarcane, potato, maize and barley. Except wheat and rice, the area under other crops is not quite large. There are marketing constraints for other crops because public procurement is effective only in case of wheat and paddy. In case of pulses, desi cotton and bajra, the productivity has almost stagnated. Overall, the Punjab agriculture is facing the problem of stagnation in production and productivity. It may be stated that actual yield in the state is already more than 80 per cent of the potential yield in case of principal crops like wheat, paddy, Bt cotton, sunflower, etc. This means that there is little scope to increase the yield of these crops at the farm level. For other crops where there is potential to increase the yield, the farmers are not willing to bring more area under those crops due to various reasons. The returns over variable cost were the maximum (Rs 28823) for sugarcane ratoon followed by sugarcane planted (Rs 26662), paddy (Rs 19826), basmati (Rs 16703), Bt cotton (Rs 16700), wheat (Rs 14874), winter maize (Rs 14759) and cotton desi (Rs 14269). Although the returns over variable cost were the highest in sugarcane ratoon and sugarcane planted being an annual crop, the farmers have preference for wheat and paddy crops due to its high and stable yield and effective public procurement at the MSP.

The Punjab agriculture which was growing fast earlier has now reached a sort of plateau in terms of productivity and production. In the wake of a declining land man ratio, it is not able to generate gainful employment and sufficient income for the growing population. Farm profitability has witnessed a decline in the recent years due to cost price squeeze. There is almost stagnation in farm income. Farming alone is not able to generate sufficient income for small and marginal farmers. Due to economic distress, 2116 farmers had committed suicides during the last 15 years in the State. At present, the rural indebtedness is to the extent of about Rs 35000 crore which work out to be about Rs 3.50 lakh per household. The Punjab farmers are in deep economic crisis. For sustainable agricultural development, non-farm employment opportunities for rural youth may be created. It is need of the hour.

References

Aulakh, K.S. (2004), Re-fixing priorities can save agro-economy, *The Tribune,* Chandigarh, Vol. 124 (73), March 15, p. 16.

Govt. of Punjab (2006), *Agricultural and Rural development of Punjab-Transforming from crisis to growth,* The Punjab State Farmers Commission, pp. 1-72.

HT Correspondent (2006), Debt trap is killing farmers, say experts, *Hindustan Times,* Chandigarh, Vol. 82 (47), Feb. 24, p. 6.

Mishra, Subash (1999), Bachelor boys, *India Today,* Vol. 24 (33), August 10-16, p.10.

Nibber, G.S. (2004), Over 2000 farmers' suicides in Punjab in 15 years: Report, *Hindustan Times,* Chandigarh, Vol. 80 (253), October 22, p. 2.

Sharma, H.L. (2006), Early paddy: Good or bad, plant we will, *Hindustan Times,* Chandigarh, Vol. 82 (94), April 21, p.6

Sidhu, M.S., A.S.Joshi and Lavleen Kaur (2006), *Problems and Prospects of Agriculture in Punjab, Research Report,* Department of Economics, PAU, Ludhiana, pp 1-41.

Singh, Kulwant (2003), Vocational shift to ease pressure on farmers, *Hindustan Times,* Chandigarh, Vol. 79 (305), December 23, p.9.

3

Agrarian Crisis in Punjab and the Way Out

M. R. Khurana

Introduction

The exasperating agrarian crisis in the present Indian Punjab portrays the enviable growth experience of an economically advanced state having gone astray. Somewhat ironical as also a matter of great national shame though it might seem to be, yet the fact of the matter is that the state which once earned the epithets such as the 'granary of India', 'cradle', ' harbinger' or 'throbbing heartland' of the Green Revolution in India with few historical parallels[1], has become pushed into deep debt and despair so much so that its farmers, who successfully rid the nation of the frequent food shortages, unable to withstand the pressures of the prevailing socio-economic ground level realities, have resorted to suicides in substantial numbers.[2] Ironical and somewhat interesting again though it might seem to be that the very people who earlier untiringly worshipped at the altar of the Green Revolution in Punjab by showering the afore-mentioned praise on the state in the bygone era are now seen frequently alleging and putting the onerous onus on the said revolution as also on the in-vogue Neo-liberal capitalist policies for spelling despair and doom for the peasantry in the state.

It is not out of context to observe in the meantime that the Green Revolution in Punjab and the Neo-liberal capitalist policies of economic Liberalization, Privatization and Globalization(popularly known as LPG strategy) have, ever since their appearance, emerged as fiercely debated issues among the peasant representatives, social activists, economists, state planners and policymakers and in more recent times the environmentalists. Broadly speaking, two opposite types of opinions have emerged on this count. At the one end of the spectrum, are those who observe that in the late 1960s, when India wobbled on the brink of famine and rural chaos, the agricultural sector in Punjab emerged as the epic-centre of the new production technology, popularly known as the Green Revolution. A widely held view of this new production technology that came to be underlined in several studies overtime was that it consisted of a highly complementary package of bio-chemical as well as mechanical innovations. While the former comprised irrigation - seed - fertilizer package, pest and disease control measures, etc., tractor, thresher, harvester, tubewell and mechanical equipments and other such items came to be included in the latter.[3] There exists mounting evidence that suggests that with a given land base, the said two components of the new farm technology tend to exert a differential impact on the timeliness and scale of field crop operations, soil structure, plants, animals, labour absorption, composition of costs on different farm sizes, so on and so forth.[4]

This apart, a characteristic feature of the Punjab's agricultural growth experience has been that depending upon its strong irrigation base, infrastructural facilities and institutional framework, Punjab emerged as the front runner in the matter of adoption of the various components of the new farm technology, and under the spurt of the technological breakthrough under reference, realized rich dividends in terms of increased yield rates of some important crops like wheat and paddy, volume of overall agricultural production and level of productivity.[5] It scarcely needs any emphasis that the introduction of the Green Revolutions technology in Punjab has, over the period of time, been accompanied by substantial economic gains in terms of appreciable increases in the yield rates of paddy and wheat, volume of agricultural production and has, as such, earned for the state a pre-eminent position. The temporal details pertaining to the progress of the Green Revolution in Punjab in terms of a few selected indicators for the period between 1970-71 and 2008-09 are presented in Tables 1 through 9.

Table 1

Temporal Pattern of Area Under High Yielding Varieties of Major Food Crops In Punjab, 1967-68 to 2008-09

('000 Hectare)

Year	*Rice*	*Maize*	*Bajra*	*Wheat*
1967-68	17	29	51	621
1970-71	130	49	126	1589
1980-81	1095	127	34	2757
1990-91	1906	160	11	3271
2000-01	2506	154	5	3408
2007-08	2610	145	4	3488
2008-09(P)	2735	143	5	3526

Note: (P) Provisional

Source: *Statistical Abstract of Punjab for Various Years*, Government of Punjab.

Table 2

Temporal Pattern of Area under Food and Non-Food Crops inPunjab, 1970-71 to 2008-09

('000 Hectare)

	Kharrif Crops			*Rabi Crops*			*Total Crops*		
Year	*Food*	*Non-Food*	*Total*	*Food*	*Non-Food*	*Total*	*Food*	*Non-Food*	*Total*
1970-71	1356	1160	2516	2773	389	3162	4129	1549	5678
	(53.90)	(46.10)	(100.00)	(87.70)	(12.30)	(100.00)	(72.72)	(27.28)	(100.00)
1980-81	1827	1324	3151	3204	408	3612	5031	1732	6763
	(57.98)	(42.02)	(100.00)	(88.70)	(11.30)	(100.00)	(74.39)	(25.61)	(100.00)
1990-91	2444	948	3392	3434	676	4110	5878	1624	7502
	(72.05)	(27.95)	(100.00)	(83.55)	(16.45)	(100.00)	(78.35)	(21.65)	(100.00)
2000-01	3072	1030	4102	3491	348	3839	6563	1378	7941
	(74.90)	(25.10)	(100.00)	(90.94)	(9.06)	(100.00)	(82.65	-17.35)	(100.00)
2007-08	2943	935	3878	3674	318	3992	6617	1253	7870
(R)	(75.89)	(24.11)	(100.00)	(92.03)	(7.97)	(100.00)	(84.08)	(15.92)	(100.00)
2008-09	3162	885	4047	3553	312	3865	6715	1197	7912
(P)	(78.13)	(21.87)	(100.00)	(91.93)	(8.07)	(100.00)	(84.87)	(15.13)	(100.00)

Note: (P) Provisional (R)Revised

Source: *Statistical Abstract of Punjab for Various Years*, Government of Punjab.

Table 3
Temporal Pattern of Net and Total Cropped Area in Punjab, 1970-71 to 2006-07

('000 Hectare)

Year	*Net Area Sown*	*Net Area Sown as percentage to total area*	*Total Cropped Area*	*Cropping Intensity*
1	2	3	4	5
1970-71	4,053	81	5,678	1.40
1980-81	4,191	83	6,763	1.61
1990-91	4,218	84	7,502	1.78
2000-01	4,250	84	7,941	1.87
2007-08(R)	-	-	7,870	-
2008-09(P)	-	-	7,912	-

Note: Differences are due to rounding of Figures in this table.
(P) Provisional, (R) Revised

Source: *Statistical Abstract of Punjab for Various Years,* Government of Punjab.

Table 4
Temporal Pattern of Gross Cropped and Irrigated Area in Punjab, 1970-71 to 2008-09

('000 Hectare)

Year	*Gross Cropped Area*	*Gross Irrigated Area*	*Percentage of Gross Irrigated Area to Gross Cropped Area*
0	1	2	3
1970-71	5678	4242.5	74.7
1980-81	6763	5781.3	85.4
1990-91	7502	7054.8	94.0
2000-01	7941	7663.8	96.5
2007-2008(R)	7870	7689.3	97.7
2008-09(P)	7912	7723.6	97.6

Note: (P) Provisional, (R) Revised

Source: *Statistical Abstract of Punjab for Various Years,* Government of Punjab.

In the meantime, it is not unimportant to mention that although several other important changes attendant to the Green Revolution technology such as the ones pertaining to factor proportions and their relative shares have also occurred alongside in Punjab, a change that, nevertheless, must not escape our attention is that of setting into motion a process of qualitative rural transformation in terms of changes in the socio-

Table 5

Temporal Pattern of Area under Principal Crops in Punjab, 1970-71 to 2008-09

('000Hectare)

Year	Rice	Barja	Maize	Wheat	Barely	Total Cereals	Total Pulses	Total Food-grains	Total Oil Seeds	Cotton	Potatoes
1970-71	390	207	555	2299	57	3,514	414	3,928	295	397	17
1980-81-	1183	69	382	2812	65	4,513	341	4,854	238	649	40
1990-91	2015	12	188	3273	37	5,525	143	5,668	104	701	23
2000-01	2612	6	165	3408	32	6,223	54	6,277	86	474	60
2007-08(R)	2609	5	154	3487	16	6,271	27	6,298	60	605	90
2008-09(P)	2735	5	151	3526	16	6,433	22	6,455	60	527	82

Notes: Cotton is cleaned cotton and is in terms of thousands bales of 170 kgs. each.
(P) Provisional (R) Revised

Source: *Statistical Abstract of Punjab for Various Years*, Government of Punjab.

Table 6
Temporal Pattern of Net Irrigated Area in Punjab by Source, 1970-71 to 2008-09

('000Hectare)

Year	*Government Canals*	*Private Canals*	*Tubewells and Wells*	*Other Source*	*Total*	*Percentages of Net Area Irrigated to Net Area Sown*
0	1	2	3	4	5	6
1970-71	1286	6	1591	5	2888	71
1980-81	1430	-	1939	13	3382	81
1990-91	1660	9	2233	7	3909	93
2000-01	962	(a)	3074	2	4038	95
2007-08 (R)	1142	-	2922	4	4068	97.2
2008-09 (P)	1110	3	2950	1	4064	97.4

Note: (P) Provisional, (R) Revised.
(a) area less than 500

Source: *Statistical Abstract of Punjab for Various Years*, Government of Punjab.

Table 7
Temporal Pattern of Growth of Tubewells in Punjab, 1970-71 to 2008-09

(in lakhs)

	Numbers of Tubewells		
Year	*Diesel Operated*	*Electric Operated*	*Total*
1970-71	1.01	0.91	1.92
	(52.60)	(47.40)	(100.0)
1980-81	3.20	2.80	6.00
	(53.33)	(46.67)	(100.0)
1990-91	2.00	6.00	8.00
	(25.0)	(75.0)	(100.0)
2000-01	2.85	7.88	10.73
	(26.56)	(73.44)	(100.0)
2007-08	2.75	9.71	12.46
	(22.07)	(77.93)	(100.0)
2008-09(P)	2.80	9.96	12.76
	(21.94)	(78.06)	(100.0)

Note: Figures in parentheses represent the percentages of the total.
(P) Provisional

Source: *Statistical Abstract of Punjab for Various Years*, Government of Punjab.

Table 8
Temporal Pattern of Production of Principal Crops in Punjab

('000 Metric Tonnes)

Year	*Rice*	*Barja*	*Maize*	*Wheat*	*Barely*	*Total Cereals*	*Total Pulses*	*Total Food-grains*	*Total Oil Seeds*	*Cotton*	*Potatoes*
1970-71	688	243	861	5,145	57	6,997	308	7,305	233	818	216
1980-81	3,233	86	612	7,677	108	11,717	204	11,921	187	1,178	767
1990-91	6,506	13	333	12,159	101	19,113	105	19,218	93	1,909	453
2000-01	9,157	5	461	15,551	109	25,283	39	25,322	88	1,199	1,166
2007-08(R)	10,486	5	525	15,716	57	26,789	20	26,809	78	2,359	1,714
2008-09(P)	11,000	5	514	15,733	55	27,307	19	27,326	73	2,285	2,014

Notes: Cotton is cleaned cotton and is in terms of thousands bales of 170 kgs. each.
(P) Provisional (R) Revised

Source: *Statistical Abstract of Punjab for Various Years,* Government of Punjab.

Table 9
Temporal Pattern of Punjab's Contribution of Rice and Wheat to the Central Pool, 1980-81 to 2008-09

(Lakh Tonnes)

	Rice	*Wheat*
Year	*Contribution to the Central Pool*	*Contribution to the Central Pool*
1	2	3
1980-81	25.2 (45.3)	42.8 (73.0)
1990-91	48.2 (41.0)	67.5 (61.0)
2000-01	69.4 (33.3)	94.2 (57.6)
2006-07	78.3 (31.2)	69.5 (75.3)
2007-08 (R)	79.8 (27.8)	68.8 (60.9)
2008-09 (P)	85.5 (25.4)	99.4 (43.8)

Note: Information of Wheat pertains to Marketing year (April to March) whereas that of Rice pertains to crop year (October to September). (P) Provisional (R) Revised

Source: Ministry of Consumer Affairs, Government of India.

economic outlook and attitudes of the different strata of the rural community in Punjab.[6] The changes associated with the process of adoption of the Green Revolution have occurred in a manner that economic values have, over the period of time, tended to become growingly more dominant over the social values. The caste which once used to be the dominant institution of the rural society in Punjab has tended to lose its influence and caste- based obligations have, in terms of time, come to occupy relatively less recognition in the economic life of the rural people compared to the pre-Green Revolution era. The caste rigidities have tended to mollify in Punjab with the passage of time. The traditional 'Jajmani' system, which had, since long, been regulating the socio economic life of the rural people, has gradually witnessed its replacement by formal contractual relations.[7] Consequently, caste- based occupational classification, has tended to gradually fade in the post-Green

Revolution period. This period has witnessed an important movement on the part of the low caste people out of their ancestral occupations in search of better economic professions. Inter-generational and intra-generational occupational mobility seems to have increased importantly and at a faster rate during the period under reference.[8] The people in the Punjab countryside seem to be becoming more and more receptive to new ideas, attitudes and values. In brief, the economic, social and institutional set up of the village economy have been experiencing important changes in diverse set of manifestations.[9] In a nutshell, the state has, with the onset of the Green Revolution in Punjab, not only filled-up India's empty granaries[10], but also has, over the period of time, been moving onto a higher trajectory of modernity and economic prosperity far exceeding its rural counterparts elsewhere in the country. These people hold that in the wake of the implementation of the policy of economic liberalization, they hold, the Punjab agriculture is bound to experience a big boost as the emergence of new trade opportunities will confer immense static as well as dynamic economic gains on it.

In sharp contrast to the above, at the other end of the spectrum are the skeptics of the Green Revolution and of the in-vogue Neo-liberal capitalist policies who frequently allege that the votaries of Green Revolution were inherently incapable of dealing with issues other than yields of wheat and rice. In support of their viewpoint, they emphatically observe that the planners and policymakers, in the over-zeal for raising the volume of production in the wake of the arrival of the Green Revolution in late 1960s , overlooked many core issues such as those pertaining to land distribution, ecological sustainability, and the long-term economic costs of an input-intensive agriculture. The gist of the argument is that the introduction of Green Revolution technologies into Punjab, while succeeding in its original assigned task of growing significantly larger volumes of foodgrains for the rest of India necessitated by rapidly growingly population, has brought about economic, environmental, and social disasters in Punjab- the impending realities not apprehended by the original advocates of the phenomenon under reference. In addition, arguing that first the Green Revolution led and later economic liberalization led process of development have adversely impacted both farmers and agro-biodiversity in the state, it has come to be maintained that the afore-mentioned production gains of new farm technology in Punjab have mainly occurred at the expense of heavy intake of pesticide use, overexploitation of groundwater resources due to excessive irrigation, growing soil infertility, and HYVs pest and disease susceptibility.[11] These processes of development, in their viewpoint, have spelt ecological disaster in Punjab. As if these were not enough, the associated health problems and increased financial burden in the wake of emergence of greed to realize higher yields through the application of higher dose of purchased farm inputs resulting into appreciable rise in the cost of cultivation have proved to be the proverbial last straw on camel's back.[12] These adversaries of Green Revolution further contend that Punjab agricultural growth experience suggests that the state agriculture, during the course of its own growth, has not succeeded in any important way in forging and strengthening the widely perceived and highly acclaimed demand and supply inter-sectoral linkages with the non-farm sector. As a result, the agricultural growth experience in Punjab did not have had the desired important bearing on the overall economic development of the state and this, in the ultimate, has led to shocking immiserization of the peasantry and even suicides on its part.[13] The current agrarian crisis, in their opinion, is a cruel counterpoint to the much-hyped excitement about the double-digit economic growth claimed to be fuelled by ongoing process of economic liberalization. It is forcefully argued that thanks to such developments that the agricultural sector in Punjab, marked by its prolonged and continuing virtual stagnation and its progressively becoming non-viable in pure economic terms overtime, is currently in a state of veritable socio-economic and environmental disaster. The spate of suicides by highly indebted farmers incurring heavy loss in farming have been continuing as an unabated phenomenon and the packaged panaceas of the governments have scarcely succeeded in stemming the suicide wave looming large in the state. The failure on the part of the government even to mollify the severity of the crisis by way of occasional packages, only proves that the Punjab agrarian crisis, far from being transitory, fractional and confined to a small area in the state, is somewhat more fundamental and structural and its aggravation is very much deep rooted in a wide variety of factors. To be more specific, the eruption of the agrarian crisis and its deepening over time and finally culminating into the phenomenon of farmers' suicides particularly in an area whose agricultural growth experience has been enviable, in the opinion of these keen observers and analysts of the prevailing agrarian reality in the Punjab countryside, is indeed one of the most tragic events of the modern times in the post-independence India.[14] These features of the Punjab agrarian crisis do not, by any stretch of imagination, mirror the image of Punjab as the granary or the throbbing heartland of green revolution in India.

Against the afore-mentioned backdrop, the moot questions that assume immense pertinence at the moment are: Why has the agrarian crisis erupted in Punjab? Can Punjab rid itself of the agrarian crisis it is presently in and regain its pristine glory of yore years in the matter of agricultural development under the prevailing conditions? If so, how? Needless to overemphasize, the meaningful answers to these and other related questions imperatively focus on the need to dissect the crisis. Motivated by this realization, we make an attempt in this paper to dismember the agrarian crisis in Punjab, locate the potent factors that contribute towards its deepening as also its plausible solutions on an enduring basis.

Though a plethora of evidence, both theoretical and empirical, exists in the wake of extensive explorations attempting to examine the agrarian crisis in Punjab, a cursory look at the existing body of literature, nevertheless, points towards a number of gaps. The first is that although the links between agrarian crisis and policymaking have come to be perceived in some well-meaning academic quarters, yet no detailed systematic and significant investigation has ever seem to have been made up till now on the causes underlying the crisis under reference. The second is that concrete policy prescriptions have not as yet been attempted possibly due to blurred vision of the planners and policy makers in terms of policy formulation to solve the agrarian crisis in Punjab.

To address the afore-mentioned issues, this paper draws upon the secondary data. These data are published annually in *'Statistical Abstract of Punjab'* by the Economic and Statistical Organisation, Government of Punjab. A part of the data have also been compiled from the published documents other official studies, and research undertaken by other research workers in the area under reference. Wherever required, percentages and averages have been worked out for carrying out the analysis in the study. The perspective offered in the present paper is that agrarian crisis and ongoing process of economic Liberalization, Privatization and Globalization(widely known as LPG strategy) are nested developments whose correlates need to be investigated. A further significant feature of this paper is that it seeks to put together various explanations of the crisis under reference. Likewise its findings might have lot of relevance not only in respect of current agrarian crisis in Punjab but also in situations identical to Punjab which like the state under reference are desperately crying for appropriate policy-mix. And yet again, the conclusions and findings emerging from analysis done in the paper might also even help the new aspirants readying themselves to replicate Punjab-like agricultural growth experience.

The paper is organized as follows. To begin with, Section 1 undertakes to understand the agrarian crisis in Punjab in terms of mirroring its characteristic features. An attempt has been made in Section 2 to make a diagnosis of the crisis under reference in terms of its causes and implications both for the state and its peasantry from the viewpoint of an economist. Section 3focuses on the elusive character of crop diversification solution. Section 4 outlines the blueprint of the proposed strategy for making the state agriculture sustainable. Finally, Section 5 presents conclusions and policy implications of our analysis.

Diagnosis of the Agrarian Crisis in Punjab

As observed above, our primary aim in this section is to carry out a diagnosis of the agrarian crisis in Punjab and to get deeper insights into it for purposes of policy formulation to this effect. In this regard, what needs to be underlined at the very outset of this section is that the said crisis has come to be viewed in terms of multi- pronged set of symptoms such as the evolving agrarian relations in the wake of the much famed Green Revolution and Neo-liberal capitalist policies, as also in that of rising input costs, declining farm produce price realization and the helplessness of farmers to abandon cultivation in the absence of economically gainful alternative livelihoods so on and so forth. It is widely observed that the agrarian crisis in Punjab is the outcome of the interplay between a wide variety of inter-connected factors. A brief recapitulation of the these various factors that account for the eruption as also for the aggravation of the crisis under reference is said to be of tremendous significance from the viewpoint of appropriate policy formulation for solving the crisis meaningfully on a lasting basis. Accordingly, in tune with this realization, we make an attempt below to locate the plausible explanations underlying the agrarian crisis in Punjab.

To provide the necessary backdrop to our attempt, it is not impertinent to make some observations in passing. *First,* it is important to mention that the agricultural sector in Punjab, after moving onto a high growth trajectory of growth for a fairly long period of time between late 1960s and early 1990s, began experiencing deceleration thereafter. In support of this contention, it has come to be maintained that with the available potential of resources and technology getting exploited closer to the maximum possible limits, a peculiar situation as characterized, among other things, by increasing costs of farm inputs, shrinking resource base, declining productivity, profitability and incomes has come to become relatively more pronounced. In its rat-race for higher growth, the Punjab peasantry, particularly the small and marginal farmers, with no alternative option to fall back upon has, over the period of time, got pushed into capital-intensive farming. The overexploitation of natural resources, particularly groundwater, further compounded the situation in that the resultant farm incomes, meagre past savings as also the fresh borrowings went into the digging of the deeper submersible pumps on an extensive scale. *Second,* there exists almost a consensus that agriculture in Punjab is characterized by slowdown and has been in a state of disarray throughout the post-economic reforms era. The reasoning that underlies this consensus is that while the Net State Domestic Product at constant prices in Punjab during the 1970s grew annually at an average of 5.4 per as against 3.4 per cent of India as a whole; in the 1980s, on the other hand, as a result of catch-up on the part of other states, Punjab with its continued growth rate of about 5.4 per cent per annum, seemed to have only a marginal edge over others, jointly clocking on yearly basis an average growth rate of 5.1 per cent during the said period. So far so good. However, it was in the 1990s that the situation in terms of growth rate catapulted for Punjab when its growth in Net State Domestic Product registered a decline to about 4.3 per cent on per annum basis, as against rest of India registering a growth rate of 6.1 per cent. In the wake of this downslide beginning somewhere in the 1990s and coinciding with the process of economic reforms in the form of Liberalization, Privatization and Globalization (popularly known as LPG Strategy) and its continuing thereafter, Punjab is reported to have lost its pre-eminent position as the highest agricultural growth achiever and also that of a highest per capita income state - the distinctions it maintained over the past four decades or so. Sadly, the state is now facing a mounting debt burden. For instance, as on March 31, 2009, the total outstanding debt of the state was estimated to be Rs. 57787 crore which, in terms of percentage, measured 37.63 per cent of the Gross State Domestic Product (GSDP). Needless to overemphasize, the high incidence of the state debt necessarily implies higher interest obligations which were estimated to be as high as Rs. 4901.68 crore during the financial year 2008-09 as against Rs. 22219 crore of Gross Revenue receipts. It has come to be pointed out that the state has been passing through a period of fiscal crisis mainly on account of inability of receipts to keep pace with the growing revenue expenditure. The revenue deficit of the state in 2008-09 is estimated to be about Rs.3856.20 crore which is only marginally higher than the 2007-08 figure of Rs. 3823.24 crore. The available evidence shows that the state sought to implement a budgeted plan of about Rs 3738.00 crore in 2008-09 as against Rs. 2934.00 crore in 2007-08. With the budgeted plan expenditure in 2008-09 registering an increase to the tune of about 27.40 per cent over the previous year, the increase in revenue and capital expenditure has led to rise in fiscal deficit which increased by roughly 45 per cent in a single year, from Rs. 4603.83 crore in 2007-08 to Rs. 6690.45 crore in 2008-09.[15] *Third,* a widely acknowledged fact about the crisis under reference is that it got underway consequent upon governments decision to dismantle, without giving adjustment time, the sophisticated mechanism that evolved in stages in the post-independence pre-reform period to protect the peasantry from the uncertainties of the market. It is indisputably true that these protectionist arrangements, comprising essentially a system of input price subsidization and output price support in the form of Minimum Support Price-Cum- Assured Purchase mechanism, notwithstanding their numerous inherent weaknesses in terms of implementation for a while, had enabled the state farmers to go in for cultivation in a predictably stable price- purchase milieu. As against this, during the post-reform period, the government not only effected a cut in the subsidies on major farm inputs, but also has attempted to absolve itself of the responsibility of producing or procuring and distributing these farm inputs at the very door steps of the farmers. As a consequence, following an important rise in the prices of farm inputs, the unscrupulous private traders engaged in the sale of farm inputs capitalized on the opportunity and pushed up the farm input prices further by way of manipulation and even by selling spurious farm inputs to the farmers in the state. The subsequent period saw the worsening of the situation in the aftermath of an increase in the rates of interest on institutional loans, on the one hand, and with the narrow window of such loans becoming all the more more narrower with the linking of loans with the ownership of land, on the other. The end result of such developments, in any case, was that the cultivating households, by and large, got pushed into the trap of the private moneylenders known for charging exorbitant interest rates as also for using other exploitative mechanisms in respect of advancing of loans to their hapless borrowers. *And finally,* as of now, the talk of the second Green Revolution has turned out to be only an empty vessel that seems to making much noise. Though a lot of excitement has been generated in respect of a second green revolution to overcome the ongoing agrarian crisis, yet no new technological breakthrough seems to be in sight in any major crop comparable to the success of the HYV varieties of the earlier Green Revolution of the late 1960s. If the prevailing grassroots realities are any indication, while the Genetically Modified(GM) crops have tended become controversial, the much-hyped Bt. Cotton seeds of Monsanto have proved to be disastrous for farmers time and again. In spite of this however, the Seed Bill 2004 does not have a liability clause to compensate the indigenous(including Punjabi) farmers in the event of their getting fleeced at the hands of gigantic Multinational Corporations and private traders involved in selling them the spurious seeds that fail them (the farmers) more often than not.

Against the afore-mentioned backdrop, we feel that the following factors have contributed to the agrarian crisis in Punjab and its deepening in terms of time:

First, it is widely believed that a comprehension of agrarian relations prevailing in a particular area is crucial for understanding of the dynamics of agricultural growth/crisis in that area. In the context of Punjab, what can scarcely be overemphasized is that the introduction of bio-chemical inputs and mechanical gadgets of the new farm technology in the form of Hybrid and in more recent times Genetically Modified(GM) varieties of seeds, chemical fertilizers, weedicides, insecticides and pesticides etc., coupled with assured means of irrigation have, over the period of time, led to appreciable rise in cropping intensity, per acre yield of various crops and mani-fold rise in the volume of production. As a consequence, Punjab agriculture has undergone perceptible commercial orientation. Thanks to the spectacular growth of the yield rates of major crops like wheat and paddy and the resultant rise in the volume of production and overall productivity in the wake of the Green Revolution since late -1960s, the state emerged agriculturally as the most advanced state amongst all the Indian states with agriculture of the state progressively becoming more and more sensitive to market conditions and signals in the process. In the meantime, it is not out of context to observe that farmers' decision in the wake of Punjab agriculture emerging as a high cost and capital intensive proposition, gets influenced, *inter alia*, by growing risk and uncertainty. The changes in farm practices and growing commercial orientation of agriculture have significantly influenced the agrarian relations in the state. Far from remaining a way of life, agriculture in Punjab has become a commercial activity where various decisions are governed by profitability/rate of return on capital investment made. Though some sections of the state peasantry in Punjab continue to be trapped in agriculture, yet they are also substantially affected by market forces and take decisions accordingly. In an important sense agriculture of the state is characterized by the dominance of capitalism. Table 10 brings out the change in terms of number of operational holdings in Punjab for the period falling in-between 1970-71 and 2005-06. This table shows that on one side, there are big farm households with operational holdings of 10 hectares and above who accounted for 7.08 per cent of the total cultivators in the state in 2005-06. These farmers, it is not out of context to mention, have, in addition to farming, diverse set of interests in urban property and business, particularly in transport, cinema, hotel, commission agent work etc. On the other extreme are agricultural labourers who constituted 24.63 per cent of work force in 1991 and 16.40 per cent in 2001(Table 11). They earn their living by selling their labour to cultivators, don't own any land and they also generally belong to the Scheduled Caste (SC) and backward caste (BC) categories of population of the state. Above the agricultural labourer but quite near to them in economic status come marginal farmers each cultivating less than one hectare of land. They constituted 13.33 per cent of the farm households in 2005-06. Above this category are small farmers cultivating land holdings of 1-2 hectare. They account for 18.24 per cent of

Table 10
Temporal Pattern of Distribution of Operational Holdings in Punjab, 1970-71 to 2005-06

Year	*Below 1 ha*	*1- 2 ha*	*2-4ha*	*4-10*	*10 and above*	*All holdings*
1970-71	517568	260083	281103	247755	68883	1375392
	(37.63)	(18.91)	(20.44)	(18.01)	(5.01)	(100.00)
1990-81	1973323	199368	287423	269072	73941	1027127
	(19.21)	(19.41)	(27.98)	(26.20)	(7.20)	(100.00)
1985-86	256259	207639	290837	260142	73553	1088430
	(23.54)	(19.08)	(26.72)	(23.90)	(6.76)	(100.00)
1990-91	295668	203842	288788	261481	67172	1116951
	(26.47)	(18.25)	(25.86)	(23.41)	(6.01)	(100.00)
1995-95	203876	183453	320340	305794	79610	1093073
	(18.65)	(16.78)	(29.31)	(27.98)	(7.28)	(100.00)
2000-01	122760	173071	328231	300954	72356	997372
	(12.31)	(17.35)	(32.91)	(30.18)	(7.25)	(100.00)
2005-06	133791	183064	319737	295777	71001	1003370
	(13.33)	(18.24)	(31.87)	(29.48)	(7.08)	(100.00)

Note: Figures in the parentheses are percentages of the total of all holdings.
Source: *Statistical Abstract of Punjab for Various Years,* Government of Punjab.

Table 11
Temporal Pattern of Workforce Structure in Punjab, 1971-2001

(Number)

Year	*Cultivators*	*Agricultural Labourers*	*Industrial Workers*	*Other Workers*	*Total*
1971	1665153	786705	442070	1018664	3912592
	(42.56)	(20.11)	(11.3)	(26.03)	(100.00)
1981	1767286	1092225	665442	1402806	4927759
	(35.86)	(22.16)	(13.50)	(28.47)	(100.00)
1991	1917210	1502123	749136	1929905	6098374
	(31.44)	(24.63)	(12.28)	(31.65)	(100.00)
2001	2099330	1498976	769047	4774407	9141760
	(22.96)	(16.40)	(8.41)	(52.23)	(100.00)

Note: Figures in the parentheses are the percentages of the total workforce.
Source: *Statistical Abstract of Punjab for various years,* Government of Punjab.

the total cultivators in the state. The marginal and small farmers together account for roughly a little less than one-third (i.e. 31.57 per cent) of the total farmers in the state (Table 10). These categories of farmers, getting sandwiched in serious crisis, are fighting for their existence which is under threat. In terms of caste, they belong to other categories of farmers. They are in a debt trap with income levels that are appreciably low. There is a large chunk of farmers who cultivate area between 2-4 hectares and 4-10 hectares. These farmers, popularly known as lower and upper medium farmers constitute 31.87 per cent and 29.48 per cent of the total farmers and put together constitute 61.35 per cent of the total state farmers. An important point worth mentioning in the case of these farmers, considered to be very active and the backbone of farming in the state, is that they are reported to be moderately under debt. The falling rates of return from cultivation, as witnessed in Punjab agriculture overtime, also seem to be affecting them in an important way.

Furthermore, as things stand today, farm cultivation in Punjab is highly mechanized and market-oriented, both in terms of acquisition of farm input and disposal of output. There is no denial to the fact that in terms of use of machinery, chemical inputs, hybrid varieties of seeds, irrigation, Punjab has, over the period of time, emerged as one of the top-ranking states in the country. The farm cultivation in the state is organized on the basis of individually owned family farms. Another important feature of Punjab agriculture that needs to be underlined in particular is that the crop production activity in the state is predominantly carried out through the use of hired labour. Though use of hired labour is common among all strata of the state peasantry, yet the dependence of medium and large farmers on hired labour is quite high. Likewise, while all categories of farmers are involved in generating a marketable surplus but the contribution of medium and large farmers, in relative terms, is much larger than their not so lucky compatriots. In the case of Punjab what needs to be underlined in particular is that regardless of prevailing differentiation among the farmers in terms of economic status, the unity in terms of caste composition, participation in the process of hiring-in of labour and selling of marketable surplus/output are some of the distinctive features which cannot be overlooked by any stretch of imagination. The differentiation also manifests itself amply in terms of educational levels of the farmers and the type of schooling their children are receiving. For instance, while the categories of small and marginal farmers as also that of the agricultural labourers, partly due to economic deprivation and partly due their being less educated in comparative terms, send their children to government schools with miserably low teaching standards in the rural areas; the ones belonging to the medium and big farmers in Punjab, on the other hand, tend to join growingly the city based private English medium schools which now seem to be penetrating the state's rural areas as well. The agriculture in Punjab has reached a point where further differentiation among the farmers is bound to fuel the ongoing process of marginalization of the small and marginal peasants in the state via multiple routes.[16] The crux of the agrarian relations in Punjab today, which also partly explains the phenomenon of the prevailing agrarian crisis including farm suicides in some regions of Punjab is that the emerging agrarian relations have over the period of time growingly replaced the traditional *Jajmani System* by the employer-employee contractual system in farm cultivation. The emergence of commercial relations overtime has importantly replaced the traditional support system for the weaker and the poorer segments of the Punjabi society and, they are progressively becoming dispossessed of their productive assets in the process. In the prevailing crisis ridden agrarian reality in Punjab, the rich seem to be involved in purchasing the land and other resources of the weaker sections rather than helping them out of it and thus are seen contributing towards the ongoing process of growing concentration in land overtime in an overall sense(Table 10).

Second, though agriculture in Punjab continues to be an important sector of the Punjab economy with a little less than one-third of the Net State Domestic Product originating in this sector alone, yet it does not seem to perform satisfactorily in terms of productivity. The share of agriculture in 2008-09 was noted to be 31.43 per cent of the Net State Domestic Product in Punjab. Within agriculture Punjab has also recorded a sluggish growth rate in the post-reform period. In the 1990s the overall growth rate in agricultural Net Domestic Product for Punjab was 2.3 per cent while the rest of India registered 3.3 per cent. This suggests a sharp decline from the 1980s when Punjab 's overall annual growth rate in agricultural income was noted to be 5.4 per cent in comparison to just 3.08 per cent for the rest of India.[17] Moreover, it has come to be observed that the cropping system in Punjab is dominated by wheat, rice, and cotton but the market for these commodities, including the foodgrains, is lacking. In the 1960s, 1970s, and to some extent in the 1980s the shortage of foodgrains in other parts of India was the major source of absorption of the surplus produced in Punjab. However, in the 1990s the deficit in other states, particularly in the northern northeast states of India, experienced reduction due to increase in the level of agricultural productivity in those areas and the market for excess supply of foodgrains from Punjab declined.

Third, another major reason that accounts for the eruption of the crisis of Punjab agriculture is the stagnation of the wheat and rice yields which, in turn, has resulted in increase in capital costs and shrinking profit margins in agricultural production. The crops such as rice and wheat require multiple watering. The use of irrigation and due to rising subsidies and falling public investments there has been an enormous waste of resources such as water and the farming system has become unsustainable. The policy of free electricity to farmers has led to excessive pumping out and hence depletion of groundwater resources resulting into the lowering of the water table to the extent of 15 centimeters per year over the past 20-25 years.[18]

Fourth, indebtedness of the peasantry is another major reason that accounts for the agrarian crisis in Punjab. It is pertinent to mention that indebtedness of the peasantry, far from occurring suddenly over night, has its roots in the credit policy that has been pursued over the period of time. Moreover, the indebtedness itself results from a mismatch in the cost of production and the Minimum Support Price that the Punjab cultivators have been receiving at the end of every cropping cycle. Another important point that deserves to be mentioned here is that heavy indebtedness has been spreading across the landholding patterns. In that context, the small and marginal farmers and the medium-sized cultivators are the most affected lot, though the large landholders in the rain- fed areas of the state, too, are seen to be experiencing strain on such counts. An important point worth mentioning in the context of availability of credit is that even after 63 years of Independence, private money-lending remains the single largest source of credit for the small and marginal farmers. This is so because the institutional sources are fast moving out of the credit delivery mechanism. There is another dimension of indebtedness in Punjab that cannot be easily glossed over. The cultivation in Punjab is primarily through tubewell irrigation in nature. Thus, the subsidy given on fertilisers and pesticides, irrigation and electricity does not reach the small and marginal landholders, as the farm cultivation in their case has, over the period of time, become deprived of an assured irrigation source. Among this lot, those who are engaged in the cultivation of cash crops requiring irrigation water facilities, have to perforce rely on the rainfall that is erratic at most of the times, and also puts the system under tremendous strain. The growing of cash crop becomes a sort of compulsion, as subsistence farming alone does not provide much needed liquid capital for the bare survival of the grower. As a result, more and more small and marginal farmers get pushed into compulsory cash crop cultivation that is having a spiral effect in terms of the debt crisis. Heavy indebtedness has been the immediate reason for most suicides by farmers. The findings emanating from 2002-03 NSSO survey on farmers' indebtedness that were published later in July 2005 are bold pointer to this effect. *First,* it came out that as many as roughly two-third(i.e. 65.4 per cent) of the total farmers in Punjab had obtained loans for one purpose or the other. More importantly, it was found that such high incidence of indebtedness clearly showed that it was, far from being just a routine indebtedness, a virtual debt trap for many farmers. For instance, according to an estimate, the total annual rural debt of the state of Punjab stood at Rs.24,000 crore in 2003-04 which in any case exceeded the state's gross annual earnings from agriculture. According to a more recent report of the National Sample Survey Organization (NSSO), on an average, each farmer in Punjab owed a debt of Rs.41,576, as against the national average of Rs.12,505 to this effect. In the light of these findings, one can argue that if the total debt is more than the gross annual earnings from agriculture and if the average debt per farmer is Rs. 41,576, that means already many small and marginal farmers in the state must have irretrievably fallen into the debt trap. Their interest commitment per year would work out to be more than their earnings/profits from agriculture. It is not surprising, therefore, that many amongst them must have been forced out of farming, losing their land in the process and unable to bear the mounting pressure and social stigma, have been found even resorting to the extreme step of committing suicides. Punjab's experience on this count is a bold pointer to the fact that under conditions of the present Indian agrarian crisis, high indebtedness is also associated with high-income but high-risk, high-investment and high-cost farming which precisely is being advocated as the solution for the crisis. Institutional credit hardly accounts for less than two-fifth of the total agricultural credit and farmers depend on private moneylenders who charge exorbitant rates of interest – up to 60 per cent and even more. In the changed scenario the banking sector has resorted to curtail their priority sector lending, especially to agriculture. Whatever institutional credit is available is cornered mostly by the big farmers who are found in recycling it as private loans to the small and marginal farmers and at times even to the medium peasants at usurious rates of interest. When it comes to repayment, these economically well - off farmers often turn out to be willful defaulters. There is no denial to the fact that that today's agricultural economy favors large farm producers. And while the large farmers have easy access to credit, the small and marginal farmers, on the other hand, have practically no option except to fall in the trap of usurious moneylenders for obtaining loans. These high interest rates, combined with the low annual income of the small and marginal farmers, have created a sort of vicious debt trap for the vulnerable segments of the Punjab peasantry. Once trapped, the small and marginal farmers must either sell or mortgage their land and thus get forced out of it becoming dispossessed of their means of livelihoods in the process. This fact has also been highlighted in some micro level studies conducted on the theme of farm indebtedness in Punjab.[19]

Fifth, studies suggests that the Punjabi farmers, guided by the objective of maximizing returns, have resorted to the overuse of fertilizers, pesticides and reliance on HYV seeds and of late, to some extent, on the Genetically Modified seeds such as the Bt. Cotton. This has led to significant rise in the cost of cultivation. Given the fact that vagaries of nature still characterize the agricultural sector in Punjab in one way or the other, the crop production business on several occasions has tended to suffer.

Sixth, the access to information base that the cultivators have largely comes from the agents of the fertilizer and seed companies. The government extension machinery is not visible in the sense that it can provide an objective database in information to the cultivators.

Seventh, the attitude of the government may be described as starkly apathetic. This is demonstrated by the fact that bulk of the suicide victims have not received any kind of compensation from the government.

Eighth, there is a total absence of safety nets for the cultivators, especially the small and the medium ones.

Ninth, it has come to be argued in some quarters that the Punjab peasantry, like its counterparts in identical situations elsewhere in the country, has been squeezed by a price precipice as evidenced by – sharply increasing input prices and stagnating output prices. The prices of all agricultural inputs such as – fertilizers, pesticides, seeds, water and even of infrastructural items such as the transportation and cold storage services have experienced a main-fold increase in Punjab over time. Owing to the perennial power crisis in Punjab, the dependence of the state farmers on diesel engines for purposes of irrigation has witnessed a considerable rise and with this getting underway, there has occurred upward revision in the price of diesel. The prices of fertilizers have also increased steadily. So have traditional seed prices and less said the better about the exorbitant monopoly prices of Genetically Modified seeds. In comparison, the increases in the Minimum Support of Prices of paddy and wheat have been too meagre to match the increases in the costs of farm inputs. Furthermore, the price crash in the case of the commercial crops has been even more dramatic. Thanks to the speculative trade lobby and fleecing middlemen, the share of the farmers in value addition, even in commodities registering considerable rise in this regard particularly in horticultural crops and vegetables, has been virtually zero. The collapse in output prices, far from resulting from of increased production or higher productivity, has been discernible even in cases where the rate of production has been falling, though the reverse should happen if the forces of demand and supply operate freely. To cut the matter short, the increase in cost of production has remained significantly at a higher pedestal in comparison to output prices which have at best risen only at a snail's pace, stagnated or even witnessed occasional declines markedly, in part due to wrong export-import policies. It has come to be observed that since late 1990s, the terms of trade have shifted 5 to 6 per cent against agriculture, and as a result, the profitability of agriculture has, depending on the crop, season and region, witnessed an erosion to the tune of about 25 to 40 per cent. Another paradoxical aspect of this price precipice has been that the increased application of farm inputs, in quantity as well as value terms, has not led to significant growth of agricultural productivity, volume of agricultural production, and earnings of farmers. Instead, it has added only to their mounting indebtedness and the related woes. To put it pithily, it can be maintained that the price precipice, aggravated by the entry of the big capital in procurement, wholesale and retail trade in agricultural commodities, and the role of the speculative big capital in forward trading, as part of the Neo-liberal capitalist policies has importantly contributed to the emergence, existence, persistence and compounding of the agrarian crisis in Punjab.

Tenth, contrary to its lip service to higher agricultural growth, the Government appears to have arrived at the conclusion that agricultural growth in Punjab is no longer important from the viewpoint of the overall future growth of the national economy. It becomes amply evidenced from the fact that the share of agriculture in the State Domestic Product has declined and even marked increase in the present growth rate of the state agriculture would not contribute much to the growth of the State Domestic Product. On close examination, however, this argument seems to be somewhat fallacious on several counts. *First,* a sizeable chunk of the workforce in Punjab continues to be dependent on agriculture. Higher incomes to them, due to higher agricultural growth, alone will help in sustaining the non-agricultural growth. *Second,* the growth of the much hyped tertiary sector cannot be sustained in the absence of sustained growth in the real productive sectors of the economy, particularly agriculture. *And finally,* high growth in State Domestic Product cannot be sustained only through higher investment, depending on foreign fund flows. To cut the matter short, if the Punjab agricultural economy has to acquire more internal dynamism, agriculture should continue to remain the mainspring its overall growth.

Eleventh, declining public investment in agriculture is yet another aspect of the Punjab agrarian crisis. Rural expenditure has fallen in an overall sense under fiscal distress in the state. In absolute terms, public investments in agriculture have been stagnating or falling over years. The Gross State Domestic Capital Formation (GSDCF) in agriculture has declined importantly to become only appallingly low.[20] To be more specific, bulk of the capital formation in the case of Punjab agriculture is attributable to the farmers. But the decline in public sector investment on the pretext of fiscal crunch in the state does not seem to have been offset by the limited increase in private investment and capital formation. This decline in public investment is reflected most ominously in the area of irrigation. Now bulk of the subsidies to agriculture are gobbled by the large farm operators in the state, while fertilizer subsidies get cornered mostly by the inefficient fertilizer units. It is often alleged that while the large and high medium farmers have been the major beneficiaries of these subsidies in Punjab, the small and marginal farmers and the low medium farmers stand to gain importantly from public sector investments.

Twelfth, the ecological problems thrown up by Green Revolution like waterlogging and the consequent new pest attacks, salinity and crop failure, decline in groundwater table, soil erosion and depletion of soil nutrients, chemical pollution due to improper use of fertilizers and pesticides etc., have cropped up in Punjab in a big way. These problems, without an iota of doubt, stand aggravated in the present phase of post-Green Revolution crisis. Although these problems can scarcely be addressed at the farm level only, yet with declining public sector investment, the government not only doesn't spend money to overcome these problems but also seems to be bereft of time even to address them. In the post Neo-liberal era, India has emerged as a huge market for all pesticides that are banned in several countries of the European Union. Unscrupulous companies mislead farmers by selling them toxic injectible enzymes and steroid stimulants to make their plants and vegetables grow bigger and gain in weight. Unfortunately, this serious ecological dimension of the present agrarian crisis has failed to evoke adequate attention and does not seem to be anybody's child in policy making circles. Furthermore, the plight of the agricultural sector in Punjab is often compounded by the natural disasters like occasional droughts and floods. As a result of the climate change, total seasonal/annual precipitation has tended to witness an important decline and with monsoons becoming more and more elusive, the rainfall pattern has also, over the period of time, tended to become erratic, spatially as well as temporally, and does not strictly coincide with the traditional agricultural seasons. The total water flows in the rivers have been receding in more recent times and the indications are that the global warming has already begun to take its heavy toll.

Thirteenth, the globalization of world agriculture throws up new challenge for Punjab agriculture. The key question is can Punjab penetrate into the world markets? The world agriculture is changing quickly with new rules of the game and with the WTO Agreement on Agreement. Market access, domestic support, and export subsidies have become three major pillars of the Agreement on Agriculture. Furthermore, sanitary and phyto-sanitary issues have come to play a major role in the Agreement on Agriculture. TRIPS have also played a major role in protecting intellectual property rights. There has been a growing presence of multinational corporations in developing countries, particularly in trading agricultural commodities. Increasing concentration and growing scale in food business in terms of processing, distribution, and retailing are required to be renegotiated. In the emerging scenario, working against Punjab agriculture, however, is also the developed country agriculture, which is highly distorted due to producer subsidies.

The impact of trade liberalization on the output prices following the signing of the Agreement on Agriculture under the WTO is said to be a key factor behind the agrarian crisis in Punjab. In certain cases, the price crash in the wake of trade liberalization has been markedly distressing. With the ushering-in of the said process of economic liberalization, the Indian markets have witnessed a glut of cheap and highly subsidized agricultural imports, which, in turn, has seriously impacted our agrarian economy. Worse, though the aggregate value of exports has increased, the unit value has declined in case of many agricultural commodities which has adversely impacted the economic fortunes of the peasantry in terms of lower earnings. The indebtedness and suicides by Punjabi cotton growing farmers in the Malwa Belt of Punjab should be viewed as a particularly disastrous outcome of the Neo-capitalist trade policies. For instance, consequent upon the implementation of export policy in respect of cotton in 1990-91 in the backdrop of high international prices, the lakhs of farmers, lured by high export prices, diversified and switched over to cotton in the Malwa Belt of Punjab, and borrowed heavily at exorbitant rates of interest for meeting the switchover costs and high input costs of cotton cultivation. But in the aftermath of the subsequent crash in the world prices of cotton taking place from the end of

1996 onwards created a situation by 2001 when earnings fell to roughly one- half of what they were in 1995. What we wish to emphasize in more precise terms is that following a crash in the international market prices and glut in cotton exports, domestic stocks of the crop under reference piled up and unscrupulous cotton millers exploited the distressed conditions of the farmers by refusing to spell out in advance the price at which they would procure or the quantity they would take. The net outcome of these developments led to distress sales on the part of cotton growers who incurred unbearable losses in the process. A well acknowledged fact of Punjab agriculture is that the state has come to enjoy a sort of comparative advantage in the production of major foodgrains, particularly wheat and paddy. In view of this the current challenge facing the Punjab agriculture is to look for external markets for the surplus foodgrains. But at the world level, when the external prices for foodgrains collapse, farmers do not seem to be sufficiently geared up to face the challenges of globalization. The rising cost of procurement, storage, and distribution acts as an important deterrent on their efforts to increase the production and distribution systems of foodgrains in Punjab. In addition, another major challenge faced by the peasantry in Punjab has been in terms of a shift in demand away from cereals due to significant rise in income over the period of time in large part of India. It has been observed that the demand for meat, milk, fruits, and vegetables has been increasing, while consumers have been switching away from the consumption of cereal foodgrains. Finally, the abolition of Quantitative Restrictions(QRs) in import of dairy products and reduction in tariff rates by the Union Government, dumping of cheaper skimmed milk powder in the Indian market and the low international prices have also, in part, transmitted the crisis to Punjab dairy farmers as well.

Fourteenth, the corporate landgrab is an extraneous factor adding to the agony of farmers suffering from the agrarian crisis and not an inherent part of the agrarian crisis itself. This unprecedented landgrab 'legitimized' under the Land Acquisition Act of the colonial era is resulting in massive displacement of agricultural population, loss of vast stretches of fertile agricultural land in many places, and outright destruction of employment and livelihood for sections of the rural poor. This is adding to their misery.

Fifteenth, agrarian crisis not only affects peasants but also agricultural labourers as rich farmers try to pass on part of the burden of their crisis onto the rural labourers. This becomes manifest in terms of declining employment and earning opportunities as also in the real wages of agricultural labourers in the state. The available evidence shows that regardless of tall claims about rapid growth of real wages of agricultural labourers during the peak period of economic liberalization between 1993-94 and 1999-2000, agricultural growth of wages in Punjab has by and large remained depressed. The Rural Labour Enquiry data for the period under reference clearly points towards very sharp wage differentials. For instance, in 1999-2000, the average daily wage per agricultural labourer was observed to be Rs. 63.44 in Punjab. The agrarian crisis has brought about a perceptible trend of wage compression in recent years in all states including Punjab. The stagnation in non-farm rural employment and wages have also tended to tighten its noose around the labour market conditions for agricultural labourers. To be more specific, during the peak liberalization era in India, while the employment growth in the whole of the economy came down, the employment growth in agriculture had almost collapsed to naught (0.10 per cent), with Punjab becoming no exception to this effect.

Finally, the stagnation of non-farm employment growth by late 1990s further compounded the problem of unemployment. The theory of growth postulates mutual inter-dependence between the farm and the non-farm growth, one acting as a stimulant for the other. The two now seem to be reinforcing each other's stagnation. Many studies have attributed the decline in rural non-farm activities to the sharp decline in public sector investment in the wake of the paradigm shift which is, *inter alia,* characterized by the implementation of Neo-liberal capitalist policies.

The preceding discussion suggests that the agrarian crisis in Punjab has many serious dimensions like increasing unremunerativeness of farming as a consequence of steep increase in input prices and a large lag of output prices, almost virtual stagnation in agricultural growth, growing indebtedness of farmers, recent deceleration of non-farm growth, the irrigation crisis, the crisis in the development of rural infrastructure, the ecological crisis and so on. Factors like the unprecedented corporate land-grab for real estate speculation and industry, declining public sector investment and capital formation in agriculture, continued dependence of farmers on private moneylenders with usurious interests, lack of adequate insurance coverage for farming in the face of frequent natural and market risks, growing stranglehold of multinational companies in seeds, fertilizers and pesticide business and, in wholesale and retail trade in agricultural commodities, heavy subsidies to agriculture in the developed countries and the inability of our farmers to compete with the heavily subsidized agribusinesses and farmers of the economically advanced countries in the international market and trade liberalization and growing opening up of the Indian agricultural sector, have all contributed to the aggravation of the present crisis. The dismantling of the state procurement and the Public Distribution System (PDS), despite the emergence of food security concerns, have also contributed importantly towards the accentuation of the agrarian crisis in Punjab. Above all, the failure to carry out meaningful land reforms and the continuing asymmetrical and skewed distribution pattern of landownership remains among the fundamental reasons of the crisis under reference. At the top of it, the issue of agrarian crisis in Punjab is inseparable from its ongoing environmental, economic and social crises. The peculiarities of these crises i.e. the particular ecological moments of falling water tables or tiring soils, are the critical points for understanding the interconnections among the afore-mentioned factors that account for the emergence, existence, persistence and aggravation of the crisis under examination. In our viewpoint, the enormity of the Punjab's agrarian crises can at best be appreciated by linking water shortages, rising input costs, crushing debt, and finally farmers' suicides. To put the record straight, the agrarian crisis in Punjab is the outcome of the interplay between a wide variety of inter-connected factors such as the rampant and widespread indebtedness among farmers due to shrinking markets, stagnating state fixed Minimum Support Prices, crop yields, and increasing production costs, ecological breakdown in both soil and water systems, social inequalities exacerbated earlier by the implementation of Green Revolution technology and now by the Neo-liberal capitalist exclusionary policies.

Crop Diversification- An Elusive Sought-After Solutions

The foregoing section seeks to diagnose the agrarian crisis in Punjab and locate its plausible causes. In particular, it is observed that the crisis under reference can be attributed to a wide variety of factors such as the adoption and domination of paddy-wheat cropping pattern in foodgrains, lust for realization of higher yield per unit of area cultivated, the deterioration experienced in terms of the fertility of the soil in the state, saturation limit reached in terms of the net area sown, cropping intensity with practically non-existent further scope for increase, stagnating productivity in the absence of breakthrough in new High Yielding Varieties and the agricultural production in the state having already reached a plateau, pressure on marketing infrastructure, dwindling ground water resources, decline in profitability, so on and so forth. Needless to overemphasize, it was noted that these major concerns of Punjab agriculture are crying for immediate attention of the planners and policymakers at the various levels. Having examined that aspect of the crisis, we now turn our attention to locate a plausible solution to the crisis under reference. Before we make an attempt in this direction, it is not out of context to observe that diversification of the existing wheat- paddy dominated cropping pattern has been suggest as the possible solution of the ongoing agrarian crisis in Punjab. The theme of diversification of Punjab agriculture has, in fact, in more recent times generated a surge of interest among the policymakers, agricultural economists, research workers, farmers' organizations, development agencies and the governments at the state and national levels alike. The evolving concern with diversification of Punjab agriculture is not totally unwarranted or unfounded due to the fact that the state economy is currently in the midst of a grave agrarian crisis. Broadly speaking, three viewpoints have emerged in respect of diversification of the state agriculture. While at the one end of the spectrum are the viewpoints of the adherents of the diversification of Punjab agriculture; at the other, on the other hand, are the viewpoints of those who are opposed to the proposed diversification. Needless to overemphasize, each of these viewpoints has specific merits to commend itself over another. And likewise, each one has its share of limitations as well. Against this backdrop, in the third approach elsewhere[21] we have argued that diversification must necessarily form an integral component of the strategy aiming at redeeming the Punjab agricultural sector of the grave crisis and as such enabling it to contribute in the overall economic development of the state economy rather than confining it in terms of inter-substitution of crops as was originally conceived in official circles. We had also argued that diversification, regardless of its brand and left to itself, is scarcely the panacea for all the social and economic ills presently characterizing the state economy in ample measure. Furthermore, without doubting or questioning the capability of diversification in terms of contributing appreciably towards the creation of material and non-material affluence in an economy in a wide variety of ways, we cautioned that it may alongside give rise to several other problems as well. Furthermore, it was also observed that with us already being in the midst of a new world economic order, while our accessibility in terms of ample scope for more diversity with regard to the models of diversification may register significant improvement; serious and well-meaning efforts, with growing focus on education, health and strengthening of the institutional-, infrastructural- and technological base of the state economy and that too with a vision and ample farsightedness for the future, nevertheless, imperatively be put in place well in time to cope up with the emerging challenges. To put the record straight, we argued for a thorough diversification of the economic base of the state economy as a whole and not for diversification merely in terms of substitution of crops as sought by the adherents of diversification for the simple reason that if Punjab has come to enjoy a sort of comparative advantage in the cultivation of crops proposed to be diversified, foregoing this may prove to be utterly detrimental not only for the state but also for the national economy as a whole, particularly in an environment when food security issues seem to be staring us in the face.

In the meantime, it is pertinent to mention that farmers actual response to the diversification package as proposed by the experts committee set up for the purpose, has been lukewarm and inadequate response. This becomes amply manifest from the information given in Table 5. It is not unimportant to observe from the said Table that of the gross cropped area in 1970-71, wheat and rice accounted for 40.49 and 6.89 per cent respectively. Together, the share of these two crops in the total cropped area was noted to be 47.38 per cent. As against this, in 2008-09, wheat and rice account for 44.57 and 34.57 per cent respectively of the total cropped area, their combined share being as high as 79.14 per cent. The information given in Table 8 further shows that even in terms of volume of production, these two crops are far ahead of others in that the production of wheat is estimated to be 15, 733 thousand metric tonnes in 2008-09 as against 5145 thousand metric tonnes in 1970-71 and that of rice at 11,000 thousand metric tonnes in 2008-09 as against only 688 thousand metric tonnes in 1970-71. It can be concluded that these two crops have, over the period of time, emerged as the overwhelmingly preferred crops of the Punjab farmers. Though several factors seem to have contributed towards the observed behaviour of the Punjab farmers in this regard, yet the role played by economic rationality on their part has possibly been the most important. It becomes manifest on many counts as given below.

First, it can be argued that wheat and paddy have emerged as the favoured crops with the state farmers owing to their being comparatively more remunerative in terms of economic returns than the alternatives available throughout the Green Revolution period. *Second,* it has come to be observed in certain well-meaning quarters that the farmers of the state have come to enjoy a sort of comparative advantage in the cultivation of these two crops and now asking them all of a sudden to move away from these is not as simple as it seems to be on the face of it. What it suggests is that it is certainly not for nothing that the farmers of the state have got stuck mainly to these crops. *And finally,* the Punjab experience shows that in crop production business there are no better and more rational allocators of the resources at their command than the farmers themselves, and they have amply demonstrated it over the years. Indeed, there exist few significant inaccuracies on their part as far as the matter of allocation of resources is concerned. On the other hand, one has reasons to believe that years of hard labour and experience have taught and enabled them in identifying and sticking to what they consider is the most optimal cropping pattern for them. The evidence from Punjab shows that in due course of time, they have tended to move away from the cultivation of pulses which used to be earlier raised in the state as the subsidiary (minor crop). Likewise, oilseeds have also not found favour with them so much so that even the groundnut which was extensively grown in the state at one point of time also became abandoned in the process of growing thrust towards wheat-paddy production cycle. Again, it is perhaps for economic reasons only that they have preferred to stick to wheat -paddy cycle rather than significantly switching-over to the cultivation of fruits and vegetables or for that matter to any other crop. To be more precise, it is the economics of wheat -paddy-cycle which has been enticing them so much so that they have not paid much attention to the proposed package. In view of this, therefore, weaning them away from what they have been doing for almost over four decades in the wake of the Green Revolution since mid -1960s is certainly a very difficult if not altogether an impossible proposition. This should, however, by no means, be construed to mean that they are likely to remain oblivious of whatever developments take place around them, and as such, go on stubbornly opposing whatever policy packages come their way in the future. If economically more remunerative options become available, there is no reason as to why they should not explore them.

Second, as observed above, the farmers and farm labourers in Punjab have, over the period of time, become experts in wheat-paddy cultivation culture. Accordingly, it might become very difficult for them to suddenly acquire the same expertise in other crop cultures, especially when major technological inputs have made the present pattern most suitable for shifting labour out of agriculture to speed up the structural transformation of Punjab agriculture. It can, therefore, be observed that double cropping on almost the entire cultivated area is possible only with wheat-paddy rotation, the proposed diversified cropping pattern does not at the moment seem to hold much ground in Punjab from this standpoint as well. It can be safely maintained that the much acclaimed Green Revolution of the 1960s and 70s was , in addition to being merely a technological revolution, also a complete cultural revolution in that it transformed irreversibly the traditional peasant soul into a cash calculating spirit, growingly imbued with commercial profit- maximization considerations over time. Owing to this very reason perhaps, the Punjab farmers, while replacing all the less remunerative crops by wheat and rice, also expanded cultivation of these two grains to the physical limit by increasing the net area sown and extending double cropping to almost entire cultivable area of the state(Tables 3 and 5). Now asking the farmers to switchover from wheat and paddy might entail significant amount of loss for various stakeholders in Punjab agriculture. Not only the farmers, the farm labourers of the state have also been seen as the handsome losers in the switchover process. Apart from these two categories of farmers and farm labourers of Punjab, there are other occupational groups such as those hiring out Harvesting Ccombines and Tractors and other Farm Machinery, Commission Agents, Marketing Committee and Mandi Board, Labour Working in Grain Markets and Truck Operators involved in grain transporting who together may also suffer importantly in pure economic terms. All this points towards the fact that switch-over from wheat and paddy is a highly uneconomical proposition for various stakeholders holders in Punjab agriculture.

Third, it is not unimportant to observe that the proposed diversification package is not the proper answer to the crisis in the state's agriculture. Rather, the farmers' continued sticking to the existing wheat-paddy dominated cropping pattern signals towards a contradiction in the perception of the farmers and that of the farm experts over the most suitable cropping pattern for Punjab. As observed above, while some farm experts prescribe diversification as the panacea for the current agrarian crisis, the Punjab farmers at the grassroots level have preferred not to change appreciably. And, this seems to have occurred in spite of expert advice and government incentives. This shows that the root of the crisis lies elsewhere rather in wheat- paddy cycle as it is usually made out to be. A detailed economic evaluation of the choices of cultivation leaves little doubt on wheat-paddy rotation being the optimal cropping pattern for Punjab agriculture. In the absence of a feasible or even a near alternative crop rotation combination that is capable of replacing wheat-paddy rotation under the present parameters and constraints, Punjab farmers, not surprisingly, continue to stick predominantly to the existing wheat- paddy cropping pattern as it yields them the most optimal return on per unit of land cultivated basis under the prevailing circumstances.

Fourth, it can be argued that the choice is not between wheat-paddy specialization versus a diversified cropping pattern, as is naively believed, but in terms of the need to explore specialization in some other crop rotation combination. The evidence shows that as of now, there has been a lack of a thorough understanding and that of a holistic approach in respect of the intrinsic compulsions of modern commercial farming which otherwise play a critical role in first clearing the prevailing uncertainty and then help in the formulation of an appropriate policy to this effect. Furthermore, it has come to be argued that production risks and market uncertainties are far more prominent in respect of alternative crops than in the case of wheat and paddy primarily because Minimum Support Price-cum- Assured Purchase (MSPAP) mechanism has been in place in respect of these crops since long. The past experience to this effect bears ample testimony that whatever quantities of wheat and paddy have been brought to the market, have been lifted by the official agencies as the buyer of the last resort. As such a development has not as yet been in vogue for want of an appropriate policy or otherwise in respect of alternatives suggested, the farmers of the state are, therefore, bound to remain away from trying their luck at other uncertain alternatives. On this count also, farmers have remained tied to wheat-paddy cycle. In our well-considered opinion, sustainable Minimum Support Price –cum- Assured Purchase (MSPAP) mechanism has been the most dominant factor amongst all the factors that has contributed towards the sustenance of the existing cropping pattern on a lasting basis.

Fifth, an important point that must not be overlooked in respect of Punjab agriculture is that the proposed diversification programme was sought to be encouraged by contract farming. As things stand today, the contract farming in large parts of rural Punjab has not as yet succeeded on any significant scale. Taking note of this fact, it is argued that diversification programme of agriculture in Punjab, as envisioned by the expert committee set up for the purpose, should have been encouraged by government guarantee of high output prices of the crops proposed to be included or by subsidization of inputs required for the purpose as it had happened earlier in respect of paddy and wheat in the wake of the Green Revolution in the state. Importantly, the rationale of such a policy is that only expectation or assurance of substantial economic gains rather than merely an inconsequential or marginal increase in income, will wean the farmers away from the existing wheat- paddy cycle and will also persuade them sufficiently to switchover to the proposed package. In support of this contention, it is plausible to argue that comparatively higher and assured profits or returns from the proposed package than from the existing one do overcome the resistance to uncertainty or risk of failure involved in the proposed switchover. And with more and more farmers becoming familiarized with the profitability of the new proposed crops, and learning the new methods efficiently, they will get enticed to shift to the new package in due course of time. This had what had happened earlier when the Green Revolution had appeared on the scene and there is no alternate route even now. If substitution of the existing wheat -paddy cycle is being resisted by the farmers of the state, it is basically on account of something missing critically in the proposed package. The possibility of the peasantry's becoming apprehensive about the likely fall in profits or household income in the event of unassured return from the proposed package cannot be dismissed as a mere fig of imagination primarily because uncertain farm incomes do not help for making the kind of adjustment envisaged through the proposed diversification programme. It is possible to argue that making any proposed package amply remunerative and lucrative in pure economic terms through appropriate price support programme is of critical importance in effecting the desired changes. Besides, it is equally important to improve the marketing and distribution channel for output as well as to establish more economical, handling, storage and warehousing facilities for the proposed products throughout the state. In our viewpoint, an improvement in handling storage, warehousing, marketing and distribution channel which reduces the cost of these services is bound to effect significant increases in the income of the peasantry of the state. In other words, what we wish to emphasize is that in the event of the introduction of any proposed package, the efficient marketing functions, including handling and transportation assume greater significance. At the same time, in the event of substitution of crops, the distribution and transportation systems also require substantial adjustment and reorientation. It is commonly agreed that the rate of expansion in the secondary and tertiary sectors should be large enough so as to absorb the resources of agriculture as are rendered surplus in the process of implementation of the proposed package. And finally, as has come to be highlighted in several studies,[22] public investment in human capital also facilitates the implementation of proposed strategy of diversification of an economy in general and to begin with its agricultural sector in particular. What we wish to emphasize is that human capital formation in the form of improved education(both in quantitative and qualitative forms, including skill formation) is both important and imperative in getting deeper insights required for triggering the process of diversification or otherwise. This is particularly so in the emerging knowledge based economy.

And finally, an important point that must not escape our attention in any future endeavour to move away from the existing wheat- paddy cycle is that the size of our population is bound to witness important rise over the next couple of decades. It is being apprehended that in terms of sheer population size, India and China may swap their positions. This requires us to assess our food requirements and supplies in terms our food security of the future. Moreover, it has come to be increasingly believed that in the emerging scenario, Punjab agriculture is fraught with the dangers of great impending crisis in that the vulnerable sections of the state peasantry, particularly the small and marginal farmers unable to compete in the face of unbridled onslaught of the global competition and getting sucked in the process, might virtually face extinction. In view of this, the planners and policymakers engaged in the task of agricultural planning of the Punjab are therefore required to be ultra alert of the impending consequences of the ongoing process of globalization for the state peasantry in general and for its more vulnerable segments in particular in the times to come. The ceremonial as well as non-ceremonial demise of diversification package both at the hands of the government and the Punjab farmers respectively sufficiently suggests that if the proposed diversification programme has had promised a significant improvement in economic efficiency at the level of the farm firm and the resultant mani-fold higher and assured returns on an enduring basis than what is offered by the existing farm practices, it would certainly would have found favour with the Punjab peasantry owing to its being economically more rewarding. As against this, if the farmers of Punjab have preferred sticking to the wheat- paddy cycle, it is because it has accelerated the development of a market-oriented capitalist agriculture which, in turn, has proved to be of immense economic gain to them. We believe that the concerns voiced in terms of the depletion of underground irrigation water resources owing to the sinking of an ever-increasing electricity and diesel operated pump-sets(Tables6 and 7), soils and environmental degradation are not altogether unfounded, and, as such, need to be addressed appropriately by designing appropriate policy packages so that these resources get preserved and augmented on a lasting basis. Deeper insights in this regard are required to be obtained through meaningful debates and discussions among the intelligentsia of the state and other outside experts who feel genuinely concerned about the sustainable development of Punjab.

And The Way Out

In the foregoing section ,we make a critical appraisal of the often perceived strategy of cropdiversification to cope up with the agrarian crisis in Punjab. In particular, we argue that on several counts farmers' response to such a strategy has at best been unenthusiastic as it is bereft of economically viable options for the state peasantry and as such is unsustainable. In such a situation, exploring a solution which might help redeeming the prevailing agrarian reality in Punjab on an enduring basis can scarcely be overemphasized. With this consideration in mind, we outline below some contours of a strategy that, in our well considered viewpoint constitutes the only way out of the morasses of the agrarian crisis in Punjab, help it regain its past pristine glory on an enduring basis.

However, before making an attempt in this direction, it is not altogether unimportant to remind ourselves that the crisis under reference is the outcome of the interplay between a wide variety of factors such as the adoption and domination of paddy-wheat cropping pattern in foodgrains, lust for realization of higher yield per unit of area cultivated, the deterioration experienced in terms of the fertility of the soil in the state in terms of low level of carbon content in soil ranging between 0.05 to 0.20 per cent as against the minimum requirement of 0.45 per cent, saturation limit reached in terms of the net area sown, cropping intensity with practically non-existent further scope for increase, stagnating productivity in the absence of breakthrough in new High Yielding Varieties and the agricultural production in the state having already reached a plateau, pressure on marketing infrastructure, dwindling ground water resources, decline in profitability, so on and so forth. Needless to overemphasize, it was noted that these major concerns of Punjab agriculture are crying for immediate attention of the planners and policymakers at the various levels. We are aware of the fact that as things stand today, the traditional land redistributive measures are neither warranted nor possible in the emerging scenario. Moreover, since it is not possible to withdraw from WTO commitments, only sweeping agrarian reforms, we feel growingly convinced, can rid the Punjab agriculture and its peasantry from the current and future agrarian crises.

In the light of the discussion in the preceding sections and realizing that the panacea for the agrarian crisis currently afflicting the countryside of Punjab imperatively calls for doing much more than mere diversification within agriculture in terms of shift in the existing wheat-paddy dominated cropping pattern as suggested in some quarters, we propose an alternative strategy to come out the morasses of the Punjab agrarian crisis with some of its broad contours in this section. It is pertinent to mention in passing that the rising commercialization of Punjab agriculture, assured and fairly equitable distribution of irrigation facilities, well developed network of village link roads and power facilities, a wide spread network of rural institutions such as village cooperative societies, fairly high level of farm mechanization, progressive state patronage etc. have been some of the distinctive features of the pre-reforms period Punjab model of rural economic transformation.[23] The advent of a new paradigm in the form of economic Liberalization, Privatization and Globalization constitutes a great change in that some of the variables, seen capturing the centre- stage in the earlier pre- reform strategy, have been experiencing significant change in the post-reform period. Against such a backdrop, given the fact that continuous and significant expansion of the overall economy in general and that of the farm sector in particular along with their progressive diversification is our primary objective in the emerging economic order, it seems that the following measures may enable the state agricultural sector to cope up with the crisis successfully while regaining its past pristine glory, and the economy in moving onto a higher trajectory of overall economic growth in the times to come:

First, since farmers' suicides are reported to be a major symptom and manifestation of the agrarian crisis in Punjab, the problem needs to be dealt with effectively at various levels, beginning from the immediate relief measures to the families of suicide victims, to long-term policy decisions covering the entire agricultural sector. For instance, for enabling the suicide victim families meet their physical survival needs, there is imperatively a need to provide monetary assistance as a part of the immediate relief package. Such assistance assumes greater significance for families where the victim happened to be the only earning member of the family. In such cases, even the waiving off the entire loan, formal or otherwise, is desired to be considered. A pension scheme to the next of kin (especially if he/she is aged and/or a non-earner) is required to be put in place to rehabilitate the grief- stricken family. Since most of the suicides are reported to be directly or indirectly related to indebtedness and economic distress, the implementation of a moratorium on the debt of the victim can play a pivotal role in mollifying the severity of the crisis under reference. Besides, important relief in the form of lowering of the rates of interest and increasing the number of interest- free installments should also be extended to the suicide victim families. In cases the victim was the sole earning member. As against this, as part of longer-term relief measures, there is urgently a need to provide for cost-free skill-oriented education in the case of minor children belonging to the suicide victim families in addition to providing economically gainful employment to the grown up children to rehabilitate the suicide victim families. This would, we feel, improve the economic capability of the victim's family to pay- off the debt and live a life of dignity as also in helping them to wash -off the stigma of being a suicide victim's kin. To ensure that such relief measures help the genuine victim families, proper identification of such families by a non-partisan organization must precede such financial compensation.

Second, any strategy aiming at solving the agrarian crisis in Punjab must necessarily seek to promote simultaneously agricultural as well as overall economic growth and structural transformation, widespread improvement of economic welfare and the sort of attitudinal changes and institutional progress in consonance with the goals of development and social modernization of the state. To be more precise, what we wish to emphasize is that the economic base of the state's rural economy needs to be progressively diversified along the lines suggested by Fisher- Clark thesis.[24] We strongly feel that there is imperatively an urgent need for synchronizing the development efforts in the farm as well as non- farm sectors of the state economy to this effect. In the farm sector itself in Punjab, there exists a remarkable scope for diversification in terms of dairying and poultry development and other such enterprises. In our viewpoint, extreme dependence on the existing cropping pattern alone or abruptly switching- over from it in one stroke as suggested in some well-meaning quarters can never be the answer to the various socio-economic problems confronting the rural economy of the state as of now. We must take note of the fact that assured and fairly equitable irrigation base as brought about by many institutional packages, coupled with the augmented availability of rural infra-structural facilities, which in several earlier studies on the theme of impact of the Green Revolution has invariably been described as the sheet – anchor of agricultural development in Punjab[25], has tended to get depleted over time.[26] In view of this, there is, therefore, an urgent need for proper water management, power and transport (or road) facilities for rural use, strengthening institutional credit mechanism to save the farmers from the ruthless economic exploitation at the hands of the commission agents, and so on. It scarcely needs to be over-emphasized that the evolution, adaptation and adoption of improved and appropriate farm technology, through well-conceived Research and Development efforts, must necessarily form the hub of the proposed strategy of diversification for Punjab. It is equally important to mention that the character of diversification is of critical significance. As far as this measure is concerned, a very cautious approach needs to be adopted. From the national perspective, well- conceived and equally well-planned national priorities need to be laid down in respect of food security. Concerted efforts are also required to be made in the direction of making the country self- sufficient in terms of accessibility as well as affordability of quality food in the future, particularly when the food requirements are bound to grow in view of sizeable additions to our population and when food security is emerging as a major issue of concern. We strongly feel that the farm subsidies, instead of being withdrawn, need to be re-oriented in the desired channels. At the same time, what must essentially be remembered is that the populist measures, implemented usually under pressure from various self-seeking lobbies and owing to vote bank compulsions entail heavy costs to the public exchequer, and thereby eventually make the process of economic growth unsustainable over time. With Punjab already in the midst of a grave fiscal crisis, the mismanagement of the state economy at various layers on such counts must stop sooner than later. To this end, the entire system ought to be over-hauled appropriately and made more efficient, transparent, accountable and geared to the genuine public needs. We strongly feel that this would save the state economy of the on-going plunder which is usually attributed to the politician-bureaucratic nexus that seems to have strengthened its stranglehold over the period of time.

Third, it is often alleged that the provision of Minimum Support Prices- cum- Assured Purchase mechanism for wheat and paddy together with the overemphasis on the said crops in terms of gearing of agriculture research and allocation of other resources (including human resource system) for producing more and more grains to meet the growing demand for food for the bourgeoning population in the country to the neglect of oilseeds, pulses, coarse cereals, fodder, other field crops, sugarcane and cotton, fruits and vegetables, livestock, horticultural crops has weakened the research in regard to the latter category of crops in terms of critical variables such as marketing policy, integrated pest and nutrient management and organic farming in the state. Furthermore, even though water has over the period of time emerged as a critical input as far as the future of agriculture in Punjab is concerned, a comprehensive research strategy for addressing various aspects of water management has been lacking. In view of the fact that growing emphasis is currently being laid on self - sufficiency in food as well as on the sustainability of the agricultural sector through diversification, there is imperatively a need for a thorough reprioritizing and regearing of the entire system. This, we feel, may be of considerable help in meeting the challenges posed by the prevailing agrarian crisis in Punjab.

Fourth, agriculture being subject to risk and uncertainty, crop and weather insurance facilities need to be provided at the very doorsteps of the farmers in Punjab at the village level . Currently, a crop insurance scheme is being implemented at the district level under the National Agricultural Insurance Scheme (NAIS). There are, nevertheless, some genuine problems in its operation. *First,* there is non-availability of reliable yield data below the state/district level. *Second,* since the claim amounts are high, the scheme is highly subsidized by both the central and state governments. *Third,* most of the claims are confined only to a few crops. *Fourth,* there is an inherent problem of moral hazard because of the possibility of collusion between implementing agencies and farmers. Given the importance of the crop insurance scheme for covering yield risks, the insurance scheme needs to be thoroughly evaluated to make it more useful to the farmers. Weather insurance schemes which are currently in operation suffer from even greater infirmities. In view of this, a comparative evaluation of crop insurance, rainfall insurance and insurance based on moisture stress indices derived from satellite imagery data is required to be made to overcome the afore-mentioned infirmities through the introduction of the necessary correctives.

Fifth, from a futuristic perspective, it can be argued that the implementation of price risk mitigation is yet another measure that can help in addressing the crisis under reference. *First,* to mitigate the impact of price collapse in cases of commodities not covered under Minimum Support Prices (MSPs), the farmers need to be provided with a financial support. *Second,* it has been observed that in the wake of trade liberalization, several agricultural commodities are facing tough competition from imports. Import policy, including variable tariffs and other World Trade Organization (WTO) compatible measures, should be used to mitigate the adverse impact of such imports. Alongside, farm producers are also required to be enabled to improve their productivity and competitiveness through investments in new technology. *Third,* it is recommended that surveillance and advance crop assessment systems should be initiated in relatively more distressed districts of the state located particularly in its Malwa belt. *Fourth,* in view of the fact that the near crumpling of the Research and Development(R&D) institutions and extension services has been one of the major factor contributing factors to agrarian distress in the state in the wake of the prevailing financial crunch, major efforts are therefore required to be made to intensify agricultural research in frontier areas like bio-technology through increased investment. The agricultural research and extension system should be revamped by providing adequate budgetary support. Besides, the strengthening of these institutions is also required for establishing links between satellite imagery data relating to soil moisture/vegetative cover and actual yields based on crop cutting experiments. *And finally,* in respect of mitigating risks from spurious inputs, there is the need for establishing an appropriate regulatory framework and rules to ensure quality inputs to the farmers. An adequate number of input testing laboratories needs to be opened at the block level to facilitate quality checks of inputs such as seeds, pesticides and fertilizers. A clear cut regulatory mechanism should be laid down for indemnifying the farmers for their losses caused the application of the spurious inputs.

Sixth, in our viewpoint, there exists huge potential for the creation and promotion of employment and earnings through non-farm activities in rural Punjab. Moreover, since non-farm employment, on an average, is economically more gainful than agricultural employment, the augmentation and supplementation of rural household income through non-farm avenues of employments seems to have the potential of mollifying the severity of income distribution in rural Punjab. In view of this, vigorous efforts are required to be made so that progressively services dominate the rural non-farm employments. At the same time such measures are also needed to be introduced as might eventually lead to relatively higher share from non-farm wage income in comparison to that of non-farm self-employment across different strata of the rural society in Punjab. What this suggests in more clearer terms is that contrary to the traditional focus on rural manufactures and self-employment, more and more attention is required to be paid overtime to develop the service sector and wage employment with locale in the rural areas of the state. This apart, what , nevertheless, needs not to be obliterated over is the fact that while the majority of the socially and economically vulnerable households in rural Punjab are involved in diversifying the structure of their employments, their access to economically more remunerative non-farm employments might be limited in terms of special skills or access to assets required for accomplishing the desired tasks efficiently and optimally. In more precise terms, what we wish to observe is that those with low education and skills and with little access to land, which not only continues to be the principal asset of production in the interior of the countryside in Punjab but also whose distribution is said to be becoming progressively more asymmetrical due to the growing proletarinization of the peasantry in the post –Green Revolution decades (Table 10 and 11), might end up in getting engaged in low return non-farm activities. In view of such eventualities, progressive diversification of economic activities in rural Punjab, it must be emphasized in particular, must ensure ever-growing productive employment for larger and larger number of people over time in the secondary and tertiary sectors of the state economy. Economically gainful supplementary activities such as dairying and poultry and development of agro- based industries together with their progressive tertiarization, in our opinion, must be encouraged and institutionally supported on a big scale in rural Punjab.[27] Moreover, through the provision of crucial requirements and adequate infra- structural facilities, other agriculture related rural non- farm enterprises and development of rural cottage and small scale industries are required to be undertaken in the state on a significant scale. To this effect, such enterprises and industries ought to be identified and developed which are characterized by high degree of technological and market interdependence.[28] It scarcely needs any over-emphasis that well co-ordinated policy packages are needed to be devised for promoting these developmental programmes in rural Punjab. In view of this, it is imperatively desired that the choice among various alternative programmes for using public and private resources to promote agriculture related rural non- farm enterprises and other rural development programmes are evaluated in terms of economic efficiency as well as in short-, medium-, and long- term social objectives underlying the state policy. In such a strategy, only such enterprises and activities need to be included as may aim at expanding the efficiency of rural infra- structural facilities on the one hand, and, improving the earning position of various segments of the rural population in Punjab, on the other. In our opinion, in the existing socio- economic and political set up of the state, the one and the only one solution of various problems confronting the state is the carefully planned and equally carefully implemented process of rapid agro-industrialization[29] together with its progressive tertiarization. Such a measure, in our well- considered viewpoint, would go a long way towards promotion of economically gainful employment and earnings for the rural workforce in Punjab. At the same time, serious efforts are required to be undertaken to promote self- employment through subsidiary agricultural sidelines as also other such non- farm activities which require relatively smaller amount of capital. This can be achieved by providing subsidized inputs, credit liberalization and providing market facilities for the products of such activities. The evidence earlier reported from the state of Punjab itself shows that such activities are helpful in mollifying the severity of in-egalitarian income distribution in the state.[30]

Seventh, it scarcely needs to be overemphasized that the rural economy of Punjab can be boosted through public investment for agricultural productivity growth. This nevertheless apart, we strongly feel that the growth of the rural non-farm sector could be an equally important complement to investments in agricultural productivity. The available evidence suggests that the growth of the rural non-farm sector is particularly pro-poor and hence 'inclusive'. In view of this, a particularly important challenge currently facing the state planners and policymakers is to devise mechanisms which might help improve the access of the socially and economically disadvantageous and dispossessed segments of the rural population of Punjab to non-farm activities that yield high and stable incomes on an enduring basis. In this regard, what must not essentially be overlooked is that with growing focus on human capital formation in more recent times, education in general and skill formation in particular has tended to emerge as a critical determinant of participation in more remunerative non-farm activities. It is contended that even the relatively moderate improvements in education are capable of triggering better employment and earning prospects in the non-farm sector. Truly speaking, if non-farm activities are to compensate for asset disadvantages or dispossession of the rural workforce in Punjab, education, to us, certainly seems to be an important instrument for alleviating economic distress. Huge amount of investment is needed to be injected in the rural education sector in Punjab along with the necessary incentives for improving access of rural youths to education to prepare them to improve their access to highly remunerative non-agricultural employments. This, in our viewpoint, will go a long way in enabling the rural households of Punjab to improve their economic lot quite appreciably in the emerging socio-economic set up. Such a measure becomes particularly important if the non-farm sector has to experience significant expansion as this sector over the period of time necessitates skills- and education-oriented employment. The state planners and policy makers must appreciate that raising the capacity of the various strata of the society in rural Punjab in economically more remunerative non-farm activities via human capital formation will be effective only if alongside the accelerated process of job creation, the prevailing socio-economic environment also becomes increasingly more conducive. To put the record straight, what we wish to reiterate in this regard is that instead of searching solutions to the diverse set of problems facing the Punjab agriculture at this juncture within this sector alone through shift in the cropping pattern, enhancing the availability and accessibility of non-farm employment and earning opportunities for the various categories of rural households must necessarily form an integral part of efforts at promoting overall development of the rural economy of Punjab. Needless to overemphasize, education including Research and Development must necessarily form an integral component of any strategy proposed to be undertaken to this effect in the times to come. In addition, pro-active concerted efforts are also required to be made to rid the rural youth of the menace of drug addiction as it has long- term implications for the health-productivity relationship in rural Punjab. To be more precise, the health status of the rural population in the state needs to be placed on a higher pedestal and appropriate mechanism needs to be put in place to this effect.

Eighth, the implementation of the afore-mentioned measures, in our well-considered viewpoint, would not only accelerate the process of growth in the farm sector, but also would pave the way for the emergence of the modern industrial sector in Punjab. As a consequence, increased demand and supply linkages would emerge and become strengthened between the two sectors, and the overall economy of the state will experience acceleration in its growth. Besides, the pernicious consequences of the over- exploitation of soil and water as well as environmental degradation can also be avoided. At the same time, wherever possible, well-intended efforts are also required to be made to ensure participatory development at the grassroots level. In this regard such developmental programmes need to be devised as might ensure the participation of all segments of the rural society in them. Ensuring equality of opportunity to socially and economically underprivileged sections of the society to effectively participate in these programmes as also in the sharing of the resultant gains trickling-down from them on an enduring basis would, we strongly feel, would give rise to a vibrant and economically active economy moving uninterruptedly on a higher trajectory of economic growth over the coming decades. This would significantly help in making a dent on various problems such as economic deprivation, unemployment, and social and economic inequalities as are being faced by the state. In addition, it would also help the promotion of relevant industrialization, and, above all, in the establishment of an egalitarian pattern of society in Punjab. Not only this, the implementation of such a strategy would also further help in combating the excessive inflationary pressures in the economy as also the much-hyped fiscal crisis which have, till date, been very severe problems facing the Punjab economy. This would be possible primarily because the proposed strategy would remove obstacles to growth with the result that rigidities would get removed and, as a result, uninterrupted economic growth ensuring distributive justice would be stimulated. An added advantage of the proposed strategy is that it would also promote decentralization of economic structure at the grassroots level. However, as the past evidence shows, since the possibility of the perceived gains from the proposed strategy getting eroded or neutralized because of the possibility of notable leakages cannot be ruled out altogether, an urgent need to evolve a result-oriented mechanism to take care of such leakages becomes today still more imperative than ever before.

And finally, the state planners and policy makers must remember that as of now we are growing as part of the global economic set up. *'Perform or perish'* [31] is the underlying dictum of such a set up. Again, in the existing set- up, performance gets propelled by the invisible hand i.e. competition. As a consequence, while such a set up bestows immense economic gains on a few, it acts as the economic doomsday of many others. In view of this, therefore, it is possible to maintain that one's success to a large extent is, *inter alia,* conditioned by outperforming one's competitors primarily because *'survival of the fittest'* is the name of the game. And to outperform the competitors, one must necessarily address all the parameters of one's concern and position oneself strategically against one's competitors. Our understanding is that it is only through comprehensive knowledge that one can strategically position oneself over time and also, accordingly, reap the benefits expected to percolate from any envisioned process of development together with securing and ensuring one's survival. Needless to overemphasize, time and resource management are likely to emerge as most critical variables in any future strategy of agricultural as well as overall development of Punjab as keeping the time stipulations in mind, coupled with appropriate management skills, will not only help in realizing rich dividends, but also in keeping one abreast of one's rivals.

In sum, the solution of the agrarian crisis in Punjab on a lasting basis, there is imperatively a need for expanding the livelihood base through the introduction of rural non-farm enterprises for the rural population. There is no gainsaying the fact that left to themselves agriculture and other land-based activities, even with a high and diversified rate of growth, will not be able to ensure employment to all the rural workers adequate levels of incomes in the long run. Rather , it is quite likely that employment potential in the growth will experience further contraction following technological advancement and institutional changes. As a consequence, the possibility of a substantial number of those underemployed in agriculture getting pushed into the category of openly unemployed workers and frantically seeking work elsewhere cannot be ironed out altogether. And given the fact that a few luckiest amongst themselves will be able to get absorbed in urban areas, what is imperatively required is that the rural economy gets diversified into non-farm activities to provide economically gainful employment to the bourgeoning rural labor force. This will also help in arresting migration from rural areas to urban areas. Such diversification and expansion of the rural economy, particularly of the non-farm sector, is possible through promotional policies and effort particularly in respect of infrastructure, improved access to credit, technological upgradation and training in entrepreneurial development and marketing support. With appropriate promotional policies, particularly those focusing on measures for orientation of credit and lending practice of banks to suit small business and manufacturing enterprises, strengthening of producers' cooperatives and assistance in marketing and technology, considerable expansion of activities with a high employment potential for rural workers can be achieved. What we wish to emphasize here is that income diversification opportunities should be created by promoting allied agricultural, agro-processing and other rural non-farm enterprises with a view to improving the sources of employment and earnings of the farmers in general and those of the small and marginal farmers and landless agricultural labour households in particular. The diversification of the economic base of the rural economy as suggested in the fore-going discussion, is the only way out of the agrarian crisis in Punjab and enabling the state economy attain sustainable growth. Nevertheless, left to itself, it scarcely is the panacea for all the social and economic problems presently confronting the state economy. Moreover, although it is capable of contributing appreciably towards the creation of material and non-material affluence in the countryside economy of Punjab in diverse set of ways, it may, it is apprehended, give rise to lots of problems as well. And with us being already in the midst of a new world economic order, while there may be ample scope for more diversity with regard to the models of diversification, serious and well-meaning efforts, with growing focus on education, health and strengthening of the institutional-, infrastructural- and technological base of the countryside economy in Punjab and that too with a vision and ample farsightedness for the future should, in our well-considered viewpoint, be made to cope up with the challenges attendant to the prevailing agrarian crisis in Punjab. The solutions, as perceived by the diversificationists in terms of mere substitution of crops, might not lead us far. In our well-considered viewpoint, a thorough diversification of the economic base of the Punjab economy as a whole along the lines suggested in this paper, on the other hand, might click to locate the plausible solution not only to the agrarian crisis under reference, but also to other socio-economic problems presently facing the state on an enduring basis.

Conclusions and Policy Implications

Our focus in this paper has been on agrarian crisis in Punjab and its solution. Taking note of the fact that the agricultural sector of Punjab has made a remarkable contribution to the state and national economies in terms of significant increases in the volume of agricultural production, kitty of foodgrains' surpluses, and labour absorption (including that of the migrants) and is said to be presently in the midst of a grave crisis, often alleged to be, *among other things,* owing to its continued focus on the existing wheat-paddy dominated production cycle and the implementation of Neo-liberal capitalist policies, the analysis in the paper notes that there is, as such, a clear rationale for examining and analyzing the said crisis, locate the cogent factors responsible for its emergence, existence and persistence, as also for searching plausible solutions in the overall context of the state economy. Such a rationale assumes greater significance in view of the prevailing belief that holds that the process of structural economic transformation of an economy like Punjab must necessary involve the shift of the workforce dependent on agriculture alongside the siphoning-off the agricultural surpluses to the more dynamic non- agricultural sectors of the state economy. It is alleged that the hitherto experienced process of structural economic transformation has, far from emerging as a healthy sign of capitalist economic development, tended to aggravate the agrarian crisis in the state and stultified its agricultural as well as overall growth. In addition, we feel that in thinking about the issues involved in respect of the crisis under reference from the prospective angle, there are numerous reasons for focusing on the various policy issues pertaining to the Punjab agrarian crisis and its worthwhile solution on a lasting basis. For instance, in the face of onslaught of the emerging challenges in the wake of the implementation of Neo-liberal capitalist policies encompassing in their fold, the ongoing processes of economic Liberalization, Privatization and Globalization, Punjab agriculture is said to be progressively assuming unsustainable proportions. The planners and policymakers of the state seem to be caught in a dilemma in regard to the choice of the necessary correctives. Earlier too, it used to be alleged that the decades of the post- Green Revolution period have witnessed the progressive depeasantization, marginalization and proletarinization of the peasantry in the State on a significant scale and predicted that this trend might get aggravated in the times to come so much so that the Green Revolution may give way to the Red Revolution. In view of this, therefore, the rationale for appropriate policy-mix in regard to agrarian crisis in Punjab along the lines suggested in this paper gets bolstered particularly when due account is taken of a large number of suicides by the farmers in the state. This apart, we nevertheless feel that the big farmers in Punjab, for reasons of their capacity to withstand the onslaught being unleashed by market forces, are probably less likely to lose in comparison to their smaller counterparts in the emerging scenario.

The tremendous boost to the economy as discernible in terms of sharp increases in incomes, production and productivity for all classes of agriculturists attendant to the introduction of the Green Revolution technology in its hey days, when viewed against the backdrop of the marked stagnation in agricultural productivity coupled with increased costs of production and almost increase-free Minimum Support Prices, growing unemployment due to mechanization of agricultural operations and lack of alternative economically gainful avenues of supplementary sources of employment and earnings, pale into insignificance and seem to label the said revolution to be only an ephemeral remedial measure to the crisis which has, over the period of time, reached unprecedented enormity. Though agrarian crisis is reported to be the outcome of the interplay of a wide variety of factors, yet factors such as crop failure, mounting indebtedness together with various problems attendant to it in the form of the pressure of the family, lenders, even mental pressure of returning the loan or face social stigma, public shame and humiliation, apprehensions concerning the loss of land in the event of failure to repay the loans, etc., seem to have been at work in tandem in the direction of deepening the crisis that has emerged in Punjab in several of its manifestations.

Though diversification of the existing cropping pattern in terms of substitution of existing wheat - paddy cycle has come to perceived as the panacea for solving the current agrarian crisis in Punjab in certain quarters, yet we firmly believe that the stark reality with regard to the present position in respect of this proposed remedy of the crisis under reference is that it has not made any significant headway thus far nor is it likely to make till the time the Minimum Support Price- cum- Assured Purchase mechanism for wheat and paddy crops remains in place. Not only this, in terms of thinking about the issues involved from the prospective angle, the emerging scenario on this count seems possibly extremely grim owing to various developments, grassroots level realities and other contemporaneous happenings such as the weakening of competitiveness of the Punjab farmers in comparison to their counterparts in the agriculturally developed world, as also in terms of their ability to become strong enough to withstand the ongoing onslaught of the global capitalism in the emerging scenario in the absence of active government support which has hitherto been available to the state peasantry. At the top of it, the fact that our workforce in the agricultural sector is not certainly so well- endowed in terms of human capital means that it is not likely to be reasonably well- equipped to find alternate jobs, possibly even in the unorganized sector. In view of this, therefore, the emerging scenario of large scale redundancy and snail-paced growth of employment and earning opportunities may, therefore, be viewed as deterioration of the situation that does not seem to portend well for the peasantry and other strata of the rural society of Punjab either in the present or in the future. In such a situation, it can be safely argued that instead of attempting the diversification of agriculture in terms of shifting the cropping pattern as proposed by the proponents of diversifications and vehemently opposed by its opponents, there is imperatively a need for diversifying the entire economic base of Punjab's rural economy. And the sooner it is done, the better it would be for the state and its people not only in the present, but also in the future. The ideal policy, therefore, would be that without dampening the on-going tempo of the wheat- paddy cycle in one go as suggested by some experts, concerted efforts are required to be made to promote rapidly the indigenous eco-friendly agro-based and labour-intensive small scale industrial and such other rural non-farm enterprises in the state with growing thrust towards tertiarization of the rural sector. We must also not forget that the immediate expansion as well diversification is, *among other things,* conditioned by the availability of the necessary infrastructure. Accordingly, particular emphasis, therefore, must necessarily be laid on the development of appropriate infra-structural facilities particularly water, electricity, etc., which have, in spite of their notable growth over the period of time, begun experiencing pressure and, as such, also started acting as a serious drag on the process of growth. In addition, serious efforts are also required to be made in the direction of evolving an effective institutional mechanism which might ensure the equitable trickling-down of the benefits from the envisaged growth over the period of time without leakages to various segments of the rural society in Punjab.

The farmers' cooperatives, sans middlemen, to produce, process and market output on the farm gates can also help the Punjab peasantry to cope up with the crisis under reference. This would not only provide the agricultural sector with a much needed diversification from the wheat-paddy rotation, but also prove to be remunerative in terms of incomes and employment on a long-term basis. The farmers' organizations must engage themselves to start collectively processing and marketing enterprises rather than purely depending on agitations for more remunerative prices. Pressing for rights along with engaging in industrial activities has the potential of eliminating the middlemen who thrive on surpluses generated through processing and marketing activities. The state government apart from supporting and extending cooperation must become innovative to articulate policies in the fast globalizing world to prod farmers' organizations to undertake such activities which integrate the processing and marketing activities on the farm gates. Farmers' indebtedness being one of the major symptom of the agrarian crisis, the state and state-run financial institutions are required to introduce such innovative system of advancing loans to the state peasantry in which loans are adequate, timely, cheap, and commensurate with demand. The problems of red tape and additional costs involved in institutional loans which make such loans highly unattractive and cumbersome are also required to be dealt with appropriately.

In areas where contract farming seems to have made its appearance, the immediate need is to identify a legislative mechanism to ensure the enforceability of such contracts in producing high value crops, on the one hand, and protect the interests of the peasantry on the other. In our opinion, the freeing up of land lease markets and computerization of land records will help in easing land transactions among farmers. Besides, the appropriate mechanisms necessary for ensuring that land tenancy laws are not a constraint to agro-industry development in the state are also required to be devised and put in place. At the same time, concerted efforts are required to be made to implement the market reforms pertaining to the rationalization of input subsidies and removal of all restrictions in terms of stocking limits, movements, and levies in transporting foodgrains.

In the emerging scenario, for redeeming the state peasantry of the agrarian crisis it is presently in, the role of tapping the international markets can scarcely be overemphasized. To this effect, while institutional innovations such as warehouse receipt system, futures trading, and establishment of commodity exchanges assume considerable importance, innovative crop insurance programmes that will help the state farmers in protecting themselves from the vicissitudes of international markets as well as from vagaries of monsoon assume still greater relevance. In our viewpoint, developing institutions for certifying quality characteristics of agricultural produces will go a long way in enabling farmers to reach out to the international markets. Appropriate institutional reforms, particularly in respect of farm inputs supplying agencies and in irrigation systems mainly veering around protection of farmers' economic fortunes, are also required to be introduced on a priority basis. And finally, for the purpose of adding value to the products produced by farmers, it is essential that farmers' associations and cooperatives to build collective bargaining power and to enter into contracts with agro-processors and supermarkets are encouraged by way of providing them much needed technical, financial and other assistance.

In the meantime, it is not out of context to remind ourselves that sustainability of farm incomes as also that of resources undeniably constitutes the core concern facing the Punjab agriculture today. And increasing production of cereals, especially wheat and rice is possibly the overriding concern facing our planners and policy makers at the national level, particularly in the wake of emerging food security issues. The hitherto experienced agricultural growth has not only helped in achieving the self-sufficiency in foodgrains but also in maintaining adequate buffer stocks to meet the food requirements of the growing population. This apart, the emergence of new challenges has given rise to new thrust areas. For example, the present thrust on the ecological and economic access to food through poverty alleviation, higher profits to farmers, sustainability of resources, import substitution, quality improvement and production for exports has led the planners to devise and implement the diversification strategies successfully. As of now, the crop sector in Punjab has not witnessed impressive diversification with impressive improvements in the share of livestock and fisheries sector in the total income from agriculture. However, the hitherto experienced diversification in Punjab has been more for mitigating the risk than for income generation. The success of any diversification programme in Punjab must essentially involve the development of crop - or enterprise-specific technologies, identification and development of market, and provision of economic incentives. In the emerging market scenario, the competitive advantage of a specific product, we strongly feel, will, *inter alia,* be determined by the market itself in that it will depend on the extent to which the crops/ commodities grown in the state are competitive in terms of productivity and cost, are remunerative to the farmers, possess marketing potential and competitiveness in terms of prices, and are able to maintain the quality desired in the market, both national and international. There is no denial to the fact that Punjab certainly enjoys a comparative advantage due to its diverse agro-eco regions in coping up with the challenge thrown up by the emerging scenario through diversification options. However, harnessing the potential of diversification pre-supposes gradual restructuring-cum-transformation of the market institutions constraining diversification, infrastructure and quality standards, and credit and fiscal setup into the ones that boost diversification in the desired directions. We strongly feel that while attempting at or accelerating diversification in Punjab in terms of shift away from the existing wheat paddy crop production cycle, it is necessary, nay imperative, to exercise certain cautions in the matter of long-term food security issues, likely fluctuations in the international market and the element of risk in transitioning from traditional to commercialized agriculture in the presence of sizeable small and marginal farmers in Punjab.

The remedy to the agrarian crisis in Punjab lies in both short-term or immediate solutions to crisis as also in long-term solutions to end the agrarian crisis itself. While immediate measures could include relief, mainly financial, to the families of suicide victims, and attempts at their rehabilitation, the long-term remedy to arrest the crisis lies in attempts at agro-based rural industrialization. In conclusion, the promotion of employment-intensive rural industrialization with market and technological inter-dependence with the outside world is one and the only one answer to resolve the agrarian crisis facing Punjab on an enduring basis. Unrestricted low-cost institutional credit should be provided for rural non-farm activities. Bold and wide-ranging policy reforms in respect of agriculture subsidies can also help in redeeming the situation quite appreciably.

The main message from the analysis done in this paper is a cautionary one. Attention to the agricultural sector, nay to all sectors of the state economy, as a means of sustained growth of the state economy must not be overlooked. Alongside, what is imperatively required on the part of our state planners and policymakers is that instead of being complacent or lackadaisical on any count, they must be wary of the impending dangers because of the potential consequences of the processes of economic Liberalization, Privatization and Globalization for social and economic deprivation of the masses in general and for the peasantry of the state in particular. The serious and meaningful efforts are required to be put in place through a well-conceived, well- planned, well- devised and equally well-implementable strategy to resolve the various trade - offs and to cope with the emerging challenges on an enduring basis. The state economy, equally important to all the stakeholders (including the peasantry, the non-agriculturists and the governments at the state and national levels), cannot be left to fend for itself in the emerging scenario. It is equally important to mention in passing that regardless of the political economy of the agrarian crisis in Punjab, we feel that there is imperatively a need for more critical and worthwhile debate on the theme of performance of the agricultural sector in relation to that of the state economy as a whole as also on the implications thereof for stimulating the overall growth of the state economy in the times to come. There are obviously many core questions that remain unanswered in respect of agrarian crisis of Punjab and its fallout. For an instance, our planners and policymakers must know who are the countries in which identical crisis have occurred, and have been successfully tackled and through which types of mechanisms? Likewise, in which countries, the strategy implemented faltered or boomeranged and for what reasons? What mix of policies have been most successful? Do the strategies always lead to the realization of goals they are introduced for or do they work only under some peculiar conditions? And, it is not impertinent to maintain that while these and other such questions must engage the attention of the planners and the policymakers of the state, any public policy for improving the performance of the state economy in general and its farm sector in particular by way of implementation of a particular strategy must be aimed at ameliorating the socio-economic lot of the peasantry and other disadvantageous strata of the rural society in Punjab. In view of this, therefore, more intense research is required to be undertaken to determine the nature, extent, strategy and consequences and strategies to cope up with the crisis so that we do not kill the goose for nothing. The outcomes of such exercises will certainly enable the state planners and the policymakers to incorporate appropriate changes as these strategies seek to evolve and fructify over the period of time. Ours this paper is just one attempt to begin the discussion and to encourage further research in this direction. Admittedly, we have only sought to explore some of the issues pertaining to the agrarian crisis in Punjab as it exists at the moment. Obviously, much has been left out and hence unexplored by us. In conclusion, what we wish to emphasize in unambiguous terms is that half- baked and equally half-heartedly implemented solutions never work. Rather, in all probability, they create much bigger problems than the ones they seek to address. We earnestly feel that there is a great deal to be learned from the careful scrutiny and close examination of cross-country experiences of those who faced the identical crisis ridden situations and came out successfully out of them.

In sum, the promotion of employment-intensive rural industrialization with market and technological inter-dependence with the outside world is, from our well-considered viewpoint, one and the only one answer to resolve the agrarian crisis facing Punjab on an enduring basis. Unobstructed low-cost institutional credit should be provided for the promotion of rural non-farm activities as supplementary sources of income and employment for the rural masses in Punjab. Bold and wide-ranging policy reforms in respect of reorientation of agriculture subsidies can also help in redeeming the situation quite appreciably. In view of this, the state planners and policy makers in Punjab need to bring the brains together to deliberate on the future development strategies for the state. In more precise terms, bringing the bankers, entrepreneurs, and farmer leaders on the same table and meeting their needs in order to make progress will be essential in the near future. Only a well- struck coordination between the interests of various stake- holders in the agricultural economy of Punjab will serve the purpose. How to accomplish it? is, in our well-considered opinion, the litmus-test for the state planners and policy makers.

(The motivation for this paper has come from Professors G.K.Chadha and H.S. Shergill. The author wishes to thank both of them. The usual disclaimers apply).

Notes

1. It is widely acknowledged that with the arrival of the Green Revolution in Punjab, the state has realized enviable economic gains in terms of substantial increases in the yield rates of paddy and wheat, volume of overall agricultural production and level of overall productivity. Punjab, in fact, has emerged as the front runner in the matter of adoption of the new farm technology, and realization of the resultant gains.
2. It has come to be observed that the farm sector in Punjab, aside from losing its earlier economic remunerativeness overtime, has also it has fallen prey to economic squeeze somuch so that 2116 farmers in the state had been forced to commit suicides owing to their getting driven into debt-trap since 1988. These estimates of farmers' suicides have been reportedly confirmed by the state government, though the non-official estimates to this effect are much higher. It is alleged that though Punjab has the highest number of rural suicides in the country, the state agencies are deliberately underplaying such suicides. Whatever be the political economy of farmers' suicides in Punjab or elsewhere, the phenomenon of the suicides is the ground level reality which cannot be overlooked easily.

3. The fact that the two said components of the Green Revolution are characterized by high degree of complementarity has been highlighted by several research workers. For the details of the said components, please see, G.K.Chadha(1979), *"Production Gains of New Agricultural Technology"*, Publication Bureau, Panjab University, Chandigarh, p.1
4. C.H. Hanumantha Rao(1975), *" Technologcal Change and Distribution of Gains in Indian Agriculture"*, The Macmillan Company of India, Limited , Delhi, pp.77.79.
5. The Indian Society of Agricultural Economics(1983), *Indian Journals of Agricultural Economics,* Vol. XXXVIII, No.4, October-December, pp. 391-434.
6. For details, please see M. R. Khurana (1992), *" Agricultural Development and Employment Patterns In India: A Comparative Analysis of Punjab and Bihar"*, Concept Publishing Company Private Ltd., New Delhi
7. M. R. Khurana (1992), *Ibid.*
8. M. R. Khurana (1992), *Ibid.*
9. M. R. Khurana (1992), *Ibid.*
10. Such a view has emerged due to Punjab's overwhelmingly high contribution to the central kitty of foodgrains, more particularly in the form of wheat and rice.
11. The idea is that even though The Green Revolution has brought about and the Neo-liberal capitalist policies promise immense economic gains of various types, the costs involved in terms of the problems associated with such developments may also be very high.
12. The opponents make this point in connection with growing unremunerativeness of the agricultural sector in Punjab.
13. It has been observed by several scholars that two types of inter - sectoral linkages namely Forward linkages and Backward linkages emerge in the course of development of the agricultural sector. These linkages in turn play an important role in accelerating the process of overall growth of an economy. For details of linkages, please see, Albert O. Hirschman (1958), *" The Strategy of Economic Development"*, Yale University Press, Inc., New Haven, Connecticut.
14. In an important sense, the shocking immiserization of the agriculture sector culminating into farmers' suicides can be

attributed to the failure of the Punjab agricultural sector in forging the linkages mentioned in 13 above.

15. Economic and Statistical Organisation(2010), *"Economic Survey 2009-2010"*, Government of Punjab.

16 The change in agrarian relations in Punjab becomes amply manifest on several counts. *First,* in the aftermath of Green Revolution, reverse tenancy has emerged as a dominant form of tenancy in the form of leasing- in land by middle and big cultivators from small and marginal owners. An important feature of this mode of tenancy is that it is informal as well as unrecorded. In hindsight, it is not impertinent to mention that in the pre-Green Revolution period, particularly during the 1950s, the small owners for purposes of supplementing their operational holdings, normally used to lease- in land from large land owners who, unable to cultivate their land, normally followed the practice of leasing it out. As against this, with commercialization of agriculture becoming more stark over the period of time in the wake of the emergence of the Green Revolution in the state, presently it is the medium owners of land who seem to be leasing-in land from small owners for increasing the size of their operational holdings. Under this informal tenancy arrangement, quite a number of marginal and small farmers with low income level, in the event of their succeeding in seeking the alterative sources of employment and earnings outside agriculture, prefer to lease- out their land and thus move out of cultivation. Although conclusive evidence on this count continues to be somewhat elusive in the absence of adequate empirical evidence, yet it makes, in part, a cogent explanation for a major shift of rural workforce away from agriculture during the last couple of decades. *Second,* the mortgaging of land has over the period of time emerged as an alternate route of shifting the land away from small and marginal owners in Punjab. It is often seen that faced with dire financial straits in the event of failure to access formal and informal sources of credit, these poor peasants generally get involved in the practice of mortgaging their land to medium and large cultivators (and at times to commission agents also). *Finally* , sale-purchase of land is yet another route contributing towards the phenomenon of land transfer to the large cultivators from small (and marginal) farmers in the Punjab countryside. Needless to overemphasize, although empirical evidence on the nature and extent of sale-purchase transactions in land for more recent times is not available, the prevailing reality confirming the existence

and continuance of this phenomenon in the Punjab countryside cannot be dismissed as a sheer fig of imagination. An important point that needs to be underlined in respect of the said mechanisms of land transfer in Punjab is that the scale of land transfers is low through mortgages and sale- purchase process in comparison to the corresponding land transfers via tenancy. The net outcome of these processes of land transfers is the growing concentration of land with medium and large cultivators at the expense of small and marginal farmers who seem to losing battle and getting growingly pushed out of land cultivation. Due to these developments, growing marginalization and growing proletarinization is on the rise in the state. For details see, Sucha S.Gill(2005), "Economic Distress and Farmer Suicides in Rural Punjab", *Journal of Punjab Studies,* Vol.12, No.2, pp.219-37.

17. It has often been argued that Punjab has over the period of time, more particularly in the wake of the introduction of the policy of economic reforms in 1990s, experienced an important deceleration in terms of growth rate of its economy, while its performing in this regard was much better in the decades of 1970s and 1980 in comparison to that of the country as a whole.

18. The concern about the decline in water table in Punjab has been voiced at a number of forums. For details, please see, Chief Minister's Advisory Committee on Agriculture Policy & Restructuring (CMACAPR) (2002), *"Agricultural Production Pattern Adjustment Programme in Punjab for Productivity Growth", Government of Punjab*

19. For the latest information in respect of farmers indebtedness, please see National Sample Survey Organisation (NSSO) (2005), *"Indebtedness of Farmer Households: Situation Assessment Survey of Farmers"*, NSS 59th Round (January-December, 2003), Report No. 498 (59/33/1), Government of India, May; also see, H.S. Shergill(2010), *" Growth of Farm Debt in Punjab"*, Institute for Development and Communication, Chandigarh.

20. The fact of declining Gross State Domestic Capital Formation (GSDCF) in Punjab agriculture has been mentioned in several official publications of the state government. For details, please see, Economic and Statistical Organisation(2010), *Op. Cit.*

21. M.R.Khurana(1992), *Op.Cit;* ---------- (2009), "Agricultural Diversification in Punjab and Beyond", *Panjab University Research Journal(Arts),* Vol. XXXV, Nos. 1-2, pp. 48-89;

and----------(2010), "The Punjab Village Economy: Looking Within and Beyond Agriculture", in R.S. Ghuman et. al. eds. (2010), *"Globalization and Change: Perspectives on Punjab "*, Essays in Honour of Professor Sucha Singh Gill, Rawat Publications Pvt. Ltd., Jaipur, pp.279-305.

22. For instance, several studies by Theodore W. Schultz, a Nobel Laureate and a staunch proponent of this line of thinking , are useful in regard to the role of investment in human beings for accelerating the process of agricultural and hence in economic development. In more recent times, following the revival of interest in the human capital theory at the hands of Kenneth J. Arrow, Robert E. Lucas Jr. and Paul M. Romer and others, this idea has received further acclaim. For details, see Theodore W Schultz (1960), "Capital Formation by Education," *Journal of Political Economy,* Vol. LXVIII, No. 6, December, pp. 571-83;-----(1961), "Investment in Human Capital", *The American Economic Review,* Vol. LI , No. 1, March, pp. 1-17; ----- (1980), *"Investing in People – The Economics of Population Quality"*, Hindustan Publishing Corporation (India), Delhi; Kenneth J. Arrow (1962), "The Economic Implications of Learning by Doing", *Review of Economic Studies,*Vol. XXIX, June, pp. 155-73(a); Robert E. Lucas Jr. (1988), " On the Mechanics of Economic Development", *Journal of Monetary Economics,* Vol. 22, pp.3-42; --------(2002), *" Lectures on Economic Growth"*, Oxford University Press, New Delhi; Paul M. Romer (1990a), " Endogenous Technological Change", *Journal of Political Economy,* Vol 98, pp. S 71- S 102; and --------(1990b), " Human Capital and Growth: Theory and Evidence", *Carnegie Rochester Conference Series on Public Policy,* Vol. 32, pp. 156- 206.

23. M. R. Khurana (1992), *op. cit.,* p. 244.

24. A. G. B. Fisher (1939),"Production, Primary, Secondary and Tertiary", *Economic Records,* Vol. 15, June, pp.24-38; C. G. Clark (1940), *" The Conditions of Economic Progress"*, The Macmillan Press Ltd., London. And for other outstanding contributions on the theme of structural transformation, see Simon, Kuznets(1966), *"Modern Economic Growth: Rate, Structure and Spread"*, Yale University Press, Inc., New Haven.25.

25. Strong irrigation base has been labeled as the sheet- anchor of agricultural development in Punjab under the green revolution technology. This indicates that the provision of assured irrigation

has been of central importance in the agricultural transformation of the state economy. For further details in this regard,see G. K. Chadha (19 86), " *The State and Rural Economic Transformation: The Case of Punjab 1950-85*", Sage Publications India Pvt. Ltd., New Delhi, p. 68.

26 Chief Minister's Advisory Committee on Agriculture Policy & Restructuring (CMACAPR) (2002), *Op.Cit.*, p.10 & p. 24.

27. Dairying and poultry including milk, milk products meat, fish and eggs, edible oils, cattle and poultry feed, liquor, malt and malt products using wheatand rice, fruits and vegetables, textiles and garments, pulp and paper including manufacturing of container boxes of paper and board, starch and starch products, wool cleansing, processing and knitting, etc are some of the agro-based industries which,in our opinion, hold a high potential for development in the state of Punjab.

28. Albert O. Hirschman (1958), *Op. Cit.*

29. M. R. Khurana (1992), *op. cit.*, p.247.

30. For instance, the fact that dairying and poultry enterprises influence the income distribution favourably in the state of Punjab has frequently been mentioned in many field level studies undertaken and published in various journals from time to time by several other research workers as well.

31. The capitalist rules of the game veer around the dictum 'survival of the fittest.' While the performers immensely gain under capitalism, those failing to withstand competition, on the other hand, are forced to meet their economic doomsday.

References

Arrow, Kenneth J. (1962), "The Economic Implications of Learning by Doing", *Review of Economic Studies,*Vol. XXIX, June, pp. 155-73(a).

Borch, Karl (1968), " *The Economics of Uncertainty*", Princeton University Press, Princeton, see especially Chapter 5

Chadha, G. K. (1979), " *Production Gains of New Agricultural Technology*", Publication Bureau, Panjab University, Chandigarh.

Chadha, G.K.(19 86), " *The State and Rural Economic Transformation: The Case of Punjab 1950-85*", Sage Publications India Pvt. Ltd., New Delhi.

Chadha, G.K.and M. R. Khurana (1989), "Backward Agriculture, Unrewarded Labour and Economic Deprivation: Bihar's Contrast with Punjab", *Economic and Political Weekly*, Vol. XXIV, No. 47, November 25, pp. 2617-2623.

Chadha, G.K. (2001), " India and WTO: Some Suggestions for Internal Corrections and External Initiatives", in G. K. Chadha (ed.), *WTO and the Indian Economy*, Deep and Deep Publications (P) Ltd., New Delhi.

Chand, R. (1999), " Emerging Crisis in Punjab Agriculture: Severity and Options for Future", *Economic and Political Weekly*, Vol. XXXIV, No. 13, Review of Agriculture, March, 27, pp.A2-A10

Clark, C. G. (1940), " *The Conditions of Economic Progress*", The Macmillan Press Ltd., London.

Fisher, A. G. B. (1939), "Production, Primary, Secondary and Tertiary", *Economic Records*, Vol. 15, June, pp.24-38.

Gill, Sucha S.(2005), "Economic Distress and Farmer Suicides in Rural Punjab", *Journal of Punjab Studies*, Vol.12, No.2, pp.219-37.

———— and Jaswinder Singh. Brar (1996), " Global Market and Competitiveness of Indian Agriculture: Some Issues", *Economic and Political Weekly*, Vol. XXXI, No. 32, August 10, pp. 2167-77.

Haggblade, Stephen, Peter B.R. Hazell, and Thomas Reardon (2007), " *Transforming the Rural Nonfarm Economy: Opportunities and Threats in the Developing World*", Oxford University Press, New Delhi.

Hazell, Peter B. R. (1988), "Risk and Uncertainty in Domestic Production and Prices", in John W. Mellor and Raisuddin Ahmed (eds), *"Agricultural Price Policy in Developing Countries"*, Oxford University Press, Delhi.

Heady, Earl O .(1952), " Diversification in Resource Allocation and Minimisation of Income Variability", *Journal of Farm Economics*, Vol. XXXIV, No. 4, November, pp. 482-96.

Heady, E.O. (1964), *"Economics of Agricultural Production and Resource Use"*, Prentice Hall of India, Pvt. Ltd., New Delhi, see especially Chapter 15, " Risk and Uncertainty in Agricultural Production, pp. 439-464.

Johl, S. S.(1986), " *Diversification of Agriculture in Punjab*", Expert Committee Report, Government of Punjab, Chandigarh.

Johl, S.S.(2002), " *Agricultural Production Pattern Adjustment Programme in Punjab for Productivity and Growth*", Expert Committee Report, Government of Punjab, Chandigarh.

Johl, S.S.(2005), " *Dithering on Diversification: Farm sector in Punjab under Squeeze"*, *The Tribune*, Friday, February 11.

Kahlon, A. S. and Karam Singh (1980), " *Economics of Farm Management in India : Theory and Practice"*, Allied Publishers Private Ltd., New Delhi, see especially, Chapter 6, " Adjustment to Risk and Uncertainty", pp. 287- 319.

Khurana, M. R. (1992), " *Agricultural Development and Employment Patterns In India: A Comparative Analysis of Punjab and Bihar"*, Concept Publishing Company Private Ltd., New Delhi

————(1999), " Swadeshi, Economic Growth and Distributive Justice", in P. P. Arya and B. B. Tandon eds. (1999), *Multinationals versus Swadeshi Today : A Policy Framework for Economic Nationalism"*, Deep and Deep Publications Pvt. Ltd., New Delhi.

————(2009), "Agricultural Diversification in Punjab and Beyond", *Panjab University Research Journal(Arts)*, Vol. XXXV, Nos 1-2, pp. 48-89.

————(2010), "The Punjab Village Economy: Looking Within and Beyond Agriculture", in R.S. Ghuman et. al. eds. (2010), *"Globalization and Change: Perspectives on Punjab "*, Essays in Honour of Professor Sucha Singh Gill, Rawat Publications Pvt. Ltd., Jaipur, pp.279-305.

Kurosaki, T. (2003), " Specialisation and Diversification in Agricultural Transformation: A Case Study of West Punjab, 1903-92", *American Journal of Agricultural Economics*, Vol. 85, No.2, pp.

Kuznets, Simon(1955), "Economic Growth and Change", The *American Economic Review*, No. 35, March, .

Lucas, Robert E. Jr. (1988), " On the Mechanics of Economic Development", *Journal of Monetary Economics*, Vol. 22, pp.3-42.

Lucas, Robert E. Jr. (2002), " *Lectures on Economic Growth"*, Oxford University Press, New Delhi.

Majumdar, N. A.(2004), " *Economic Reforms Sans Development"*, Academic Foundation, New Delhi.

Mukhopadhyay, Swapna and Chee Peng Lim eds.(1985), *"The Rural Non-Farm Sector in Asia"*, Asian and Pacific Development Centre, Kuala Lumpur, Malaysia.

National Sample Survey Organisation (NSSO) (2005), *"Indebtedness of Farmer Households: Situation Assessment Survey of Farmers"*, NSS 59th Round (January-December, 2003), Report No. 498 (59/33/1), Government of India, May.

Rao, C. H. Hanumantha (2001), " WTO and Viability of Indian Agriculture", *Economic and Political Weekly*, Vol. XXXVI, No. 36, September 08, pp. 3453-57.

Romer, Paul M.(1990a), " Endogenous Technological Change", *Journal of Political Economy*, Vol 98, pp. S 71- S 102.

Romer, Paul M.(1990b), " Human Capital and Growth: Theory and Evidence", *Carnegie Rochester Conference Series on Public Policy*, Vol. 32, pp. 156- 286.

Schultz, T. W. (1960), "Capital Formation by Education," *Journal of Political Economy*, Vol. LXVIII, No. 6, December, pp. 571-83.

Schultz, T.W. (1980), *"Investing in People – The Economics of Population Quality"*, Hindustan Publishing Corporation (India), Delhi.

Schultz, T.W.(1961), "Education and Economic Growth," in Henry, N.B. ed (1961), *"Social Forces Influencing American Education ,"* University of Chicago Press, Chicago.

Schultz, T.W.(1961), "Investment in Human Capital", *The American Economic Review*, Vol. LI , No. 1, March, pp. 1-17.

Shand, R.T. ed. (1986), *"Off-Farm Employment in the Development of Rural Asia"*,Volume I and II, National Centre for Development Studies, Australian national University, Canberra, Australia.

Shergill, H. S.(2002), *"Crop Adjustment Programme for Diversification of Punjab Agriculture: Can it Deliver the Goods?"*, Working Paper, Department of Economics, Panjab University, Chandigarh.

————(2005), *" Wheat and Paddy Cultivation and the Question of Optimal Cropping Pattern for Punjab"*, Occasional Paper, Institute for Development and Communication, Chandigarh.

————(2010), *" Growth of Farm Debt in Punjab"*, Institute for Development and Communication, Chandigarh.

Sidhu, R. S. and S. S. Johl (2002), " Three Decades of Intensive Agriculture in Punjab: Socio- Economic and Environmental Consequences" in S. S. Johl and S. S. Ray (eds), *" Future of Punjab Agriculture"*, Centre for Research in Rural and Industrial Development, Chandigarh.

Singh, Jasdev (1998), "Dynamics of Input- Use and Potential to Improve Productivity of Wheat and Paddy in Punjab", *Journal of Agricultural Development and Policy*, Vol. 10, No. 2, July-December, pp.47-60.

Singh, Joginder and R. S. Sidhu (2004), Factors in Declining Crop Diversification: Case Study of Punjab", *Economic and Political Weekly*, Vol. XXXIX, No. 52, Review of Agriculture, December 25, pp.5607-10.

Singh, Karam , Rangi, P. S. and Sajla Kalra (2004), "Wheat Production and Sustainability in Punjab: Growth and Varietal Diversity", *Indian Journal of Agricultural Economics*, Vol. 59, No.4, October-December, pp.745-71.

Singh, S. (2004), " Crisis and Diversification in Punjab Agriculture: Role of State and Agribusiness", *Economic and Political Weekly*, Review of Agriculture, Vol. XXXIX, No. 52, Review of Agriculture, December 25, pp. 5583-90.

Vaidyanathan, A. (1992), " Instability in Agriculture: Extent, Causes and Consequences", *Indian Economic Review*, Vol. XXVII, No.2, pp.211-22.

4

Agricultural Development and Productivity Stagnation in Punjab

Sanjay Kumar & Parminder Singh

Introduction

Punjab agriculture has registered spectacular progress since the country became independent in 1947. At the time of independence, the Punjab agriculture was reeling under the prevalence of fragmented and scattered unirrigated holdings under zamidari system, indebtedness of farmers from moneylenders, outmoded farming techniques, subsistence farming and fluctuation in crop output. It was only after independence that an era of planning began when the first five-year plan started in 1951. The main emphasis of the five-year plans in agriculture sector was to overcome these problems. During the plans, emphasis was laid down on the consolidation of holdings, land reforms, irrigation infrastructure, power, research and extension service, credit, marketing and transport network along with effective price policy and facilities for procurement and distribution of farm inputs. Consequently, the food-grain production in the state increased from 3 million tonnes in 1961 to 25.6 million tonnes in 2009-10 which accounted for about 13 per cent of total food-grains production in the country with only 1.75 per cent of total geographical area in the country. Punjab is also a major contributor of food grains to the central pool, although its share has declined for paddy from 45 per cent in 1980-81 to 34 per cent in 2006-07, while for wheat the contribution has remained at the same level (75 per cent) during the same period. But still, Punjab is the largest contributor of wheat to the central pool while it ranks second after Andhra Pradesh for contribution of paddy.

Effective price policy coupled with relatively better technology available, has resulted into the emergence of paddy and wheat crops as the most secure and profitable ones in the state. The area under other cereals, gram and oilseeds has declined significantly since the emergence of the Green Revolution period. Successive failures of cotton and low returns from this crop, have pushed the farmers to grow paddy even on marginal lands, which is another cause of concern that can thwart the efforts of diversification. The productivity of paddy and wheat has recorded a significant growth of 4.33 and 3.30 per cent per annum for the period of 1965-66 to 1989-90, but it has shown the signs of stagnation since nineties. But still the yield rates of the major crops in the state are quite high as compared to the national average. This was made possible by the Punjab state taking a big leap forward in terms of irrigation facilities, use of chemical fertilizer, pesticide, high yielding varieties, mechanization etc.

The transformation of Punjab agriculture has started showing signs of new set of problems since the nineties. The productivity of major crops like wheat and rice has stagnated leading to increase in cost of production resulting in reduced profitability making many small and marginal farmers unviable. It is important to note that the growth in recent past as well as during the last three decades has been attributed due to adoption of innovative technologies. Thereafter, the impacts of technology have slowed down mainly because of soil fatigue resulting in decline in fertilizers use efficiency. A strong tendency is developing among small and marginal farmers to lease out their land due to uneconomic holdings. The predominance of paddy-wheat monoculture is posing a great threat to soil health, resulting in depletion of underground water.

Hence, the present paper tries to examine the agriculture development scenario and constraints in the agricultural sector in Punjab. Further, it also seeks to find out the causes and remedial policies to deal with the stagnation of productivity in the state.

The present paper has been divided into f sections. Section I is introduction. It gives a brief account of the agricultural development and subsequent changes in agricultural policy measures in Punjab and the emergence of problems/constraits of development in Punjab agriculture and outline the objectives of the present study. Section II highlights the methodology adopted for the data collection and analysis. Agricultural development scenario of the state and problems/constraits are discussed in Section III, where development pattern of the land use, input use, cost structure; prices and capital formation of the state agriculture economy are analyzed. The section IV highlights the conclusions and policy implications emerging out of the present study.

Methodology

This paper is part of the larger study entitled "Determinants in Stagnation of Productivity of Important Crops in Punjab" completed by AERC, Ludhiana and funded by Ministry of Agriculture, New Delhi (Kumar and Singh, 2010). The present study was based on the secondary data and various sources were tapped to achieve the stipulated objectives of the study. The requisite data for the study relating to area, production, productivity of various crops, minimum support prices, harvest prices, wholesale prices, input use, land holding structure and major growth parameters have been collected from the various sources such as *Centre for Monitoring Indian Economy, Statistical Abstracts of Punjab, Agricultural Statistics at a Glance,* and Directorate of Agriculture, Punjab. The data relating to the estimates of cost of cultivation/production of paddy, wheat and cotton have been collected various issues of *CACP (Commission for Agricultural Costs and Prices) Reports.*

The compound annual growth rates were calculated by fitting the following exponential function to different aspects of prices, infrastructure and agricultural growth parameters of Punjab State.

$$Y = ab^x$$

$$\text{Log } Y = \log a + x \log b$$

Compound annual growth rate = (Antilog b-1)X 100

Where : Y = Absolute value

x = Time (years)

Recent Developments in Agriculture in the State and Constraints Faced

The Punjab state manifests the growth in agriculture sector achieved by India after the green revolution period. This structural transformation was the result of new farm technology in the form of high yielding seeds, fertilizers as well as irrigation infrastructure and agricultural credit. Rapid dissemination and adoption of new technologies, development of necessary infrastructure and setting up of institutional mechanisms for the supply of agricultural inputs and procurement of agricultural produce created an enabling environment in enhancing agricultural production. However, the state agriculture is currently facing many difficulties which are hampering its potential for realizing higher growth in future. The agriculture sector is in crisis and the negative impacts of intensive agriculture have manifested in many forms. The present section highlights the development of agriculture in the state and subsequently the constraints faced in its sustainability.

Irrigation Status

The excellent network of irrigation facilities is serving the Punjab agriculture. Irrigation coverage, which was about 76 per cent of net sown area in triennium ending 1972-73, has increased to the level of about 97 per cent in triennium ending 2006-07 (Table 1). Canals and tube wells are the main sources of irrigation in the state. The canal irrigation system irrigated 13,08,000 hectare land in triennium ending 1972-73 while only

Table 1

Proportion of Gross Irrigated Area and Net Irrigated Area from different Sources of Irrigation, Punjab, Triennium Ending Average (TE) 1972-73 to 2006-07

Particulars	*1972-73*	*1982-83*	*1992-93*	*2000-01*	*2003-04*	*2004-05*	*2005-06*	*2006-07*
Gross Irrigated Area (000,ha)	4396.8	5965.2	7102.9	7619.4	7632	7692.2	7679.7	7657.4
Per cent GIA to GCA	76.1	86.8	94.4	96.3	96.9	97	97.6	97.4
Source of Irrigation: Percentage to Net Irrigated Area								
Govt. Canals	44.69	40.76	38.67	26.34	27.76	27.29	27.93	29.16
Private Canals	0.18	0.00	0.15	0.00	0.00	0.17	0.10	0.10
Tubewells & Wells	54.62	58.92	60.97	73.53	72.07	72.34	71.77	70.75
Other sources	0.51	0.32	0.20	0.12	0.17	0.20	0.20	0.00
Net Irrigated Area (000 ha)	2927.7	3446.7	3903.3	4017	4032.0	4035.0	4060.0	4078.0
	(100.0)	(100.0)	(100.0)	(100.0)	(100.0)	(100.0)	(100.0)	(100.0)

Note: TE indicates Triennium Ending Average

Source: Various issues of Statistical Abstracts of Punjab

11,41,000 hectare was irrigated in triennium ending 2006-07. While canal irrigation has been declining over the years, tube well irrigation, particularly in the central and northern region of Punjab has been on an increase. This is mainly due to availability of cheap credit and free supply of electricity in the state. But the extensive use of canal irrigation and reckless use of ground water through tube wells have caused water logging problems in some areas and lowering of the ground water table in other areas.

Land Use Pattern

Punjab is a tiny state with total geographical area of 50.33 lakh hectares (Table 2). There has been continuous increase in the net sown area in the state since 1960-61 and the proportion of net sown area to total geographical area, which was 75.83 per cent in triennium ending 1962-63 has reached to 83.14 per cent by triennium ending 2006-07. This was made possible by the adoption of short duration dwarf varieties of wheat and rice, along with the expansion in the irrigated area, fertilizer consumption and growth of farm mechanization in the state. There has been significant increase in area under forests in the state as proportion of area under forests to total geographical area increased from 0.68 per cent in triennium ending 1962-63 to 5.42 per cent by triennium ending 2006-07. There has been significant decrease in area under permanent barren and unculturable land and current fallow over the study period of 1960-61 to 2006-07. There has been marginal increase in net area sown from 3.81 million ha in triennium ending 1962-63 to 4.18 million ha by triennium ending 2006-07, though the gross cropped area increased from around 4.84 million ha to 7.87 million ha during the same period. This has resulted in an increase in the cropping intensity from around 127 per cent in triennium ending 1962-63 to about 189 per cent in triennium ending 2006-07. This increase was higher during the period of 1960-61 to 1980-81 as compared to the later period and it has not increased substantially since the year 1995-96. Because of the absence of any scope to increase the cultivated area of the state horizontally, the vertical expansion of area has become

Table 2

Changes in the Land Use Pattern, Punjab, Triennium Ending Average (TE) 1962-63 to 2006-07

(Per cent to total geographical area)

Type of Land use	*TE 1962-63*	*TE 1972-73*	*TE 1982-83*	*TE 1992-93*	*TE 2000-01*	*TE 2006-07*
Forests	0.68	2.35	4.38	4.77	5.89	5.42
Barren and un culturable land	Na	4.13	1.84	1.53	4.65	0.52
Land put to non-agricultural uses	Na	8.28	8.61	7.52	3.47	9.35
Culturable waste	Na	1.56	0.77	0.64	0.59	0.16
Permanent pastures & other grazing lands	Na	0.1	0.08	0.12	0.08	0.08
Land under Misc tree crops and groves	Na	0.08	0.07	0.15	0.09	0.07
Current fallows	5.49	2.56	0.8	1.7	0.85	0.79
Other fallow lands	Na	Na	0.02	0.37	0.09	0.01
Net Area sown	75.83	80.93	83.60	83.26	84.29	83.14
Area sown more than once	20.50	33.92	53.09	66.23	76.64	73.56
Geographical Area (Lakh ha)	5038	5036	5036	5036	5036	5036

Note: TE indicates Triennium Ending Average

Source: Various issues of Statistical Abstracts of Punjab

increasingly limited due to already achieved higher levels of cropping intensity and some topographical and irrigational constraints in some pockets of the state. Therefore, sustainability in the growth of production per unit of land area has to come through raising the input use efficiency or upward shift in the use of technology.

Changing Structure of Landholdings

Since the introduction of the green revolution technology, the agrarian structure of Punjab has witnessed interesting changes. Till 1980-81, the number of marginal and small holdings declined sharply, while those in the higher-size categories showed a modest increase. These changes occurred primarily due to the reasons that with the onset of the green revolution technology, crop production activities became economically attractive, which created an active land-market for leasing and selling land. In the later period (1980-81 to 1990-91), when profitability in farming started falling and growth of employment opportunities in the non-farm sector became limited, the absolute number of holdings in the state increased, even with a significant decline in the total operated area. Consequently, the average holding size in the state fell sharply from 4.07 hectare in 1980-81 to 3.61 hectare in 1990-91 (Table 3). All except the small farmers registered a decline in average landholding size. The number of marginal farmers increased steeply from 1,97,323 in 1980-81 to 2,95,568 in 1990-91 (an increase of more than 50%), while their operating land base, during the same period, increased from a total of 1,26,000 hectare to around 1,64,000 hectare (i.e., an increase of about 30%). Small farms too increased but marginally, with more than a proportionate increase in their total operated area, primarily due to progressive subdivision of medium and large farms under the law of inheritance. These negative developments in Punjab agriculture had slightly arrested in 2000-01 when the average holding size in the state had improved to nearly 4.03 hectare but there was marginal decrease to 3.95 hectare in the recent years (2005-06). In 2000-01, except marginal and small farms, all other categories of farms have considerably increased.

Table 3
Changing Structure of Land Holdings and Area Operated, Punjab, 1970-71 to 2005-06

Holdings	*Number of holdings*					*Area Operated (000 hectare)*				
	1970-71	*1980-81*	*1990-91*	*2000-01*	*2005-06 (P)*	*1970-71*	*1980-81*	*1990-91*	*2000-01*	*2005-06 (P)*
Marginal	517568	197323	295568	122761	134000	NA	125	164	77	83
(Below 1.0 ha)	(37.63)	(19.21)	(26.46)	(12.31)	(13.36)		(3.02)	(4.07)	(1.91)	(2.09)
Small	260083	199368	203842	173071	183000	NA	291	328	242	258
(1.00-1.99 ha)	(18.91)	(19.41)	(918.25)	(17.35)	(18.25)		(6.98)	(8.13)	(6.02)	(6.51)
Semi-Medium	281103	287423	288888	328231	319000	NA	841	841	876	855
(2.00-3.99 ha)	(20.44)	(27.98)	(25.86)	(32.91)	(31.80)		(20.16)	(20.86)	(21.78)	(21.57)
Medium	247755	269072	261481	300977	296000	NA	1672	1622	1731	1701
(4.00 -9.99 ha)	(18.01)	(26.20)	(23.41)	(30.18)	(29.51)		(40.09)	(40.23)	(43.04)	(42.91)
Large	68883	73941	67172	72356	71000	NA	1241	1077	1096	1067
(10.00 & above)	(5.01)	(20)	(6.01)	(7.25)	(7.08)		(29.75)	(26.71)	(27.25)	(26.92)
All	1375392	1027127	1116951	997396	1003000	NA	4171	4032	4022	3964
	(100.0)	(100.0)	(100.0)	(100.0)	(100.00)		(100.0)	(100.0)	(100.0)	(100.00)
Average						NA	4.07	3.61	4.03	3.95

Note: P denotes Provisional.
Source: Various issues of Statistical Abstracts of Punjab.

As a result, the average operating land base for all categories of farms had declined, except for the marginal ones. The state of agrarian structure was due to the fact that marginal and small size farming, though the largest in numbers, were fast becoming unviable and were leasing out land to large farmers but the trend seems to be reversing marginally in 2005-06.

Changes in Cropping Pattern

Cereals, particularly rice and wheat dominate the cropping pattern scenario in the state. This has been made possible through the technological breakthrough in wheat and rice crops along with higher use of fertilizers and HYV seeds and assured price policy for these crops in the state. Due to these policies, the country has become net exporter of food grains as compared to the position of net importer in the early 1960s. Punjab has also been significantly contributing rice and wheat to the national pool. Although, wheat was grown on about 30 per cent of gross cropped area in the state in triennium ending 1962-63 but Punjab was not a traditional rice grower as it occupied only about 5 per cent of GCA in the state. The dominance of rice in the cropping pattern, which has occupied about 33 per cent of the GCA in the state in triennium ending 2006-07, has serious implications on the indiscriminate and uncontrolled use of ground water resources. A perusal of the Table 4 also revealed that the increase in area under paddy and wheat in the state was at the expense of area under oilseed, pulses, maize and bajra crops. The proportion of area under oilseed and pulses to the gross cropped area which was about 23 per cent in triennium ending 1962-63 has come down to the level of about one per cent in the year triennium ending 2006-07. Area under gram, which used to be the most important pulse crop in the state during the sixties, has recorded a sharp decline from about 8,37,493 hectare in triennium ending 1962-63 to less than 10,000 hectare in triennium ending 2006-07. Yield of gram, which stagnated till 1990-91, has started improving, though it has not yet become attractive enough to arrest the decline in its area and production.This tremendous decrease in area under these crops may be attributed to the absence of technological improvements and ineffective price policy for these crops in the state. Cotton is also one of the important crops in the state but due to severe attack of insect-pest and variation in prices, the area and productivity of this crop has very wide fluctuations. Areas under crops such as sugarcane, potato, etc., have not remained stable (Table 4).

Table 4
Changes in the Cropping Pattern, Punjab, Triennium Ending Average (TE) 1962-63 to 2006-07

(Per cent to Gross Cropped Area)

Crop	*TE 1962-63*	*TE 1972-73*	*TE 1982-83*	*TE 1992-93*	*TE 2000-01*	*TE 2006-07*
Rice	4.8	7.6	19.3	27.3	31.8	33.5
Maize	4.9	9.6	5.0	2.5	2.0	1.9
Jowar	0.1	0.1	0.0	0.0	0.0	0.0
Bajra	2.7	2.8	0.8	0.1	0.1	0.1
Wheat	30.0	40.6	42.7	43.4	41.7	44.0
Barley	1.3	0.9	1.1	0.6	0.4	0.2
Other cereals	0.3	0.0	0.0	0.0	0.0	0.0
Total Cereals	44.1	61.6	67.9	73.9	76.0	79.7
Black gram	17.3	5.8	3.0	0.5	0.1	0.1
Other pulses	1.4	1.0	1.2	1.0	0.7	0.3
Total pulses	18.7	6.8	4.2	1.5	0.8	0.4
Total Food grains	62.8	68.4	72.1	75.4	76.8	80.1
Groundnut	1.5	2.9	1.2	0.2	0.1	0.1
Total Oil seeds	3.9	5.6	3.2	2.3	1.3	1.0
Cotton-A	4.6	4.0	7.9	8.4	4.9	6.5
Cotton-D	5.0	4.0	2.1	1.0	1.3	0.6
Sugarcane	2.6	1.9	1.4	1.4	1.4	1.1
Tobacco	NA	NA	NA	NA	NA	NA
Dry Chillies	0.0	0.3	0.1	0.0	0.0	0.0
Fruits	NA	NA	0.3	1.0	0.6	0.7
Vegetables	NA	NA	0.6	0.8	1.5	1.4
Gross Cropped Area (in ha)	4841000	5778000	6869000	7524000	8099000	7887000

Note: TE indicates Triennium Ending Average

Source: Various issues of Statistical Abstracts of Punjab

Area, Production and Productivity Growth

The temporal changes in the area, production and productivity of different crops in the Punjab state has been presented in Table 5 and the productivity level of important crops are shown in Figure 1. To ascertain the temporal growth in area, production and productivity of different crops in the Punjab state, the analysis were done for the four periods viz. period I (1960-61 to 1966-67); period II (1967-68 to 1979-80); period III (1980-81 to 1989-90) and period IV (1990-91 to 2006-07).

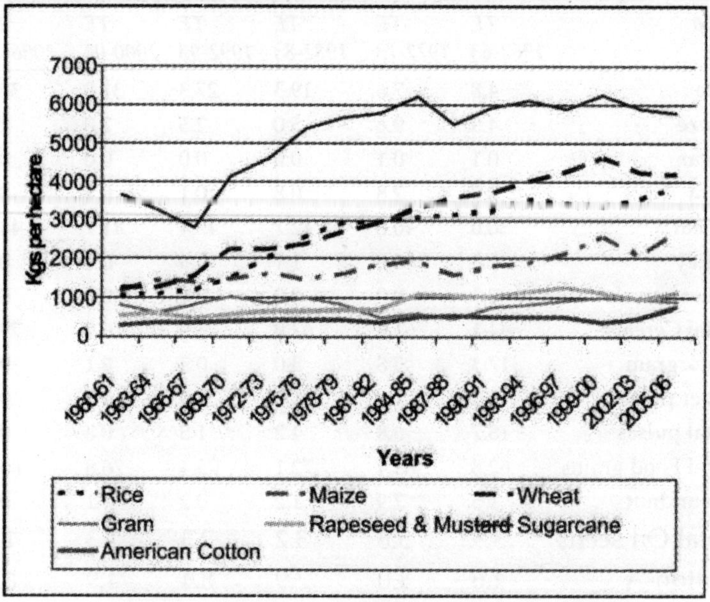

Figure 1: Productivity of Major Crops, Punjab

There was tremendous increase in area, production and yield under paddy for all the periods under study. Wheat also showed the same trend but the increase was at lesser pace than for the paddy. Increase in area and productivity of these crops are the main movers for this increase in production of these crops in the state. All other crops showed either decrease in area or the insignificant increase in area during this period. It clearly reveals that the paddy and wheat crop rotation became

Table 5

Average Annual Compound Growth Rates of Area (A), Production (P) and Yield (Y) of Major Crops in Different Periods, Punjab

(Per cent per annum)

	1950-61 to 1966-67			*1967-68 to 1979-80*			*1980-81 to 1989-90*			*1990-91 to 2006-07*		
YEAR	*A*	*P*	*Y*	*A*	*P*	*Y*	*A*	*P*	*Y*	*A*	*P*	*Y*
Rice	4.86**	7.18**	2.2	11.17**	18.90**	6.95**	5.34**	6.70**	1.3	1.86**	2.95**	1.07**
	(0.75)	(1.76)	(1.40)	(0.78)	(0.79)	(0.70)	(0.62)	(1.23)	(0.78)	(1.86)	(0.23)	(0.22)
Bajra	6.83	10.57	3.97	-8.54**	-9.04**	-0.55	-18.63**	-21.34**	-3.07*	-3.45*	-4.61**	-0.98
	(3.93)	(6.56)	(4.67)	(1.80)	(1.94)	(0.80)	(2.31)	(2.21)	(1.24)	(1.26)	(1.48)	(0.6)
Maize	23.6	10.14*	5.11	-1.47	-1.38	-0.08	-5.64**	-6.83**	-1.27	-1.42**	1.68*	3.13**
	(20.51)	(3.65)	(3.82)	(0.82)	(0.85)	(0.83)	(0.55)	(1.49)	(1.74)	(0.19)	(0.65)	(0.57)
Wheat	2.20**	5.44*	3.17	2.95**	5.42**	2.40**	1.25**	4.29**	3.0**	0.45**	1.31**	0.29
	(0.35)	(1.89)	(1.74)	(0.40)	(0.70)	(0.37)	(0.25)	(0.67)	(0.65)	(0.07)	(0.29)	(2.72)
Barley	4.54	8.59*	3.76	-4.98	-1.26	3.87**	-7.92**	-2.99	5.55**	-5.32**	-4.0**	1.38**
	(4.27)	(3.68)	(3.43)	(3.35)	(3.32)	(0.87)	(1.71)	(2.50)	(1.38)	(0.52)	(0.68)	(0.28)
Other cereals	-32.60*	0.0	-	-1.89	-7.69**	-	1.42	-3.67	-	0.68	5.63	-
	(11.95)	(9.90)		(1.89)	(1.29)		(6.82)	(6.27)		(2.18)	-5.41)	
Total Cereals	4.23**	6.64**	-	3.05**	6.36**	-	1.81**	4.55**	-	0.92**	1.90**	-
	(1.23)	(1.53)		(0.2)	(0.53)		(0.26)	(0.57)		(0.10)	(0.23)	
Gram	-5.64**	-6.95	-1.39	-2.86*	-3.27	0.12	14.15**	-10.20*	4.52	-13.61**	-12.30**	1.46**
	(1.07)	(3.53)	(3.22)	(1.19)	(1.83)	(0.95)	(2.15)	(3.83)	(2.84)	(0.90)	(0.94)	(0.48)

Contd...

(Per cent per annum)

	1960-61 to 1966-67			1967-68 to 1979-80			1980-81 to 1989-90			1990-91 to 2006-07		
YEAR	*A*	*P*	*Y*	*A*	*P*	*Y*	*A*	*P*	*Y*	*A*	*P*	*Y*
Other pulses	-4.96*	-5.29*	-	0.71	0.01	-	0.88	1.89	-	-7.28**	-7.94**	-
	(2.43)	(2.30)		(1.18)	(1.46)		(1.64)	(3.32)		(0.72)	(0.72)	
Total pulses	-5.58**	-6.87*	-	-2.51*	-2.63		-8.21**	-5.04*	-	-8.71**	-9.01**	-
	(1.14)	(3.43)		(1.0)	(1.68)		(1.54)	(2.50)		(0.57)	(0.62)	
Total Food grains	0.89	4.24*	-	2.46**	5.96**	-	1.58**	4.46**	-	0.81**	1.88**	-
	(0.52)	(1.77)		(0.17)	(0.48)		(0.32)	(0.57)		(0.10)	(0.23)	
Arhar	-	-	-	14.59**	18.05**	3.02*	2.40	0.55	-1.81	-3.16**	-3.79**	-0.66
				(3.23)	(3.64)	(1.03)	(4.93)	(5.83)	(1.71)	(0.49)	(0.76)	(0.69)
Moong	-11.34**	-6.38	5.62**	0.8	2.53	1.71	10.46**	8.78*	-1.52	-9.64**	-10.10**	-0.51
	(3.68)	(4.62)	(1.85)	(2.82)	(2.89)	(1.01)	(2.66)	(3.9)	(1.51)	(1.10)	(1.15)	(0.88)
Rapeseed & mustard	-0.52	0.34	0.87	0.90	2.06	3.19*	-0.04	5.51	5.49**	-3.78**	-3.37**	0.41
	(2.70)	(1.27)	(3.02)	(2.58)	(3.08)	(1.25)	(2.57)	(3.59)	(1.66)	(0.83)	(0.93)	(0.55)
Sunflower	-	-	-	-	-	-	-	-	-	-1.39	-1.16	0.07
										(4.75)	(4.84)	(0.56)
Sesamum	7.85	9.61*	1.64	0.73	0.70	-0.03	-1.85	-1.2	0.67	-4.01**	-4.23**	-0.22
	(5.94)	(4.79)	(3.65)	(2.27)	(2.16)	(0.74)	(2.12)	(1.73)	(1.59)	(0.88)	(1.01)	(0.57)
Total Oilseeds	8.42**	15.40**	-	-3.30**	-3.33*	-	-4.53*	-2.56	-	-5.76**	-6.22**	-
	(1.85)	(2.11)		(1.10)	(1.18)		(1.72)	(2.38)		(1.24)	(1.63)	
Sugarcane	3.91	2.50	-1.32	-3.41**	0.77	4.31**	2.07	2.71	0.64	0.15	-0.13	0.29
	(2.87)	(3.47)	(1.99)	(0.92)	(1.30)	(0.65)	(1.59)	(1.56)	(0.70)	(1.18)	(1.21)	(0.25)

Contd...

(Per cent per annum)

	1960-61 to 1966-67			1967-68 to 1979-80			1980-81 to 1989-90			1990-91 to 2006-07		
YEAR	A	P	Y	A	P	Y	A	P	Y	A	P	Y
Dry chillies	-	-	-	-0.98	-1.18	-0.2	-14.48**	-9.47**	2.28	-3.73*	-3.12*	0.64**
				(2.72)	(2.59)	(0.79)	(2.03)	(2.22)	(0.93)	(1.39)	(1.44)	(0.20)
	9.46**	10.57*	0.95	10.31**	15.00**	4.32**	-2.37**	-2.47	0.29	8.07**	8.02**	-0.19
Potato	(2.51)	(3.87)		(1.29)	(1.90)	(0.84)	(1.62)	(1.65)	(2.59)	(1.24)	(1.33)	(0.46)
Cotton A	-1.23	1.8	3.04**	7.67**	8.17**	-0.12	2.44	11.28**	8.61*	-2.32*	-0.85	1.51
	(2.01)	(2.51)	(0.90)	(0.77)	(0.76)	(0.42)	(1.70)	(2.81)	(1.85)	(0.86)	(2.39)	(2.03)
Cotton D	0.38	0.01	-0.36	-0.94	-2.35	-1.96**	-10.83**	-5.72	5.71	-2.10	1.18	3.32*
	(1.96)	(2.33)	(0.51)	(1.15)	(1.53)	(0.46)	(1.85)	(3.16)	(2.91)	(1.840)	(1.72)	(1.25)

**significant at I per cent level

* Significant at 5 per cent level

Note: Figures in the parentheses indicate Standard error

predominant at the cost of maize, other cereals, oilseed and pulses in the state. A cursory glance on the table revealed that the productivity of paddy was consistently improving over the years but the growth has slowed down in period III, particularly during nineties. The productivity of rice increased at the significant rate of 6.95 per cent per annum during period II, but then it plateau during the period III and did not show any significant growth. Recently, the productivity of wheat also showed the signs of stagnation but the decline in the wheat yield was more dramatic as compared to paddy. It shows that the genetic potential of wheat was exploited till 1980s and then got stabilized while in paddy crop, the process has been continuing but the rate of growth has slowed down. The monoculture of paddy and wheat has also caused resurgence of pest and diseases and weeds, which have adversely affected the crop yield. Cotton (American) showed significant increase in area during the period II and III and replaced the area under Cotton (Desi). But due to the persistent attack of insect pest on the Cotton (American) crop, its area and production was badly hit during nineties. The productivity of sugarcane and potato have also stagnated during the recent years. Recently, the productivity growth was notable for maize in the state, but the area was still decreasing at a significant rate.

Changes in Inputs Use

Agricultural Credit

The adoption of high yielding varieties (HYVs) itself might not have occurred on a large scale, if the state had not taken the complementary steps of expanding the availability of rural credit through formal credit institutions, such as co-operative societies, co-operative banks, land mortgage banks, regional rural banks and commercial banks. Besides institutional credit, a substantial amount of credit flows to the farmers from non-formal channels, i.e. commission agents or arhtias. The use of agricultural loans for the unproductive purpose like marriage, social functions, medical treatment etc. has resulted in the present situation of indebtedness in the state (Grover et al.;

2003). Compared to other states, the spread of banks is fairly well developed in Punjab. Overall, on an average, the total availability of agricultural credit has increased form Rs 945 million during 1971-75 to Rs. 88838 million in 2001-05 (Table 6). Till mid 1960s primary agricultural cooperative societies were the only formal agency for the disbursal of rural credit. This availability of credit was augmented through Land Development Banks (LDB) and later through commercial and regional rural banks.

Fertilizer

Fertilizer, the most important component of new technology, has played a very important role in enhancing the agricultural production in the state. The availability of high fertilizer responsive varieties of seed along with assured source of irrigation increased the consumption of chemical fertilizers in the state. Total consumption of NPK in Punjab, which was merely 276 thousand nutrient tones during 1971-75, has continuously increased over time and reached to a level of 14.52 lakh nutrient tones by the period 2001-05 (Table 6). Now, Punjab has the highest consumption of chemical fertilizer per hectare in the country. It consumed about 184 kgs/ha of fertilizers in the period 2001-05 as compared to average of 47kgs/ha during 1971-75. While the productivity of crops increased during the first two decades, on account of increasing nutrient use efficiency, it began to decline thereafter on account of imbalances in the use of N, P and K, along with the deficiencies of micro nutrients. The use of nitrogenous fertilizers showed a significant growth of 2.52 per cent while phosphatic and potassic fertilizers showed a negative growth rate over the period of 1985-86 to 1999-2000 (Singh et al., 2002). This has further distorted the NPK ratio in favour of nitrogenous fertilizer, which is disturbing the soil structure of the Punjab farms.

Agricultural Machinery

The rapid adoption of green revolution technology in Punjab has led to a sharp increase in farm mechanization. The Punjab

Table 6
Major Inputs Use, Punjab, 1971-72 to 2005-06

Year	Gross Area under HYVs (000,ha)	Agriculture Credit (in lakhs)	Tractor (Number)	No. Pump set(Number)		Fertiliser consumption (NPK)	
				Electrical	Diesel	Per ha GCA(kg)	Total (000, nutrients tonnes)
1971-75	2232.60	9451.12	39469	120600	182600	47.03	275.80
1976-80	3375.60	23798.33	82400	234400	343400	75.04	484.40
1981-85	4450.60	76278.70	143100	384600	281200	130.09	901.20
1986-90	4995.20	124328.39	226600	548000	211600	153.18	1117.60
1991-95	5432.40	205677.15	293000	648200	190000	162.72	1233.00
1996-00	5691.60	394593.03	375951	732000	173000	168.74	1321.40
2001-05	6120.80	888386.07	450691	827000	242400	183.96	1452.80

Source: Various issues of Statistical Abstracts of Punjab and Directororate of Agriculture, Punjab

agriculture is highly mechanized in nature. The density of tractors per thousand hectares is 64 in Punjab, which is highest in India. It has increased from the level of mere 5 tractors per thousand hectares of land during 1960-61. On an average, there is now one tractor for every eight hectare of net cultivated land, and in some districts the area operated by a tractor is even lower. There are numerous farmers in Punjab with little land, owning a tractor, while many large farmers have more than one tractor. The available stock of tractors in the state is not fully utilized. In addition, lack of facilities for the service and maintenance of farm equipment near the villages results in raising the cost of production. Excessive farm tractorization has caused damage to physico-chemical characteristics of soils, particularly where puddling is done for rice cultivation. With the loss of soil characteristics, biological activities are also impaired and in the long run, such soils are likely to become unproductive. Similarly, electric tube wells are increasing rapidly in Punjab and it has crossed the figure of 8.27 lakh by 2001-05 (Table 6). Diesel engines are also increasing in the state but at lesser pace than the electrical tube wells. It was due to the policy of supply of free electricity of the state Govt. The number of diesel tube wells has reached 2.42 lakh by 2001-05. The large-scale farm mechanization has led to increase in cropping intensity and commercialization of Punjab agriculture. But in turn, there has been decline in the use of agricultural labour and underutilization of farm machinery, which has led to increase in the cost of production of agriculture in the state.

Seed

As already discussed, the impact of Green Revolution was achieved due to the adoption of high yielding varieties (HYVs), particularly for paddy and wheat and presently almost all the area under rice, wheat and bajra has been covered by the high yielding variety seeds. Punjab was never known for rice cultivation. It was only after the adoption of short stature HYVs of rice IR8 in 1968 and Jaya in 1971, along with the expanded tube well irrigation facilities, the area under rice showed a tremendous increase. The area under HYVs of rice, wheat and bajra was about 57, 72 and 45 per cent respectively in triennium ending 1972-73 (Table 7). For maize, the area under HYVs increased tremendously from 7 per cent in triennium ending 1972-73 to about 95 per cent by triennium ending 2006-07. Overall, the area under HYVs increased from about 21 lakh hectares in the triennium ending 1972-73 to about 63 lakh hectares during triennium ending 2006-07. The introduction of HYVs of different crops resulted in big jump in the productivity of these crops in the state. It is this remarkable increase in productivity of rice and wheat in the state that came to be known as green revolution. But the saturation of yield of rice and wheat in the recent years calls for an urgent need for further genetical improvement in the present day varieties used in the state.

Table 7
Area under HYV Crops of the State, Punjab, Triennium Ending Average (TE) 1962-63 to 2006-07

(Percentage Area to total area under the Crop)

Crop	*TE 1962-63*	*TE 1972-73*	*TE 1982-83*	*TE 1992-93*	*TE 2000-01*	*TE 2006-07*
Rice	NA	56.6	94.4	93.6	97.0	100.0
Maize	NA	6.8	36.4	89.4	91.3	94.5
Bajra	NA	44.9	60.6	96.7	68.8	100.0
Wheat	NA	72.4	98.8	100.0	100.0	100.0
Gross area under HYVs (in ha)	NA	2058000	4238000	5356000	6030000	6258000

Note: TE indicates Triennium Ending Average
Source: Various issues of Statistical Abstracts of Punjab

Changing Cost Structure of Principle Crops

The cost and return analysis have been done for paddy, wheat and cotton for the five periods viz. period I (1970-71 to 1979-80); period II (1980-81 to 1989-90); period III (1990-91 to 1999-00); period IV (2000-01 to 2005-06) and period V (1990-91 to 2005-06) and presented in Tables 8 to 10.

Table 8 indicated that in paddy cultivation the level of most of the major input use, except for human labour, has increased

Table 8
Trends in Cost Structure of Paddy Crop, Punjab, 1970-71 to 2005-06

(Rs./Ha)

Crop	*1970-71 to 1979-80*	*1980-81 to 1989-90*	*1990-91 to 1999-00*	*2000-01 to 2005-06*	*1990-91 to 2005-06*
Operational costs	2230	4371.02	8502	14973	10928
Seed	112	139	309	585	412
Manure	28	106	127	129	128
Human Labour	873	1525	2928	4581	3548
Bullock/Animal Labour	136	154	55	53	54
Pesticides/chemicals	29	158	608	1305	869
Irrigation	354	759	1324	2653	1822
Fertilisers	478	903	1482	2221	1759
Tractor/ Machine labour	162	511	1444	3032	2040
Misc. Expenses	-	-	1	17	7
Interest on working capital	58	116	224	12691	10152
Fixed Costs	927	2756	7099	12691	6449
Rental value of owned land	651	1787	5118	8668	6449
Rent paid for leased-in land	67	376	879	2425	1459
Land revenue, cesses & taxes	5	4	3	-	2
Depreciation on implements & buildings	28	96	161	173	165
Interest on fixed cost	176	493	938	1425	1121
Total cost (C2)	3157	7127	15601	27664	20124
Paid out cost A1	1940	3918	7546	13272	9694
Total Cost C3	3473	7840	17161	30430	22136

Source: Various issues of *CACP (Commission for Agricultural Costs and Prices) Reports.*

significantly in period IV (2000-01 to 2005-06) as compared to other periods. The total human labour use for paddy cultivation was significantly lower at Rs. 2928/ha in period III (1990-91 to 1999-00) as compared to Rs. 4581/ha in period IV (2000-01 to 2005-06). The bullock/animal labour was found to decline over the period of time in the wake of mechanization of various operations especially the preparation of fields and harvesting of paddy as well as increased dependence on chemicals for weed control. The expenditure on weedicides and insecticides increased overtime from Rs. 29/ha in period I (1970-71 to 1979-80) to Rs. 1305/ha in period IV (2000-01 to 2005-06). Over this time period, the amount spent on seeds (value of paddy nursery) increased from Rs. 112/ha to Rs. 585/ha and the fertilizer use increased from Rs. 478 kg/ha to Rs. 2221/ha. Similarly, the total machine labour in paddy crop increased from Rs. 162/ha to Rs. 3032/ha during the same period. The operational costs increased at a lower rate than the fixed costs and the cost C3.

Table 9 indicated that in wheat cultivation the use level of most of the major inputs has increased significantly in period IV (2000-01 to 2005-06) as compared to other periods. The total human labour use for wheat cultivation increased marginally from Rs. 2349/ha in period III (1990-91 to 1999-00) as compared to Rs. 2457/ha in period IV (2000-01 to 2005-06) as the total machine labour increased in wheat crop, particularly during harvesting and its expenses increased from Rs. 1478/ha to Rs. 3479/ha during the same period. The bullock/animal labour was found to decline over the period of time in the wake of mechanization of various operations especially the preparation of fields. The expenditure on weedicides and insecticides increased overtime from almost negligible (Rs.3/ha) in period I (1970-71 to 1979-80) to Rs.1068/ha in period IV (2000-01 to 2005-06). Over this time period, the amount spent on seeds increased from Rs. 105/ha to Rs. 801/ha and the fertilizer use increased from Rs. 367/ha to Rs. 2683/ha. The operational costs increased at a lower rate than the fixed costs and the cost C_3.

Table 10 indicated that in cotton cultivation the use level of most of the major inputs has increased significantly in period IV (2000-01 to 2005-06) as compared to other periods. The total human labour use for cotton cultivation increased marginally from Rs. 4204/ha in period III (1990-91 to 1999-00) as compared to Rs. 4819/ha in period IV (2000-01 to 2005-06) as the total machine labour increased in cotton crop and its expenses increased from Rs. 1039/ha to Rs. 2803/ha during the same period. The bullock/animal labour was found to decline over the period of time in the wake of mechanization of various operations especially the preparation of fields. The expenditure on weedicides and insecticides increased overtime from Rs. 47/ha in period I (1970-71 to 1979-80) to Rs.5661/ha in period IV

Table 9
Trends in Cost Structure of Wheat Crop, Punjab, 1970-71 to 2005-06

(Rs./Ha)

Crop	*1970-71 to 1979-80*	*1980-81 to 1989-90*	*1990-91 to 1999-00*	*2000-01 to 2005-06*	*1990-91 to 2005-06*
Operational costs	1449	2995	7213	11461	8807
Seed	105	223	543	801	640
Manure	14	14	21	43	30
Human Labour	426	784	2349	2457	2390
Bullock/Animal Labour	189	125	57	88	69
Pesticides/chemicals	3	91	347	1068	617
Irrigation	119	165	278	479	353
Fertilisers	367	866	1911	2683	2201
Tractor/ Machine labour	186	634	1178	3479	2228
Misc. Expenses	3	12	35	44	38
Interest on working capital	37	81	194	319	241
Fixed Costs	936	2220	7367	12174	9170
Rental value of owned land	632	1361	5081	7976	6167
Rent paid for leased-in land	97	338	999	2117	1418
Land revenue, cesses & taxes	6	4	3	0	2
Depreciation on implements & buildings	52	95	204	236	216
Interest on fixed cost	149	422	1080	1845	1367
Total cost (C2)	2385	5215	14580	23635	17977
Paid out cost A1	1336	2771	6632	10756	8178
Total Cost C3	2624	5737	16038	25999	19775

Source: Various issues of *CACP (Commission for Agricultural Costs and Prices) Reports*

(2000-01 to 2005-06). Over this time period, the amount spent on seeds increased from Rs. 29/ha to Rs. 1519/ha. The increase was recorded highest during the current decade due to more use of Bt hybrid, which costs more. The fertilizer use increased from Rs. 145/ha period I (1970-71 to 1979-80) to Rs. 1207/ha during period IV (2000-01 to 2005-06).

Trends in Agricultural Prices

The Compound Annual Growth Rates (CAGRs) have been calculated to know the comparative growth of minimum support price (MSP), average wholesale prices (WSP) and farm

Table 10
Trends in Cost Structure of Cotton Crop, Punjab, 1970-71 to 2005-06

Particulars	*1970-71 to 1979-80*	*1980-81 to 1989-90*	*1990-91 to 1999-00*	*2000-01 to 2005-06*	*1990-91 to 2005-06*
Operational costs	1237	2840	9027	17344	12147
Seed	29	91	311	1519	764
Manure	21	16	18	24	20
Human Labour	641	1395	4204	4819	4435
Bullock/Animal Labour	155	217	117	173	138
Pesticides/chemicals	47	332	2203	5661	3500
Irrigation	75	164	372	653	415
Fertilisers	145	299	652	1207	860
Tractor/ Machine labour	97	261	1039	2803	1701
Misc. Expenses	-	-	-	5	2
Interest on working capital	27	65	211	480	312
Fixed Costs	811	2121	6159	9350	7139
Rental value of owned land	589	1479	4315	6436	5110
Rent paid for leased-in land	65	244	732	744	597
Land revenue, cesses & taxes	9	17	29	481	138
Depreciation on implements & buildings	37	79	195	258	202
Interest on fixed cost	111	302	888	1431	1092
Total cost (C2)	2048	4961	15186	26694	19286
Paid out cost A1	976	2206	7159	16107	10515
Total Cost C3	2253	5457	16705	29363	21215

Source: Various issues of *CACP (Commission for Agricultural Costs and Prices)* Reports

harvest price (FHP) over the years for three important crops of the state viz., paddy, wheat and cotton for the two periods viz. period I (1980-81 to 1989-90) and period II (1990-91 to 2006-07). Table 11 shows that although procurement price, wholesale price and farm harvest price showed significantly consistent growth over the years but for paddy and maize crops, the growth of MSP in period I was higher than for the growth in WSP and FHP, whereas reverse was the situation in period IV. The growth rate of MSP, WSP and FHP were very close to each other in case of wheat and there was an evident improvement in growth rates for period II as compared to period I for all the three types of prices. For cotton, in period II, the growth was

Table 11
Average Annual Compound Growth Rates of Wholesale Price Index (WPI), Farm Harvest Prices (FHP) and Minimum Support Prices (MSP) of Major Crops in different periods, Punjab

	1980-81 to 1989-90			*1990-91 to 2006-07*		
YEAR	*WPI*	*FHP*	*MSP*	*WPI*	*FHP*	*MSP*
Rice	7.58**	7.66**	5.47**	5.90**	6.23**	6.66**
	(0.80)	(0.71)	(0.41)	(0.49)	(0.44)	(0.49)
Maize	6.29**	7.58**	4.01**	4.19**	5.06**	6.95**
	(0.95)	(1.03)	(0.45)	(0.65)	(0.79)	(0.41)
Jowar	5.23**	6.95**	4.01**	5.63**	7.87**	7.39**
	(0.72)	(1.68)	(0.45)	(0.69)	(0.73)	(0.35)
Bajra	5.98**	6.25**	4.01**	3.62**	5.96**	7.39**
	(1.33)	(1.38)	(0.45)	(1.09)	(0.75)	(0.35)
Wheat	5.13**	3.56**	4.37**	6.14**	7.72**	8.46**
	(0.58)	(0.34)	(0.43)	(0.46)	(0.45)	(0.44)
Barley	6.34**	4.79**	3.83**	7.73*	7.46**	7.76**
	(0.81)	(1.05)	(0.42)	(3.21)	(0.77)	(0.48)
Gram	10.16**	8.26**	9.65**	7.56**	8.64**	8.56**
	(1.98)	(1.70)	(2.34)	(0.75)	(0.78)	(0.30)
Rapeseed	-	6.34**	4.52**	-	5.12**	
6.87**(0.26)		(1.73)	(0.88)		(0.62)	
mustard						
Cotton	6.70**	7.70**	6.33**	4.18**	4.41**	6.82**
	(1.51)	(1.46)	(0.73)	(0.89)	(0.97)	(0.62)
Chillies	8.68**	-	-	6.66**	-	-
	(2.78)			(1.03)		
Sugarcane	-	-	6.37**	-	-	9.69**
			(0.65)			(0.59)

** Significant at 1% level, * significant at 5 % level

Note: figures in the parentheses indicate Standard error

Source: Various issues of Statistical Abstracts of Punjab

the highest for MSP while in period I, it was the highest for FHP. The price policy was effective for paddy, wheat, cotton and sugarcane as the government has made the arrangements for procurement of these crops in the state. But for all other crops only the MSP was announced and no procurement is done by the Government agencies.

Capital Formation in Agriculture

The proportion of gross capital formation in Punjab agriculture at current prices to the gross capital formation showed a decline from 21.7 per cent in 1980-81 to around 11 per cent till 2003-04 but then decreased up to 9.8 per cent by the year 2005-06 (Table 12). The growth of capital formation in public sector was lesser as compared to the private sector since 1980s. The capital formation in public sector at current prices increased from Rs 42 crores in 1980-81 to about Rs 198 crores in 2005-06, while the growth in private sector during the period was from Rs 108 crores to about 1797 crores. Therefore, the private sector contributes more as compared to the public sector in the capital formation in Punjab agriculture.

Entirely different picture emerges when we look at the trends in expenditure on agricultre in the state during this period (Table 13). It is the story of almost stagnant real expenditure on agriculture (at 1980-81 prices). Another dismal feature of the expenditure was, the exenditure on capital account was negative during some of the years under study. The total expenditure on agriculture, which was Rs 14.55 crore during 1981-85, declined to Rs 9.44 crore during 1996-00 and became Rs. 55.67 crore during the period 2001-05. In a similar way, the expenditure at 1980-81 prices declined from Rs 13.58 crore to Rs 1.93 crore and further increased to Rs. 9.69 crores. Such trends undermines the extension delivery system of the state department for dissemination of latest technologies. The decline in expenditure on agriculture sector therefore has severe implications for the growth of Punjab agriculture. A look at the per hectare budgetary expenditure on agriculture in Punjab further establishes the stagnation trends during the period of study. No doubt, the expenditure on agriculture on current prices more than quadrupled from 1981-85 to 2001-05, there was a decrease in such expenditure at the constant prices.The share of agriculture in expenditure on budetary expenditure at current prices declined continuously from 11.86 per cent during 1981-85 to mere 0.69 per cent during 1996-00 and then jumped to 2.41 per cent during 2001-05. While at constant prices,it declined continuously from 13.91 per cent during to 2.75 per cent during 1996-00 and then jumped to 11.85 per cent during the latest period under study. Hence, it appears that the agriculture sector has been totally neglected in the planned development efforts of the Government of Punjab despite the fact that around 31 per cent of state GDP comes from agriculture.

Table 12

Trends in Capital Formation in Agriculture and its share in total GCF, Punjab, 1980-81 to 2005-06

(Rs in crores)

Year	*Public*	*Private*	*Total*	*% share of total GCF in agriculture to total CGF*
1980-81	42.0	108.0	150.0	21.74
1995-96	415.19	1031.26	1446.45	11.65
2000-01	303.29	1305.99	1609.28	11.91
2003-04	72.8	1566.33	1639.13	11.30
2004-05	142.73	1665.07	1807.8	9.22
2005-06(P)	197.82	1797.32	1995.17	9.86

P-provisional

Source: Economic and Statistical Adviser, Punjab

Table 13

Public Investments in Agriculture (Average), Punjab, 1978-79 to 2005-06

	Capital Expenditure on Agricultural & allied heads Rs. Crore/year		*Capital Expenditure per hectare of net sown area Rupees Per year*		*Share of Budget expenditure on agriculture*	
Year	*at Current prices*	*at 1980-81 prices*	*at Current prices*	*at 1980-81 prices*	*at Current prices*	*at 1980-81 prices*
1978-80	-13.70	-18.14	-33.0	-43.0	Na	Na
1981-85	14.55	13.58	35.0	32.0	11.86	13.91
1986-90	-7.39	-3.0	-18.0	-7.0	Na	Na
1991-95	28.76	8.90	68.0	21.0	3.30	8.52
1996-00	9.44	1.93	22.0	5.0	0.69	2.75
2001-05	55.67	9.69	151.0	26.0	2.41	11.85

Source: Economic and Statistical Adviser, Punjab.

Conclusion and Policy Implications

Predominance of paddy-wheat rotation has serious repercussions in the form of soil health due to toxicity, alkalinity/salinity, micronutrient deficiencies and depletion of groundwater due to excessive mining of water and therefore the productivity of these crops has almost become stagnant. Considering these hazardous effects of mono-culture, paddy-wheat rotation needs diversification towards more sustainable cropping system and at least 10 per cent area under paddy should be diverted to other crops like oilseeds, cotton, maize, pulses and fruits and vegetables which demand less water.

The rice-wheat cropping system is loosing its sustainability considering the slowing growth in production and productivity and its adverse impact on vital resources such as water and land. The productivity of both rice and wheat seems to be plateauing. This is despite the monsoon remaining favourable in the last decade. The productivity of other crops such as sugarcane, cotton, oilseeds and pulses has either stagnated or increased marginally.

The rice-wheat cropping system has strained the water and land resources. The over-exploitation of groundwater resulted in a sharp decline in the ground water table and rendered a sizable area less productive because of salination. Salts have accumulated in the upper layer of the soil surface and could render vast stretches useless for cultivation. Besides, about 70 blocks in the State are in the dark category, where water exploitation seems much more than what nature can replenish. The excess utilisation of water, especially in rice, has created water-logged conditions in the canal command areas (Southern Punjab) and a sizable area is getting saline for want of adequate drainage. Free electricity and highly subsidised water have compounded problems. Research findings also indicate that irrigation practices are outmoded and need to be replaced. The flooding of fields can no longer be the right technology. Research has also established that proper field preparation, timely planting and irrigation techniques can lead to higher water-use efficiency.

The high profitability of rice-wheat crop production has led to the higher, if not excessive, input use. More reliance on chemical fertilisers and their imbalanced use has affected soil health. The micronutrient deficiency in soil has increased. A large area has become deficient in zinc, copper, iron and manganese. Besides, the gap in nutrient application and what is depleted by the crop has also increased. Integrated use of balanced chemical fertilizers in conjunction with organic manures (compost and green manure), rotation of cereals with legumes and use of bio-fertilizers and vermiculture have to be undertaken to maintain the health of the soil. To enhance fertilizer-use efficiency under different cropping systems, continuous technological inputs are needed to make them cost-effective. The use of farm compost and recycling of crop residues seems to have become a practice of the past. The crop residue management has become a major problem in the State and many farmers are burning paddy and wheat straw which were earlier fed to the cattle and finally found its way into the fields as manure. Thus, the already low organic carbon content in the soil has decreased further. As per a recent report of the Indian Council of Agriculture Research, in most areas of Punjab, the soil is deficient in organic carbon, which has come down from 0.5 per cent in the 1960s to 0.2 per cent. Organic-carbon improves the biological activity in the soil, helps retain soil moisture longer and reduces the leaching of plant nutrients.

The spectrum of use of pesticides has been changing over the years in response to emerging pests- and weed-problems due to intensive cultivation. Excessive and indiscriminate use of pesticides and weedicides has led to several new problems, such as development of pest resistance, pest resurgence and outbreaks, and adverse effects on such non-target organisms as predators, pollinators and honey bees. Development of resistance in the American boll worm, because of abuse and misuse of pesticides in cotton, accounts for the inability to control cotton pests in cotton belt of the state. Similarly, abuse and misuse of pesticides is rampant on fruit and vegetable crops, which pose great health hazards to consumers. The strategy for effective management of pests- and weed-problem lies in the use of integrated pest management technology (IPM), wherein agronomic practices, intercropping and forecasting of pests and diseases are essential components, besides use of pesticides. On the other hand, the pesticides available in the market, particularly at the village level, are usually unbranded, often adulterated or date-expired, and the advice on how to use pesticides is given by relatively ignorant pesticide sellers or commission agents.

This inadequacy in the use of pesticides is not only wasteful but also dangerous, as it contributes heavily to the pollution of air, water and soil, in addition to health hazards.

Farm mechanization, no doubt, has been beneficial for the intensive use of land and has helped considerably in overcoming the risk of unfavourable effects of weather on maturing crops. The shift from animal to mechanical power has also indirectly affected soil health. In turn, there has been a decline in the use of agricultural labour, which has created serious social and economic problems, as alternative avenues for employment of displaced labour are few. The level of efficiency of farm implements, in terms of time and energy-consumption, needs to be improved through extensive research. Besides, there is also need to develop more innovative and inexpensive instruments, which could be used as timesaving devices and also for additional operations of cleaning, grading, packing, etc. For efficient water management the technologies like laser levelling of fields, optimal paddy transplantation date, diversification of agriculture to less water-requiring crops, bed or furrow planting, renovation of village ponds, roof-top rainwater harvesting and scheduling of irrigation for paddy by use of tensiometer, etc. need to be more popularised.

Increase in indebtedness, though officially attributed to the increasing cost of inputs, is high really because of unproductive spending habits of farmers; the relative ease with which credit is made available encourages farmers to spend it often on social ceremonies and excessively on domestic consumption. The arhtia-farmer relationship is traditionally very old and bitter, because of the excessive interest they charge. On the other hand, no institutional credit can match the services the arhtias provide —speedy supply of credit on demand and on short notice. Sometime the artias manipulate the repayment, by giving more loans at a still higher interest rate, until the farmer is forced to sell a part or whole of his land, to meet the debt obligations. Nevertheless, with the increasing opening up of the rural economy, a system of direct linkages should be encouraged through face to face contact of the producers with the investors or marketing and processing agencies. The role of the corporate sector in such a venture needs full policy and governmental support in order to minimize the role of commission agents and arhtias.

Recently, the decline in public investment in Punjab was mainly due to the diversion of resources in the form of subsidies for fertilisers, rural electricity, irrigation, credit and other agricultural inputs rather than on creation of assets. The declining trend in public sector agricultural investment needs to be reversed by augmenting agricultural credit and increasing allocation for agriculture. Since the Centre and States are facing a resource crunch, public investment can be increased only if the present level of subsidy on agricultural inputs such as power, water and fertilisers is readjusted.

Due to poor financial resources most of the States extension workers have no facility to undertake field visits and educate farmers with the latest developments in agriculture. With far-reaching changes in communication technology and breakthroughs in space technology, remote sensing, satellite broadcasting and the media spread revolution, extension workers will have to be totally re-oriented and re-trained to adapt themselves to these developments and emerging opportunities. Research and extension would need to be focussed on environmentally sustainable diversification and intensification of agriculture, location-specific technologies tailored to suit local needs and greater efficiency in the use of inputs. To accelerate growth in agriculture, the transfer of technology has to be made more effective and the present extension needs to be reoriented to provide farmers the proper technology.

References

Grover D. K.; Sanjay Kumar and Kamal Vatta (2003), *Market Imperfection and Farmers' Distress in Punjab*, Agro Economic Research Centre, PAU, Ludhiana.

Kumar, S. and Singh P. (2010), *Determinants of Stagnation in Productivity of Important Crops in Punjab.* Agro Economic Research Centre, Punjab Agricultural University, Ludhiana.

Singh, K.; Kamal Vatta and Sanjay Kumar (2002), *Impact of Minimum Support Prices on Agricultural Economy in Punjab*, Agro Economic Research Centre, PAU, Ludhiana.

5

Institutional Mechanisms in Punjab's Agricultural Sector: A Smallholder Perspective

Sukhpal Singh

Introduction: Institutions and development

Institutions and institutional context are important determinants of development. There are various terms and concepts used to refer to this in literature e.g. institutions, institutional framework, institutional environment, institutional capacity, institutional arrangements and institutional mechanisms. Institutional analysis is also being used to understand the processes of globalisation and economic reforms and restructuring of economic and social systems. In economic geography, the institutional analysis focus has been described as the institutional turn in the discipline which has focussed on the question of 'to what extent and in what ways are the processes of geographically uneven capitalist development shaped and mediated by the institutional structures in and through which those processes take place?". Coming from different disciplines like economics, sociology, political science and development studies, various approaches to institutions confirm that institutions and organisations do matter and economic outcomes can not be disentangled from the concrete social worlds in which they lie.

Institutions refer to 'rules of the game' in a society or more formally, the humanly designed constraints that shape human interaction. They are made up of formal constraints like rules and laws, informal constraints like norms of behaviour or codes of conduct, and their enforcement characteristics according to North and they altogether define the incentive structure of the societies and more so economies.

North also differentiates between institutions and organisations – the former being the rules of the game and the latter the players in the game. But, both of them influence each other interms of what organisations come up and how they evolve is determined by the institutional framework (rules of the game) and they in turn influence how the institutional framework itself evolves. Further, the institutional economics also differentiates between institutional environment and institutional mechanisms or arrangements. The former refers to the fundamental political, social, and legal ground rules that establish the basis for production, trade/exchange and distribution and the latter are arrangements between and among economic units that governs the ways in which these units can compete and/or co-operate.

These institutions are further embedded in local social and cultural systems which leads to institutional thickness which refers to dense presence of organisations in a local area, their strong interactions in local area, their domination due to this high level of interaction and there is a shared commitment to a common cause, though all of this need not be formal. This relationship between regional institutions and local economic development led to the realisation that there is a need for policy and public institutions to facilitate a common context of co-ordination (Neilson and Pritchard, 2009).

In the above framework, this paper examines the various institutions and policies in the agricultural sector of Punjab. This section also profiles the smallholders of the state followed by discussion of the nature of crisis in the farm sector in general in section 2. Section 3 examines the role of corporate sector and section 4 of the state and its agencies and policies. Section 5 concludes the paper with major conclusions and policy suggestions for smallholder benefit and sustainability of the farm sector.

Small Farmers in Punjab

In Punjab, only 30% holdings are small or marginal and account for only 8% of operated area (*Statistical abstract of Punjab*, 2007; Singh, 2008). Infact, small farmers in Punjab are moving out of farming due to the phenomenon of reverse tenancy under which they lease out their farm lands to the bigger operators like medium or large holders who have resources and linkages for modern farming or rather agribusiness. Infact, Punjab is the only state in India where the size of operational holding is increasing unlike other states and the all India trend of declining average size of operated holding. A recent study shows that during the last decade, 1.28 lakh smallholders had leased out their land to larger holders and operators and were themselves out of farming. Another 72000 had infact sold their land to larger farmers. Out of these two lakh smallholders, about 22% has joined the ranks of agricultural or other labour (Singh et al, 2009). This, in a situation of mechanised farming in the state which had led to lower labour intensity in general over the last few decades as most of the work on two major crops is carried out with machines like paddy transplanters, harvesters and reapers.

Punjab is also the state where the number of smallholdings has been declining over time. The small and marginal holdings declined by as much as two lakh over the decade of 1990s when the overall decline in holdings was only 1.2 lakh holdings. This indicates growing concentration of land in fewer hands in the state. Majority of the farmers from marginal and small categories left farming (2/3rd) after 2000 only and +low income from farming was the major reason followed by too small size of holding and repayment of debt. Half of those who left farming had totally or partially sold their land and one third of those selling land were worse off after leaving farming and those who only leased out land were not worse off in general (Singh et al, 2009).

The suicides by farmers and farm labourers are a manifestation of the agrarian crisis in its economic and social dimensions as non-viability of farm enterprise pushes small farmers and farm labour into this "honor suicide" as selling land or being exposed to be indebted is worse than death and in order to save family honor, heads of households or earning members take this extreme step (Singh, 2006).

Nature of crisis in Punjab Agriculture

There has been negligible growth in crop productivity after 1990 and none of the districts in Punjab figures among the top 10 in land productivity in India. The largest casualty of agricultural development and its intensification has been the groundwater due to its over-pumping by farmers. Already more than 1,000 of the 5,723 geographic blocks of India are either overexploited or critical. In Punjab, 79% of groundwater blocks are classified as overexploited or critical with average annual rates of decline being of the order of 0.7 to 1.07 meters during the early 1990s (Chopra and Bathla, 2004). Punjab has a tubewell for every 9 acres of land (Singh, 2009b) (Figure 1).

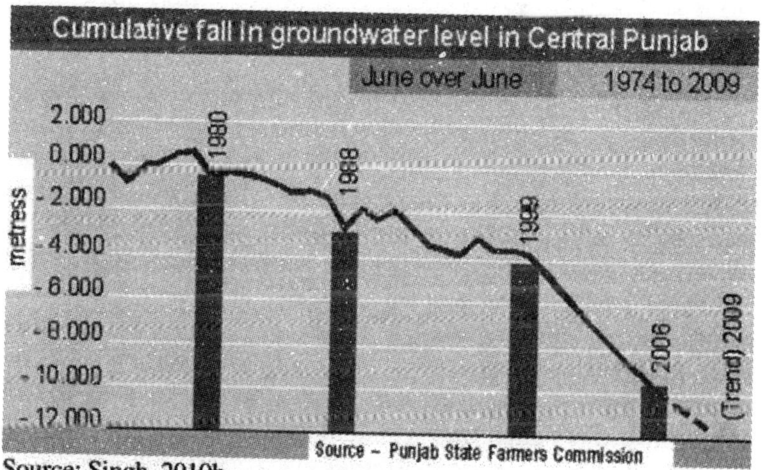

Source: Singh, 2010b.

Figure 1

M S Gill, present union sports minister and former Development Commissioner, Punjab, and former Secretary to Government of India, Department of Agriculture writes: "However, the nine lakh shallow tubewells now dangle dry. The rich have started digging deep, to 300 feet or more, with submersible pumps, to grab the water. The small farmers who predominate, cannot afford the cost and are being dried out. One deep tubewell will dry up a hundred around it. The water table has gone far down and this situation will lead to social tension. We read every day that 95 per cent of East Punjab's development blocks are in the grey area for tubewells". He goes on,

"Time has come to license and regulate tubewell sinking including the permissible depth. All must share fairly, and not take the maximum by means of wealth and power. – –it is very easy in the computer age to monitor all nine lakh tubewells all the time to know the depletion and the recharge; to be able to plan and administer the fair sharing and use of groundwater.– I would appoint a High Commissioner for Ground Water Management for Punjab with full scientific staff, and powers, reporting only to the Chief Minister– Punjab is not a great agriculture state. It is only a grain growing factory and factories have lock outs. We are facing one now" (Gill, 2010).

Further, there has been soil degradation and soil/water salination e.g. in aquaculture in Andhra Pradesh and water logging in parts of Punjab. Decline of forest cover (deforestation), toxicity, micro-nutrient deficiency, chemical residues in food and loss of biodiversity are other fall outs of the agricultural transformation in India (Shiva, 1991). The intensive production has led not only to monocultures in general in the states of Punjab due to rice and wheat rotation and, within these two crops in particular, but also higher incidence of pests and diseases. Pollution due to burning of crop residues of paddy and wheat in the fields after mechanical harvesting of these crops is another environmental externality of the intensive farming system practiced in irrigated regions like Punjab.

Corporate Farming for Agricultural Development?

Punjab is at the forefront of corporatising its farming since the 1990s. Field Fresh -an equal partnership venture between Bharti Enterprises (Airtel group) and Rothschild- has acquired 300 acres of land from the Government of Punjab for its model R&D farm called the 'Field Fresh Agri Centre of Excellence' near Ludhiana. The primary focus is on crop and varietal trials, progressive farming techniques, and identification and adoption of appropriate technologies. The farm includes 42 acres of state-of-the-art protected cultivation including poly-houses, glass and green houses, and net houses. All Field Fresh farms are Hazard Analysis and Critical Control Points (HACCP), GlobalGap, and British Retail Consortium (BRC) accredited. It also leased in 4000 acres and was using those former owner cultivators as farm managers on these leased farms. Distribution of fresh fruits and vegetables was done to the European Union, Eastern Europe, South East Asia, Middle East and the Commonwealth of Independent States (CIS) countries. It had sent the first consignment of vegetables to the UK included okra, bitter gourd and chilli. The project claimed that the marginal leasee farmer livelihoods have improved compared to when they were cultivator owners as the project pays minimum wages (Rs. 80/day). Thus, a farmer whose land is leased in by the company gets Rs. 15,000 per acre lease rent and if two of his family work on these leased out farms as labour, earn Rs. 57,600 annually. Thus, a two-acre farmer can earn about Rs. 90,000 (30000 rent plus 60,000 wages) annually compared with what he gets from his farm (Rs. 50,000) as gross output (without any cost deductions) if he goes for wheat and paddy crop cycle which is very common in Punjab. It was also working with other agribusiness firms like Rajtech Agro Plantations, Jaipur and Satluj Agriculture, New Delhi for leased land production of fruits and vegetables. Rajtech had last year leased 200 acres from 17 farmers near Chomu at the rate of Rs. 7000 per acre and was paying Rs. 5000 per month to supervising farmers. The company (Rajtech) was paid 17% of the profits made by Fieldfresh on the sales of the supplies made.

Similarly, Satluj Agriculture Pvt. Ltd. New Delhi leased in land @Rs. 17,000 per acre for 2.5 years, Leaser farmer provided all farm machines and operator/s. Minimum 25 acres with valid 10 HP tubewell connection in one place was a condition for lease. Local leasee farmers/sons (minimum +2 pass) were employed as managers for Rs. 6, 000/month. Land was leased in a local large farmer's name without any written agreement; It supplied to Field Fresh; paid labour @ Rs. 85 per day for men/women, excluding Provident Fund contribution with 8AM-5PM work hours. It had 5,000 acres at three places (Fatehgarh Sahib, Sangrur and Jalandhar districts). Now, all of these projects have been withdrawn as Field fresh could not sell what was produced on these farms and has to be bailed out by another agribusiness company.

Besides these, Nijjer Agro, Amritsar which is now into bulk supply of tomato paste to nestle and vegetables to NDDB's SAFAL project in Delhi, and many potato kings lease in thousands of acres of land for corporate farming. Most of these are Punjab's 'Progressive farmers' and cultivate more than 50 acres each and are educated and eager to increase their incomes through diversification and new technologies. It is important to note that Punjab's progressive or large farmers (8% of total) are larger than India's large farmers (1% of total). They lease in large chunks of land, from Non-Resident Punjabis in the area which is known for immigration or even sometimes from local small and marginal farmers as a 'reverse tenancy' practice which is well connected with Punjab's Green Revolution now (as against tenancy practice elsewhere in India) for commercial farming for open markets or for contract farming (hereafter CF). They live in palatial houses mostly outside the main village and frequently own multiple tractors and tubewells, combine harvesters, or other machines for modern farming, and cars for personal use. They are eager to get the land ceilings Act relaxed and for promotion of agro exports. For these farmers, state support in the form of CF or extension support is a bonus as even otherwise they would have grown these new crops. Thus, the state support was mis-targeted and had a political economy angle wherein in the name of small farmers, larger ones corner the policy benefits (Witsoe, 2006).

The potato kings include three families that collectively cultivate 12000 acres of seed potato on leased in land and possess cold storage facilities capable of storing their entire produce. The lease is typically for three years through informal contracts as formal tenancy laws, designed to protect the interest of small producers, do not permit such long leases. The largest of these three potato kings- described locally as the largest seed potato farmer in the word –cultivates 5500 acres and has built this empire over twenty years and now leases land in dozens of villages. His farm employs 5000 labourers during peak periods, mostly migrant labour from Bihar who live in make shift tents next to the potato fields. They are recruited through 'contractors' and managed by mangers specially hired for this purpose (Witsoe, 2006).

The Jalandhar Potato Growers' Association, which was initially organised to protect the interest of relatively smaller potato seed growers (with holdings of above 50 acres each) and later joined in by the potato kings, has a membership of 125 active members, and 500 secondary members. There is a criterion for active membership and secondary membership i.e. land holding of atleast 50 acres for the active membership and less than 50 acre for secondary membership. It is associated with 257 cold storages, in which 70% stored potato is seed potato. These association members either take land on lease or organize CF with other smaller growers for potato production, with each one working with about 50-70 growers each. Association provides seeds and extension services free of cost to the members and other costs are borne by farmers. The main markets for produced seed potatoes are West Bengal, Gujarat, Karnataka, Maharashtra, MP etc. Earlier the transportation cost via truck was Rs.3-4 per bag to Karnataka, now they have started transporting seeds via train and the cost has gone down by Rs. 0.67/- per bag. The prices for procurement are fixed, like for Kufri Jyoti the price is Rs. 234/- per bag (50 kg). It goes up to Rs. 250 /bag. after grading, sorting, cleaning and packaging. The price received in Karnataka is about Rs. 1100/ql. The

Association has contract with Haldiram - an Indian snack food company - at the rate of Rs. 5 / kg and with Pepsi, for 2-3% of its total requirement.

It has recently begun export of potatoes to Pakistan in collaboration with Markfed (a state run co-operative) and is in the process of getting GlobalGAP certification for its members for exports to Europe. Their farms are all lined for GlobalGAP inspection with separate bath rooms for labourers, safety signs for workers and storage for various chemical inputs. Some of them are also going organic partly. They are very confident of dealing with competition from MNCs and say that they will give the MNCs a run for their money as they have local contacts, long experience with the crop and business of seed potato, and a large scale of operations in a niche market (claiming 50% of the Indian market for seed potatoes (field observations). They are now competing with Chambal Agritech of the Birla Group specialising in seed potatoes which has around 2000 acres under contract and sells F1 seed tubers. The major difference in their strategies is that whereas potato kings do self cultivation, the corproates use CF system and work with relatively small farmers, though big by any other standards (Witsoe, 2006).

The association also carries out certified seed production for state and private agencies. For example, the National Seed Corporation provided 700 qtl. breeder seeds and the Association would provide 50,000 qtl. certified seeds in 2008. They have produced 700 qt of breeder seed like F1, F2 etc and monitoring is done by Punjab State Seed Corporation. According to the association, total requirement of seed potatoes is ten million (one crore) bags (50 kg). Its members meet in a hotel in Jalandhar every Friday and discuss their common problems and make presentation to potential business partners on their plans and activities. They also agitate for compensation for damaged potato crops and this time (2007) even staked claim for a local legislative assembly seat from the main political parties. The large farmers in the potato belt of the state are aware of potato market and therefore do not find Pepsi's fixed price contract attractive and it also avoids them.

More recently, there has been a split in the association and another one –POSCON –Potato Growers' Confederation has been formed under the patronage of a former state minister of agriculture. The State has also set up Potato Development Board with 11 members and it is by and large dominated by the potato kings.

Corporate Farming by the State?

As part of the diversification plan, the following four special purpose vehicles (SPVs) were created in the state:

Council for Citrus and Agri Juicing

Organic Farming Council of Punjab

Council for Value Added Horticulture

Viticulture council of Punjab.

Surprisingly, set up in 2006 - Council for Citrus and Agro Juicing in Punjab (A joint venture SPV of Pepsico and Govt. of Punjab (PAFC)) had also resorted to leasing and corporate farming to promote horticulture. It has 75 acre nursery in three locations in Punjab for growing citrus saplings which is on land owned by Punjab Agro and is managed by Pepsi. Council leased land @Rs.8-12,000/ acre for 12 years from farmers under two options: 20% increase in rent every 3 years OR 2% increase for 6 years and then 50:50 sharing of fruit profits; minimum 5 acres with assured irrigation is needed. It had leased in 2000 acres and the target was to cover 21000 acres by 2007. Pepsi sold fruit plants @Rs. 50 each to PAFC and planted farms were managed by the council. These did not perform and there is an initiation of an enquiry into the funds misappropriation through these agencies by the present government recently.

The Council for Citrus and Agro Juicing aimed to bring 20,000 acres under citrus fruit varieties imported by multinational Pepsico. However, even as trials at the experiment sites of the Punjab Agriculture University (PAU) and Punjab Horticulture Department were still on, the Council invited farmers to offer their land on lease under two schemes spanning six and 12 years. In 2007, reports of poor fruit retention in the imported plants, non-compatibility of rootstocks and no juice in a few varieties started trickling in from the sites. Following media reports, the Council was asked to reduce the land to 5,000 acres. The government stopped funding the Council and refused to stand guarantee for further loans to be raised by it. It was instead asked to hunt for a venture capitalist. Even Pepsico, which had by this time created lakhs of plants at its nursery in Jallowal near Jalandhar, later brought in a few new varieties to replace the non-performing ones. However, it was too late for farmers who had already bit the diversification bait in 2006 and early 2007. The farmers are now alleging breach of contract by the Council and demanding their land back so that they can go back to growing wheat and paddy. While no citrus plantation has come up on lands of many farmers, varieties grown on farms of several others have failed. To make matters worse, farmer are not being paid lease money timely nor is the Council monitoring the orchards.

A farmer Jasbir Singh Sidhu said though the Council defaulted on timely payment of lease money and monitoring of orchards, they were themselves tending to their farms with the hope of reaping a good harvest. "However, out of the four varieties planted on our fields, two have shown to have no juice at all. The fate of others would only be known by the end of this year. For the last eight months, the labourers have not been paid; we are paying them from our own pockets to save the orchards. We also incurred an additional Rs 1-2.5 lakh on constructing water tanks for installing drip irrigation," he said. Sidhu, who leased out his 24 acres in Doomwali village of Bhatinda to the Council, said he has raised kinnow and guava orchards with the help of subsidy under the National Horticulture Mission on his other farm in the village. "Look at the contrast between the two farms," he says. "No plantation has been done on 26 acres land of my brothers in Doomwali village", said Sidhu while Sukhdev Singh Grewal of Tahliwala Jattan village in Ferozepur said "Citrus varieties have been planted in just 15 acres out of his 25 acres of land. The remaining land was lying waste" (Singh, 2010c).

Two of the units set up by the council for multipurpose juicing at Hoshiarpur and Abohar are lying idle since last two years and are planned to be privatised. They failed partly because of Tropicana stopping to buy juice from them when it had cheaper alternative (Singh, 2001).

Role of the State

The state and its agencies impact development in many ways by incentivising or disincentivising some activities over others. These systems and policies are discussed below:

State Sponsored CF, and Retail Chain 'Contact Farming'

The state sponsored programme of CF did not deliver in Punjab. Most of the problems farmers faced related to production and quality (like quality of seed and extension) and not marketing of produce (except peas) as open market could take care of contract produce). There have also been instances of corruption and malpractice in the state agency run CF program due to conflicts of interest among implementing agencies and lack of monitoring. For the programme of CF to be successful, it should have taken into account the aspects of selection of crops for contracting, development of quick and effective contract enforcement and dispute resolution system, limiting fiscal risks to the state government, limiting the number of parties in a contractual arrangement, and developing farmers' organizations capable of contracting with sponsors, with a view to reduce transaction costs, increasing information flow, and improving farmers' negotiation position (WB, 2003; WB 2004).

Further, CF influences the direction of ecological change through two actors. One, the contracting agency lays down the production schedule for the farmers at the farm level. By determining the crop to be grown and the husbandry practices the farmer has to follow, the contracting agency influences the impact CF will have on the environment. The government is the second actor as the main source of conservation measures i.e. advisory, financial and material. The farmer's access to these measures is, to a large extent, is determined by the government policy. Thus, the contracting agency and the government have a larger role to play in environmental/ecological change than the farmer, since they occupy a 'privileged' position in the realm of decision making. Contracts tend to be concerned with land management measures which ensure crop growth and quality and production levels only in the short-term agricultural cycle. Land management measures geared to maintaining resource quality over the long term are not specified. The grower is responsible for decisions about investment in the long-term maintenance of land quality and productive capacity in conditions where contracting companies influence the land use practices through contracts which tie growers to larger markets and encourage production growth. Environment is also impacted through rejection of some produce of the grower by the contracting agency as the cost of not harvesting results in soil loss through tillage and excessive use and wastage of chemicals causing nutrient depletion (Singh, 2010e).

The environmental implications of CF include monocultures leading to depletion of soil quality, and effect of fertilizers and pesticides on natural resources, environment, humans and animals. The contracting firms tend to aggravate the environmental crisis as most of the contracts are short term (one or two crop cycles) and the firms tend to move on to new growers and lands after exhausting the natural potential of the local resources, particularly land and water, or when productivity declines due to some other reason. The over-exploitation of groundwater, salination of soils, decline in soil fertility, and pollution are examples of environmental degradation due to CF. The firms do not pay heed as the costs of such effects are externalised so far as the firm is concerned (Singh, 2010e).

Repeated cultivation of the same crop without rotation can lead to a variety of soil infestations, most commonly nematodes, which has happened in many situations in the case of tomatoes. In fact, sometimes, the land becomes unfit for any kind of crop cultivation. Irrigation intensity of contract crops, i.e. tomato, potato and chilly, was more than that of wheat in the Indian Punjab during the late 1990s under Pepsi Foods (a Pepsico subsidiary) CF. For example, potato required 8-12 irrigations compared with only 5-6 for wheat and other crops. Pesticides and fertilisers were also used at much higher levels than in the traditional crops. For example, potato cultivation required 108 kg. of NPK (chemical fertiliser) per acre as against only 78 kg. for wheat and 60 kg. each of phosphorus and potassium per acre. Tomato crop required 60-90 kgs. of nitrogen, 60-100 kgs. of phosphorus, and 60-120 kgs. of potash per acre depending on the quality of soil. Similarly, the chip potato crop required 4-5 pesticide sprays and the seed potato crop 6-7 sprays (Singh, 2002). This, despite the fact that the company (Pepsico) website states that it follows a policy of "application of environmentally sound agricultural practices with its suppliers of agro-materials (Singh, 2010e). Tomato crop under contract required as many as 14 sprays, which was even higher than that in cotton (Singh, 2002). This in a situation of low awareness of the implications of high chemical input use is a serious cause for concern (Singh 2010e).

More recently, in Punjab, it was found that CF promoted by the provincial government to encourage diversification of cropping pattern away from wheat and paddy led to less water consumption on contract farms as against non-contract farms. The water consumption for paddy was 265.71 hours per acre compared with only 183.86 hours for Basmati paddy promoted and grown under CF arrangement. Similarly, maize cultivation under CF led to water use of the order of only 18.35 hours per acre. This meant that crops being grown under CF arrangement were water saving. That was so due to the provincial government plan to promote those crops. Overall, contract growers' weighted water consumption per acre was 120.49 hours compared with 129.58 hours in case of non-contract growers. But, reduced water consumption on contract farms was due to greater area devoted to the new crops (Basmati and Maize) and not due to any new agricultural practices promoted by the contracting agencies. In fact, the contract farmers were practicing more intensive agriculture than the non-contract farmers and were devoting significantly higher number of water hours to basmati and maize than that by non-contract farmers across all crops. Thus, increased commercialisation of the various crops under CF propelled these contract farmers to use various inputs more intensively. Further, crop combination of potato and sunflower promoted under CF was more water intensive, though more remunerative than wheat (the alternative traditional crop) and therefore, defeated the very purpose of CF in the state (Singh 2010e).

On the other hand, modern retail chains being promoted to create market linkages for farmers have not had a good start in Punjab and most of them have either wound up or do not have any linkages with growers. A study of ITC's Choupal Fresh showed that it procured about 60% of fruits and vegetables from mandi and 40% from 'contact' (not contract) farmers through the consolidator. The farmers were paid *mandi* price and 10% premium on A grade produce. The consolidator was paid a net commission of Re. 0.37 per kg. of produce and Rs. 700/ day to transport the produce from the field to the retail store in Chandigarh. Of the total farmers interviewed, 54.5% were local and the rest leasee migrant farmers. The average operated area of retail chain farmers (9.91 acres altogether) and of the leasee and the local farmers separately (8 and 11.5 acres respectively) was higher than the average size of the operational holding at the state level - 9.36 acres.

Small farmers accounted for only 36% of the total growers of the retail chain. The proportion of small operators was higher among the leasee category (50%) and only 25% among local landholders compared with the proportion of small and marginal holders in the state- 35.4%. But, leasee migrant farmers, on an average, put about 60% Gross Cropped Area under vegetables compared to only about 23% in case of local farmers although cropping intensity across both categories was similar (211 and 221).

ITC procured about 23% of cauliflower and bottle gourd each from leasee migrant farmers compared to only 15.5% of cauliflower and bottle gourd each in case of local farmers. The rejection rate was only 2%. However, rejection rate of leasee migrant farmers' produce was lower (1.7%) as compared to that of local farmers (2.25%). The average yield was higher in case of leasee migrant farmers (85 qtls. in cauliflower and 104 qtls. in bottle gourd) than that in case of local farmers (81.11 qtls in cauliflower and 97.8 qtls. in bottle gourd). The farmers realized somewhat higher price in ITC channel (about Rs. 5.5/kg in cauliflower and Rs. 4.2/kg in bottle gourd) compared to that in mandi channel (Rs. 5.1-5.4/kg in cauliflower and Rs 3.9-4/kg in bottle gourd) but the sales to retail chain was only of A grade produce. Leasee migrant farmers realized lower price in mandi as compared to that realized by local farmers. The average cost of production was higher among local farmers (Rs 3.89/kg) compared to that in case of leasee migrant farmers (Rs. 3.35/kg). The ITC farmers did not incur any marketing cost (except the packing cost in polythene for bottle guard) since the produce was picked from farm itself. The net income for each crop in each channel was higher for leasee migrant farmers than that for local farmers.

Major reasons for selling to ITC were: no transportation costs, time saving, higher price, and free supply of crates, to pack vegetables. But, about 77% farmers were not satisfied in linking with ITC. The major problems faced were: low volumes procured and low price overtime.

The leasee farmers being professional vegetable growers had better yields as well as better quality produce. The chain was not able to make an impact on the growers as it was procuring too little because it was not able to sell the procured produce in the market where it faced competition from other retail chains and local vendors and farmer's market. Finally, the chain wound up its retailing and procurement operations in the region in April, 2009 (Singh and Singla, 2010).

Direct Payments to Farmers

This issue has been around for almost four years now with plenty of going back and forth in terms of its implementation despite the fact that there are no two arguments about the issue that a seller of the produce should be paid directly by the buyer of the produce especially when the produce is bought by the state procurement agencies. The recommendation for direct payment to farmers by the procurement agencies was made by the state farmers' commission in 2006 and the then Congress government had even issued a notification in this regard but due to the pressure from arthiya/commission agent lobby, it was withdrawn and a committee of ministers suggested that since the arthiyas were willing to devise and implement a code of conduct, there was no need for any legal provision from the state's side.

This issue and debate brings forth the role of interlocking of factor markets in Punjab even after its so called commercialisation of agriculture after the green revolution. Still, 40% of the total debt of the farmers in the state is owed to the commission agents (arthiyas) of whom there are 33975 in grain markets and 2933 in fruit and vegetable markets. On an average, each arthiya lent Rs. 4.6 million to farmers. In grain markets, this business was in the hands of 20232 families which meant that each family owned more than one (1.6) licenses. An average arthiya served 120 farmers across 11 villages. Though 90% farmers are in favour of direct payments as it will save them from interlocking which leads to higher implicit price for inputs which they buy from arthiyas and their poor quality at the same time as when a farmer buys on credit, he/she can not ask for the best quality. This interlocking is conducted through a slip (parchi) system wherein the arthiya gives a slip to the farmer showing which he/she can get inputs or groceries on credit from other shops or traders of such inputs or goods and the arthiyas deducts these loans at the time of sale of produce. The nature of lobbying by arthiyas has also changed as now there are a large number of arthiyas who come from farming background and have political clout. Only 35% arthiyas are from traditional money lending and trading background (Bania caste) and the rest have come from new backgrounds like farming and trade and other occupations like government or private job. One-fourth each of the total were with farming background and mostly Jat Sikhs by caste, and with grocery and trading business background (Khatris) and 8% were Brahmins. 60% of all commission agents had atleast one more business other than commission agency and these included farming (48%), grocery shop (23%), agricultural input dealership (17%), and rice shelling (16%) (Singh and Dhaliwal, 2011). It is argued that this new class of arthiyas has changed the way business of money lending and agricultural produce handling is conducted as the new entrants are not as humble, clever and low key. They are more aggressive, dominating and repressive and also have land as their main interest while dealing with farmers. Their increasing lobbying power is also reflected in the fact that they have been able to get the commission charged increased from 1.5% in 1961 to 2% during 1990-98 and 2.5% after that though there was no need for this as the increasing produce price and higher arrivals in markets due to higher farm production in the state would have automatically meant higher income for arthiyas (Singh, 2009c).

Subsidy to Large Farmers

The Punjab Government has announced a subsidy for farmers for the purchase of transplantation machines. Based on the recommendations of the Farmers Commission, the state will extend a subsidy of Rs. 75,000 on each transplanter machine and in addition, farmers who will help fellow farmers with paddy transplantation with these machines, will be given an additional subsidy of Rs 5,000 per acre. Two models of Japanese planters are available in the market, one that has to be manually pulled costs about Rs. 2.5 lakh while another model that is motorised and can be driven costs between Rs. 8-10 lakh. With the help of these machines, about 5 acres can be planted in a day as compared to five persons taking a day to plant one acre. In the past, transplantation machines have not been very successful on account of following reasons: one farmers were not trained in the use of these machines and secondly, they are not fully conversant with the preparation of a "matt nursery" required for these machines. Besides, machines imported from China performed poorly as compared to the machines imported from Japan. The Agriculture Department has announced an assistance of Rs. 5,000 per acre to those growing paddy nursery for mechanised transplantation this year.

The state farmers' commission has given 80 'happy seeders', machines that sow wheat among standing rice stubbles free of cost and the remaining 120 machines at a 50 per cent subsidy to the PACS to reduce burning of paddy crop residues in fields. The state government has introduced two wonder machines to manage paddy residue and recycle it into fuel generation and animal feed. Named as "Baler", these machines have been imported from the United State of America. Though the cost of each machine is Rs 11 lakh but a special subsidy package has been extended that has brought its cost at Rs 5 lakh per machine. The machines, with the help of its specially designed spokes automatically collects the paddy waste and puts it into another unit to bind it with the help of a nylon strip. Thereafter, these bales can be transported to sugar mills to be reused for fuel purposes. The farmers will be paid Rs. 75 per quintal for their paddy waste. The PSFC also provides Rs. 20,000 as subsidy to farmers for setting up of net house for vegetable growing which costs Rs. 48,000 per kanal.

Earlier, for three years, the PAFC was reimbursing Rs .150/- per acre to any agribusiness company which was providing extension to contract growers in the state under which many companies claimed large amounts just by showing lists of farmers they had signed contracts with which farmers never knew. Johl writes about this "Another flop case is of Mohindra Shublabh entering into a contract with farmers through Punjab Agro for the production of maize. They sold the seed, got the extension costs, but never visited the farmers and the scheme failed miserably" (Johl, 2008). Further, reimbursing extension cost irrespective of the size of holding of the contract growers defeats the purpose as it does not ensure that small and marginal farmers who can not afford to pay for extension and need to be brought into the contract system are included.

PSFC and Organic Farming for Sustainability

In 2009, a Punjab State Farmers' Commission (PSFC) report on feasibility of organic farming in Punjab concluded that by and large, it is not possible and advisable to go for organic farming in Punjab. The report asks: Is organic farming more profitable? This question itself is biased as why should one expect organic farming to be more profitable than conventional farming, especially when it has many non-business benefits like improved soil health, safer food and a better environment? Could conventional farming in the state be viable without the

MSP? Though the report recognises the sustainability of soil health and the eco system as a crucial concern, it does not recognise the role of organic production processes in that. The report asks questions like: Does organic food taste better or is it more nutritious and safer?

The important question to ask is: Is conventional farming as practised today viable only because of subsidies on chemical inputs and the MSP or on its own? On the other hand, there are no subsidies for organic production. To that extent, the profitability comparison is unfair. It is also difficult to understand that if mainstream field crops are not viable organically, how milk, meat or eggs, as recommended by the PSFC, can be so, when all of them require organic inputs like fodder or poultry/cattle feed? If organic farming is so unviable and not suitable for Punjab, why was it being promoted during the Congress regime as part of its crop diversification programme with a special purpose vehicle and why was it not questioned?

So far as its concern with food security is concerned, the report has not bothered to ask the question: If food production or its availability was the only way to ensure food security, why has not India achieved it even today i.e. after four decades of chemical-based farming?(Singh, 2009a).

Conclusions

The above analysis of the various aspects of farm policy and practice shows that the policy either ignores smallholders or pays a lip service to their concerns. This has resulted in corporatisation of the farm sector wherein larger operators are increasingly taking control of the sector and manipulating agricultural policies to their advantage in the name of smallholders and farm crisis. Exclusion of smallholders is perpetuated through selection of crops, farmers, farm technologies and practices, and market linkage models for diversification and agricultural growth.

A striking absence of any farmer or producer organizations at the village level points to the potential for farmer organization through various alternatives like SHGs, farmer groups, farmer associations, and co-operatives, especially new generation co-operatives. Infact, compared with 2.2% farmers in India being members of any farmer association and 4.8% of any Self-Help Group (SHG), in Punjab, only 0.3% and 1.5% farmers respectively were member of any such association and such SHG (Witsoe, 2006). On the political organisation side, the farmer movement is highly fragmented. 16 farmer unions which altogether claim to represent farmers- a total of 10 lakh farmer families in the state, and another 9 which represent workers (30% of rural hhs) have their own political affiliations and disagreements on major issues facing farmers and farm workers (see the list below)[1]. None of them have been able to really represent the smallholder interest in policy and practice. They also keep dithering between larger issues of world trade and more immediate issues like free electricity for irrigation or direct payments to producers for their produce bought by state agencies.

Since corporate interface with growers is going to spread across crops and regions, it is important to protect the growers' interest, especially of the small growers wherever and in whatever measure they are into it. The contract growers' groups can be a way to do so. Not only the state should encourage such groups but also the local development agencies should organise contract growers into groups for their inclusion into these value chains and for collective negotiation with contracting agencies (Singh, 2008a).

New institutional mechanism like groups, associations, co-operatives, New Generation Co-operatives (NGCs) and other collectivities or networks are needed to reach small and marginal producers more effectively. A New Generation Co-operative is one which has restricted or limited membership, links product delivery rights to producer member equity, raises capital through tradable equity shares among membership, enforces contractual delivery of produce by members, distributes returns based on patronage, goes for value addition through processing or marketing, and makes use of information efficiently throughout the vertical system. However, it retains one member- one vote principle for major policy decisions. This kind of restructuring helps co-operatives to tackle problems; of free riding by membership, of horizon which is at the root of financial constraint, and that of opportunism, both of the members as well as of the co-operative. This arrangement by co-operatives has helped them become economically efficient, financially viable, and obtain member loyalty wherever it has been tried. Additionally, non-member procurement and quantity or acreage contracts have been also used by co-operatives to tackle supply side problems. Some of the co-operatives like those dealing with sapota (chickoo) in south Gujarat have also attempted quality based grading and pooling system, and contractual relations with members for procurement, along with market orientation strategies like multiple outlets, and efficient use of market information to achieve better business performance. Similarly, sugar co-operatives in south Gujarat have been able to mobilize enough capital by informally trading in co-operative shares which gives producers right to deliver specified acreage sugarcane to the co-operative which is the only way to access the market for sugarcane. Their shares sell at a premium.

The amended Companies Act 2003 permits registration of produce companies but there has been lack of adequate awareness and support from state agencies and NGOs for this which has led to no momentum for this type of co-operative companies (Singh, 2008b). It is ironic that a corporate joint venture with a foreign wholesaler (Tata-Total Produce) is the first one in Punjab to organise fruit and vegetable producers in central Punjab into producer companies, instead of a state agency or an NGO.

For sustainability and local economy reasons, regional decision makers in Punjab need to encourage diversification from crops like paddy and wheat to high value crops like potato, sunflower, basmati, garlic, etc, most of which consume less water and are more remunerative though risky and hi-tech. Fast depleting ground water is a very serious problem in the state. Drip and Sprinkler (micro irrigation) is being promoted in states like Gujarat and AP by dedicated agencies for the purpose. But, there are no similar efforts in Punjab.

Though recently, the central water authority has proposed a ban on new tubwells and the permission from District Collector will be required to dig a tubewell, this is not in favour of small producers who still lack access to water for irrigation, unless alternatives measures are adopted which can be institutional in nature like water sharing, public tubewells and rationing of water.

Creating markets and making them accessible to farmers at large is required in case of new crops as right now these crops face competition from traditional crops like wheat and paddy which have MSP. Also, speedy and direct payment from government procurement agencies should be ensured so that farmers are in a position to make use of MSP.

There is a need to provide for ecological concerns into CF programs and policies. This can be done by way of land use planning based on soil depth, soil quality, land slope and suitable water availability. It is also important to understand previous land use and make it mandatory to follow crop rotation, if necessary. The role of the government should be enabling and developmental in nature. That credit support to CF projects by the state is crucial has been emphasized earlier as well in other contexts. The state policy, including CF, needs to be changed in favour of small producers because it does not help the small producers particularly (Singh, 2010e).

On the other hand, the functioning of open regulated markets (APMC) needs to be improved to enhance their cost efficiency which can help reach a better share of the consumer rupee to the primary producers. The measures needed, besides the setting up of private markets which the amended APMC Act allows, are: mandatory adoption of open auction system, more competition in these markets in terms of number of buyers, provision of better facilities like cold storage and improving transparency through access to market information to farmers through ICTs. It is important to ensure better functioning of these markets as small farmers may still depend on these markets, and these markets can also serve as competitors to CF to help deliver better value to contract growers (Singh, 2008a).

Note

1. The farmer unions are: Bharti Kisan Union Ekta (Ugrahan), Kirti Kisan Union, Bharti Kisan Union Ekta (Dakaunda), Punjab Kisan Sabha, Kirti Kisan Sabha Punjab, Punjab Kisan Union, Kisan Sangharsh Committee (Kanwalpreet Pannu), Jamhoori Kisan Sabha, Bharti Kisan Union (Krantikari), Bharti Kisan Union Ekta (Sidhupur), Khetibari Kisan and Vikas Front, Kisan Sangharsh Committee (Satnam Pannu), Punjab Kisan Sabha, Bhartiya Kissan Union (Lakhowal) and Bhartiya Kissan Union (Rajewal).

   The farm worker unions are: Punjab Khet Mazdoor Union, Pendu Mazdoor Union Punjab, Mazdoor Mukti Morcha, Pendu Mazdoor Union (Mashaal), Krantikari Pendu Mazdoor Union, Dihati Mazdoor Sabha, Krantikari Dihati Mazdoor Sabha, All-India Khet Mazdoor Union and Punjab Khet Mazdoor Sabha (Singh, 2010a).

References

Johl S S (2008), "Corporates in agriculture: They must promote scientific farming", *The Tribune*, Chandigarh, October 22.

Gill M S (2010), "Water crisis in East and West Punjab-Let's tackle it with a steady application of science", *The Tribune*, perspectives, May 23, Chandigarh.

Neilson J and B Pritchard (2009), *Value Chain Struggles- Institutions and governance in the plantation districts of south India*, Wiley-Blackwell, Chichester (UK).

Singh, J (2010b), Elusive Water 1 and II, *The Tribune*, Chandigarh, June 12 and 13.

Singh, J (2010c), "Farmers divided over citrus council's role", *The Tribune*, Chandigarh, April 6.

Singh, J (2010d), 'Kinnow experiment flops, plants up for sale', *The Tribune*, September 26, Chandigarh

Singh, K, S Singh and H S Kindra (2009), "Agrarian Crisis and Depeasantisation in Punjab-status of small/marginal farmers who left agriculture", *Indian Journal of Agricultural Economics*, 64(4), 585-603.

Singh, P (2010a), "Farm workers, farmers join hands for struggle", *The Tribune*, Chandigarh, March 10.

Singh, S. (2002), "Contracting Out Solutions: Political Economy of Contract Farming in the Indian Punjab", *World Development*, 30(9), September.

Singh, S (2008a), "Marketing channels and their implications for smallholder farmers in India", in McCullough, E.B., Pingali, P.L. and Stamoulis, K.G.: *The Transformation of Agri-food Systems: Globalization, Supply Chains, and Smallholder Farmers*, FAO, Rome and Earthscan Press, London, 2008, 279-310.

Singh, S (2008b), "Producer Companies as New Generation Co-operatives" *Economic and Political Weekly*, 43(20), May 17.

Singh, S (2009a), "Organic farming is worth it- Farmers' commission report illogical", *The Tribune*, Chandigarh, op. ed. page, Jan.15.

Singh, Sukhpal (2009b), "Punjab de kheti sector da badlada muhandara", *Lal Parcham (in Punjabi)*, March-April, 15-17.

Singh, Sukhpal (2009c), "Arthiya system ate faslan di sidhi adayigi da masla", *Lal Parcham (in Punjabi)*, Sept.-Oct, 26-29.

Singh, S and Naresh Singla (2010), "Linking Small Primary Producers with Markets through Fresh Food Retail Chains in India: How Inclusive and How Effective?" in Ghuman R S, Surjit Singh and J S Brar (eds.): *Globalisation and Change-Perspectives from Punjab* (Essays in honour of Prof. SS Gill), Rawat, Jaipur, 2010, 275-302.

Singh, Sukhpal and T K Dhaliwal (2011), *Taking more than commission- a critique of the commission agent system in Punjab Agriculture*, Aakar, Delhi.

Singh, S (2010e), "Globalisation and Sustainability Issues in Agriculture in Asia- A Case of India", in S S Gill, L Singh and R Marwah (eds.): *Economic and Environmental Sustainability of the Asian Region*, Routledge, Delhi.

WB (World Bank) (2003), India: *Revitalising Punjab's Agriculture*, Rural Development Unit, South Asia Region, The World Bank, Washington.

WB (World Bank) (2004), *Resuming Punjab's Prosperity-The Opportunities and Challenges Ahead*, The World Bank, Washington and New Delhi.

6

Squeezing Size of Land Holding: And Sustainability to Farming in Punjab

M. K. Sekhon, Manjeet Kaur,
M. S. Sidhu & Amrit Kaur Mahal

Indian agriculture continues to bear the burden of increasing population pressure. As a consequence, the number of marginal and small holding in India increased from 74.05 million during 1985-86 to 98.93 million during 2000-01. They are expected to increase further with the increase in population, not getting any avenues elsewhere in the economy.

Different type of situation prevails in the Punjab state relating to operational size of holdings. The numbers of small and marginal farmers increased form 3.96 lakh during 1980-81 to 4.99 lakh during 1990-91; and after that start declining and became 2.96 lakh during 2000-01. With the onset of the development crisis in agriculture marginal and small farmers have been finding it difficult to survive, with the result many marginal farmers left agriculture in distress. Over the next 5-6 years, the situation is not likely to change significantly that means more number of marginal and small farmers will lease out/sell their land to other categories of farmers.

Table 1
Number and projection of operational holding in Punjab Overtime

(000 No.)

Year	*Marginal (Up to 1 ha)*	*Small (1-2 ha)*	*Semi-medium (2-4 ha)*	*Medium (4-10 ha)*	*Large (10 & above)*	*Total*
1970-71	518	260	281	247	68	1373
1980-81	197	199	287	269	74	1027
1985-86	256	208	291	260	74	1088
1990-91	295	204	289	261	67	1117
1995-96	204	183	320	306	80	1093
2000-01	123	173	328	301	72	997
Projected						
2004-05	107	165	335	309	73	989
2009-10	90	156	344	320	73	983
2014-15	76	147	353	331	74	982

It is projected that the number of small and marginal farmers would decrease to 2.23 lakh up to 2014-15. Agriculture for a marginal and small farmer in pursuit of adopting latest technology to increase output would still yield low family incomes as their unit cost of production becomes high. Even if farmers cultivate the best possible crops or combination of crops, the return will remain meager (Singh et.al.2009). They are unable to form viable and workable cooperatives and face discrimination in the contract farming. They are also unable to take up any additional agriculture business and make value additions which aggravate their disadvantages. Thus, small farms are only viable when they are supported with some supplementary income (Chandra 2001). A farm is said to be viable when it generates sufficient income to maintain a family at reasonable level by employing the family labour effectively. If such viabilities assured on regular basis then the farm can also be called sustainable. Studies from different regions (Maji et.al. 1990; Acharya and Verma, 1990, Haque T, 1996) showed that although marginal and small farms are as efficient as large farm (if not more), they do not generate sufficient income to sustain land holder's family. Why these farmers are leaving out crop production? What are the reasons behind this? This study is an endeavor to answer these questions by examining the income and expenditure pattern of these farmers and their viability on the basis of farm and family income, with the specific objectives: (i) to study the source of income and expenditure pattern of different farm size categories in Punjab; (ii) to examine the viability of farm household using different viability criteria under different income scenarios, and iii) to identify the factors differentiating viable farmer from non-viable farmer.

Methodology and Analytical Techniques Used

The present study was undertaken in the Punjab state a most agriculturally advance state of the country. The state is divided into three regions i.e. sub-mountainous region 9% (I), central plain region 65% (II) and south western region 26% (III). Three stages stratified random sampling technique was used for the selection of the sample households. At the first stage of sampling two blocks from region I namely Mukerian and Anadpur Sahib, and five blocks from region II i.e., Verka, Chogawan, Phagwara, Khanna and Moga and three blocks from region III i.e. Muktsar, Dhuri and Faridkot were randomly selected. Two villages from each block were randomly selected (total 20 villages) at the second stage of sampling. At the final stage farm families were selected on the basis of size of operational holding. A sample of five marginal (up to 1 ha), five small (1.01 to 2 ha) and five from other categories of farmers were selected. Thus the total sample size comprised of 100 marginal, 100 small and 100 other categories of farmers; which consists of 60,150 and 90 families from sub-mountainous, central and south western region was 300 farm families. The primary data were collected through personal interview method for the year 2005-06. Comprehensive schedule was prepared which included the information on various parameters like family size, operational holding, input cost for crops and dairy, production of crops, other sources of income, consumption pattern, etc. was gathered for the purpose of study. Simple averages, percentage and tabular analysis were used to achieve the objectives of the study. The analysis was performed for different categories of farm households for the

Punjab state. By calculating income and expenditure pattern, the farmers were categorized into viable and non-viable farmers. Linear discriminant function was used to disseminate the socio-economic characteristics of the viable and non-viable farmers of different categories among different regions of the state.

Results and Discussion

Socio-economic Background of the Respondents

As the study was focused on small and marginal farmers, their economic characteristics have great bearing on the viability of the farmer, and varied among different regions. Average size of operational holding of marginal farmer was worked out as 0.66, 0.70 and 0.62 ha in respective regions. Small farmers operate 1.59, 1.65 and0.62 ha of land and other category 6.54, 6.74 and 7.20 ha of land respectively. It was mentioned here that small farmers lease in land whereas marginal farmers leased out the land. Education is an important determinant of socio-economic conditions of the farm family, measured as number of year in a school. It varied directly with the farm size. Education was the lowest for marginal farmers among all the three categories of farmers; and among regions in south western region of the state. Marginal farmers have lower asset position and so the land size. As marginal farmers were resource poor farmers their ownership in terms of machinery was also significantly lower. These farmers (marginal and small) are entrapped in the vicious circle of small holding with less production and low marketable surplus. Herd size composition on different size categories showed the direct relationship in all the regions.

Income Level of Farm-Family

The average family income of marginal, small and other categories of sample farmers worked out to be Rs 96,593, 1,50257 and 3,57917 respectively per household per annum for the year 2005-06 for the Punjab state. This is highest in the central region followed by south western region (Table 3).

Table 2
Socio-economic Background of the Respondents in Different Regions of Punjab, 2005-06

	Farm size categories		
Characteristic	*Marginal*	*Small*	*Others*
Sub-mountainous region			
Owned land (ha)	0.72	1.57	5.56
Leased in land (ha)	0.01	1.10	1.0
Leased out land (ha)	0.07	0.08	0.02
Operational holdings (ha)	0.66	1.59	6.54
Family size (No.)	4.65	1.59	6.54
Educational level of head of the family	8.70	11.0	11.8
Herd size (No)	4.61	5.64	12.88
Tractor (%)	-	10	55
Electric motor (%)	85	100	100
Central region			
Owned land (acres)	0.97	1.60	5.72
Leased in land (acres)	0.04	0.14	1.02
Leased out land (acres)	0.32	0.09	0.01
Operational holdings (acres)	0.70	1.65	5.92
Family size (No.)	4.28	4.52	5.92
Educational level of head of the family	8.12	8.66	10.82
Herd size (No)	4.60	5.24	12.40
Tractor (%)	6	40	194
Electric motor (%)	88	172	466
South west region			
Owned land (acres)	0.84	1.56	6.19
Leased in land (acres)	0.04	0.06	0.10
Leased out land (acres)	0.26	0.06	0.10
Operational holdings (acres)	0.62	1.56	7.21
Family size (No.)	4.5	5.0	7.07
Educational level of head of the family	8.3	10	9
Herd size (No)	4.05	5.5	11.35
Tractor (%)	10	40	110
Electric motor (%)	30	73	250

The share of farm income to the total family income increased with the increase in farm size, as the farm income heavily depends on farm size. Adhoc income includes income from service, pension, labour wages, business and land rent, etc. was about one per cent in case of marginal farmers and

Table 3
Income From Different Sources Per Farm Among Different Farm Size, Punjab, 2005-06

	Farm size categories		
Particulars	*Marginal*	*Small*	*Others*
Sub-mountainous region			
A. Farm income (Returns over A_1 costs)	33764 (44)	51269 (31)	159517 (65)
B. Off-farm income	43990 (55)	60800 (37)	57700 (24)
C. Adhoc income	-	52500 (32)	27250 (11)
D. Total income	77754	164569	244467
Per capita income	16721	23593	39493
Central region			
A. Farm income (Returns over A1 costs)	72157 (66)	129487 (86)	363871 (85)
B. Off-farm income	35930 (33)	16402 (11)	42544 (10)
C. Adhoc income	1600 (1)	3870 (3)	19720 (5)
D. Total income	109687	149759	426135
Per capita income	25254	32276	68651
South west region			
A. Farm income (Returns over A1 costs)	46447 (54)	93108 (81)	288205 (90)
B. Off-farm income	40900 (46)	18133 (16)	25966 (8)
C. Adhoc income	-	3633 (3)	5683 (2)
D. Total income	87347	114875	319855
Per capita income	19410	22248	44437
Punjab			
A. Farm income (Returns over A1 costs)	56760 (59)	102931 (69)	300300 (84)
B. Off-farm income	39033 (40)	33801 (22)	40602 (11)
C. Adhoc income	800 (1)	13525 (9)	17015 (5)
D. Total income	96593	150275	357917
Per capita income	21673	29030	55162

Note: Figures in parentheses are percentage to total income

higher in case of small and other categories of farmers. The per capita income worked out to be Rs21673, 29030 and Rs 55163 for marginal, small and other categories of farmers of the Punjab state. It was observed that marginal farmers were as efficient as other category of farms, the per capita income of other categories of farmers was more than two and half times than the per capita income of marginal farmers. The income level of farmers in the central region was higher among other regions, and also from the state average. It is obvious from the above discussion that increases in off-farm income may save the marginal and small farm family in the long run. As farm income from the small piece of land was already reached at the highest level as efficiency was considered, although less than small farmers.

Technical efficiency estimates were worked out as 71.04 per cent for marginal, 77.49 per cent for small farms and 72.25 per cent for other categories of farms. More than 70 per cent of the frontier output of given technology was achieved and above 30 per cent can be increased with the given set of inputs (Sekhon, et. al. 2008).

Domestic Expenditure Pattern of the Sample Households

Domestic expenditure pattern of sample households includes expenditure on food items and non-food items (Table 4). The table indicated that the total expenditure incurred by marginal, small and other categories of farm households varied directly with the farm size, lower on marginal farms followed by small and other categories of farms, whereas the expenditure on food items varies directly with the farm size in absolute terms and inversely with the farm size in proportionate terms. This in line with the Engel's law of consumption which states that the proportional expenditure on food items decline with the increase in income. Major portion of expenditure of marginal farmers was on food items i.e. 58, 55 and 51 percent respectively among different regions. Among non-food items expenditure on social ceremonies was higher (24.82%), followed by education and health in sub mountainous region. In the central region marginal farmers spends a lot on education (30.33%) of their wards, social ceremonies were the next major item of expenditure. Highest expenditure on social ceremonies was in south western region to the tune of 30.40 percent of non food expenditure. It is observed that the total expenditure was directly related to farm size. Among the food items, around 50 per cent of food expenditure was made on milk followed by wheat. It was pointed out by Bhalla and Chadha (1982) that per capita expenditure on milk and milk products were over estimated during 1982, when the proportionate expenditure on this item was about 33 per cent. It is still obvious from the data that cultivators in Punjab spend much on milk and milk products. This fact may be due to the reason that farmers sometimes over estimated such kind of products. All the categories of farm household followed the same pattern in case of spending on different items of food. The expenditure on meat and fish found to be directly related to farm size. Even miscellaneous items covered more than five per cent and up to 10 per cent of the total food expenditure. Among the non food items more than one fourth expenditure were made on social ceremonies, and it was the highest for small farm size categories being at 41 per cent of the non-food expenditure.

It has worsened the economic condition of farmers. It was observed that the major portion of the income of small and marginal farmers goes on food items and remains on social ceremonies, education and health.

Viability on the Basis of Economic Surplus

The concept of viability relates to a situation where the particular economic unit under the discussion is capable of sustaining itself. In the present study the viability of sample farm households have been examined on the basis of farm business income. Economic surplus is the income left with the household after meeting the food and non food expenditure of the farm family. The economic surplus of all the selected farm families was calculated by subtracting the total domestic expenditure from the corresponding farm business income from crops and dairy respectively for each selected farm family. The farm business income from crops and dairy has been calculated at two costs concepts. Cost A_1 (operational costs). Cost C_1 includes cost A_1 plus rent paid for lease in land, interest on value of owned fixed capital and imputed value of family labour. Returns over C_1 cost measures the efficiency of owned land and management. The overall economic surplus was estimated by adding the off-farm income of the marginal and small farmers in the farm business income of the respective category of the farmers and then deducting the domestic expenditure from their total income.

The viability of sample farm households shows that the number of viable farm income varies directly with the farm

Table 4
Proportionate Expenditure on Food Items by Sample Households, Punjab 2005-06

	Farm size categories					
Items	*Marginal %age to food expdt./Non Food expdt*	*Small %age to total expdt.*	*Others %age to food expdt. / Non Food expdt*	*%age to total expdt.*	*%age to food expdt. / Non Food expdt*	*%age to total expdt.*
Sub mountainous						
A. Food items	23873	58.26	29638	22.30	55383	32.77
B. Non-food items	17102	41.74	103286	77.70	113606	67.23
1. Clothing*	29.49	12.31	8.25	6.39	13.69	9.20
2. Education	19.76	8.25	3.74	2.90	12.53	8.43
3. Expenditure on health	12.50	5.22	4.77	3.71	21.49	14.45
4. Sociol- ceremonies	24.82	10.36	79.00	61.40	42.30	28.44
5. Total expenditure	40975		132924		168989	
Central region						
A. Food items	26132	54.85	29192	47.93	62536	38.45
B. Non-food items	21514	45.15	31712	52.07	100103	61.55
1. Clothing*	27.09	12.23	21.31	11.09	16.98	10.46
2. Education	30.33	13.69	19.61	10.29	13.42	8.26
3. Expenditure on health	12.09	5.46	13.11	6.83	14.49	8.92
4. Sociol- ceremonies	19.22	8.68	34.82	18.13	40.85	25.14
5. Total expenditure	47646		60904		162639	

Contd...

Items	Farm size categories					
	Marginal %age to food expdt./Non Food expdt	Small %age to total expdt.	Others %age to food expdt. / Non Food expdt	%age to total expdt.	%age to food expdt. / Non Food expdt	%age to total expdt.
South west region						
A. Food items	23035	51	32236	53	64431	48
B. Non-food items	21756	49	28210	47	69032	52
1. Clothing*	29.75	14.64	25.79	12.18	21.65	11.36
2. Education	15.12	7.35	26.62	12.42	24.05	12.44
3.Expenditure on health	15.26	7.41	12.09	5.64	13.47	6.97
4.Sociol- ceremonies	30.40	14.77	26.36	12.30	29.08	15.04
5.Total expenditure	44792		60446		133463	

* Clothing includes expenditure on washing, footwear and fuel and lighting.

size and non-viable indirectly with the farm size. As per the Table 5 there were 81, 62 and 39 per cent of marginal, small and other farm households who were non-viable on the basis of (C_1 costs) crop income, and this number declined to 64, 31 and 32 when dairy income is added to the crop income for these respective categories of farmers. As family income constituted of farm and off farm income, the percentage of non-viable farmers declined further to 23, 18 and 24 per cent among marginal, small and other categories of farm household respectively. The highest number of non-viable farmers was in the sub- mountainous region subsequently south-western region.

Table 5
Non-viable Sample Farms on the Basis of Different Sources of Income in Punjab, 2005-06

	Crop income		*Farm business income*		*Family income*	
Region/farm sizecategory	*Cost A1*	*Cost C1*	*Cost A1*	*Cost C1*	*Cost A1*	*Cost C1*
1. Submountaious region						
a. Marginal	100	100	65	95	5	25
b. Small	95	95	60	70	30	45
c. Others	60	60	50	85	45	5
2. Central region						
a. Marginal	72	72	36	50	10	20
b. Small	32	42	4	20	2	12
c. Others	8	28	4	26	4	18
3. South western region						
a. Marginal	75	75	48	60	18	24
b. Small	42	66	6	21	0	9
c. Others	12	27	3	6	0	3
4. Punjab						
a. Marginal	81	81	47	64	12	23
b. Small	49	62	16	31	7	18
c. Others	24	39	13	32	11	24

Viability Analysis: Discriminant Function Approach

Discriminant analysis is a statistical technique used to differentiate between two or more classes of persons or objects based on the common variables, which are thought to be relevant. With the discriminate function; it is possible to measure the net effect of the variables by holding the other variables constant. The farmers were categorized into two groups on the basis of economic surplus left with the farm family i.e viable farmers and non-viable farmers for different regions of the state.

Sub-mountainous Region

It was revealed that total fixed investments, off farm income and domestic expenditure were the factors which differed significantly on viable and non-viable farms in sub-mountainous region (Table 6). Total fixed investments and domestic expenditure was significantly lower on viable farms (Rs 82589.23; Rs 54478.73) as compared to non-viable farmers (Rs 160645.50; Rs 85395) respectively while on the contrary to this, off farm income was significantly higher on viable farms (Rs 103283.90) as compared to non-viable farms (Rs 30296.30). The contribution of total fixed investment, off farm income and domestic expenditure were 143532.73 and 17.00 per cent respectively towards total distance between the two groups of farms in sub-mountainous region. Thus it is clear that the increase in off farm income, rationalization of domestic expenditure and fixed investment is required to make the non-viable farm as viable ones.

Central Region-II

Education expenditure on social and religious ceremonies and the net income from dairy were the two factors which differed significantly between viable and non-viable farms in central region (Table 7). The average expenditure on education was more of viable farmers (8.92) as compared to non-viable farmers (6.08) on social ceremonies was significantly lower on viable farms (Rs 10356.57) as compared to non-viable farms (Rs 96730.77), while on the contrary the net income form dairy was significantly higher on viable farms (Rs 53667.7) as compared to non-viable farms (Rs25217.7).These factors contributed 21.00, 51.26 and 16.32 per cent respectively towards total distance between the two groups of farm in central region.

Table 6
Particulars of Discriminant Function in Sub-mountainous Region of Punjab, 2005-06

Variables	*Mean*		*Mean difference (di)*	*Discriminant coefficient (Li)*	*Discriminating distance (Li) (di)*	*Per cent contribution to the total distance*
	Viable	*Non-viable*				
Age (yrs) X_1	43.13	46.85	-3.72282	-0.0533024	0.198435	3.64
Education (yrs) X_2	8.77	9.70	-0.92951	-0.0146086	0.013579	0.25
Farm size (acres)X_3	8.63	5.98	2.64705	0.2455084	0.64987	11.91
Family size (no)X_4	4.81	5.26	-0.45281	-0.3782836	0.17129	3.14
Total fixed investment (Rs)X_5	82589.23	160645.50	-78056.3*	-0.000000032	0.783068	14.35
Off- farm income (Rs)X_6	103283.90	30296.30	72987.57***	0.000002446	1.785459	32.73
Domestic expenditure (Rs)X_7	54478.73	85395.00	-30916.3*	-0.000002999	0.927256	17.00
Expenditure on social & religious ceremonies (Rs)X_8	11106.45	85437.04	-74330.6	-0.000001026	0.76281	13.98
Value productivity from crops (Rs) X_9	66523.16	56026.15	10497	0.000000701	0.07362	1.35
Net income from dairy (Rs)X_{10}	26521.13	20000.25	6520.88	0.000003837	0.09023	1.65
D square					5.455617***	100.00

*, **, *** significant at 10, 5 and 1 per cent respectively

Table 7

Particulars of Discriminant Function in Central Region of Punjab, 2005-06

Variables	*Mean*		*Mean difference (di)*	*Discriminant coefficient (Li)*	*Discriminating distance (Li) (di)*	*Per cent contribution to the total distance*
	Viable	*Non-viable*				
Age (yrs) X_1	39.17	36.85	2.321729	0.3678678	0.085409	2.59
Education (yrs) X_2	8.92	6.08	2.842785**	0.24307216	0.691002	21.00
Farm size (acres)X_3	7.65	5.90	1.741993	0.05557697	0.096815	2.94
Family size (no)X_4	4.90	5.15	-0.25604	-0.104534543	0.026765	0.81
Total fixed investment (Rs)X_5	202024.30	182109.00	19915.33	-0.0000007469	-0.13437	-4.08
Off- farm income (Rs)X_6	32827.01	18961.54	13865.47	0.0000001229	0.017049	0.52
Domestic expenditure (Rs)X_7	67965.35	72629.85	-4664.5	-0.00000096816	0.04516	1.37
Expenditure on social & religious ceremonies (Rs)X_8	10356.57	96730.77	-86374.20***	-0.000001952	1.686486	51.26
Value productivity from crops (Rs) X_9	135014.00	106529.40	24484.65	0.0000008369	0.238394	7.25
Net income from dairy (Rs)X_{10}	53667.7	25217.70	28450.00**	0.00000188776	0.537067	16.32
D square					3.28978*** (18.10)	100.00

*, **, *** significant at 10, 5 and 1 per cent respectively

Thus, it is pointed out to increase education level and the net income from dairy whereas to rationalize the expenditure on social ceremonies for non-viable farms in order to make them viable in the central region.

South Western Region-III

The education, farm size, family size and value productivity from crops per acre were calculated to be the significant discriminating factors with 12.81, 47.27, 12.10 and 20.39 per cent contributing respectively towards total distance between viable and non-viable farmers (Table 8). The education, farm size, family size and value productivity was higher on viable farms with average of 9.23 years, 8.63 acres, 5.69 members and Rs 1,66,200.3 per farm for these variables respectively and lower for non-viable farms with average of 7.0 years, 3.00 acres, 4.42 members and Rs 54,049.73 per farm respectively. The smaller size of farm, lower education level and the lower returns per farm make farms non-viable. The improvement in these variables is required to make the farms viable as in south western region of Punjab.

The region-wise analysis highlights the major factor affecting the viability level of farmers. In sub mountainous region increase in off farm income, rationalization of domestic expenditure and fixed investment is required to make non-viable farmers to viable.Major factor contributed in the central region to differentiate the viable farmer from non viable were expenditure on social festivities and lower income from dairy which needs to rectify at this stage through mass campaigning. In the south-western region factor mainly education, farm size, family size and gross value productivity from crops were calculated to be discriminating these two groups of viable and non-viable. It was observed in the socio-economic profile of the farmers that low education level still prevalent in south western region.

State as a Whole

Table 9 presents the results of the discriminant function analysis for the Punjab state and observed that age of the head of the

Table 8

Particulars of Discriminant Function in South Western Region of Punjab, 2005-06

Variables	*Mean*		*Mean difference (di)*	*Discriminant coefficient (Li)*	*Discriminating distance (Li) (di)*	*Per cent contribution to the total distance*
	Viable	*Non-viable*				
Age (yrs) X_1	37.52	39.17	-1.64103	-0.0332624	0.54585	0.76
Education (yrs) X_2	9.23	7.08	2.147436**	0.42639799	0.915662	12.81
Farm size (acres)X_3	8.63	3.00	5.628205*	0.60020699	3.378088	47.27
Family size (no)X_4	5.69	4.42	1.275641*	0.6777505	0.864566	12.10
Total fixed investment (Rs)X_5	152571.50	67387.50	85184.04	-0.00000008	-0.06818	-0.95
Off- farm income (Rs)X_6	31435.90	8166.67	23269.23	0.0000021	0.488681	6.84
Domestic expenditure (Rs)X_7	78857.86	72036.96	6820.91	-0.00000879	-0.59961	-8.39
Expenditure on social & religious ceremonies (Rs)X_8	11871.29	8464.58	3406.71	0.0001044	0.355617	4.98
Value productivity from crops (Rs) X_9	166200.30	54049.73	112150.6*	0.000001299	1.457357	20.39
Net income from dairy (Rs)X_{10}	42813.69	15340.87	27472.83	0.000001091	0.29963	4.19
D square				7.146397***		

*, **, *** significant at 10, 5 and 1 per cent respectively

Table 9
Particulars of Discriminant Function, Punjab, 2005-06

Variables	*Mean*		*Mean difference (di)*	*Discriminant coefficient (Li)*	*Discriminating distance (Li) (di)*	*Per cent contribution to the total distance*
	Viable	*Non-viable*				
Age (yrs) X_1	39.15	42.57	-3.42773*	-0.03254412	0.111553	4.26
Education (yrs) X_2	9.00	8.30	0.703704	0.04898354	0.03447	1.32
Farm size (acres)X_3	7.75	6.88	0.863464	0.162417601	0.140242	5.36
Family size (no)X_4	5.14	5.02	0.119693	0.13347675	0.015976	0.61
Total fixed investment (Rs)X_5	171293.40	145314.70	25978.68	0.0000001356	0.035328	1.35
Off- farm income (Rs)X_6	41264.63	22083.33	19181.30*	0.000001204	0.230957	8.83
Domestic expenditure (Rs)X_7	69719.54	79619.75	-9900.21	-0.00000223	0.220388	8.42
Expenditure on social & religious ceremonies (Rs)X_8	10931.34	68386.57	-57455.20*	-0.00000118	0.67922	25.96
Value productivi-ty from crops (Rs) X_9	134948.60	74368.29	60580.30**	0.00000137	0.829671	31.70
Net income from dairy (Rs)X_{10}	45983.54	23739.40	22244.14***	0.00000143	0.319016	12.19
D square					2.616821***	100.00

*, **, *** significant at 10, 5 and 1 per cent respectively

family, off farm income, expenditure on social ceremonies, net income from crops per farm, and net income from dairy were significant factors discriminating viable farms from the non viable farms. Net income form crops came to be most discriminant factor with average income from crops at Rs 134948.6 for viable farms and Rs 74368.29 for non viable farms. Its contribution towards total distance was 31.70 per cent. The second major discriminating factor was found to be the expenditure on social and religious ceremonies which was significantly lower on viable farms (Rs10931.34) as compared to the non- viable ones (Rs 68386.57). Its contribution towards total distance was 25.96 per cent. Net income form dairy, off-farm income and age of the head of the family contributed 121.9, 8.83 and 4.26 percent respectively towards total distance. To curtail this distance, income from crops, off farm income from dairy, less expenditure on social ceremonies could lead to the non viable farm to become viable ones.

The region-wise analysis showed some details about the regional variation of which affects the viability level of the farmers. In sub-mountainous region off farm income, domestic expenditure and investment as fixed assets in agriculture were the main reason which drags the viable farmer into non-viable groups. As agriculture income level has been low in this region it became pertinent to increase the income from other sources and it is difficult to lessen the domestic expenditure. As domestic expenditure is concerned it is already low in this region. The region actually demand the off farm employment opportunities. In the central region farmers spends a lot on education of their wards and made an extravagant expenditure on social ceremonies which worsened their economy. In the south-western region education of the farmer and farm size; when they were lower, shifts the family into non-viable group of farmers. Hence, education has great bearing on the decision making of the farmers and to gain technical know-how about the farm operations. Therefore, south-western region demand education for farm wards

Thus, it is concluded from the discriminant analysis that the provision of more off-farm opportunities of income, improvement in crop productivity and education ought to be given due attention and curtailing expenditure on social and religious ceremonies should also be educated to make the non-viable farms viable ones. Education of farmers also plays an important role in improving the economic condition of the farmers.

Conclusions and Strategies

Although green revolution had made impressive strides in Punjab agriculture and achieved many land marks to enhance the income of the farmers. Nevertheless, success still eludes marginal and small farmers. These resource poor farmers are unable to get their fair share in the cake. The development process in agriculture improved the living standards of all categories of farmers, but due to division of land holding and also due to stagnation in agriculture, marginal and small farmers became unable to keep the living standards at par which they had achieved once. With the on set of the development crisis in agriculture, marginal and small farmers are finding it difficult to survive, with the result that many marginal farmers left farming in distress. It is projected that up to the year 2015 this number will decrease further to 76 thousand, which will be about eight per cent of the total holdings, whereas it was about 38 per cent during 1970-71 and 19 per cent during 1980-81.

These marginal farmers with surplus family labour of zero opportunity cost needs chance to survive by employing their family labour effectively. Under the impact of new economic policy of liberalization, there is an emphasis on export led agricultural growth through integration of our village economy with the rest of the world while such trade linkages may have some advantages, this cannot be relied upon as an efficient strategy of development. The present situation of declining income of farmers particularly marginal and small, their sustainability demands some concrete steps. It is also a cause of concern for policy makers, research workers and development administrators. It warrants immediate steps to improve their living standards in the short run and strategies for improving their income in the long run. The following steps are suggested:

Provision of Off-farm Employment Opportunities

The study reveals that off farm income is an important weapon to cut down the level of non viability in farmers. The marginal and small farmers who were non-viable in the tune of 81 per cent and 62 per cent reduced to 31 per cent and 18 per cent when off farm income was included. Without other source of income most of the marginal farmers were non viable. Marginal and small farmers urgently required employment at their village/town level so they can work and come back home.

Provision of Education and Public Health Services

The fact clearly emerged from the study that education improves the human capital formation and income of the farmers definitely. It was also observed that still illiteracy dominant particularly amongst the marginal farmers, it is higher in south western region. Same way public health services are also crucial, and these are found to be very costly. In the matter of expenditure on these two items lower strata of farm families have decisive disadvantages. The picture regarding future living standard of this category of farm families became quite disconcerting. It is only through a policy of active state intervention that such families can be saved from further erosion of their living standards. Free education up to matriculation and health services at reasonable charges should be provided at the village level and monitored effectively.

Provision of Custom Hiring Services Through Cooperatives

Marginal and small farmers are the resource poor farmers having inadequate investments on machinery and implements. The cooperative societies in the village should be strengthened to provide these services on hiring basis particularly to the marginal and small farmers and in general to all farm size categories.

Strengthen the Fair Price Shops

To provide the essential goods at reasonable prices fair price shops should be strengthened at the village level. These shops will be particularly for marginal and small farmers and other poors in the village. it was observed that more than 50 per cent of consumption expenditure goes on food items of marginal and small category of farmers. This requires definite some measures to save this vulnerable section.

Campaign Against Extravagant Expenditure on Social Festivities

The mass campaign should be launched against this extravagant expenditure on social festivities like marriages and other socio-religious ceremonies. Some observation showed that extravagant expenditure put the farmers in the category of non viable; which other-wise are the viable ones. For this purpose village leader/panchayat, youngster can play an important role to save the peasantry of Punjab.

Farmers Advised to Continue Joint Family System

So all should not be done by the state government or village leader/panchayats, farmers have some responsibility to avoid the crisis in agriculture. Joint family system should be encouraged to work upon the economies of scale in expenditure pattern and also to keep the farm size reasonably better than subdivided holding. This was observed in the study that joint family system is a significant discriminates variable which helps in improving viability of the farm family.

Issue Passbooks to Facilitate the Flow of Institutional Services to Small and Marginal Farmers

Issue a passbook to the farmer which includes land records i.e. owned land, leased in and leased out land, from the revenue officer of the village and countersigned by village Sarpanch. This passbook should be a valid document for presentation to banks and other institutions for availing the necessary services. Recording of these services should be made mandatory so that proper monitoring can be done.

References

Acharya, S.S. and Sunita Verma (1990), Viability and sustainability of agriculture in Rajasthan in Proceedings of the National Seminar held at NIRD, Hyderabad, October 8-10, 1990.

Bhalla, G. S. and Chadha, G. K. (1982), Green Revolution and the small peasant: A study of income distribution in Punjab agriculture, Economic and political weekly, May, 1982.

Chandra, D. (2001), Crucial agriculture problems facing small farmers, *Political Economy Journal of India*, 10: 1-4.

Haque, T. (1996), Sustainability of small holder agriculture in India, Concept Publishing Company, New Delhi -110 059.

Maji, C.C. and T. Haque (1990), Economics of marginal and small farms in West Bengal, Paper presented at the National Seminar on Economics of agriculture with special reference to viability and sustainability of small and marginal farmers held at NIRD, Hyderabad, Oct. 8-10, 1990.

Sekhon, M.K., Sidhu, M.S., Kaur Manjeet and Kaur Amrit (2008), Production, marketing and institutional constraints: Strategies for small and marginal farmers, U.G.C. funded project report, Punjab Agricultural University, Ludhiana.

Singh, Mandeep, Bhullar, A.S. and Joshi, A.S. (2009), Factors influencing economic viability of marginal and small farmers in Punjab, *Agril. Economics Research Review*, 22 (2): 269-279.

7

Agrarian Crisis, Indebtedness and Farmers' Suicides in Punjab

Sukhpal Singh, H. S. Kingra & Sangeeta

Punjab's agrarian economy has been facing deep economic crisis. Due to neo-liberal policies, farm profitability has declined which has adversely impacted the socio-economic base of the rural community. Agricultural growth rate in Punjab state was 4.6 per cent in 1980's which declined to 2.5 per cent in 1990s. Even it was lower than the national average growth rate of 3.2 per cent in 1990s. The growth rate of Punjab agriculture further decelerated to 1.9 per cent in the 2000s. A large number of proximate and structural factors have pushed the farming and farmers towards distress conditions. As a result, economic condition of the farming population is deteriorating at a fast rate and the number of poor in the farming population is constantly increasing. About 11 per cent of the farming population of the state lives below poverty line (Singh *et al*, 2009). The green revolution model increased the financial need of the farmers which increased their dependency on non-institutional sources of finance. An abrupt rise in the number of suicide cases every year is clearly an indication of remorseful state of the agrarian structure of the Punjab. As a result, as much as 89 per cent of the farmers of the state were indebted. On an average a farmer was indebted up to 64 per cent of his annual income but the marginal, small and semi-medium farmers up to 4 ha were indebted up to about 90 per cent of their annual income (Singh, Sukhpal *et al*, 2007). The condition of peasantry is so much wobbly that out of five lakh small farmers, about two lakh left farming during last 15 years. Generally, these farmers have joined the labour market and some other low paid activities. Agrarian crisis further has many manifestations like economic hardness, marginalization and even suicides. Increase in number of suicides each year is a clear indication of the sorry state of affairs of the rural economy. Keeping in view the above said condition of the Punjab agriculture, the present paper attempts to examine the nature and magnitude of crisis in farm sector of the state.

Changing Structure of Workforce

Agriculture is still considered as the main occupation, even though income from agriculture keeps declining. According to census of 2001, 23 per cent of the population in Punjab is still dependent on agriculture as the main occupation (Table 1). The share of employment in the agriculture sector has declined with time as the proportion of cultivators to the total workforce has decreased i.e. it showed a decline of -7.86 per cent from 1971 to 1981, -2.36 per cent during 1981 to 1991, and -9.35 per cent from 1991 to 2001. From 1971 to 2001, a negative decline of about 20 per cent was there in the number of cultivators.

The study further revealed that during the decade 1991-2001, the number of labourers in the agriculture sector declined significantly (by -7.94 per cent). Correspondingly, in other sectors there was about 17 per cent rise in employment. This trend broadly suggests that the agrarian distress has driven cultivators out of agriculture sector in search of employment in the Rural Non Farm (RNF) sector leading to shift of workforce from agriculture sector to non- agriculture sector in Punjab.

This is also an indication towards a fact that the Punjab agriculture's capacity to absorb labour has declined over time.

Table 1
Changing Structure of Workforce in Punjab, 1971 to 2001

(Thousands number)

Occupation category	*1971*	*1981*	*1991*	*2001*
Cultivators	1665	1710	1973	2099
	(42.57)	(34.71)	(32.35)	(23.00)
Agricultural labour	786	1216	1488	1503
	(20.10)	(24.68)	(24.41)	(16.47)
Others	1460	2001	2637	5525
	(37.33)	(40.61)	(43.24)	(60.53)
Total No of workers (000)	3911	4927	6098	9127
	(100)	(100)	(100)	(100)
Per cent Shift	*1971-1981*	*1981-1991*	*1991-2001*	*1971-2001*
Cultivators	-7.86	-2.36	-9.35	-19.57
Agricultural labour	4.58	-0.27	-7.94	-3.63
Others	-3.28	2.63	17.29	23.20

Note: Others include allied activities, manufacturing, processing and repairing, construction, trade, transport and communication

Source: GOP, Statistical Abstract of Punjab, various issues

Calculations by PAU, Ludhiana have shown that Punjab agriculture employment elasticity with respect to aggregate output is less than 0.2 which implies that even 5 per cent rate of growth in agricultural output creates only one per cent growth on the employment front (PAU, 1998). In the peak liberalization era, while the employment growth in the whole of the economy came down from 2.06 per cent per annum in 1983-84 to 1993-94 period to 1.82 per cent in 1993-94 to 2004-05 period, the employment growth in agriculture had collapsed to almost zero (0.10 per cent) (*www.flipkart.com*).

In the wake of globalization, a progressive opening up of the domestic agriculture to the world market since the mid 1990s has been a source of considerable distress for rural people in general and for farmers in particular. By now, it is well acknowledged that as a result of liberalization of imports, several crops have been hit by unfavourable price trends. During the post-liberalization period, agricultural commodity prices in the world market have witnessed a secular downtrend. Combination of these factors has increased the vulnerability of the farming and farmers of the state and there exists an undue competitive pressure on already resource poor farmers. About 40 per cent of farm households, given the choice, would like to quit farming to take some other vocation, while another 27 per cent farmers do not like farming because it is not being profitable (GOI, 2005). This scenario shows that farming is not a profitable and lucrative venture.

Process of Depeasationsation

The transformation of workforce from farming to non-farming sector can be divided into two categories namely, growth-led transformation and distress-induced transformation. The growth-led transformation is related with the development factors like mechanization of agriculture, increasing employment and income, high education level, urbanization, development of secondary and tertiary sector and even state intervention for generating employment opportunities. These factors are known as 'pull factors', which contribute to 'pull' the workforce from farming to more lucrative non-farm activities. On the other hand, distress-induced transformation is based on the hardship or crisis driven factors like, falling productivity, increasing costs and decreasing returns, unemployment and underemployment, crop failure due to natural calamities, supply of spurious chemicals and other inputs, indebtedness and even suicides. These factors are known as 'push factors', which 'push' the agriculture workforce from farming towards non-farm activities to eke out their livelihood (Singh, Karam *et al*, 2007). The present shift of workforce from farming towards non-farm activities in Punjab seems to happen with push factors which is a distress-induced transformation, generally known as depeasatisation.

Punjab is an agriculturally developed but land scarce economy. Due to law of inheritance and soil fertility differentials, there is a division and sub-division of land holdings. This process has increased the number of holdings in Punjab agriculture up to 1991. But the wide scale mechanization and capitalization has made the small sized farming less remunerative as the scale of technology does not suit to small farms. The number of operational holdings in the state decreased from 11.17 lakh in 1990-91 to 10.03 lakh in 2004-05 (Table 2). The number of marginal and small farmers decreased significantly from 5 lakh in 1991 to 3.18 lakh in 2005. This shows that about two lakh small and marginal farmers shifted from farming activity during last 15 years and the maximum shifting (about 55 per cent) was noted for the marginal farmers, from 3 lakhs in 1991 to 1.34 lakhs in 2005. The decline in number of marginal and small holdings since 1991 is a pointer to the fact that the small holdings have turned non-viable and finding it increasingly difficult to maintain their living from the farming activity alone, the small and marginal farmers prefer to start other occupation rather to stick with non-remunerative farming on tiny farm holdings. In a NSSO study, it has been reported that 40 per cent of the Indian farmers and 37 per cent of the Punjab farmers expressed their desire to leave farming, as it is not a profitable occupation (NSSO, 2005).

Table 2

Distribution of Number of Operational Holdings in Punjab, 1981 to 2005

	No. of operational holdings (Lakh)			*%age of total holdings*		
Categories of holdings	*1981*	*1991*	*2005*	*1981*	*1991*	*2005*
Marginal (< 1.0 ha)	1.97	2.96	1.34	19.21	26.48	13.36
Small (1-2 ha)	1.99	2.04	1.84	19.41	18.25	18.25
Semi-medium (2-4 ha)	2.87	2.89	3.19	27.99	25.85	31.80
Medium (4-10 ha)	2.69	2.61	2.96	26.20	23.41	29.51
Large (> 10 ha)	0.74	0.67	0.71	7.19	6.01	7.08
Total	10.27	11.17	10.03	100.00	100.00	100.00

Source: GOP, Statistical Abstract of Punjab, various issues.

An analysis of the composition of labour market in the study shows that the inertia among the small farmers against inter-sectoral mobility has gradually declined. Under the pressure of agrarian crisis, the marginal farmers in particular and small farmers in general have been finding very hard to live on farming income alone and thus have been forced to push out of agriculture towards some other activities. Correspondingly, the RNF employment has increased which is distress-driven strategy of households to seek employment in other sectors.

Similar trend was observed in the study as it was found that migration was considered as a last option and a way to meet ends. During the study period, it was found that the farmers who started following RNF activities formed about 80 per cent of the total farmers leaving farming as their main occupation while another about 20 per cent of the small farmers started doing labour (4.24 per cent as agricultural labour, 3.06 per cent as factory labour and 12.73 per cent as other labour) as shown in Table 3.

Table 3

Occupational Shift of Farmers After Leaving Farming in Punjab

Sl. No.	*Activity*	*Marginal (< 1 ha)*	*Small (1-2 ha)*	*Semi-Medium (2-4 ha)*	*Large (> 4 ha)*	*Overall*
1.	Labour	20.10	20.00	12.70	-	20.03
(a)	Agricultural labour	6.90	4.10	1.40	-	4.24
(b)	Factory labour	3.70	4.20	1.50	-	3.06
(c)	Other labour (Construction etc)	17.50	12.50	9.80	-	12.73
2.	Entrepreneur	27.20	26.60	25.40	13.00	27.68
3.	Service	23.00	22.40	25.40	13.00	22.41
4.	Distress-rentier	2.30	13.50	16.40	37.00	10.80
5.	Dairy & Milkman	10.1	8.80	10.40	6.60	9.49
6.	Abroad	6.90	6.80	6.70	8.70	6.79
7.	Trader/Dealer	0.90	1.00	2.20	6.60	1.59
8.	Others*	1.40	-	0.70	15.10	1.21
	Total	100.0	100.0	100.0	100.0	100.0

Note: *Others include vegetable vendor, construction contractor (commission agents in case of large farmers) etc.

Source: Singh, Karam *et al*, 2007

Among these, the maximum about 28 per cent self employed themselves, about 22 per cent joined the service sector, about 10 per cent turned to dairy activity, about 11 per cent as distress-rentier. Similarly, about 7 per cent migrated to other countries, about two per cent became traders/dealers and the rest 1.21 per cent followed vending and contracting activities to meet their ends. Different studies (Singh, 2003; Gupta, 1988 and Verma, 2006) also point towards this fact.

Different studies from different regions of India were also studied for the causes and strategies of shifting labour from one sector to another. In a study of Gujarat (Breman, 1974) it was found that with growing monetization of consumption, the landowning upper class of rural society of South Gujarat realized that it was cheaper to replace a permanent workforce with casual labour. So influx of bonded labour from elsewhere was evidenced for which local shortage of labour was not the reason but it was so that the land poor and landless preferred to migrate out of their villages to work in far-away brick kilns to earn their livelihood.

In another study in Tamil Nadu (Breman, 2010), it was found that about one-fourth of the workers (23.4%) in wet zones and more than one half in dry zones (55.7%) had opted for brick kilns as a source of livelihood when they failed in meeting ends with agriculture. For two-third of them, it was a temporary option, used irregularly when work in agriculture was not available. In wet zones, migration is mainly considered as a coping strategy in case of economic hardship and lack of employment opportunities.

In a study for Andhra Pradesh seasonal migration of landless and marginal landholders as a coping strategy during droughts and famines was also noted (Deshingkar and Start, 2003) due to influx of migrant agricultural labourers from other states; some local agricultural labourers had to change their profession.

Farming is attached with some social status in the agrarian society, particularly in Punjab. Thus, it is very difficult for the farmers to leave this occupation and join lower paid jobs or lower social status jobs or other activities in the economy. Some people who have found job in public sector or joined other better paid activities were satisfied from their new professions while others were almost dissatisfied from their new occupations. Thus, one-fourth of these persons want to go to further new professions. This is symptomatic of the lack of opportunities available to such distress farmers (Singh, Karam *et al*, 2007).

Extent and Magnitude of Indebtedness

The green revolution model increased the financial need of the farmers which increased their dependency on non-institutional sources of finance. The productivity of almost all the crops increased, but the profitability is quite low in Punjab. Also distinct slowdown in agricultural growth adversely impacted the socio-economic base of the rural community. Thus, the peasantry is reeling under debt. On the basis of sample survey of 300 farmer households from different agro-climatic regions of Punjab during the year 2008-09, it is observed that 90 per cent of the farmers of the state are under severe debt (Table 4).The position of medium and semi-medium farmers is very shaky as about 96 per cent and 94 per cent farmers of these categories, respectively are indebted. The capitalist model of agriculture has made almost all the categories of farmers indebted. Not only small and marginal farmers but 80 per cent of the large farmers who have land holding of more than 6 hectares are also living under debt.

Table 4
Extent of Indebted Farm Households in Punjab, 2008-09

Size of holding	*Average Farm Size (ha)*	*Sample Size*	*No. of Indebted Households*	*Percentage of Indebted Households*
Marginal	0.72	40	35	87.50
Small	1.60	50	45	90.00
Semi-Medium	2.93	90	85	94.44
Medium	5.11	55	53	96.36
Large	7.87	65	52	80.00
Average	3.88	300	270	90.00

Source: Field Survey, 2009.

Despite the fact that institutional network of finance has been significantly developed in the state, the non-institutional sources, particularly commission agents are still the important source of credit to the Punjab farmers. There seems to be little doubt left to the mind as who is profiteering from the indebtedness. From banks and big farmers to commission agents and other petty money lenders, money lending seems to be the most lucrative business. Table 5 reveals that about 37 per cent of the total credit of Punjab farmers is being advanced by the non-institutional sources. This proportion is higher in case of marginal (41 per cent) and small farmers (39.9 per cent) than the large farmers (33.87 per cent) as the large farmers have a better access to institutional loans.

Table 5
Magnitude of Farmer's Debt in Punjab, 2008–09

(Rs.)

Size of holding	*Debt/ Household*	*Debt /ha*	*Institutional*	*Non-institutional*
Marginal	118820	165028	69510 (58.50)	49310 (41.50)
Small	187325	117078	112582 (60.10)	74743 (39.90)
Semi-Medium	315804	107783	196431 (62.20)	119373 (37.80)
Medium	361550	70753	227295 (62.87)	134255 (37.13)
Large	516614	65643	341638 (66.13)	174976 (33.87)
Average	320022	85907	202653 (63.32)	117369 (36.68)

Note: Others include shopkeepers, relatives and friends.
Source: Field Survey, 2009.

On an average Punjab farmer household is indebted to the tune of Rs. 320022. The amount of debt is directly related with the farm size. It is the highest in case of large farmers and the lowest in case of marginal farmers. However, in relation to the size of land, the association is negative. The burden of debt is Rs. 165028 per hectare on marginal farmers and Rs. 65643 per hectare on large farmers. This shows that the relative indebtedness on the smaller farmers is two and half times higher than that of the larger farmers.

The declining phase of the green revolution started in the early nineties as the farm profitability was the lowest in mid-1990s. So, different studies were analyzed for their estimates for rising debt burden and the source of credit for the farmers (Table 6). During this period, academicians, popular discourse, and media started raising a hue and cry regarding the worst economic position of peasantry. In this critical period, the first popular report was brought out by H.S. Shergill (1998), which was widely circulated among scholar, media, and policy planners. The report highlighted that Punjab peasantry was indebted of Rs. 5700 crores in 1997, out of which 46.32 per cent was owed by the commission agents. After five years, another study concluded by Singh and Toor (2005) showed that during 2002-03 the debt burden on Punjab peasantry increased to the tune of Rs. 9886 crores, out of which share of commission agents was 50.51 per cent.

Table 6
Increasing Debt Burden on Punjab Peasantry – Various Estimates

		Non-institutional (Rs./crore)			
Year	*Institutional (Rs./crore)*	*Commission Agent*	*Others*	*Total Debt (Rs./crore)*	*Studies*
1997	2654	2641	406	5700.91	Shergill
	(58.50)	(46.31)	(7.12)	(100.00)	(1998)
2002–03	4139	4994	753	9886	Singh & Toor
	(60.10)	(50.51)	(7.62)	(100.00)	(2005)
2005–06	13047	6736	1281	21064	Singh, Kaur &
	(62.20)	(31.98)	(6.08)	(100.00)	Kingra (2007)
2007–08	15407	13179	1808	30394	Shergill (2010)
	(62.87)	(43.36)	(5.95)	(100.00)	
2008-09	20265	11610	127	32002	Field Survey,
	(63.32)	(36.28)	(0.40)	(100.00)	2009

In 2005–06, Singh, Kaur and Kingra (2007) estimated that the debt burden on Punjab farmers has increased to Rs. 21064 crores. The share of commission agents, though, increased in absolute term, but significantly declined from 51 per cent to 31.98 per cent due to liberal credit polices of the government for agricultural sector. Recently H.S. Shergill (2010) again conducted a study on farmers debt and estimated that during 2007-08, the debt burden on Punjab farmers increased to Rs. 30394 crores and the share of the commission agent increased to 43.36 per cent. Similarly, our present field survey revealed that the Punjab farmers are indebted to the amount of Rs. 32002 crores during 2008-09. The share of the non-institutional source is 36.68 per cent out of which Rs. 11,610 crores (about 36 per cent of total debt) was owed by the commission agents and the remaining 0.4 per cent is provided by the relatives and friends. This scenario shows that the debt burden on Punjab peasantry has been significantly increasing since the mid-1990s. This phenomenon is said to be the phase of falling farm profitability and increasing indebtedness. The analysis conferred that almost all the sections of Punjab peasantry have been facing the problem of severe debt burden and the commission agents have still dominant status in rural credit market.

Farmers' Suicides

The most gruesome and chilling manifestation of agrarian crisis has been farmers' suicides. An abrupt rise in the number of suicides is a clear indication of this fact. During last one decade several studies were conducted by the scholars regarding rural suicides (Table 7).

Table 7
Suicides in Rural Punjab-Various Studies

Item	*Bhalla et al. 1998*	*Iyer and Manic 2000*	*AFDR 2000*	*Chahal 2005*	*PAU 2009*
Suicide cases studied (No.)	53	75	79	42	
2890Census					
Cultivator(%)	55	67	85	100	60
Agricultural labour(%)	45	33	15	-	40
Small and marginal farmers (%)	25	84	66	55	79
Suicides due to debt (%)	38	79	62	55	73
Debt exclusively from moneylenders (%)	37	68	27	9	N.A.
Debt from money lenders and others (%)	NA	81	71	52	90

Sources: Bhalla et al. (1998), Iyer and Manick (2000), AFDR (2000), Chahal (2005) and PAU (2009).

All the studies conferred similar conclusions that farmers and agricultural labourers have been committing suicides primarily due to economic hardship and indebtedness. Small and marginal farmers are the main victims, as they are not in a position to eke out their lives with meager earnings reaped from their tiny size of holdings, which of course are capital intensive. The large numbers of suicide victims were indebted either exclusively of private money lenders or both the private and public agencies.

The first ever census survey on the issue of farmers and agricultural labourers' suicides was conducted by Punjab Agricultural University (PAU), Ludhiana. The study revealed that as much as 2890 farmers and agricultural labourers have committed suicides in Bathinda and Sangrur district during 2000-08. Although National Crime Record Bureau (NCRB) data focuses the Punjab state among the least suicide prone areas of the country but PAU census survey revealed that the number of farmers suicides is far higher than that of the figure provided by the NCRB. Moreover, the farmers' suicide rate is almost one-and-half times more than the general suicide rate. According to NCRB data almost 15 farmers per lakh farmers annually had committed suicide in India since 1997. This figure for general suicide is just 10. PAU census survey conferred that the farmer suicide rate is four times more than that of the figure provided by the NCRB. In Bathinda and Sangrur districts of Punjab, 63 farmers per lakh farmers annually have committed suicides whereas this figure is just 15 in case of Indian farmers. It is important to note that 79 per cent of these farmers are the owners of less than 2 hectares of land which shows that the small farmers are living under stressful conditions, that is why they are the main victims of this phenomenon. It is also interesting to know that 73 per cent of the suicide victims were under heavy debt burden of commission agents and banks. They ended their life due to unbearable stress of day-by-day increasing debt burden due to exorbitant interest rate of non-institutional agencies.

Although the tone and tenor of state and the popular discourse have been posing sociological and psychological aspects as the primary reasons for happening these suicides, but actually suicide phenomenon is purely an economic one. However, in some situations, this economic aspect is triggering them towards the other non-economic factors. Declining farm profitability in general and debt burden of private money lenders in particular, are the main reasons behind this act of finishing precious human lives.

Conclusions

Agriculture sector in Punjab is under an unprecedented and multi-facet crisis. And, the agrarian crisis has been manifested in the decelerated growth in agricultural output, declining employment opportunities and squeezing farm profitability. In the wake of trade liberalization, the undue competitive pressure shattered the economy of already resource poor farmers. Due to agrarian crisis, small and marginal farmers of the state have undergone the process of pauperisation and immiserisation. The prevalence of depeasantisation gained momentum since 2000 which has resulted in low income, under consumption and indebtedness among the peasantry.

The gravity of indebtedness is continuously escalating as the debt burden of Punjab peasantry increased from Rs. 5700 crores in 1997 to Rs. 32002 crores in 2009. Heavy farm input loans along with exorbitant interest rates particularly of private moneylenders and commission agents are disturbing dimensions of economic scenario of peasantry. The farmers have borrowed heavily for purchase of expensive farm input, farm machinery, digging/deepening of tube wells and replacement of old bore wells with submersible pumps. Un-remunerative prices of crops, successive crop failures and high costs of cultivation have landed the peasantry, particularly small farmers, into clutches of debt.

Although suicide is a complex phenomenon but the dominant factors behind this act are economic ones as majority of the farmers have been committing suicides due to heavy debt burden. Majority of the suicide cases were happened due to heavy debt burden along with harassment by moneylenders/commission agents/bank officials, economic hardship, family discord and social reasons. In some situations, the loss of status due to harassment by the moneylender in the form of continuous visits to victims' house, insult in front of villagers and public, threat to file a case and threat to take possession of house/land also perceived as a precipitating factor of suicides. Thus the government should exercise a strong check on the activities of non-institutional credit agencies and provide institutional credit to the farmers. The easy repayment facilities with low rates of simple interest will help reduce mounting debt burden on Punjab peasantry.

The whole issue of agrarian distress begs holistic framework in which the long term policy measures for raising farm incomes on sustainable basis and developing rural physical and social infrastructure through large investments in agriculture should be focused. Also, there is an urgent need to diversify state's agrarian economy not only in narrow sense of diversification within crop sector but also in its wider sense of going in for allied agricultural and non-farm activities. To tackle the problem of unemployment and underemployment in the state, something on the lines of Chinese model of employment where surplus rural labour workforce engaged in the non-farm sector, appears to be the answer. Similarly, cooperative farming can also provide good employment opportunities and income to small and marginal farmers. By rationalizing the existing resources through cooperative sector, human labour and costly farm implements can be used optimally which, in turn, will reduce the cost of cultivation and increase the income of the farmers in the state.

All these measures will be helpful for improving the economic conditions and human health of agricultural workforce which, in turn, become the deriving force to solve the agrarian crisis of the state.

References

AFDR (2000), "*Suicides in rural areas of Punjab-A Report*" Association for Democratic Rights (AFDR), Patiala Unit, Punjab.

Bhalla, G. S., S. L. Sharma, N.N. Wig, S. Mehta and P. Kumar (1998), *Suicides in Rural Punjab*. Chandigarh: Institute for Development and Communication (IDC).

Chahal, T.S. (2005), *Forced Fall: A Case of Punjab Farmers*. Amritsar: Institute of Development and Planning.

Breman J. (1974), *Patronage and Exploitation-Changing Agrarian Relations in South Gujarat*, India. University of California Press, Berkeley.

Breman J. (2010), *The Political Economy of Un Free Labour in South Asia: Determining the Nature and Scale of Debt Bondage*, European Conference on

Modern South Asian Studies (ECMSAS), Conference in Bonn on Contemporary and Historical Aspects of Labour Regulations and Labour Standards: 26-29 July.

Deshingkar P and Daniel S (2003), *Seasonal Migration for Livelihoods in India: Coping, Accumulation and Exclusion*, Working paper 220 (London, UK: Overseas Development Institute).

Government of India (2005), Indebtedness of Farmer Households, 59th round, Publication No. 498, NSSO, Ministry of Statistics and Programme Implementation, New Delhi, May.

GOP (Government of Punjab), *Statistical Abstract of Punjab*, Various Issues.

Gupta A K, Arora D R and Aggarwal B K (1988), Sociological Analysis of Migration of Agricultural labourers from Eastern to North-Western region of India, *Indian Journal of Industrial Relation*, 23 (4): 429-45.

Iyer K G and M S Manick (2000), *Indebtedness, Impoverishment and Suicides in Rural Punjab*, India Publishers and Distributors, New Delhi.

NSSO (2005), *Situation Assessment Survey of Farmers: Indebtedness of Farmer Households*, National Sample survey Organisation, 59th Round, (January-December) May.

PAU (1998), *Punjab Agriculture 2020: Farmers and Farming in Punjab*, Research Report, PAU, Ludhiana

PAU (2009), *Farmers' and Agricultural Labourers' Suicides due to Indebtedness in the Punjab State- Pilot Survey in Bathinda and Sangrur districts*, PAU, Ludhiana.

Shergill H S (1998), *Rural Credit and Indebtedness in Punjab*. Chandigarh: Institute for Development and Communication.

Shergill H S (2010), *Growth of Farm Debt in Punjab* 1997 to 2008. Chandigarh: Institute for Development and Communication.

Singh, Sukhpal and M.S. Toor (2005), 'Agrarian Crisis with Special Reference to Indebtedness Among Punjab Farmers', *Indian Journal of Agricultural Economics*, Vol. 60, No. 3, pp 335–46.Singh,

Sukhpal, M. Kaur and H. S. Kingra (2007), *Flow of Funds to Farmers and Indebtedness in Punjab*. Research Report, The Punjab State Farmers' Commission, Government of Punjab.

Singh R (2003), *Socio-Economic Implications of Migrant Labour on Punjab Economy*, Ph. D thesis, Punjab School of Economics, Guru Nanak Dev University, Amritsar: 131.

Singh, Sukhpal, Manjit Kaur and H S Kingra (2007), *Flow of Funds to Farmers and Indebtedness in Punjab*. The Punjab State Farmers Commission and Punjab Agricultural University, Ludhiana.

Singh, Karam, Sukhpal Singh and H S Kingra (2007), *Status of Farmers who left Farming in Punjab*. The Punjab State Farmers Commission and Punjab Agricultural University, Ludhiana.

Singh S, Sharma V K and Kingra H S (2009), *A Study into the Economy of Farming and the Pattern of Income and Expenditure in the Punjab Agriculture*. Report submitted to Department of Economics and Sociology, Punjab Agricultural University, Ludhiana, Punjab: 86.

Verma A K (2006), Pattern of Wages and Loans among Migrant and Local Agricultural Labourers in Punjab, *J Agri Develop. & Policy* 18(1&2):135-41.

www.flipkart.com/ agrarian-crisis-farmers-suicides-livelihood-book-8189886622- Cached- CPI (ML) Resolution on Agrarian Crisis and the Way Out.

8

Globalisation and Growth of Farmer's Indebtedness in Punjab

H. S. Shergill

The drastic shift in policy environment triggered by liberalization and globalization of Indian economy since 1991 impacted Punjab agriculture quite severely owing to its highly commercialized and specialized production structure and intense market involvement. The developments on pricing and marketing side generated by the paradigm shift made wheat and rice cultivation in the State unprofitable. During the same period cotton farmers of the State also suffered considerable losses due to repeated attacks of American boll-weevil. The deficit in farm economy caused by these negative developments resulted in considerable increase in farm debt since the mid nineteen nineties. The main objective of this paper is to picture the extent of change in the quantum, composition and burden of farm debt in Punjab since the paradigm shift to liberalization and globalization. Although the shift to liberalization of the economy started in 1991, but its full impact started manifesting only after India joined W.T.O. in 1995 and became fully integrated in the world economy. The policy changes and other economic events that impacted Punjab agriculture during the last about one and a half decade are summarized in section one to describe the economic scenario in which farm debt grew in the State. The empirical basis of farm debt estimates used to capture the change in the quantum, composition and burden of farm debt during this period is described in section two. In section three, the growth in the magnitude of farm debt since the mid 1990's is discussed and the change in the composition of farm debt is described in section four. The growth in the burden of farm debt is evaluated in section five and the incidence of debt trap in section six. The supply side changes in farm credit market are described in section seven and the salient feature of change in farm debt situation over this decade are encapsulated in the last section.

Punjab Agriculture in the Era of Globalisation

The economic reforms introduced since 1991 and joining of W.T.O. in 1995 drastically changed the policy environment in which Punjab's modern commercialized wheat and rice farming has been operating for almost three decades. The cosy regime of guaranteed minimum support prices and assured purchase of entire marketed surplus of these two grains experienced serious strain as the state started withdrawing from the economic sphere under the paradigm shift in favour of the market economy. As a result minimum support prices of wheat and paddy grew at a slow pace during the 1997 to 2001 period, and were virtually frozen between 2002 to 2005. The farm input subsidies were slashed to make the farmers pay market prices for these inputs. Even the complete scrapping of the minimum support prices system and dismantling of Food Corporation of India was recommended by some zealots of globalization. These negative developments on the marketing side coincided with some adverse trends on the production side. The yield of wheat and paddy started stagnating and the fall in water table made existing water pumping technology non-functional. As a result Punjab farmers had to invest huge amount in the upgradation of tubewell technology by installing submersible pumps. The stagnation of yield rates, over-capitalisation of farm operations, rising prices of farm inputs, and fall in water table combined to push up the cost of production of wheat and paddy, the main commercial crops of the state. These developments on the supply side combined with the virtual freezing of minimum support prices manifested in eroding the profitability of wheat and rice cultivation in the State. The economics of wheat and rice production in Punjab looked so unfavourable in the initial years of the present decade that many farm experts started doubting the sustainability of current levels of production of these two grains in the State. To tackle the emerging agrarian crisis, a major scheme to shift 10 lakh hectares of area from wheat and paddy to other crops was prepared by Punjab Government and submitted to the Central Government for approval and funding. Alongwith the worsening economics of wheat and paddy cultivation, the cotton production in the state also suffered a severe shock from the continuous failure of the cotton crop for a number of years during this period due to American Boll-Weevil attack. The farm situation in the state looked very grim indeed in the middle years of the current decade.

Luckily, then the economic wheel turned and food prices in the world market soared, and the danger of food shortage emerging in the country looked real. Government had to import huge quantity of wheat at high prices to build the buffer stocks. This sudden development on the food front forced the Central Government to reverse the farm policy course, and a major jack up in minimum support prices of wheat and paddy was made in 2007 and that positive change in wheat/paddy pricing policy is continuing since then. The handsome increase in minimum support prices of wheat and paddy since 2007, has restored the profitability of wheat and rice cultivation in the State to some extent. The cotton economy has also improved considerably in recent years owing to the introduction of Bt Cotton and the consequent rise and stability of cotton yield. But the substantive problems of stagnant yield rates of wheat and paddy, falling water table and over-capitalisation of farm operations being unresolved, the question mark on the long run sustainability of wheat and rice specialization of Punjab farms has not completely disappeared. This is the economic scenario in which farm debt situation in Punjab evolved since the introduction of economic reforms and globalization of the economy.

Empirical Basis of Farm Debt Estimates

The change in the farm debt situation in the state is pictured on the basis of farm debt estimates for two points of time, 1997 and 2008. The farm debt estimate for 1997 almost coincides with the period when the impact of globalization on Punjab agriculture started manifesting after the joining of W.T.O. in 1995. So the comparison of farm debt situations in 1997 and 2008 pictures adequately the growth in indebtedness of Punjab peasantry in the era of globalization. For record and reference the empirical basis of these two farm debt estimates is briefly described. The information on farm debt situation in 2008 is based on a primary survey of 300 farms carried out by the author in June-August, 2008. The information pertains to the agricultural year 2007-08 and gives the farm debt estimate as in June-August, 2008. The sample was stratified both region wise as well as farm size wise and 300 farms were selected randomly from 30 villages of the state. The results of this farm debt survey were published in the form of a research monograph by *Institute for Development and Communication*, Chandigarh in January, 2010 (6). The information on farm debt situation in 1997 is based on a primary survey of 260 farms carried out by the author in December, 1997 under a research project sponsored by the Punjab Government (4). This information pertains to the full year covered by Rabi and Kharif Crops harvested in 1997. The sample design and methodology used in the two primary surveys was almost the same; the only major difference being in the size of two samples. The farm debt estimates of these surveys are broadly comparable and have been largely accepted by economists researching on and interested in Punjab agriculture. These two estimates are used to capture the nature and extent of growth in farm debt in Punjab during the globalization period. The exact time gap between these two farm debt surveys is about 10.5 years, and in computing the growth rates and ratios that exact period of

10.5 years is used. However, for ease of expression and presentation this period is referred as a decade in the text of this paper.

Growth of Farm Debt Over 1997-2008

In the post W.T.O. era farm debt in Punjab grew at a quite fast rate, more than doubling between 1997 and 2008. The information on the quantum of farm debt in Punjab in 1997 and 2008 is presented in Table 1. At current prices the amount of farm debt grew at the annual rate of 17.28 per cent; the 2008 amount (Rs. 30394.12 crore) being more than five times the 1997 amount (Rs. 5700.91 crore). At constant prices, the amount of farm debt more than doubled in this decade: growing at the annual rate of 8.81 per cent. The per farm household debt grew at a still faster rate of 18.36 per cent per year (at current prices), and at 9.83 per cent per year at constant prices. The faster growth of per farm household debt, compared to total farm

Table 1
Growth of Farm Debt in Punjab Over 1997-2008

Aspect of Farm Debt	*Amount*		*2008 as multiple of 1997*	*Growth Rate (Per cent per year)*
	1997	*2008*		
Total farm debt at current prices (Rs. crore)	5700.91	30394.12	5.33	17.28
Total farm debt at constant prices (Rs. crore)	5700.91	13829.32	2.43	8.81
Debt per farm household at current prices (Rs. lakh)	0.52	3.05	5.86	18.36
Debt per farm household at constant prices (Rs. lakh)	0.52	1.39	2.67	9.83
Debt per operated acre at current prices (Rupees)	5721	28708	5.02	16.60
Debt per operated acre at constant prices (Rupees)	5721	13062	2.28	8.18

Notes: 1. Source of Farm Debt Estimates: H.S. Shergill (1997, 2008)
2. Weighted Index of prices of 21 agricultural commodities grown in Punjab is used to estimate debt at constant prices. *Source of Price Index:* Statistical Abstract of Punjab, various issues.

debt, was caused by the fall in the number of farm households in the state over this period. On the same lines debt per operated acre also more than doubled (at constant prices), and became more than five times at current prices. The information presented in Table 1 leaves little doubt about total farm debt, debt per farm household, and debt per operated acre more than doubling in real terms (i.e. constant prices) in the decade following the joining of W.T.O. and global integration of the Indian economy.

Change in Composition of Farm Debt

During this post W.T.O. period not only the quantum of farm debt increased at a fast rate, even the composition of farm debt also under went considerable change. The composition of farm debt is captured into two ways i.e. (i) by the proportion of outstanding debt, short-term recurring crop loans and mortgage debt in total farm debt; and (ii) by the share of marginal/small farms and medium/big farms in total farm debt. The growth of outstanding debt, short-term farm loans and mortgage debt over the reference period is shown by information presented in Table 2. It may be seen that out of these three components of farm debt, outstanding debt grew at the highest rate; 23.03 per cent per year at current prices and 14.13 per cent per year at constant prices. The debt equivalent of short-term loans grew at a relatively slower rate; at 12.74 per cent per year at current prices and at 4.59 per cent per year at constant prices. Since most of the outstanding debt amount is the unpaid portion of long/medium term loans, the obvious inference is that long term/medium term loans grew faster than short-term loans during this period. Surprisingly, the amount of mortgage debt actually declined over these ten years; at the rate of 4.94 per cent per year at current prices, and at the rate of 13.09 per cent per year at constant prices. It seems the practice of raising loans by mortgaging out land is disappearing in the Punjab rural side. Owing to the variation in the growth rate of these three components of farm debt, their share in total farm debt also changed considerably. The share of outstanding debt in total farm debt increased from 38.16 per cent in 1997 to 63.05

per cent in 2008. On the other hand, share of debt equivalent of short-term loans declined from 54.72 per cent in 1997 to only 36.14 per cent in 2008. The share of mortgage debt has become negligible (just 0.81 per cent in 2008), though in 1997 it accounted for 7.12 per cent of total farm debt.

Table 2

Growth of Farm Debt Components and Change in Farm Debt Composition

Farm Debt Component	*Amount*		*2008 as multiple of 1997*	*Growth Rate (Per cent per year)*
	1997	*2008*		
Outstanding debt at current prices (Rs. crore)	2175.26 (38.16)	19165.11 (63.05)	8.81	23.03
Outstanding debt at constant prices (Rs. crore)	2175.26	8720.13	4.01	14.13
Mortgage debt at current prices (Rs. crore)	406.02 (7.12)	245.05 (0.81)	0.60	(-) 4.94
Mortgage debt at constant prices (Rs. crore)	406.02	111.50	0.28	(-) 13.09
Debt equivalent of short-term loans at current prices (Rs. crore)	3119.33 (54.72)	10983.96 (36.14)	3.52	12.74
Debt equivalent of short-term loans at constant prices (Rs. crore)	3119.33	4997.36	1.60	4.59

Notes: 1. For source of information see legend under Table 1.
2. Figures in bracts indicate per cent share of debt component in total farm debt.

The share of marginal/small farms and medium/big farms in total farm debt has also undergone considerable change over this period because the two grew at different rates (Table 3). The debt of marginal/small farms group grew at a slower rate than the debt of medium/big farms. The marginal/small farms debt grew at the slow rate of 2.48 per cent per year at constant prices and at 10.46 per cent per year at current prices. In contrast the debt of medium/big farms grew at the rate' of 9.97 per cent per year at constant prices and at 18.53 per cent per year at current prices. The reasons for this big difference in the growth rate of marginal/small farms debt and medium/big farms debt are not fully clear, but three plausible explanations

Table 3
Growth in Debt Position of Farm Size Groups and Change in Their Share in Total Debt

Farm Size Category wise Debt (Rs. crore)	*1997 (As in December 1997)*	*2008 (As in June-August 2008)*	*2008 Amount as multiple of 1997 amount*	*Growth Rate (Per cent per year)*
Debt of marginal and small farms at current prices	1229.58	3495.26	2.84	10.46
Debt of marginal and small farms at constant prices	1229.58	1590.34	1.29	2.48
Debt of medium and big farms at current prices	4471.33	26653.81	5.96	18.53
Debt of medium and big farms at constant prices	4471.33	12127.48	2.71	9.97
Marginal and small farms share in total farm debt (Per cent)	21.57	11.59	(Per cent points) -9.98	(Per cent change) 46.27
Medium and big farms share in total farm debt (Per cent)	78.43	88.41	9.98	12.73

Notes: 1. Source of Farm Debt Estimates: H.S. Shergill (1997, 2008)

2. Farm debt amount for 2008 does not include mortgage debt because it could not be apportioned between the two farm size classes owing to small number of sample observations.

may be advanced. One is that some sort of saturation point seems to have been reached in the demand for loans by marginal/small farms stratum; they are already financing most of their farm input purchases and domestic expenditure by borrowed money. The second is that a limit of sorts may have been also reached so far as their borrowing capacity is concerned; because of their poor asset base. The third is that medium/big farms are on the way of becoming fully mechanized and consequently have been borrowing at a fast rate to purchase Tractors and other farm machines. On account of the different rates of growth of debt of marginal/small and medium/big farms, their respective share in total farm debt has also changed. The share of marginal/small farms stratum in total farm debt has declined by 9.98 per cent points; from 21.57 per cent in 1997 to 11.59 per cent in 2008. There is a corresponding rise in the share of medium/big farms group in total farm debt from 78.43 per cent in 1997 to 88.41 per cent in 2008. Despite this decline in the share of marginal/small farms in total debt, their debt share in 2008 (11.59%) was much higher than their share in the total operated area of the state (7.56 per cent). It means in per acre terms marginal/small farms debt is considerably higher than medium/big farms debt per acre.

Growth of Debt Burden

The increase in the absolute amount of farm debt per se does not convey much information on the increase or decrease of burden of debt on the farm sector. Only in comparison with farmer's income and value of assets does the farm debt amount reveals the direction and extent of change in the burden of debt on the peasantry. The burden of farm debt on the farm sector can be estimated in a number of ways that are alternatives as well as complements of each other. The indicators of debt burden used in this study are detailed in Table 4, and can be divided into two categories. In the first set (serial number 3 to 5) the amount of farm debt is compared with value of assets and income of Punjab farmers, and in the second set (serial numbers 6 to 9) the annual interest charge on farm debt is compared with different indicators of repaying capacity of the farmers. It may be noted that between 1997 and 2008 farm debt as proportion of Net State Domestic Product (NSDP) originating in agriculture increased by 16.26 per cent points; from 67.60 per cent in 1997 to 83.86 per cent in 2008. In simple per cent terms this is an increase of 24.55 per cent in this proportion. Farm debt as proportion of the value of Machinery owned by farmers rose from 15.04 per cent to 52.88 per cent i.e. by 37.84 per cent points over these 10 years. Similarly, farm debt as a proportion of the total value of land owned by farmers rose by 0.70 per cent points (from 3.31 per cent to 4.01 per cent) over this period, despite the steep rise in farm land prices in the state in recent years. So in terms of each of these three indicators debt burden on Punjab farm sector has increased substantially during the post W.T.O. period.

The comparison of annual interest charge on farm debt with repaying capacity of the farm sector (serial number 6 to 9, Table 4) also reveals considerable increase in debt burden on the Punjab farm sector over this period. The annual interest charge on farm debt increased from 10.96 per cent of NSDP (Agriculture) in 1997 to 14.44 per cent in 2008; an increase of 3.48 in per cent points, and 31.75 per cent in standard per cent terms. Similarly, annual interest charge on debt as proportion of annual rental surplus of farm land increased from 21.48 per cent in 1997 to 33.15 per cent in 2008; an increase of 54.33 per cent in this proportion in 10 years following the W.T.O. membership. So, in whatever way one compares the conclusion is almost the same; that interest burden of farm debt on Punjab farmers has gone up substantially over the 1997-2008 period.

From Debt Burden to Debt Trap

The substantial increase in burden of farm debt indicated by comparison of 1997 and 2008 debt pictures (Table 4) does not reveal the full story of the severity of debt burden on Punjab peasantry. A more detailed disaggregated (according to debt burden) analysis of 2008 debt survey data (Table 5) showed considerable variation in debt burden among the sample farms. The severity of debt burden on a farm family was assessed by comparing the annual interest charge on its debt amount with

Table 4
Change in Burden of Farm Debt Over 1997-2008

Sl. No.	*Indicators of Debt Burden*	*Value of Indicator in* 1997	2008	*Change in indicator (2008 value as multiple of 1997 value)*
1.	Debt per farm household at constant prices (Rs. lakh)	0.52	1.39	2.67
2.	Debt per operated acre at constant prices (Rupees)	5721	13062	2.68
3.	Debt as per cent of NSDP originating in agriculture	67.60	83.86	16.26*
4.	Debt as per cent of value of machinery and tubewells owned by farmers	15.04	52.88	37.84*
5.	Debt as per cent of value of farm land owned by farmers	3.31	4.01	0.70*
6.	Annual interest charge of farm debt at constant prices (Rs. crore)	1102.78	2512.33	2.28
7.	Annual interest charge of farm debt as per cent of NSDP originating in agriculture	10.96	14.44	3.48*
8.	Annual interest charge of farm debt per operated acre at constant prices (Rupees)	1074	2263	2.11
9.	Annual interest charge of farm debt as per cent of cash rent per acre	21.48	33.15	11.67*

Notes:
1. Source of Farm Debt Estimates: H.S. Shergill (1997, 2008)
2. Price per acre of farm land prevailing in sample villages is used to compute the value of farm land owned by farmers.
3. Cash rent per acre prevailing in the sample villages is used for figures reported in row 9.
4. *indicates change in terms of per cent points.

the annual rental surplus of its owned land. The average cash rent per acre prevailing in the sample villages was used as a rough and ready measure of surplus revenue generated from farming after meeting material costs of production, wages of hired labour and imputed wages of family labour. It may be mentioned that owned land, rather than operated area, is the relevant factor for this purpose. The cash rent of leased in area goes to the leasing out household, and if the farmer has leased out some of his owned area than he gets the cash rent for it. So the total cash rent equivalent of the owned area gives a fairly good estimate of the surplus revenue generated by a farmer after meeting the material costs of production, wages of hired labour and imputed wages of family labour. The rental surplus thus defined is the notional maximum amount a farmer can spare to meet the annual interest charge on his loan. In fact, in most cases, this maximum amount cannot be spared (or saved) because in that case family consumption expenditure has to be kept down at the level of imputed wages of family labour; a very difficult, if not an impossible feat. If the annual interest charge on the loan amount is more than the rental surplus of the owned area, then some of the interest will remain unpaid and get added to the principal amount even if the indebted farmer pays the entire rental surplus to the credit provider. In such a case the loan amount will go on inflating over time, and the chance of the loan being paid back out of savings from current farm income will be almost nil. Such a farmer cannot

Table 5
Distribution of Farms by Debt Burden

	Number of Farms				
Debt Amount Per Owned Acre (Rupees)	*Number*	*Proportion*	*Mean Owned Area (Acres)*	*Amount of Debt Per Farm (Rs. lakh)*	*Amount of Debt Per Owned Acre (Rupees)*
80 thousand & Above	51	17.00	4.69	5.99	127709
60 to 80 thousand	32	10.67	8.04	5.73	71228
40 to 60 thousand	60	20.00	7.60	3.85	50651
20 to 40 thousand	74	24.67	9.24	2.71	29311
Upto 20 thousand	72	24.00	10.97	1.18	10778
Nil	11	3.67	9.27	-	-
All Farms	300	100.00	8.42	4.37	51858

Source: H.S. Shergill: Growth of Farm Debt in Punjab: 1997 to 2008, IDC, Chandigarh, January 2010.

extricate himself from debt without selling some land. Such farmers are virtually in debt trap out of which they cannot get out without selling some of their owned land. This is the definition of debt trap used to identify the debt trapped farmers.

To identify the debt trapped farmers the benchmark loan amount per owned acre was estimated on the basis of average cash rent per acre prevailing in the sample villages and the rate of interest usually charged by Commission Agents and Money Lenders in these villages. It worked out to Rs.80 thousand per owned acre. So all those farmers who owe Rs.80 thousand or more per owned acre were deemed to be in debt trap. The distribution of farms by debt amount per owned acre given in table 5 reveals that 17 per cent of sample farmers were in debt trap in this sense, and another 10.67 per cent were on the doors of debt trap because their debt amount per owned acre was between Rs. 60 to Rs. 80 thousand. The debt burden on these 27.67 per cent farmers is very severe indeed. On the average a debt trapped farmer owes a total amount of Rs.5.99 lakh; which comes to Rs. 1.28 lakh per acre of his owned land. Most of the debt trapped farms (92.13 per cent of all debt trapped farms) belong to marginal, small and medium farm size categories (Table 6). Out of these three farm size classes, the marginal and small farms are more seriously involved; almost 40 per cent of marginal and 31 per cent of small farms being in debt trap. These debt trapped farms cannot extricate themselves from indebtedness through their own efforts; howsoever hard they work and tighten their belts. They have to, sooner or latter, sell some of their owned land to liquidate their debt, unless some debt relief measure is provided by the state to extricate them from the debt trap.

Change In Supply Side of Farm Debt

The liberalization and privatization of the economy impacted the farm credit market through many different channels. The interest rate and other credit subsidies to the farm sector were reduced, and the public sector credit agencies (Commercial Banks and Cooperative Credit Institutions) were asked to gradually shift to provision of farm credit on a cost effective

Table 6
Farms in Debt Trap: Farm Size Wise Distribution
(Debt Per Owned Acre Rs. 80 Thousand and Above)

Farm Size Class (Acres)	*Number of Sample Farms*	*Number of Farms in Debt Trap*	*Per cent of Farms of Size Class in Debt Trap*	*Share of Size Class in Debt Trapped Farms of State (Per cent)*	*Debt Amount Per Farm (Rs. lakh)*	*Debt Amount Per Owned Acre (Rs. lakh)*
Marginal upto 2.5	38	15	39.47	29.41	2.70	2.21
Small 2.5 to 5.0	51	16	31.37	31.37	4.82	1.35
Medium 5.0 to 10.0	100	16	16.00	31.37	7.56	1.16
Big 10.0 to 25.0	80	4	5.00	7.84	16.77	1.12
Large 25.0 & Above	31	-	-	-	-	-
All Farms	300	51	17.00	100.00	4.37	1.28

Source: H.S. Shergill, Growth of Farm Debt in Punjab: 1997 To 2008, IDC, Chandigarh, January, 2010.

and competitive basis. The two public sector credit agencies, Commercial Banks and Cooperative Credit Institutions, responded differently to this change in policy regime. The Commercial Banks responded by introducing new farm credit products and aggressive but farmer friendly marketing practices. The Cooperative Credit Institutions, on the other, languished as the government started reducing its patronage and support and competition in the farm credit market increased. The change in the share of main credit agencies in farm debt in Punjab over the 1997-2008 period is pictured by information displayed in table 7. In absolute terms all the three main credit agencies owned in 2008 a much bigger amount of farm debt based assets compared to 1997. But their share in farm debt has undergone visible change in the course of these ten years. The most conspicuous change is in the share of Cooperative Credit Institutions; their share in farm debt declined from 27.14 per cent in 1997 to 18.91 per cent in 2008. This change indicates a fall of 8.23 per cent points, and of 30.32 per cent in standard per cent change terms in their share of farm debt. The share of Commission Agents and Money Lenders in farm debt also declined, but only marginally by 2.96

per cent points or 6.32 per cent in standard per cent terms. The Commercial Banks, on the other hand, have increased their share in farm debt substantially; by 12.36 per cent points or by 63.65 per cent in standard per cent terms. However, despite of the big increase in the share of Commercial Banks in farm debt, Commission Agents and Money Lenders still remain (in 2008) the largest single farm credit agency in terms of amount of farm debt and share in total farm debt. The new liberlised economic environment and the policy changes accompanying it, seems to have hit the Cooperative Credit Agencies quite hard and these institutions find it difficult to withstand the intense competition in farm credit market both from Commercial Banks as well as Commission Agents. The Commercial Banks, however, has shown considerable resilience in adapting to change in policy regime and have been successful in increasing their share in farm debt.

Table 7
Change in Share of Main Credit Agencies in Farm Debt Over 1997-2008 (Amount in Rs. Crore at Current Prices)

Credit Agency		*1997*	*2008*	*Change Over 1997-2008 Amount: 2008 as Multiple of 1997 Share: Change in Per cent Points*
Commission Agents &	Amount	2640.52	13179.09	4.99
Money Lenders	Share (%)	46.32	43.36	(-) 2.96
Commercial Banks	Amount	1106.95	9659.81	8.73
	Share (%)	19.42	31.78	12.36
Cooperative Credit	Amount	1547.42	5748.85	3.72
Institutions	Share (%)	27.14	18.91	(-) 8.23
Others	Amount	406.02	1806.37	4.45
	Share (%)	7.12	5.95	(-) 1.17
All	Amount	5700.91	30394.12	5.33
	Share (%)	100.00	100.00	-

Source: H.S. Shergill (1997 and 2008)

Conclusions

The paradigm shift to liberalization and globalization impacted wheat and rice farming in Punjab very severely owing to its highly commercialized and specialized character. The unfavourable turn in economics of wheat and rice production and continuous failure of cotton crop for many years resulted in increased indebtedness of Punjab peasantry. In the post W.T.O. period (1997 to 2008) total farm debt in the state more than doubled in real terms; and outstanding loan amount quadrupled in real terms over the same period. The annual interest charge on farm debt now eats up almost one-third of the entire rental surplus generated by Punjab agriculture. The increased burden of debt has pushed about 17 per cent of state farmers into a virtual debt trap in the sense that they are not in a position to pay even the annual interest charge on their loans out of current farm income. Sooner or latter, they have to sell some of their farm land to extricate themselves from the debt trap.

References

Govt. of India (2005), *Indebtedness of Farm Households,* NSSO, New Delhi

Govt. of India (2007), *Report of the Expert Group on Agricultural Indebtedness,* Ministry of Finance, New Delhi.

Govt. of Punjab (2002), *Report of the Expert Committee on Agricultural Production Pattern Adjustment Programme in Punjab,* Chandigarh

Shergill, H.S. (1998), *Rural Credit and Indebtedness in Punjab,* Institute For Development and Communication, Chandigarh

Shergill, H.S. (2007), "Sustainability of Wheat and Rice Production in Punjab: A Re-Examination", *Economic and Political Weekly,* December 29th

Shergill, H.S. (2010), *Growth of Farm Debt in Punjab: 1997 To 2008,* Institute for Development and Communication, Chandigarh

Singh Sukhpal, Manjeet Kaur, *Flow of Funds To Farmers and Indebtedness in Punjab,* and H.S. Kingra (2007), Punjab Agricultural University, Ludhiana.

9

Finances and their Management in North-Western States

Sucha Singh Gill & Sanjay Gupta

Introduction

Adequate availability of finances with the government enables it to undertake a large number of development activities. The role of government has transcended from traditional law and order into development activities. The undertaking of development activities requires a large quantity of financial resources. Some activities are designed by the state/provincial administration depending on its revenue/financial availability. But there are a large number of centrally sponsored schemes, which demand some state government share. Earlier there were 210 such schemes in the Tenth Plan, which have been compressed to 99 now, in Eleventh Five Year Plan (Grewal, 2010). There is incentive in implementation of these schemes as in many cases this allows a massive (90 per cent) contribution by the Union Government. But the implementation is possible if the states are able to raise their matching resources. Some states are finding it difficult to raise matching resources to take benefit of such centrally sponsored schemes. The Constitution of India has clearly demarcated between the State List and the Union List from the Concurrent List for purposes of revenue raising and development in those areas. But in terms of responsibilities, the constitution assigns predominant role to the state governments in provision of social services and equal role in the provision of economic services with the Union Government. At present, the states raise about 40 per cent of the combined revenue of the state and union government and account for 58 per cent of the aggregate/combined expenditure (Rao and Shah, 2009). This has led to chronic dependence of states on the Union Government for resource transfers. There are two channels of resource transfers from the Union Government to the state governments. One is statutory channel, established under the Constitution of India via the institution of Finance Commission established after every five years for this purpose. The second channel is through Planning Commission, which transfers resources to the states for various development projects and programmes generally on sharing basis. When the states are unable to meet their needs through their own resources and resources transferred from the Union Government, they resort to borrowing from the Union Government as well as from the financial institutions. They are also permitted to borrow from the public through issue of specific financial instruments. The complex nature of financing their expenditure in different states has chartered their own course for management of their finances. In the present paper, an attempt has been made to examine finances of four North-Western states of India, viz. Punjab, Haryana, Himachal Pradesh and Jammu & Kashmir.

The paper has been organized into four sections. Section one introduces the theme. The second section examines the performance of different states using various indicators of fiscal health. Section three examines the debt liability and its composition of chosen states. The last section makes concluding observations.

Fiscal Performance of States

The analysis of fiscal performance of states in the North-Western region has been done by dividing states in two categories. One, the states of Punjab and Haryana belong to

General Category States, while Himachal Pradesh and J & K belong to Special Category States. The Special Category states get transfers from the Planning Commission in the form of loans as 10 per cent and 90 per cent grant while General Category states receive 70 per cent as loans and 30 per cent as grant (Grewal, 2010). Moreover, the special category states of Himachal Pradesh and J & K along with other states have been given special package of tax concession by the Union Government since 2003 which have been extended in 2008 for next five years for newly established industrial units.

The data on gross fiscal deficit of the four states is in Table 1. The data bring out that gross fiscal deficit of Punjab and Haryana respectively stood at 3.37 per cent and 3.78 per cent during 1980-81 to 1982-83 (three years average). In case of Punjab, this increased to 8.03 per cent during 1989-90 to 1991-92 (three years average) but this declined to 3.23 per cent in case of Haryana in the corresponding period. This divergence can be explained due to disturbed political conditions in Punjab, while Haryana continued to be a normal state. In Himachal Pradesh, the gross fiscal deficit as percentage of NSDP increased from 3.38 per cent during 1980-81 to 1982-83 to 9.65 per cent during 1989-90 to 1991-92 (gross fiscal deficit moved almost in Punjab way). In case of J & K state, it increased from 11.87 per cent during 1980-81 to 1982-83 to 20.97 per cent during 1989-90 to 1991-92. Again being a disturbed state since the mid-1980s, the jump in fiscal deficit has been phenomenal (9.10 per cent point). The period between 1989-90 to 1991-92 and 1999-2000 to 2001-02 saw a narrowing down of gross fiscal deficit as percentage of the NSDP between the two sets of the states. The fiscal deficit in Punjab decreased to 5.98 per cent during 1999-2000 to 2001-02 compared to 8.03 per cent during 1989-90 to 1991-92. In case of Haryana, this increased to 4.44 per cent from 3.23 per cent during the corresponding period. The gross fiscal deficit also declined marginally to 8.26 per cent from 9.65 per cent in case of Himachal Pradesh and drastically in J & K state to 9.95 per cent from 20.97 per cent in the corresponding period. In case of Punjab, this improvement has been indicative of normalcy in the state, which made its fiscal indicators to move

Table 1
Gross Fiscal Deficit

(Rs. In crores)

States	1980-81	1981-82	1982-83	1983-84	1984-85	1985-86	1986-87	1987-88	1988-89	1989-90	1990-91	1991-92	1992-93	1993-94	1994-95	1995-96	1996-97	1997-98	1998-99	1999-00	2000-01	2001-02	2002-03	2003-04	2004-05	2005-06	2006-07	2007-08	2008-09 (RE)	09-10 (BE)
Punjab	160	178	183	262	479	566	343	968	833	909	1242	2151	1252	1495	1785	1365	14[illegible]5	2478	3779	3195	3904	4958	4401	488	4036	2656	4384	1604	6856	9660
Haryana	112	102	189	134	235	230	170	216	289	393	386	375	444	480	535	986	10[illegible]9	1128	2240	2133	2285	2740	1471	2933	1206	286	-1179	1264	3708	8557
H.P	-35	57	74	58	80	35	89	129	254	226	279	224	372	152	620	521	5[illegible]2	1202	1662	190	1845	1511	2342	2384	1810	720	921	552	1864	1592
J & K	145	136	142	198	248	247	244	417	410	524	861	449	204	88	-23	97	1[illegible]6	444	1054	1339	2166	748	1245	-17	1008	1588	1461	2609	2325	2205

Net State Domestic Product at Factor - State Wise (At Current Prices)

(Rs. In crores)

States	1980-81	1981-82	1982-83	1983-84	1984-85	1985-86	1986-87	1987-88	1988-89	1989-90	1990-91	1991-92	1992-93	1993-94	1994-95	1995-96	1996-97	1997-98	1998-99	1999-00	2000-01	2001-02	2002-03	2003-04	2004-05	2005-06	2006-07	2007-08	2008-09 (RE)	09-10 (BE)
Punjab	4449	5285	5838	6456	7381	8347	9174	10816	12495	15055	16738	20245	23280	27068	30528	34218	3911[illegible]	43099	49612	61139	67779	71280	73494	79840	85781	96108	107591	128303	148008	173993
Haryana	3032	3498	4004	4351	4747	5788	6081	6743	8878	9919	12238	14639	15416	19422	23138	20168	3134[illegible]	33909	38358	47329	53518	60158	66457	75918	85562	96857	119285	141602	168322	193519
H.P	723	848	897	1023	1031	1237	1363	1539	1933	2184	2521	2975	3411	4250	5192	5930	680[illegible]	7807	9507	12467	13852	15215	16751	18127	20299	22482	24787	27523	30923	
J & K	1050	1195	1362	1549	1747	1929	2134	2086	2548	2688	2908	3250	3565	5500	6001	6973	785[illegible]	8858	11128	13533	14328	15458	17400	18992	20724	22623	24747	27100		

GFD/NSDP Ratio (in percentage)

States	1980-81	1981-82	1982-83	1983-84	1984-85	1985-86	1986-87	1987-88	1988-89	1989-90	1990-91	1991-92	1992-93	1993-94	1994-95	1995-96	1996-97	1997-98	1998-99	1999-00	2000-01	2001-02	2002-03	2003-04	2004-05	2005-06	2006-07	2007-08	2008-09 (RE)	09-10 (BE)
Punjab	3.60	3.37	3.13	4.06	6.49	6.78	3.74	8.95	6.67	6.04	7.42	10.62	5.38	5.52	5.85	3.99	3.7[illegible]	5.75	7.62	5.23	5.76	6.96	5.99	0.61	4.71	2.76	4.07	1.25	4.63	5.55
Haryana	3.69	2.92	4.72	3.08	4.95	3.97	2.80	3.20	3.26	3.96	3.15	2.56	2.88	2.47	2.31	4.89	3.5[illegible]	3.33	5.84	4.51	4.27	4.55	2.21	3.86	1.41	0.30	-0.99	0.89	2.20	4.42
H.P	-4.84	6.72	8.25	5.67	7.76	2.83	6.53	8.38	13.14	10.35	11.07	7.53	10.91	3.58	11.94	8.79	8.4[illegible]	15.40	17.48	1.52	13.32	9.93	13.98	13.15	8.92	3.20	3.72	2.01	6.03	
J & K	13.81	11.38	10.43	12.78	14.20	12.80	11.43	19.99	16.09	19.49	29.61	13.82	5.72	1.60	-0.38	1.39	2.1[illegible]	5.01	9.47	9.89	15.12	4.84	7.16	-0.09	4.86	7.02	5.90	9.63		

Source: "Handbook of Statistics on State Government Finances" in 2010, RBI Occasional Publication
"Handbook of Statistics on Indian Economy", RBI Publication

Note: NSDP (at current prices) for HP, 2009-10 (BE) not available

Note: NSDP (at current prices) for J&K, 2008-09 (RE) and 2009-10 (BE) not available

closer to neighboring state of Haryana. In all the four states, there has been an implementation of pay commission reports showing higher burden of the salaries of the employees yet the states could manage to show better results due to better fiscal management. This is further reflected in the improvement of the own tax revenue of the states. The Punjab's own tax revenue as percentage of NSDP has decreased from 7.83 per cent during 1989-90 to 1991-92 to 6.81 per cent during 1999-2000 to 2001-02. In Haryana, the share of own tax as percentage of NSDP declined from 8.93 per cent to 7.92 per cent during this period. In Himachal Pradesh, this share declined from 6.46 per cent to 5.42 per cent while in J & K it fell from 5.21 per cent to 5.01 per cent (Table 2). Similarly the share of central taxes to NSDP also fell in all the four states during this period (Table 3). This is in line with all India trend. This is period of time, when the share of the central gross tax revenue as percentage of GDP dropped from 10.2 per cent to 8.2 per cent for years 1991-92 to 2001-02. Consequently, transfers to the states from the Union Government fell by one per cent point during this period (Rao and Jena 2009). The states during this period began to depend more on the commercial borrowings to manage their fiscal debt. The three year average ratio of market borrowings rose from 0.21 per cent of NSDP during 1990-91 to 1992-93 in Punjab to 0.84 per cent during 2000-01 to 2002-03. In case of Haryana, this increased from 0.46 per cent to 0.64 per cent while in Himachal Pradesh this ratio rose from 0.85 per cent to 2.72 per cent. In J & K, this ratio rose from 1.03 per cent to 2.23 per cent during this period. In fact, this period (the decade of 1990s) opened the way of high debt burden on the states (Table 4).

Realizing that the most of the states in country were falling neck deep in the fiscal crisis, the Twelfth Finance Commission suggested that the states pass Fiscal Responsibility Legislation with target of reducing fiscal deficit to 3 per cent of the NSDP by nearby future. Punjab state passed Fiscal Responsibility Act (FRA) in May 2003, Haryana in July 2005 and Himachal Pradesh in April 2005 with cap of guarantee for borrowings to 80 per cent of the revenue receipt and target for fiscal deficit to be brought at 3.00 per cent by March 2010 (Srivastava, 2009). This

Table 2
Own Tax Revenue

(Rs. in crores)

States	1980-81	1981-82	1982-83	1983-84	1984-85	1985-86	1986-87	1987-88	1988-89	1989-90	1990-91	1991-92	1992-93	1993-94	1994-95	1995-96	1996-97	1997-98	1998-99	1999-00	2000-01	2001-02	2002-03	2003-04	2004-05	2005-06	2006-07	2007-08	2008-09 (RE)	09-10 (BE)
Punjab	349	432	491	544	567	670	803	916	1041	1228	1291	1543	1759	2150	2599	2651	2735	3045	3262	3948	4895	4820	5711	6146	6945	8989	9017	9899	11547	14062
Haryana	234	291	337	366	406	502	566	664	795	910	1070	1300	1447	1589	1888	2169	2143	2369	3120	3518	4312	4972	5550	6348	7440	9079	10926	11618	14301	14647
H.P	34	42	48	54	61	74	92	103	118	142	161	193	222	256	299	342	412	476	572	620	728	916	888	984	1252	1497	1656	1958	2301	2700
J & K	38	60	62	71	79	104	118	123	138	133	163	165	207	225	244	285	289	367	437	578	748	858	976	1152	1400	1689	1903	2290	2693	3011

Own Tax Revenue/NSDP Ratio (in per cent)

States	1980-81	1981-82	1982-83	1983-84	1984-85	1985-86	1986-87	1987-88	1988-89	1989-90	1990-91	1991-92	1992-93	1993-94	1994-95	1995-96	1996-97	1997-98	1998-99	1999-00	2000-01	2001-02	2002-03	2003-04	2004-05	2005-06	2006-07	2007-08	2008-09 (RE)	09-10 (BE)
Punjab	7.84	8.17	8.41	8.43	7.68	8.03	8.75	8.47	8.33	8.16	7.71	7.62	7.56	7.94	8.51	7.75	6.99	7.07	6.58	6.46	7.22	6.76	7.77	7.70	8.10	9.35	8.38	7.72	7.80	8.08
Haryana	7.72	8.32	8.42	8.41	8.55	8.67	9.31	9.85	8.95	9.17	8.74	8.88	9.39	8.18	8.16	10.75	6.84	6.99	8.13	7.43	8.06	8.26	8.35	8.36	8.70	9.37	9.16	8.20	8.50	7.57
H.P	4.70	4.95	5.35	5.28	5.92	5.98	6.75	6.69	6.10	6.50	6.39	6.49	6.51	6.02	5.76	5.77	6.06	6.10	6.02	4.97	5.26	6.02	5.30	5.43	6.17	6.66	6.68	7.11	7.44	
J & K	3.62	5.02	4.55	4.58	4.52	5.39	5.53	5.90	5.42	4.95	5.61	5.08	5.81	4.09	4.07	4.09	3.68	4.14	3.93	4.27	5.22	5.55	5.61	6.07	6.76	7.47	7.69	8.45		

Source: "Handbook of Statistics on State Government Finances" in 2010, RBI Occasional Publication
"Handbook of Statistics on Indian Economy", RBI Publication

Note: NSDP (at current prices) for HP, 2009-10 (BE) not available

Note: NSDP (at current prices) for J&K, 2008-09 (RE) and 2009-10 (BE) not available

Table 3
Share in Central Taxes

(Rs. in crores)

States	1980-81	1981-82	1982-83	1983-84	1984-85	1985-86	1986-87	1987-88	1988-89	1989-90	1990-91	1991-92	1992-93	1993-94	1994-95	1995-96	1996-97	1997-98	1998-99	1999-00	2000-01	2001-02	2002-03	2003-04	2004-05	2005-06	2006-07	2007-08	2008-09 (RE)	09-10 (BE)
Punjab	82	92	99	112	122	114	147	156	171	208	248	293	349	379	424	442	528	657	587	539	719	611	649	754	902	1227	1566	1975	2378	2527
Haryana	61	68	73	81	94	86	97	108	121	154	186	219	562	282	317	361	432	539	480	525	345	449	757	601	620	1201	1296	1634	1922	1922
HP	22	25	27	30	33	101	121	143	176	154	188	240	276	290	369	400	440	651	727	921	330	325	348	450	537	493	629	794	968	1035
J&K	29	35	38	44	48	136	170	174	229	257	325	413	496	509	569	643	822	1135	1212	1232	645	729	709	825	1003	1164	1488	1655	2053	1880

Share in Central Taxes/NSDP Ratio (in per cent)

States	1980-81	1981-82	1982-83	1983-84	1984-85	1985-86	1986-87	1987-88	1988-89	1989-90	1990-91	1991-92	1992-93	1993-94	1994-95	1995-96	1996-97	1997-98	1998-99	1999-00	2000-01	2001-02	2002-03	2003-04	2004-05	2005-06	2006-07	2007-08	2008-09 (RE)	09-10 (BE)
Punjab	1.84	1.74	1.70	1.73	1.65	1.37	1.60	1.44	1.37	1.38	1.48	1.45	1.50	1.40	1.39	1.29	1.35	1.52	1.18	0.88	1.06	0.86	0.88	0.94	1.05	1.28	1.46	1.54	1.61	1.45
Haryana	2.01	1.94	1.82	1.86	1.98	1.49	1.60	1.60	1.36	1.55	1.52	1.50	3.65	1.45	1.37	1.79	1.38	1.59	1.25	1.11	0.64	0.75	1.14	0.79	0.72	1.24	1.09	1.15	1.14	0.99
HP	3.04	2.95	3.01	2.93	3.20	8.16	8.88	9.29	9.11	7.05	7.46	8.07	8.09	6.82	7.11	6.75	6.47	8.34	7.65	7.39	2.38	2.14	2.08	2.48	2.65	2.19	2.54	2.88	3.10	
J&K	2.76	2.93	2.79	2.84	2.75	7.05	7.97	8.34	8.99	9.56	11.18	12.71	13.91	9.25	9.48	9.22	10.47	12.81	10.89	9.10	4.50	4.72	4.07	4.34	4.84	5.15	6.01	6.11		

Source: "Handbook of Statistics on State Government Finances" in 2010, RBI Occasional Publication
"Handbook of Statistics on Indian Economy", RBI Publication

Note: NSDP (at current prices) for HP, 2009-10 (BE) not available

Note: NSDP (at current prices) for J&K, 2008-09 (RE) and 2009-10 (BE) not available

led to containment of fiscal debt in the subsequent period to near the target in case of Punjab (3.32 per cent) during 2006-07 to 2008-09, 0.70 per cent in Haryana, 3.92 per cent in Himachal Pradesh and 7.77 per cent in J & K (table-1). Though fiscal deficit has been contained but this is largely due to resorting to market borrowing by the states. For Punjab, this has increased from 0.84 per cent (three year average) at the beginning of 21st century to 2.26 per cent of NSDP during 2006-07 to 2008-09. In Haryana, this has declined to 0.40 per cent while in Himachal Pradesh it has increased from 2.72 per cent to 4.12 per cent and in J & K it has increased from 1.34 per cent to 3.76 per cent during the 2005-06 to 2007-08 (Table 4). In view of the fiscal crisis faced by various states, the Union Government relaxed the fiscal deficit target under the FRA to 3.5 per cent in 2008-09 and 4.0 per cent of their GSDP in 2009-10. This has been done to allow fiscal stimulus packages to meet recessionary situation arising out of global crisis (Chakraborty and Badra, 2010)

Market Borrowing and Rising Debt of the States

In view of fast increasing expenditure of the states on revenue accounts, the pressure of the Union Government to contain fiscal deficit the states resorted to market borrowing. In fact, the Twelfth Finance Commission (TFC) had fixed a cap on the outstanding debt of the state governments. The cap existed in the form that debt will not exceed 30.8 per cent of the GSDP by 2009-10 and during any year the borrowing would not exceed 3.0 per cent of GSDP. If the debt of the North Western states is examined in terms of the cap fixed by TFC, Haryana is the only state, which has remained within this limit with its debt - NSDP ratio stood at 20.84 per cent up to 2009-10. The Punjab exceeded this cap as its debt - NSDP ratio stood at 38.93 per cent. The Himachal Pradesh reached very high level by 2008-09 with debt - NSDP ratio of 64.4 per cent. J & K has the highest ratio in the region at 81.56 per cent in 2007-08. In the subsequent years, this ratio has further gone up. There are three major sources of internal loans of the states. They are state development loans, loans from National Small Saving Fund, and loans from banks and financial institutions. The outer

Table 4
Market Borrowings

(Rs. in crores)

States	1990-91	1991-92	1992-93	1993-94	1994-95	1995-96	1996-97	1997-98	1998-99	1999-00	2000-01	2001-02	2002-03	2003-04	2004-05	2005-06	2006-07	2007-08	2008-09	2009-10
Punjab	37	41	47	37	171	221	243	268	345	545	345	397	1062	2005	1660	978	738	3793	4645	4361
Haryana	54	67	76	64	109	134	147	162	193	218	218	261	715	1086	930	387	-147	-253	2505	3684
H.P	23	26	26	24	34	40	44	49	137	223	233	364	684	856	852	425	468	1322	1752	1177
J & K	29	37	34	42	58	66	73	80	89	88	239	264	578	477	416	227	618	2108	1629	1482

Marketing Borrowings/NSDP Ratio (in per cent)

States	1990-91	1991-92	1992-93	1993-94	1994-95	1995-96	1996-97	1997-98	1998-99	1999-00	2000-01	2001-02	2002-03	2003-04	2004-05	2005-06	2006-07	2007-08	2008-09 (RE)	2009-10 (BE)
Punjab	0.22	0.20	0.20	0.14	0.56	0.65	0.62	0.62	0.70	0.89	0.51	0.56	1.45	2.51	1.94	1.02	0.69	2.96	3.14	2.51
Haryana	0.44	0.46	0.49	0.33	0.47	0.66	0.47	0.48	0.50	0.46	0.41	0.43	1.08	1.43	1.09	0.40	-0.12	-0.18	1.49	1.90
H.P	0.91	0.87	0.76	0.56	0.65	0.67	0.65	0.63	1.44	1.79	1.68	2.39	4.08	4.72	4.20	1.89	1.89	4.80	5.67	
J & K	1.00	1.14	0.95	0.76	0.97	0.95	0.93	0.90	0.80	0.65	1.67	1.71	3.32	2.51	2.01	1.00	2.50	7.78		

Source: "Handbook of Statistics on State Government Finances" in 2010, RBI Occasional Publication
"Handbook of Statistics on Indian Economy", RBI Publication

Note: NSDP (at current prices) for H.P, 2009-10 (BE) not available

Note: NSDP (at current prices) for J&K, 2008-09 (RE) and 2009-10 (BE) not available

sources of loans include loans advanced by the Union Government, borrowings from Provident Fund. The data given in Table 5 bring out that the loans advanced by the Union Government constitute 4.00 per cent to 7.24 per cent of the outstanding debt of the North Western states. The rest represent loans which are borrowing from the sources with high interest rates. The specific mention can be made of National Small Savings Fund loans and Provident Fund loans accounting for more than 45 per cent of the outstanding loans for both Punjab and Haryana at 36.13 per cent for J & K and 38.19 per cent for Himachal Pradesh.

Table 5
Composition of Outstanding Loans of the States 2009-10 (BE)

(Rs. in crore)

State	*SDL*	*NSSF*	*Loans from Banks & FIs*	*Advance from the Central Govt*	*Provident Fund*	*Total (including other source)*
Punjab	23426	20857	4851	3502	10177	67721
	(34.58)	(30.79)	(7.15)	(5.17)	(15.03)	(100.00)
Haryana	10530	10284	3037	2489	8093	40324
	(26.11)	(25.50)	(7.52)	(6.17)	(20.07)	(100.00)
Himachal Pradesh	9008	4018	2583	905	4854	22619
	(39.83)	(17.17)	(11.42)	(4.00)	(21.02)	(100.00)
J&K	8093	3665	3783	1695	5794	26179
	(30.91)	(14.00)	(14.15)	(7.24)	(22.13)	(100.00)

Source: RBI, State Finances: A Study of Budgets 2009-10, Mumbai, 2010
Note: Figures in parentheses are in percentage

Due to rising and higher than the ratio specified by TFC (30.8 per cent), interest liability of Punjab, Himachal Pradesh and Jammu & Kashmir has been rising very fast. Interest payment as a percentage of NSDP has risen very fast. In case of Punjab, this ratio was less than 2 per cent for years 1980-81 and 1992-93, it has remained around four per cent up to 2006-07 when this source became visible. In case of Himachal Pradesh, this ratio rose sharply from less than 2 per cent between 1980-81 to 1983-84 and then ranged between 2 – 4 per cent up to 1990-91 and then rose to 5 per cent during 1991-92 and 1992-93 then rose to above 7 per cent from 2001-02 till 2005-

06 and fell to 6 per cent in the subsequent years. The same is the case with J & K where this ratio increased from 3.0 per cent during 1980-81 to 1982-83 and then rose to 10 per cent in 1992-93 and subsequently varied between nearly six to seven per cent. Haryana is the sole exception among North Western states where this ratio has never become 3.00 per cent but recently it has fallen below 2.0 per cent (Table 6). All other three states are using very high proportion of their tax revenue to make interest payments. If payment of principal amount is added, then the debt serving in these states accounts for nearly 50 per cent or more of their total tax revenue. This has reduced the capacity of the states to finance capital spending.

The reduction in capital spending by the government negatively affects private capital formation. The capital expenditure - NSDP ratio remained above six per cent and some years 10 per cent in Punjab and nearly 8 per cent in Haryana up to 1987-88, declined and now vary between 3-4 per cent. There is also declining trend of capital expenditure in Himachal Pradesh and J & K (Table 7). The states of Himachal Pradesh and J & K have been beneficiaries of the special package tax concession by the Union Government since 2003 and their growth rates have not dipped like that of Punjab. Haryana partly benefits from its proximity to National Capital Zone and has been experiencing high growth. At the same time the state's debt burden as proportion of the state income is not only within the stipulated limit but also lowest in the region. A detailed study of Punjab's fiscal problem (Sood, 2010) covering the period of 1980 to 2010 brings out that it is neither centre's neglect nor growing burden of salaries in wake of implementation of pay commission reports have created this crisis. In fact, the grants plus transfers (of taxes) from the Union Government constituted 20.69 per cent of the revenue receipts in Punjab during 1980-85 which increased to 22.00 per cent during 1985-90, 20.22 per cent during 1990-95 fell to 16.25 per cent during 1995-2000 but has jumped to 23.80 per cent during 2005-2010. In the case of salaries, their share in total non-plan revenue expenditure stood at 51.81 per cent during 1980-85 and has fallen consistently to 47.05 per cent during 1985-90, 42.33 per

Table 6
Interest Payments

(Rs. in crores)

States	1980-81	1981-82	1982-83	1983-84	1984-85	1985-86	1986-87	1987-88	1988-89	1989-90	1990-91	1991-92	1992-93	1993-94	1994-95	1995-96	1996-97	1997-98	1998-99	1999-00	2000-01	2001-02	2002-03	2003-04	2004-05	2005-06	2006-07	2007-08	2008-09 (RE)	09-10 (BE)
Punjab	62	74	84	90	152	147	175	161	219	234	332	361	411	1042	1244	1490	1634	849	2317	2637	2343	3178	3434	3712	3982	3715	4152	4527	4856	5349
Haryana	37	46	52	59	81	98	133	150	161	206	242	322	343	422	487	556	716	820	997	1357	1492	1625	1946	2113	2235	2100	2265	2346	2354	3001
H.P	10	12	17	18	28	31	42	49	69	88	111	148	177	210	223	285	313	372	498	597	798	1042	1172	1473	1641	1563	1669	1703	1883	2049
J & K	33	31	42	57	68	91	102	115	198	213	219	3869	359	276	577	440	489	593	665	845	845	1086	1159	1100	1175	1300	1201	2031	1600	1726

Interest Payments/NSDP Ratio (in per cent)

States	1980-81	1981-82	1982-83	1983-84	1984-85	1985-86	1986-87	1987-88	1988-89	1989-90	1990-91	1991-92	1992-93	1993-94	1994-95	1995-96	1996-97	1997-98	1998-99	1999-00	2000-01	2001-02	2002-03	2003-04	2004-05	2005-06	2006-07	2007-08	2008-09 (RE)	09-10 (BE)
Punjab	1.39	1.40	1.44	1.39	2.06	1.76	1.91	1.49	1.75	1.55	1.98	1.78	1.77	3.85	4.07	4.35	4.18	.29	4.67	4.31	3.46	4.46	4.67	4.65	4.64	3.87	3.86	3.53	3.28	3.07
Haryana	1.22	1.32	1.30	1.36	1.71	1.69	2.19	2.22	1.81	2.08	1.98	2.20	2.22	2.17	2.10	2.76	2.28	.42	2.60	2.87	2.79	2.70	2.93	2.78	2.61	2.17	1.90	1.66	1.40	1.55
H.P	1.38	1.42	1.90	1.76	2.72	2.51	3.08	3.18	3.57	4.03	4.40	4.97	5.19	4.94	4.30	4.81	4.60	.76	5.24	4.79	5.76	6.85	7.00	8.13	8.08	6.95	6.73	6.19	6.09	
J & K	3.14	2.59	3.08	3.68	3.89	4.72	4.78	5.51	7.77	7.92	7.53	119.05	10.07	5.02	9.62	6.31	6.23	.69	5.98	6.24	5.90	7.03	6.66	5.79	5.67	5.75	4.85	7.49		

Source: "Handbook of Statistics on State Government Finances" in 2010, RBI Occasional Publication
"Handbook of Statistics on Indian Economy", RBI Publication

Note: NSDP (at current prices) for HP, 2009-10 (BE) not available

Note: NSDP (at current prices) for J&K, 2008-09 (RE) and 2009-10 (BE) not available

Table 7

Capital Expenditure

(Rs. in crores)

States	1980-81	1981-82	1982-83	1983-84	1984-85	1985-86	1986-87	1987-88	1988-89	1989-90	1990-91	1991-92	1992-93	1993-94	1994-95	1995-96	1996-97	1997-98	1998-99	1999-00	2000-01	2001-02	2002-03	2003-04	2004-05	2005-06	2006-07	2007-08	2008-09 (RE)	09-10 (BE)
Punjab	267	376	433	614	785	800	627	990	798	866	880	816	785	7177	1463	1369	622	1636	2578	1784	2398	2982	2511	4633	3796	2244	7753	3458	6081	5378
Haryana	207	2[illegible]1	350	338	359	461	542	375	436	419	464	453	577	708	539	770	1064	1188	1562	1407	1978	2072	1240	5005	3035	2190	3276	4553	5111	6624
H.P	150	[illegible]4	90	101	134	177	183	196	216	209	217	1358	301	339	394	446	486	754	833	892	939	1093	1475	2508	2242	2120	2447	2322	3211	2854
J & K	154	252	178	198	238	294	336	408	439	530	772	754	539	825	1015	1057	1123	1414	940	1055	1144	1927	2325	2221	2939	3743	3806	5361	6303	7652

Capital Expenditure/NSDP Ratio (in per cent)

States	1980-81	1981-82	1982-83	1983-84	1984-85	1985-86	1986-87	1987-88	1988-89	1989-90	1990-91	1991-92	1992-93	1993-94	1994-95	1995-96	1996-97	1997-98	1998-99	1999-00	2000-01	2001-02	2002-03	2003-04	2004-05	2005-06	2006-07	2007-08	2008-09 (RE)	09-10 (BE)
Punjab	6.00	7.11	7.50	9.51	10.64	9.58	6.83	9.15	6.39	5.75	5.26	4.03	3.37	26.51	4.79	4.00	1.59	3.80	5.20	2.92	3.54	4.18	3.42	5.80	4.43	2.33	7.21	2.70	4.11	3.09
Haryana	6.83	6.08	8.74	7.77	7.56	7.96	3.91	5.56	4.91	4.22	3.79	3.09	3.74	3.65	2.33	3.82	3.39	3.50	4.07	2.97	3.70	3.44	1.87	6.59	3.55	2.26	2.75	3.22	3.04	3.42
H.P	20.75	9.91	10.03	9.87	13.00	14.31	13.43	12.74	11.17	9.57	8.61	45.65	8.82	7.98	7.59	7.52	7.14	9.66	8.76	7.15	6.78	7.18	8.81	13.84	11.04	9.43	9.87	8.44	10.38	
J & K	14.67	21.03	13.07	12.78	13.62	15.24	15.75	19.56	17.23	19.72	26.55	23.51	15.12	15.00	16.91	15.16	14.30	15.96	8.45	7.80	7.98	12.47	13.36	11.69	14.18	16.55	15.38	19.78		

Source: "Handbook of Statistics on State Government Finances" in 2010, RBI Occasional Publication
"Handbook of Statistics on Indian Economy", RBI Publication

Note: NSDP (at current prices) for HP, 2009-10 (BE) not available

Note: NSDP (at current prices) for J&K, 2008-09 (RE) and 2009-10 (BE) not available

cent during 1990-95, 41.91 per cent during 1995-2000, 39.19 per cent during 2000-05 and 35.80 per cent during 2005-10. The share of pension has increased from 3.10 per cent of the non plan revenue expenditure during 1980-85 to 13.76 per cent during 2005-10. The combined share of salaries and pensions of non plan revenue expenditure stood at 54.91 per cent during 1980-85 has declined to 49.56 per cent during 2005-10. Thus registering a decline of 5.35 per cent point. The real culprit remains the mounting debt burden and interest payments. Interest payments accounted for 14.92 per cent of the non plan revenue expenditure during 1980-85 has now increased to 24.95 per cent during 2005-10. This analysis equally applies to Himachal Pradesh and Jammu and Kashmir. The fiscal crisis indicated by growing fiscal debt as percentage of NSDP is mainly due to the method of management of fiscal resources. Instead of depending on raising tax NSDP ratio, the states have found easy way of financing expenditure to borrowing channels available to them, which are high cost/interest rate debts.

Concluding Observations

The analysis brings out that all the states in the North Western region face inadequacy of resources to meet their constitutional obligations. Consequently, all of them are accumulating debt over a period of time. All the states except Haryana are facing serious crisis and are unable to keep within limits their expenditure requirements from all sources of revenue receipts. There is need to provide the assured sources of revenue to make them sustainable in terms of fiscal management. This is important in view of changing nature of economy from commodity producing to service dominant economy. This requires restructuring of centre-state financial relations. There is already building opinion countrywide on this issue.

The Central Government has surplus funds with it over and above its expenditure nearly by 40 per cent. The Union Government spends 42 per cent of the combined expenditure of the Union and state governments and receives 60 per cent of the combined revenue receipts of the union and state governments. The states are chronically dependent on the central government for resource transfer for meeting their expenditure needs. The transfer of resources from the centre to the states needs to be made objective and transparent; making some states as special category states (hill states) in terms of tax concession package has hit some states like Punjab. They need to be compensated or added to this category of states. There is transparency for statutory transfers but arbitrariness is visible in case of non statutory transfers.

It has been observed that all states in North West India except Haryana are facing acute fiscal crisis and their debt-NSDP ratio is much higher than the cap (30.8 per cent) fixed by the TFC. This indicates that these states are spending much more than their revenue collection. These states need to examine thoroughly their fiscal management and resort to better tax compliance on one side and also need to economize on the expenditure side. Under present circumstances they need to avoid populist spending by rationalization of such spending. The path is shown by Haryana through better tax compliance. Punjab and other states need to really work hard for this.

There is a lot of scope to avoid fiscal collapse by better debt management. Most of the debt of these states is high cost debt from NSSF or loans from provident fund. The state governments can seek those sources of loans, which are cheap and have longer maturity period. The central government should increase its contribution to states in the form of loans and at concessional rates and save states from falling into debt trap through commercial borrowings.

These states have to take a combination of steps to make their fiscal system sustainable in the long run. They include transfer of some dynamic resources from the centre to the states, increasing the share of states in the pool of taxes and revenue collected by the Central Government, making tax compliance more effective and efficient in the states and also making debt management better and keeping it within the permissible limit. By making the states self-sustaining in the fiscal resources, an environment can be created for improved performance of functioning of the state governments to make federal system viable and successful.

References

Chakraborti, Lekha and Bhadra, Kaushik K. (2010), "Subnational Public Finance in Times of Recession", *Economic and Political Weekly,* August 28, Vol. XIV No. 35

Grewal, H.I.S (2010), *Genesis of Economic Scenario of Punjab in the context of Constitution of India,* Mimeograph, Chandigarh.

Handbook of Statistics on State Government Finances, 2010, Mumbai: Reserve Bank of India.

Handbook of Statistics on Indian Economy, 2009-10, Mumbai: Reserve Bank of India.

Rao, G. and Jena P.R. (2009). "Recent Trends in State Finances", in Govinda Rao & Anwar Shah (Eds.) *States' Fiscal Management and Regional Equity: An Overview,* New Delhi: Oxford University Press, M.

Rao, G. and Shah, A., Eds. (2009), *States' Fiscal Management and Regional Equity: An Overview,* New Delhi: Oxford University Press.

Sood, Atul (2010), "Shadow - boxing in Punjab on Government Finances", *Economic and Political Weekly,* June 12, Vol. XLV, No.24.

Srivastava, D.K. (2009), "Debt Management in States: Emerging Issues" in Govinda Rao & Anwar Shah (Eds.), ***States' Fiscal Management and Regional Equity: An Overview,*** New Delhi: Oxford University Press.

State Finances: A Study of Budgets 2009-10, Mumbai: Reserve Bank of India.

State Finances: A Study of Budgets 2008-09, Mumbai: Reserve Bank of India.

10

Public Expenditure on Education in the North-West Region during Reforms Period

Angrej Singh Gill & Jaswinder Singh Brar

Introduction

The role of public resources in the educational progress in any politico-administrative set up can not be over-emphasized. It has been well-established by economic theory, empirical constructs, and the actual development and growth experience of the present day educationally and economically advanced countries and regions. The public resources create the basic structure for the development of educational activities and programs and hence provide the needed dynamism to the educational sector in order to realize the various types of educational and social goals. The countries which somehow managed to provide the sufficient quantum of public funds to the education sector on sustainable basis under a well functional educational-delivery mechanism have realized not only higher growth rates but also plethora of other benefits in the form of improved general standards of living for the vast majority of populace.

The indispensability of public resources in the education sector is far more crucial in case of developing countries like

India in which population suffers from acute poverty, inequality, illiteracy, huge number of first-generation learners, child labor, unemployment, malnutrition, and multiple social and economic disparities and discriminations. The Constitution of India, since its adoption, very aptly demarcates a strong role for the state in the domain of education. The Article-45 in unequivocal terms states that 'the state shall endeavor to provide, within a period of ten years from the commencement of the constitution, for the free and compulsory education for all children until they complete the age of fourteen years'. To fulfill the constitutional mandate, the Government of India has constituted the First Education Commission, i.e. Kothari Commission during 1964–66 (GOI, 1966). It had recommended, by taking into account large number of parameters, transfer of resources worth six per cent of state income to education sector through the medium of public funds.

The education financing structure in the country witnessed major change with the placing of the education on the concurrent list through the Constitutional Amendment of 1976, which has made the education as the joint responsibility of centre and state governments. The provision of public resources to the extent as suggested by the Kothari Commission was subsequently upheld by the National Policy on Education (1968), New Education Policy (1986) and its revised version of 1992 (GOI, 1986 and 1991). It was decided to attain the target of transfer of six per cent of national income to the education from Eighth Five-Year Plan (1992–93 to 1996–97) onwards. Subsequently, it was again decided to realize the target at the end of Tenth Five-Year Plan (i. e. 2006–07). Importantly, the target of transfer of six per cent of income to education was also the part of the UPA government's Common Minimum Program (CMP) (Tilak, 2006).

The 86th Constitutional Amendment of 2002 led to the inclusion of a new Article 21-A in Part III of the Constitution which has made education as a Fundamental Right (GOI, 2008: 249). Consequently, Right of Children to Free and Compulsory Education Act, 2009 (known as RTE Act 2009) has made it mandatory for the state to provide Free and Compulsory

Education to all children of the 6 to 14 years of age (Jha and Parvati, 2010). The RTE Act 2009 received the Presidential assent on 26 August, 2009. The universalization of elementary education as envisaged under the new act requires the country to arrange huge amount of public resources to create the necessary infrastructure. It is held that the additional resource requirement under the RTE Act 2009 would be in the range of Rs. 1.78 lakh crore spread over a period of next five years (Mukual, 2009). Thus, attempts are under way towards providing adequate level of public funds to the education sector in order to fulfill the constitutional goals, provisions and mandates.

The education sector in the country experienced drastic changes during about the last one and half decades under the overall environment of national level economic reforms initiated in the country since 1991. The mutual roles of the state and market changed substantially under the processes of privatization, marketization, liberalization and globalization. Economic reforms have influenced the education delivery mechanism for all types and levels of education. The private suppliers of education entered in a big way by their own network of educational institutions. The strengthening of the public sector institutions slipped away from the top priority of the authorities. These institutions experienced the dwindling supply of public resources under the stabilization phase of economic reforms. The public authorities tried to control the overall level of public expenditure by adjusting the expenditure levels across or within the various sectors. Consequently, the budgetary back up to the education sector remained inadequate with adverse implications for the delivery of quality education.

The financing of the education at the level of the country and for the individual states have been analyzed in some studies (World Bank, 1986; Shiva and Babu, 1998; Qamar and Zahid, 2002; Duraisamy and Duraisamy, 2003; Gill et al 2008). But, no comprehensive study is available which examines the public expenditure on education by focusing exclusively upon the North-West Region as a separate category of analysis and more specifically during the reforms period. The North-West region constitutes about 11.33 per cent of the geographical area of the country (SAI, 2004-05); 6 per cent of the population as per Census of 2001; and 8.17 per cent of the aggregate Net State Domestic Product (GDP) of the country during 2004-05(GOI, 2008). Moreover, within this region, as per estimates pertaining to 2004-05, the per capita income differences were found to be on lower side among three states, viz. Punjab (Rs. 32,945), Haryana (Rs. 35,044) and Himachal Pradesh (Rs. 31,140). But, the per capita income of the Jammu & Kashmir was quite low, i.e. 18,630 (GOI, 2008). This region comprises the states with medium level of human resources development when viewed on the basis of Human Development Index (HDI). The HDI values during 2005 were in the following order: Punjab (0.679), Haryana (0.644) and Himachal Pradesh (0.681), and Jammu & Kashmir (0.601). The HDI value at the all India level stood at 0.612 (Wikipedia, 2010).

Though the number of educational institutions increased manifold in this region, yet the average level of educational and social indicators of the region are not in tune with the requirements of the modern day knowledge society. There prevail wide disparities across the states within the region so far Gross Enrollment Ratios (GER) is concerned. The Gross Enrollment Ratio refers to the percentage of enrollment in the particular stage of education to the estimated population in the relevant age group. While Himachal Pradesh stood apart from the rest and achieved higher levels of GER which is even comparable to the developed countries, the other states including the rich ones (viz. Punjab and Haryana) fared badly on such account. All the states of the North-West Region (except Himachal Pradesh) fared very badly so far the GER for classes IX-XII are concerned. The GER ranges between 35 per cent and 40 per cent (S.E.S., 2004-05). This may be contrasted with above 90 per cent GER in developed countries and between 40 per cent and 50 per cent in several developing countries (Tilak, 2008). In case of elementary education, the GER were in the following order: Punjab (72.57 per cent), Haryana (80.01 per cent), Himachal Pradesh (108.74 per cent), and Jammu & Kashmir (74.45 per cent). Interestingly, the GER in case of All

India was 93.54 per cent (GOI, 2008). The GER of more than hundred points indicates the presence of over-age or under-age or both categories of the students in the particular stage of education. Moreover, it is noteworthy that GER (for classes IX-XI) for some social groups like Scheduled Castes (SC), Scheduled Tribes (ST) and other marginalized sections is very low.

The balancing of educational progress across the genders is another serious challenge before any project of universalization of education. It is generally measured by the use of Gender Parity Index (GPI). The GPI values vary considerably across the states of the North-West Region. Gender Parity Index (GPI) is calculated by dividing girls' GER by boys' GER for a given level of education. It measures the progress towards gender-equity in education. GPI value equal to one indicate that there is no gender-disparity. The learning opportunities are available for girls equally to that of boys. GPI value less than one indicates that the girls are not getting the learning opportunity equal to that of boys. The GPI values for the state in case of secondary education of the North-West Region were as follows: Haryana (0.88 per cent), Himachal Pradesh (0.93 per cent), Jammu & Kashmir (0.81 per cent), and Punjab (1.02 per cent). It shows that the girls in all these states except Punjab have lesser access to secondary education as compared to boys (S.E.S., 2004-05). Moreover, with rapid growth of population in these states, it is quite natural that the demand for education would grow at a fast rate. Therefore, the North-West Region still have miles to go in generating adequate provision of education for the masses which involves huge budgetary resources.

The rest of the paper is divided into the following sections. Section II discusses the methodology, data sources, and overall framework of analysis. Section III examines the level of public expenditure on education by the North-West Region in the comparative perspective. It also provides the level of educational expenditure by the various states of the North-West Region. Section IV deals with the share of education budget in general budget and income. Section V provides in comparative terms the per-capita levels of education expenditures of the concerned states. Section VI provides the sectoral distribution of the educational expenditure for the various sub sectors of the education. Section VII provides the composition of educational expenditure under the various heads of spending. Section VIII provides the picture related to the growth of the various variables relevant to the public spending on education. Section IX summarizes the main findings of the study.

Methodology and Data Sources

The primary purpose of the study is to examine the various facets of public spending on education by the North-West Region. Therefore, the spending on education by any type of the private or non-government sources has not been included in the study in any way. It is worthwhile to state here that the non-government sources of finance to the education refer to any sort of income which accrues to the educational institutions other than from the direct government sources. It can take numerous forms such as student fees, other funds, voluntary donations, private endowments, rental incomes, etc. The government sources include the expenditure made by the union government, state governments and various local bodies for the development of the education. The study is restricted to the financing of education direct from the governmental sources which in specific way refer to public spending on education. The data sources provide information about public expenditure on education under two categories, viz. revenue account and capital account. The revenue account consists of the expenditure incurred on the items such as administration, direction, and inspection; salary bill of teaching and non-teaching staff; scholarships and student aid programs; maintenance of buildings, apparatus, equipment and furniture; laboratory consumables; games and sports; and teaching and learning material, etc. This type of expenditure has to be incurred every year in order to run the system and hence also called the recurring-expenditure. The capital account includes the expenditure made on the construction of buildings, libraries and laboratories; purchase of equipment and furniture, etc. It is also known as non- recurring expenditure. It actually represents the physical capital formation side of education system. The study has been limited to the expenditure on revenue account as it constituted the overwhelming proportion of the public educational expenditure on education. The share of capital account in the total public expenditure on education sector was just 1.25 per cent in the North-West Region during 2004-05.

The study is practically confined to four states of North-West Region. These are: Punjab, Haryana, Himachal Pradesh, and Jammu & Kashmir. The term North-West Region in the study refers to these four states only. It needs to be further cleared that the study is confined to that component of public educational expenditure which is incurred by the education departments of the respective states on the development of education in their concerned states. The study does not include the expenditure incurred by the government departments other than that of education department such as labour, agriculture, rural development or any other on the formal and on-job training of their respective manpower. The period chosen for analysis is fifteen financial years staring from 1990-91 to 2004-05. The figures for all the years show actual budgetary spending and not the budgeted or revised amount as mentioned in the various budgeted documents. It is important to note here that there prevails huge differences in the amount actually spent for a particular year and amount mentioned as budgeted or revised for that year. Thus, the real efforts made by a state for the development of education can be captured only by using the actual amount spent during the particular period.

The study analyses the public spending on education by North-West Region by comparing it with All States and that of the whole country. The term All States used in the study exclusively refers to all the states of the country. It does not include any of the Union Territory. It also does not include the expenditure made by the Union government on the development of education in the country. The public expenditure on education in absolute and relative terms has been analyzed both at the current and constant prices. The expenditure at nominal prices has been converted into real prices by using the implicit-NSDP deflator with base at 1993-94. This type of deflator is preferred because of two reasons: first, no separate education-specific deflators are available; and second, state-specific price indexes are also not prepared in the country. The annual trend growth rates for educational expenditure, NSDP, and state budgetary expenditures have been worked out by using the semi-log form. The study is based exclusively on the secondary sources of data. The various data sources used are: Analysis of Budgeted Expenditure on Education (MHRD); Selected Educational Statistics (MHRD); Statistical Abstract of India (GOI); Human Development Report (UNO); Census of India (GOI); and Economic Survey (GOI).

North-West Region

The comparison of the education budget of the North-West Region with that of the other states and all India threw some interesting tendencies as is clear from the data contained in Table 1. The total education budget, i.e. public spending on education, of the North-West Region increased consistently from Rs. 1279.33 crore during the Triennium Average (TA) (1990-93) to Rs. 5453.69 crore during TA (2002-05). The education budget of All States increased from Rs. 16,948.70 crore to Rs. 63188.77 crore during the corresponding trienniums. By this, the share of education budget of the North-West Region in the overall educational budget of all states of the country increased from 7.55 per cent to 8.63 per cent. The North-West Region has spent 16.09 per cent of its general budget on education during TA (1990-93), which declined over the study period and reached to 14.38 per cent during TA (2002-05). Similar situation comes up when education budget of the North-West Region is viewed against the collective income of the region. The proportionate share of education budget of the North-West Region in the overall income of the region declined from 4.73 per cent to 4.19 per cent during the chosen reference periods.

The another important tendency which emerges from the perusal of the data is that the proportionate spending on

Table 1
Education Budget of North-West Region versus India

	North-West Region			** All States*			
Year (T.A)	*Education Budget (Rs. Crore)*	*% age of General Budget*	*% age of Income (NSDP)*	*Education Budget (Rs. Crore)*	*% age of General Budget*	*% age of Income (NSDP)*	***India*
1990-93	1279.33 (7.55)	16.09	4.73	16948.70 (100)	18.90	6.63	3.69
1993-96	1773.52 (7.30)	13.78	4.34	24282.78 (100)	17.96	5.78	3.40
1996-99	3207.37 (8.67)	15.72	4.92	37000.80 (100)	18.14	5.76	3.45
1999-02	4680.61 (8.71)	16.08	5.09	53711.78 (100)	17.82	5.87	3.66
2002-05	5453.69 (8.63)	14.38	4.19	63188.77 (100)	15.95	5.14	3.92

Note: 1. The figures in brackets indicate the percentage share of the total.
2. *All states stand for the States only. It does not include the Uts and the Centre.
3. ** This column indicates the percentage share of the public spending on education by the India(all states, Uts, and Centre) as proportion of the National Income, i.e. NNP.
4. T. A. for Triennium Average of concerned financial years.

Source: 1. *Analysis of Budgeted Expenditure on Education*, MHRD, New Delhi (various issues).

education in terms of budget and income in the case of North-West Region was on the lower side as compared to that of the All States. However, the spending on education by the India as a whole (all States, Union Territories, and Centre government) hovers between 3.40 per cent and 3.92 per cent during study period. It declined almost continuously during first four tricnniums reported in the table but some how rose during the last triennium, i.e. 2002-05. Thus, the North-West Region has spent smaller proportion of its budget and income on education than that of all states. Furthermore, the education budget of the region experienced a decline in proportionate terms during the economic reform period. But, the proportionate share of the education budget of the region in the overall educational spending of All States registered some increase over the period. Hence, the education spending by the North-West Region was less than that of the constitutionally agreed required level of six per cent of the income level.

The proportionately lower level of spending resulted in lower level of per capita expenditure by the North-West Region than that of the all states. The per capita public spending of the North-West Region varied between 84.44 per cent and 85.94 per cent that of all states during first two trienniums of study, i.e. TA (1990-93) and TA (1993-96). But, the situation improved in the later period and the North-West Region catches up and in the end the per capita spending was slightly lower than that of all states. It was between 99.64 per cent and 99.96 per cent of the all states. But, it once again declined in the subsequent triennium to 97.88 per cent during TA (2002-05). It means the North-West Region supply resources to education with less degree of stability than that of the all states (Table 2).

Table 2
Per Capita Public Expenditure on Education; North-West Region versus India

(Revenue Account) (Rupee) (Current Prices) (T. A.)

Year (T. A.) 1	*North-West Region* 2	*India (Overall)* 3	*Gap (Rs.) 4=3-2*	*Percentage 2 of 3*
1990-93	268.67	318.16	49.49	84.44
1993-96	379.28	441.31	62.03	85.94
1996-99	614.42	635.75	21.33	96.64
1999-02	880.37	880.74	0.37	99.96
2002-05	1000.58	1022.21	21.63	97.88

Source: 1. *Analysis of Budgeted Expenditure on Education*, MHRD, New Delhi (various issues).

The overall educational spending and that of educational progress in any region has strong connections with the individual level of spending by its various constituents. In terms of absolute level of spending on education during all of the trienniums reported during the study period the state of Punjab occupies the highest position, followed by Haryana, Himachal Pradesh and Jammu & Kashmir (Table 3). In the total education budget of the North-West Region, the proportionate share of Punjab declined over the period from 44.55 per cent during

TA (1990-93) to 38.56 per cent during TA (2002-05). The proportionate share of Haryana by and large remained stable with small yearly variations. But, the respective shares of Himachal Pradesh and Jammu & Kashmir registered an increase. The share of Himachal Pradesh rose from 15.81 per cent TA (1990-93) to 17.61 per cent TA (2002-05). And, the proportionate share of Jammu & Kashmir rose from 10.92 per cent TA (1990-93) to 15.85 per cent TA (2002-05) (Table 4).

Table 3
Public Expenditure on Education in the North-West Region, 1990-91 to 2004-05

(Revenue Account) (Rs. Crore) (Current Prices) (T. A.)

State	*1990-93*	*1993-96*	*1996-99*	*1999-02*	*2002-05*
1. Punjab	569.98	685.15	1321.33	1761.00	2102.88
2. Haryana	367.37	537.55	922.70	1318.08	1526.12
3. Himachal Pradesh	202.27	308.26	534.88	820.84	960.55
4. Jammu & Kashmir	139.71	242.56	428.46	780.69	864.14
Total (1+4)	1279.33	1773.52	3207.37	4680.61	5453.69

Note: The figures in brackets indicate the percentage share of the total

Source: 1. *Analysis of Budgeted Expenditure on Education*, MHRD, New Delhi (various issues).
2. *Statistical Abstract of India*, GoI (various years).

Table 4
Percentage Distribution of Public Expenditure on Education in the North-West Region (1990-91 to 2004-05)

(Revenue Account) (Rs. Crore) (Current Prices) (T. A.)

State	*1990-93*	*1993-96*	*1996-99*	*1999-02*	*2002-05*
1. Punjab	44.55	38.63	41.20	37.62	38.56
2. Haryana	28.72	30.31	28.77	28.16	27.98
3. Himachal Pradesh	15.81	17.38	16.68	17.51	17.61
4. Jammu & Kashmir	10.92	13.68	13.36	16.68	15.85
Total (1+4)	100.00	100.00	100.00	100.00	100.00

Note: The figures in brackets indicate the percentage share of the total

Source: 1. *Analysis of Budgeted Expenditure on Education*, MHRD, New Delhi (various issues).
2. *Statistical Abstract of India*, GoI (various years).

Education, General Budget and Income

The educational priorities in any region become clear when the educational spending is being adjudged against the income and general budget of that region. The education budget of the North-West Region as proportion of the general budget of the region declined over the period with strong yearly variations (Table 5). The amazing fact which emerges is that the education budget as proportion of general budget declined in case of all of the states of the region. The proportionate decline was the least in case of Jammu & Kashmir and the highest in case of Punjab. For Punjab, it declined from 17.05 per cent TA (1990-93) of general budget to 12.94 per cent TA (2002-05), i.e. about 4.11 basis points. During the corresponding years, the decline in the case of the rest of the states was as follow: Haryana (1.73 basis points), Himachal Pradesh (0.93 basis points), and Jammu & Kashmir (0.08 basis points). But, the spending by Himachal Pradesh was continuously higher than that of the average of the region through out the study for every triennium reported. And, that of the Jammu & Kashmir was considerably lower than that of the regional-average during some trienniums to the extent of four per cent also. It means the presence of the Himachal Pradesh raised the regional-average and that of the Jammu & Kashmir has suppressed it.

The education budget of the North-West Region on an average registered a decline in proportionate terms in the overall income of the region (Table 6). It constituted 4.73 per cent of the income during TA (1990-93) and with ups and downs has attained the level of 4.19 per cent during TA (2002-05). It attained its level of 5.09 per cent during TA (1996-99). Interestingly, the proportionate share of education budget declined in case of all the states except Jammu & Kashmir. In case of Punjab, it declined from 3.29 per cent to 2.94 per cent; for Haryana from 3 per cent to 2.38 per cent; and for Himachal Pradesh from 7.90 per cent to 6.10 per cent from TA (1990-93) to TA (2002-05). Within the region, only Himachal Pradesh has continuously allocated more than six per cent of its state income to the education sector during all the trienniums. Jammu & Kashmir has allocated only once, viz. during TA (1999-02), more than six per cent of its income to the education sector.

Another interesting feature of the education budget of the region pertains to the lower proportionate share of the plan expenditure in the overall education budget. Plan expenditure is earmarked for the formulation of new programs and schemes. The non-plan expenditure is absorbed in the maintenance of existing activities. The share of plan expenditure hovered between 13.68 per cent and 21.99 per cent during the study period. Himachal Pradesh has allocated the highest proportion of its education budget on the plan account. It has increased continuously from about 22 per cent to 46 per cent from TA (1990-93) to TA (2002-05). Jammu & Kashmir too has allocated good proportion of its education budget through the plan account. The spending by Haryana through the plan account too was on the higher side for larger part of the study. But, Punjab, has by and large allocated smaller proportion of its budget through plan process. It was just 5.24 per cent during TA (2002-05). For this state, the education budget has become the function of non-plan spending only (Table 7).

Table 5
Public Expenditure on Education as a Proportion of General Budget of the North-West Region (1990-91 to 2004-05)

(Revenue Account) (Per Cent) (T.A.)

STATE/UT	*1990-93*	*1993-96*	*1996-99*	*1999-02*	*2002-05*
1. Punjab	17.05	13.11	17.98	15.26	12.94
2. Haryana	16.46	11.15	12.62	17.35	14.73
3. Himachal Pradesh	18.55	18.83	20.43	19.28	17.62
4. Jammu & Kashmir	12.31	12.01	11.86	12.42	12.23
Total	16.09	13.78	15.72	16.08	14.38

Source: Same as Table 1

Table 6
Public Expenditure on Education as Proportion of Income of the North-West Region

(Revenue Account) (Rs. Crore) (Current Prices) (T. A.)

STATE/UT	*1990-93*	*1993-96*	*1996-99*	*1999-02*	*2002-05*
1. Punjab	3.29	2.54	3.40	3.25	2.94
2. Haryana	3.00	2.78	3.03	3.05	2.38
3. Himachal Pradesh	7.90	7.20	7.81	7.58	6.10
4. Jammu & Kashmir	4.74	4.83	5.43	6.48	5.35
Total(1+4)	4.73	4.34	4.92	5.09	4.19

Note: The income data in case of Chandigarh is not available
Source: Same as Table 1

Table 7
Share of Education Budget (Plan) in Total Education Budget of North-West Region, 1990-91 to 2004-05

(Revenue Account)(Per Cent) (T.A.)

STATE/UT	*1990-93*	*1993-96*	*1996-99*	*1999-02*	*2002-05*
1. Punjab	3.40	14.29	12.27	11.64	5.24
2. Haryana	6.84	16.70	19.83	12.25	4.89
3. Himachal Pradesh	22.18	21.09	30.76	44.81	46.24
4. Jammu & Kashmir	22.03	16.67	15.59	19.06	19.14
Total	13.68	17.35	19.60	21.99	18.89

Source: Same as Table 1

Per-Capita Level

The ultimate and real picture of the availability of public educational spending emerges when educational budget is viewed on the basis of the per capita level at real prices. Such types of data are presented in Table 8. The perusal of the data shows that the per capita education budget of the region increased consistently from Rs. 322.85 [TA (1990-93)], to Rs. 460.55 [TA (1996-02)], and to Rs. 567.56 [TA (2002-05)]. It means the region on an average has provided more resources to the education in real terms. Such was the behavior in case of all the states but for Punjab. In case of Punjab, though the education budget on per capita basis in real terms in general increased but it also registered a decline during TA (1993-96). Moreover, the availability of education budget during TA (2002-05) was higher

Table 8
Per Capita Public Expenditure on Education in the North-West Region, 1990-91 to 2004-05

(Revenue Account) (Rupee) (T.A.) (Constant Prices)

STATE/UT	*1990-93*	*1993-96*	*1996-99*	*1999-02*	*2002-05*
1. Punjab	337.23	294.07	435.09	476.15	487.12
2. Haryana	267.86	281.14	359.26	412.54	406.28
3. Himachal Pradesh	469.48	519.81	696.73	885.18	890.30
4. Jammu & Kashmir	215.66	266.84	348.96	511.31	481.77
Total	322.85	341.54	460.55	570.21	567.56

Note: The current prices have been converted into constant prices by using WPI deflators with 1993-94 as base year

Source: Same as Table 1.

than that of its level during TA (1990-93) by the following order: Punjab (1.44 times); Haryana (1.52 times); Himachal Pradesh (1.90 times); and Jammu & Kashmir (2.23 times).

Sub-Sectoral Distribution

The distribution of the overall budget of the educational sector among the various sub-sectors of education highlights the priorities provided within the education (Tables 9, 10, 11, and 12). The North-West Region in overall allocates almost equal proportion of its general education budget to elementary and secondary education (about 40 per cent each). So far elementary education is concerned, Himachal Pradesh has allocated the highest proportion (between 54.02 per cent and 57.83 per cent); followed by Jammu & Kashmir, Haryana, and Punjab. Punjab has allocated the highest proportion to the secondary education.

Table 9
Percentage Share of Elementary Education in the Overall Education Budget of the State

	Punjab	*Haryana*	*Himachalh Prades*	*Jammu & Kashmir*	*North-West Region*
1990-93	31.63	45.02	54.02	45.50	40.53
1993-96	25.65	45.95	54.35	47.11	39.73
1996-99	29.84	46.13	56.03	48.22	41.35
1999-02	27.93	45.76	57.83	47.54	41.47
2002-05	26.14	48.05	55.75	47.45	40.86

Source: *Analysis of Budgeted Expenditure on Education*, MHRD, New Delhi (various issues).

Table 10
Percentage Share of Secondary Education in the Overall Education Budget of the State

	Punjab	*Haryana*	*Himachalh Prades*	*Jammu & Kashmir*	*North-West Region*
1990-93	50.65	35.65	33.75	36.40	42.12
1993-96	54.77	35.21	34.33	35.69	42.68
1996-99	55.76	38.18	31.69	36.70	44.14
1999-02	57.83	35.50	32.52	35.96	43.45
2002-05	59.61	34.96	35.21	38.33	45.04

Source: *Analysis of Budgeted Expenditure on Education*, MHRD, New Delhi (various issues).

The next in importance fall the university and higher education for all the states. Amazingly, the technical education has received the lowest proportion of the education budget in case of each and every state of the region.

Table 11
Percentage Share of University and Higher Education in the Overall Education Budget of the State

	Punjab	*Haryana*	*Himachalh Prades*	*Jammu & Kashmir*	*North-West Region*
1990-93	13.92	14.14	7.77	12.07	12.81
1993-96	15.41	14.20	7.37	11.02	13.05
1996-99	10.68	11.88	7.28	11.63	10.58
1999-02	11.36	14.27	7.53	11.98	11.61
2002-05	11.85	13.44	6.99	11.41	11.37

Source: *Analysis of Budgeted Expenditure on Education*, MHRD, New Delhi (various issues).

Table 12
Percentage Share of Technical Education in the Overall Education Budget of the State

	Punjab	*Haryana*	*Himachalh Prades*	*Jammu & Kashmir*	*North-West Region*
1990-93	2.50	3.24	1.37	3.40	2.63
1993-96	2.25	3.49	1.44	4.26	2.76
1996-99	2.74	2.81	1.66	2.66	2.57
1999-02	2.08	3.85	0.99	2.96	2.53
2002-05	1.57	2.89	0.75	2.28	1.91

Source: *Analysis of Budgeted Expenditure on Education*, MHRD, New Delhi (various issues).

Composition of Educational Budget

Another way of assessing the educational spending patterns comes from the analysis of the relative spending on the various types of educational activities and functions pertaining to the educational institutions in terms of ownership. From the Table 13, it is clear that the very small proportion has been used for the purpose of direction and administration in case of the three states reported here, i.e. Punjab, Haryana and Himachal Pradesh. The proportion was lowest in case of Punjab (0.78 per cent) and highest in case of Himachal Pradesh (3.04 per cent).

All of the three states were found to be spending more on government institutions. The highest being the Himachal Pradesh which has spent about 90 per cent of its education budget on government institutions. Punjab has spent 76.90 per cent and Haryana 78.28 per cent of their respective budgets on government institutions. A small proportion of Himachal Pradesh's education budget has been transferred to non-government private institutions in the form of various types of assistance. But, Punjab and Haryana has provided respectively 11.65 per cent and 16.66 per cent to the non-government private institutions.

Table 13
Functional Distribution of Education Budget, 2002-05 (Per cent)

Head	*Punjab*	*Haryana*	*Himachal Pradesh*
1. Direction & Administration	0.78	3.04	1.68
2. Spending on Government Institutions	76.90	78.25	90.30
3. Assistance to Non-Government Institutions	11.65	16.66	3.24
4. Others	10.67	2.05	4.78
Total	100.00	100.00	100.00

Note: Jammu & Kashmir is not included here because of data paucity.
Source: *Analysis of Budgeted Expenditure on Education*, MHRD, New Delhi (various issues).

Comparative Growth Rates

The differential growth in economic variables over a longer period results in the noticeable difference in the ultimate level of the various variables involved in the economic process. The economic variable which starts with small base but subject to high growth over the considerable period obtain very higher level and occupy strong presence in the system. During the reforms period from 1990-91 to 2004-05, in case of the North-West Region, the real prices based growth in the three variables under study (Table 14) were as follows: education budget (7.88 per cent), income (8.25 per cent), and general budget (6.52 per cent). It means the growth in educational budget was less than that of the state income and slightly more than that of general budget.

For states, the growth in education budget was found to be more than that of the respective general budget of the state in case of each and every state. The respective growth rates in case of education budget and general budgets for the studied states were as follow: Punjab (6.76 per cent and 6.45 per cent); Haryana (6.23 per cent and 2.18 per cent); Himachal Pradesh (7.73 per cent and 7.58 per cent); and Jammu & Kashmir (9.48 per cent and 9.04 per cent). The education budget recorded less growth than that of the state income in case of Haryana and Himachal Pradesh. And, it had recorded more growth than that of the state income in case of Punjab and Jammu & Kashmir. Thus, the education sector got more from the general budget for every state and the region as a whole.

Table 14
Growth of Public Spending on Education and Related Variables in North-West Region, Real Prices, Base 1993-94 (1990-91 to 2004-05)

State	*Education Budget*	*Income (NSDP)*	*General Budget*
1. Punjab	6.76	5.85	6.45
2. Haryana	6.23	8.16	2.18
3. Himachal Pradesh	7.73	9.88	7.58
4. Jammu & Kashmir	9.48	8.47	9.04
North-West Region	7.88	8.25	6.52

Note: The current prices have been converted into constant prices by using WPI deflators with 1993-94 as base year

Source: 1. *Analysis of Budgeted Expenditure on Education*, MHRD, New Delhi (various issues).
2. *Statistical Abstract of India*, GoI (various years).

Summing up

The foregoing analysis of availability of public resources to the education sector during the reform period highlights certain crucial trends and patterns pertaining to the public educational spending in the North-West Region of the country as a whole and separately for the four states analyzed under this region, i.e. Punjab, Haryana, Himachal Pradesh, and Jammu & Kashmir. The North-West Region has actually provided comparatively smaller proportion of its budget and income to education than that of all states of the country taken together.

The education budget of the region declined as proportion of the general budget and collective state incomes of the region during the period of economic reforms. The marginal improvement in the share of the educational budget of the region in the overall educational spending of all States was not sufficient enough to raise the proportionate levels of educational budget (i.e. education budget as proportion of general budget and income) as compared to that of all states. Even the per capita expenditure of the North-West Region was found to be on lower side than that of all states. In overall, the education spending by the North-West Region was less than that of the constitutionally agreed required norm of six per cent of the state income. Within the region, only Himachal Pradesh has continuously allocated more than six per cent of its state income to the education sector.

Out of the total educational budget of the region, the share of Punjab remained the largest through out. It was followed by Haryana, Himachal Pradesh and Jammu & Kashmir. But, the notice worthy fact is that the proportionate share of Punjab too registered a decline over the study period. And, that of Haryana by and large remained stable. But, the respective shares of Himachal Pradesh and Jammu & Kashmir registered somewhat increase. Further, the education budget of the North-West Region as proportion of the general budget of the region generally declined over the period. The amazing fact which emerges is that the education budget as proportion of general budget of the respective state declined in case of all of the states of the region. The proportionate decline was the least in case of Jammu & Kashmir and the highest in case of Punjab; the state which occupy the highest share of the education budget of the region in absolute terms. But, the spending by Himachal Pradesh was continuously higher than that of regional-average (i.e. education budget as proportion of general budget) through out the period of the study. And, that of the Jammu & Kashmir was considerably lower than that of the regional-average. The presence of the Himachal Pradesh in the region has raised the regional-average and that of the Jammu & Kashmir suppressed it. Himachal Pradesh, Jammu & Kashmir and Haryana have allocated higher proportion of their respective educational budgets through the plan account. But, Punjab has routed very smaller proportion of its budget through the plan process. The region on an average has provided more resources to the education as the per capita education budget of the region increased consistently in real terms.

The North-West Region in overall has allocated almost equal proportion of its general education budget to elementary and secondary education (about 40 per cent each). Himachal Pradesh has allocated the highest proportion of its educational budget to elementary education; followed by Jammu & Kashmir, Haryana, and Punjab. But, Punjab has allocated the highest proportion to the secondary education. The next in importance fall the university and higher education for all the states. Amazingly, the technical education has received the lowest proportion of the education budget in case of each and every state of the region. The three states, i.e. Punjab, Haryana and Himachal Pradesh have allocated very small share of their education budget under the heading direction and administration. All of the three states were found to be spending more on government institutions. A small proportion of Himachal Pradesh's education budget has been transferred to non-government private institutions in the form of various types of assistance. But, Punjab and Haryana has provided higher funds to the non-government private institutions.

The growth in educational budget of the region was less than that of the collective incomes of the concerned states and slightly more than that of their general budgets during the study period. Further, the growth in education budget was found to be more than that of the respective general budget of the state in case of each and every state. The education budget recorded less growth than that of the state income in case of Haryana and Himachal Pradesh. And, it had recorded more growth than that of the state income in case of Punjab and Jammu & Kashmir.

The providing of resources to education depends upon the complex interplay of large number of factors which have deep connection with the politico, economic and social processes under way in that region. These processes have crucial role in the formation of the state priorities which have been reflected through the budgetary spending. The states which have consistently provided more resources to education sector through public funds along with better resources for direction, administration and plan account have definitely performed better on the educational front as is the case of Himachal Pradesh. However, it is to be noted that even in case of this state, there has been considerable decline in the share of public spending on education as proportion of state income, though technically it remained above the six per cent norm during the reform period.

In overall, the supply of public funds to the education sector in the region remained restrictive and inadequate. Interestingly, all of it happened even in the situation of adoption of many constitutional measures and policy pronouncements which stand for enhanced supply of public resources to the education sector. It may be having some deep linkages with the grossly changed educational scenario in the region as is the case in the country as a whole. The emergence of private education system in the region on a large scale has considerably reduced the interest of the elite sections of society in the public institutions. It has reduced the collective and systematic pressure on the governments to provide more to the education sector along with better governance of public educational institutions in order to improve the productivity of public resources which goes to education sector. The passing of the RTE act has now constitutionally enabled the stakeholders in the public education institutions along with civil society organizations for making available more resources to the education sector. Thus, public spending on education in the region need correction when viewed and analyzed in the context of other states, spending norms, educational goals, and requirements of human capital formation.

References

Duraisamy, P. and M. Duraisamy (2003), 'Public Expenditure and Grants-in-Aid for Secondary Education in Tamil Nadu,' *Journal of Educational Planning and Administration,* Vol. 17, No. 4, pp. 449-80.

Gill, S.S., Sukhwinder Singh and J.S. Brar (2008), 'Punjab: Financing of Secondary Education: Sources, Patterns and Emerging Issues' in J.B.G. Tilak (ed.) *Financing of Secondary Education in India: Grants-in-Aid Policies and Practices in States,* Shipra Publications, New Delhi.

GOI (1966), *Report of Education (Kothari) Commission, 1964-66,* New Delhi.

GOI (1986), *National Policy on Education, 1986,* Government of India, New Delhi/

GOI (1991), *Report of the Committee for Review of National Policy on Education, 1986 (Rama Moorthy Committee),* Government of India, New Delhi

GOI (2005), *Report of the CABE Committee on Financing of Higher Education and Technical Education,* Central Advisory Board of Education, Ministry of Human Resource Development, Government of India, New Delhi, *http://www.education.nic.in*

GOI (2008), *Economic Survey 2007-08,* Government of India, Oxford University Press, New Delhi.

Jha Parveen and Pooja Parvati (2010), Right to Education Act 2009: Critical Gaps and Challenges, *Economic and Political Weekly,* Vol. XLV, No. 13, pp.20-23.

Mukual, Akshaya (2009), Cost of right to Education: Rs. 1.78 lakh crore, *Times of India,* 29th September.

Qamar, F. and M. Zahid (2002), *Financing of Secondary Education in Delhi: Principles and Practices of Grants-in-Aid System,* National University of Educational Planning and Administration (NUEPA), New Delhi.

SAI (2004-05), *Statistical Abstract of India,* Government of India, New Delhi

SES (2004-05), *Selected Educational Statistics,* Ministry of Human Resource Development, New Delhi

Shiva, R. and M. Babu (1998), *Financing of Secondary Education in Andhra Pradesh,* paper presented in National Conference on Management of School Education, Organized by National Institute of Educational Planning and Administration, New Delhi.

Tilak, JBG (2006): On Allocating Six Per cent of GDP to Education, *Economic and Political Weekly,* Vol. XLI , No. 7 , pp. 613-618.

Tilak, J.B.G. (2008), *Financing of Secondary Education in India: Grants-in-Aid Policies and Practices in States,* (Editor's Introduction: P. XV), Shipra Publications, New Delhi,

Wikipedia (2010), *Wikipedia,* down loaded on 22 November, 2010.

World Bank (1986), *Financing of Secondary Education in Developing Countries,* World Bank, Washington, D.C.

11

Microfinance In North-West India

R. K. Mahajan & Deepty Bansal

Introduction

Microfinance programme has emerged as an innovative programme of generating self-employment and alleviating poverty. The unique feature of microfinance programme is that it focuses on women for development. In this programme micro-loans are provided to the poor people through the Self-help Group-Bank Linkage Model (SHG-BLM) and Microfinance Institution (MFI) Model. The SHG-BLM has been developed by NABARD in 1992. In this model the informal self-help groups (SHGs) are credit linked with the formal banking system. In the MFI model, the MFIs provide financial services to the individuals or to the groups like SHGs, Joint Liability Groups (JLGs) and Grameen groups. However, the SHG- Bank Linkage Model is widely prevalent throughout the country.

The success of this programme is globally accepted. The present paper is a modest attempt to find out the impact of microfinance programme, its problems/challenges and policy implications to make this programme effective in rural Punjab.

The specific objectives of the study are:

(1) To find the achievements of microfinance programme in terms of employment generation, poverty alleviation and women empowerment.

(2) To study the problems and challenges to the programme.

(3) To give some suggestions to make this programme effective.

The study is divided into four sections. Section-I is related with the methodology and the status of microfinance in Punjab. The section-II deals with the impact of microfinance programme on employment, poverty and women empowerment. Section-III is represents the challenges and problems of microfinance programme. Section-IV incorporates some policy implications.

SECTION-I

Methodology

The main target of the microfinance programme is the rural poor women. A primary study has been conducted among two types of households: participants and non-participants. Participants are the members of the SHGs who have been benefited from the scheme and have received the bank loans (credit linked) up to March 2006. Non-participants are those women who have newly joined this programme through new SHGs and had not availed the bank loan till the time of survey. Multistage random sampling method is used for collecting the primary data. In the first stage, Punjab is agro-climatically divided into three regions: Alluvial Plains, Hilly Sub-Mountainous Strip and Sandy Region or South Western Region. From these regions Jalandhar, Hoshiarpur and Bathinda districts are selected, respectively. In the second stage, three blocks from each of these districts are selected where there are a large number of credit linked SHGs. In the third stage, five per cent of the credit linked SHGs in the three districts are selected. As a result 30, 25 and 9 SHGs are selected from Jalandhar, Hoshiarpur and Bathinda districts respectively. These SHGs are taken proportionately from the selected blocks according to their total number in that block. In the last stage, three members from each SHG are selected randomly and interviewed. In this way, 90, 74 and 26 participants are surveyed from the selected blocks of Jalandhar, Hoshiarpur and Bathinda districts respectively. Matching number of non-participants, i.e., 190 are also selected from the same areas with the same method. The data is collected with the help of a pre-tested schedule.

Status of Microfinance in Punjab

Microfinance programme in Punjab is relatively a new concept. The programme was started in India in the year 1992 but in Punjab it was started in 1998-99 and it gained momentum only after the year 2000. In Punjab, microfinance is provided only through the SHG-BLP and there is no role of MFIs. SHGs are formed by bank officials, aanganwadi workers, social workers and by the NGOs. These groups are provided loans by the formal financial institutions.

Table 1 shows the number of credit linked SHGs and the bank loan disbursed in Punjab. It is found that 3091 SHGs are provided about 146 million of bank loans up to March 2005 and the number of credit linked SHGs increased to 8965 with the bank loan of 620 million up to March 2008. This progress of the programme in Punjab is very limited as compared to many other states in India.

Table 1
Number of SHGs Linked to Banks and the Amount of Bank Loan in Punjab

Year	*Number of SHGs*	*% Growth*	*Bank loans (in million Rs.)*	*% Growth*	*Per SHG Loan*	*% Growth*
Up to March 2005	3091	–	145.76	–	47156	–
March 2006	4561	47.56	238.86	64.05	52370	11.06
March 2007	6454	41.50	356.60	49.29	55252	5.50
March 2008	8965	38.91	620.00	73.86	69157	25.17

Source: NABARD annual reports

SECTION-II

Impact of Microfinance Programme

The primary data collected from 380 participants and non-participants of the programme is used to measure the impact of microfinance programme in generating self-employment opportunities, eradicating poverty by generating income and in the empowerment of women participants.

Impact of Microfinance on Employment

Analysis of primary data reveals that the loans provided under microfinance programme are mainly utilised for productive purposes. The programme has diversified the economic activities of the programme participants. It is observed that along with the traditional economic activities as rearing milch animals, stitching and embroidery etc. the participants have also started manufacturing and small business activities like petty shops, dairy, garland making, rope making, surf making, running STD/PCOs etc.

These activities have helped the programme participants to increase their level of employment. The employment status of the participants before and after joining this programme (pre-SHG and post-SHG) is compared in Table 2. A perusal of the table provides that before joining the microfinance programme 49 per cent of the total participants were employed and 51 per cent were unemployed. But microfinance programme changed this scenario. The participants started utilising the loan to adopt economic activities. As a result, 80 per cent of the participants are employed in post-SHG situation. Hence, 31 per cent of the participants who were unemployed in pre-SHG situation gained employment.

In order to measure the impact of programme, participants are also compared with the non participants. The employment status of non-participants is almost similar to the employment status of the participants in their pre-SHG situation. The table shows that 48 per cent of the non-participants are employed and 52 per cent are unemployed.

Table 2
Employment Status of the Participants and Non-Participants

Status of Employment	*Participants*								*Non-participants*			
	Pre-SHG				*Post-SHG*							
	Jal.	*Hsp.*	*Bti.*	*Pun.*	*Jal.*	*Hsp.*	*Bti.*	*Pun.*	*Jal.*	*Hsp.*	*Bti.*	*Pun.*
Employed	38	44	12	94	70	61	21	152	44	31	17	92
	(42)	(59)	(46)	(49)	(78)	(81)	(81)	(80)	(49)	(42)	(65)	(48)
Unemployed	52	30	14	96	20	13	05	38	46	43	09	98
	(58)	(41)	(54)	(51)	(22)	(19)	(19)	(20)	(51)	(58)	(35)	(52)
Total	90	74	26	190	90	74	26	190	90	74	26	190
	(100)	(100)	(100)	(100)	(100)	(100)	(100)	(100)	(100)	(100)	(100)	(100)

Source: Field survey 2008.

Note: The figures given in parentheses indicate percentages of participants and non-participants. The value of Chi-square (χ^2) is 22.22 between participants and non-participants. The table values at 5 per cent and 1 per cent with 1 degree of freedom are 3.84 and 6.63 respectively.

Chi-square (χ^2) test shows the significant difference among the participants and non-participants regarding their level of employment.

The study also shows that microfinance programme not only increases the number of persons employed but also helped in increasing the number of employment days. Table-3 shows the employment of the respondents measured in person days per annum. It is found that participants were employed for 80 person days before joining the microfinance programme. But after receiving the benefits of the programme the participants are employed for an average 160 person days. Thus, microfinance programme has generated 80 additional days of employment per annum for the programme participants. The table also shows the comparison of participants with the non-participants in terms of their employment status. It is found that the non-participants are employed for just 78 days per annum as compared to 160 days for the participants. The table reveals that there is 100 per cent increase in employment for the programme participants in their post-SHG situation over the pre-SHG situation, while there is 105 per cent increase in employment days for the programme participants as compared to the non-participants.

Table 3
Employment Generated in Person Days per Annum

	Employment Status			*Increase in Employment Days*	
	Participants				
District	*Pre-SHG*	*Post-SHG*	*Non-participants*	*Pre- and Post- SHG Analysis*	*Participants Non-participants Analysis*
Jalandhar	79	163	85	84 (106)	78 (92)
Hoshiarpur	83	153	61	70 (84)	92 (151)
Bathinda	73	166	99	93 (127)	67 (68)
Punjab	80	160	78	80 (100)	82 (105)

Source: Field survey 2008.
Note: The figures given in parentheses indicate percentage increase in employment.

Determinants of Employment (Regression Analysis)

Simple linear regression equation is fitted to the field data in order to determine the factors affecting the employment level of the participants. The independent variables selected for this purpose are: age of the participant, education level of the participant, age of the SHG, number of group loans received, amount of group loans used for productive purposes, employment days of the participants in pre-SHG situation, and the level of household income. Employment days in post-SHG situation are taken as dependent variable. The coefficients of employment are calculated with the help of following linear equation:

$$EMP = b_0 + b_1 AGE + b_2 EDU + b_3 GAGE + b_4 NLON + b_5 LROD + b_6 EPSG + b_7 TINCM$$

Where :

EMP = Employment in post-SHG in person days

AG = Age of the participant in years

EDU = Education level of the participant

GAGE = SHG age for maturity of the group

NLON = Number of times loan taken

LROD = Amount of loan used for productive purpose in Rs.

EPSG = Employment in Pre-SHG

TINCM = Total household income in Rs.

The results of this regression equation are shown in Table 4. A perusal of the table provides that the coefficients of age and education level of the participants appear in the negative. It may be due to the fact that as the age of participants increases, they spend less time for work and more time for other jobs or leisure. Similarly, increase in education level of the participants has led to limited involvement in self-employment activity. However, both these variables are not statistically significant. Maturity of the group, i.e., group age is considered to be very important variable for increasing employment. The regression coefficient of group age is high and significant which shows that maturity of an SHG leads to significant addition in the employment. The coefficient of number of group loans received shows that the large number of group loans leads to high employment level but this coefficient is also not statistically significant.

Table 4
Results of Regression Analysis

	Standardised Coefficients			
Variables	*Jalandhar*	*Hoshiarpur*	*Bathinda*	*Punjab*
Constant	(0.373)	(0.197)	(1.339)	(1.405)
Age of the participants	-0.098	-0.012	0.017	-0.041
	(-1.330)	(-0.159)	(0.170)	(-0.839)
Education level of the	-0.063	0.013	-0.070	-0.041
participants	(-0.810)	(0.181)	(-0.645)	(-0.808)
Maturity of the Group	0.317	0.116	0.147	0.198
	(4.382)*	(1.603)	(1.273)	(4.038)*
Number of times loan	0.120	0.001	-0.176	0.002
taken	(1.567)	(0.011)	(-1.658)	(0.040)
Amount of loan used for	0.294	0.324	0.392	0.337
productive purposes	(3.888)*	(4.964)*	(4.109)*	(7.212)*
Employment in	0.543	0.707	0.788	0.597
pre-SHG	(7.611)*	(9.775)*	(6.936)*	(12.80)*
Total household Income	0.097	0.183	-0.195	0.105
	(1.375)	(2.488)**	(-1.524)	(2.188)**
R^2	0.656	0.751	0.862	0.647

* Significant at 1 per cent level. ** Significant at 5 per cent level.

Source: Own calculation from field survey data 2008.

Note: The figures given in parentheses indicate t-values.

The amount of loans utilised for productive purposes is significantly influencing the employment of the participants. The amount of loans utilised for starting new ventures or expanding the existing business contribute positively towards the employment generation. The employment of participants in the pre-microfinance is also taken as a variable. The coefficient for this variable is positive, very high and statistically significant showing that the participants who are already employed in pre-SHG situation are getting more benefits of microfinance regarding employment. In other words, it may be interpreted that well-established participants have more benefits of microfinance than those who are new entrants in any economic activity. Family income of the participants is also positively related to the level of employment. The value of this coefficient is positive and significant which shows that the sound financial position of the family contributes to increase the level of employment. The magnitude of R^2 is 0.647 for Punjab, which shows that the regression equation explains about 65 per cent of the total variations.

Impact of Microfinance Programme on Poverty

Poverty is the lack of basic minimum necessities such as food, clothing, water, and shelter needed for proper living. In this study impact on poverty is mainly measured through changes in income of the programme beneficiaries. Analysis of primary data shows that microfinance programme has improved the level of income of the programme participants and has resulted in alleviating poverty. Table 5 provides that the average income of the participants is Rs. 1,725 per month in post-SHG as compared to only Rs. 718 per month in pre-SHG situation, i.e., 2.5 times increases in income in post-SHG over the pre-SHG situation. The income of the participants has been significantly higher as compared to non-participants. It is also found that the average income of non-participants is just Rs. 638 per month as compared to Rs. 1,725 per month for the participants. It

Table 5
Income of the Participants and Non-Participants Per Month

	Average Income (in Rs.)			*Increment in income*	
	Participants				
District	*Pre-SHG*	*Post-SHG*	*Non-participants*	*Pre- and Post- SHG Analysis*	*Participants Non-participants Analysis*
Jalandhar	657	1,546	646	889 (135)	900 (139)
Hoshiarpur	772	1,915	573	1,143 (148)	1,342 (234)
Bathinda	773	1,804	799	1,031 (133)	1,005 (131)
Punjab	718	1,725	638	1,007 (140)	1,087 (170)

Source: Field survey 2008.
Note: The figures given in parentheses indicate percentage increase in income.

shows that the income of the participants has increased substantially. The average income of the participants is 2.7 times more than the average income of non-participants.

Composite Poverty Index

The overall impact of microfinance programme on various dimensions of poverty has been measured by preparing a Composite Poverty Index (CPI). For this purpose, 10 score based socio-economic parameters have been identified. These indicators are almost similar to the 13 indicators, recommended by the Expert Group constituted by the Ministry of Rural Development for BPL census for 10th Five-Year Plan. However, some of these 13 indicators have been omitted/modified in the present study according to the state/field conditions. These ten indicators include: per capita household income per month, major source of household income, per capita consumption expenditure per month, highest education level of the household, condition of house, source of drinking water, cooking fuel used, basic household amenities, ownership of consumer durables and value of land owned. These indicators are assigned arbitrary scores between 0-4 as shown in Appendix-1. Thus, the sum of scores of these 10 indicators ranges between 0-40. The participants and non-participants who scored between 0-10 are classified as extreme poor. Similarly, the scores between 11-20, 21-30 and 31-40 are classified as moderate poor, threshold non-poor and non-poor respectively. The results of this poverty index are shown in Table 6.

Table 6
Scores of Composite Poverty Index

Category	*Score*	*Number of Participants*	*Number of Non-participants*
Extreme Poor	0-10	01 (<1)	02 (01)
Moderate Poor	11-20	63 (33)	86 (45)
Threshold Non-poor	21-30	89 (47)	80 (42)
Non-poor	31-40	37 (19)	22 (12)
Total		190 (100)	190 (100)

Source: Field survey 2008.
Note: The figures given in parentheses indicate percentage of participants and non-participants.

A perusal of the table shows that a negligible percentage of both participant and non-participant households are in the extreme poor category. Thirty-three per cent of the participants and 45 per cent of the non-participants are moderate poor and 47 per cent of the participants and 42 per cent of the non-participants are threshold non-poor. Nineteen per cent of the participants and 12 per cent of the non-participants are non-poor. Thus, it may be said that microfinance programme has benefited the moderate poor and they have uplifted to the non-poor categories. This result shows that the medium poor people are the actual beneficiaries of the microfinance programme.

Determinants of Poverty (Regression Analysis)

In order to determine the factors affecting the poverty level of participant households, simple linear regression equation is fitted to the field data. The independent variables selected for this purpose are group maturity, amount of group loans used for productive purposes, household members, household income and highest level of education in the family. Poverty index is taken as a dependent variable. The coefficients of poverty determinants are calculated with the help of the following linear equation:

$$CPI = b_0 + b_1\, G\_AGE + b_2\, LOAN\_PROD + b_3\, HH\_MEM + b_4\, HH\_INCOM + b_5\, HL\_EDU$$

Where :

CPI	=	Composite poverty index
G_AGE	=	Group age shows maturity of the group in years
LOAN_PROD	=	Amount of loan used for productive purposes in Rs.
HH_MEM	=	Total number of household members
HH_INCOM	=	Household income in Rs.
HL_EDU	=	Highest level of education in the family.

The results of regression equation are shown in Table 7. A perusal of the table shows that the maturity of group leads to lower levels of poverty. It is already found in the previous discussion that as the group matures, the participants become more economically empowered. The value of this coefficient is significant. The variable of loan amount used for productive purposes is positively influencing the poverty index but this is not very significant.

Table 7
Results of Regression Analysis

	Standardised Coefficients			
Variables	*Jalandhar*	*Hoshiarpur*	*Bathinda*	*Punjab*
(Constant)	(7.209)	(5.747)	(5.053)	(9.751)
Group age	0.129	0.013	0.100	0.090
	(1.896)***	(0.151)	(0.884)	(1.892)***
Group loans used for productive purposes	0.010	0.028	-0.085	0.000
	(0.138)	(0.333)	(-0.907)	(0.011)
Number of household members	-0.276	-0.196	-0.452	-0.234
	(-4.038)*	(-2.411)**	(-3.992)*	(-4.974)*
Household income	0.504	0.569	0.886	0.575
	(7.385)*	(6.286)*	(6.414)*	(11.482)*
Highest level of education in the HH	0.499	0.296	0.265	0.374
	(6.929)*	(3.372)*	(2.288)**	(7.442)*
R^2	0.862	0.841	0.876	0.628

* Significant at 1 per cent level. ** Significant at 5 per cent level.
*** Significant at 6 per cent level.

The table shows that the coefficient of household members is negatively related with the value of poverty index. This explains that higher number of family members reduce the score of poverty index, which indicated a greater incidence of poverty. The levels of education and household income are very significantly influencing the poverty level of the participants. This shows that higher level of education leads to lower level of poverty, and the participants with higher level of household income can afford better living standards. The magnitude of R^2 is 0.628 for Punjab, which shows that the regression equation explains about 63 per cent of the total variations.

Impact of Microfinance on Women Empowerment

Women empowerment is a multidimensional process of improvement in the status and abilities of women. The present study takes into consideration twenty-one indicators of women empowerment under four domains which measure economic; socio-cultural and familial; political; and education, skill and training empowerment.

In order to quantify the level of women empowerment a Composite Empowerment Index (CEI) is prepared. The indicators influencing women empowerment are assigned arbitrary scores as shown in Appendix-II and then the scores of these indicators are added together. The respondents whose total score ranges between 0-20 are classified as less empowered. The respondents who score between 21-30, 31-40 and 41-50 are classified as medium, high and very high empowered respectively. Punjab is a prosperous state; and women residents of this state are relatively more empowered as compared to their counterparts living in other states. So, index score of 20 is assumed to be the minimum expected score from the respondents surveyed. The results of CEI are exhibited in Table 8.

Table 8

Composite Empowerment Index of Participants and Non-participants

Level of Empowerment	*CEI Score*	*Number of Participants*	*Number of Non-participants*
Very high empowered	(41–50)	11 (06)	01 (01)
High empowered	(31–40)	69 (36)	12 (06)
Medium empowered	(21–30)	79 (42)	79 (41)
Less empowered	(0–20)	31 (16)	98 (52)
Total		190 (100)	190 (100)

Source: Field survey 2008.

Note: The figures given in parentheses indicate percentages of participants and non-participants.

Chi-square (χ^2) = 44.07. Table values at 5% and 1% with 3 d.f. = 7.81 and 11.3 respectively.

A perusal of the table provides that only six per cent of the participants and one percent of the non-participants are found to be very high empowered. Thirty-six per cent of the participants are high empowered, whereas this percentage in the case of non-participants is just 6 per cent. Forty-two per cent of the participants and 41 per cent of the non-participants fall in the medium empowered category. However, 16 per cent of the participants and 52 per cent of the non-participants fall in the less empowered category. The Chi-square (χ^2) test also shows very significant differences between the level of empowerment of the participants and non-participants.

Regression Analysis

The experiences of the field survey and the review of literature give an idea that maturity of the SHGs, amount of group loans used for income generating activities, age of the participants, their level of education, level of employment, household income and their confidence in moving out of their houses may be the significant determinants of empowerment of the programme participants. The present study also finds out the impact of these variables on the level of women empowerment. A multiple linear regression is used to statistically measure the impact of all these determinants on the level of Composite Empowerment Index (CEI). The following regression equation is used to measure the effect of key indicators on CEI.

$$CEI = b_0 + b_1 AGE + b_2 EDU + b_3 GAGE + b_4 PLOAN + b_5 EMPL + b_6 HHIN + b_7 MOBTY$$

Where :

CEI	=	Composite empowerment index
AGE	=	Age of the participant in years
EDU	=	Education level of the participant
GAGE	=	Group age sows maturity of the group
PLOAN	=	Amount of loan used for productive purposes
EMPL	=	Employment in person days in Post SHG
HHIN	=	Household income of the participant
MOBTY	=	Level of mobility of the participant.

Table 9 highlights the coefficients of these variables. The regression results in the table show that all the coefficients have positive values except variables of age and loan used for productive purposes in Bathinda. The coefficients of regression variables, e.g. education, group age, household income, employment, amount of loans used for productive purposes and spatial mobility of the participants are playing an important and significant role in women empowerment. The magnitude of R^2 is 0.847 for Punjab, which shows that the regression equation explains about 85 per cent of the total variations.

Table 9
Results of Regression Analysis

	Standardised Coefficients			
Variables	*Jalandhar*	*Hoshiarpur*	*Bathinda*	*Punjab*
Constant	(1.555)	(0.154)	(2.671)	(2.438)
AGE	0.072	0.175	-0.172	0.053
	(1.537)	(3.002)*	(1.941)	(1.620)
EDU	0.446	0.390	0.218	0.379
	(9.007)*	(6.370)*	(2.070)**	(10.781)*
GAGE	0.069	0.175	0.136	0.117
	(1.385)	(2.919)*	(0.191)	(3.473)*
PROLOAN	0.055	0.085	-0.011	0.069
	(1.175)	(1.564)	(0.097)	(2.142)**
EMPL	0.439	0.438	0.418	0.420
	(8.199)*	(6.999)*	(3.690)*	(11.878)*
HHINC	0.117	0.031	0.157	0.083
	(2.550)**	(0.546)	(1.324)	(2.610)*
MOBTY	0.379	0.299	0.383	0.383
	(8.716)*	(5.358)*	(3.521)*	(12.021)*
R^2	0.862	0.841	0.876	0.847

* Significant at 1 per cent level. ** Significant at 5 per cent level.

Source: Field survey 2008. Note: The figures given in parentheses indicate t-values.

SECTION- III

Challenges to Microfinance Programme

No doubt, microfinance programme has shown impressive achievements, but there are many problems/challenges associated with this programme. Some of the main problems have been discussed in the following paragraphs.

Regional Disparity

The region-wise spread of microfinance programme under 'Self Help Group- Bank Linkage Model' (SHG-BLM) and MFI models has been depicted in Table 10.

Table 10
Region-wise Spread of Microfinance Programme (up to 2008)

Region	*Cumulative Number of SHGs*	*Number of SHG Members*	*Number of MFI Clients*	*Total Microfinance Clients*
Northern Region	2,30,740	29,99,620	1,13,102	31,12,722
	(6.63)	(6.63)	(0.80)	(5.25)
Punjab	8965	116545	Nil	116545
	(0.26)	(0.26)		(0.20)
North Eastern Region	1,19,857	15,58,141	1,75,589	17,33,730
	(3.45)	(3.45)	(1.25)	(2.92)
Eastern Region	6,72,201	87,38,613	34,75,622	1,22,14,235
	(19.33)	(19.33)	(24.70)	(20.60)
Central Region	4,05,707	52,74,191	10,14,202	62,88,393
	(11.67)	(11.67)	(7.21)	(10.61)
Western Region	3,74,561	48,69,293	15,85,681	64,54,974
	(10.77)	(10.77)	(11.27)	(10.89)
Southern Region	16,74,811	2,17,72,543	77,04,449	2,94,76,992
	(48.15)	(48.15)	(54.77)	(49.73)
Total	34,77,965	4,52,13,545	1,40,68,645	5,92,82,190
	(100)	(100)	(100)	(100)

Source: Srinivasan (2009)
Note: The figures given in parentheses indicate percentages of SHGs and microfinance members.

The table shows that the programme is mainly concentrated in the southern region and spread of the programme is limited in the north, north-eastern and western regions of the country. Out of the total microfinance outreach in India only 5.25 per cent and 2.92 per cent of the clients belong to north and north-eastern region, respectively. In the table the spread of the microfinance programme is shown separately for the Punjab state. The table shows that the programme outreach is very limited in Punjab and there are just 0.2 per cent of the total microfinance clients of India. The table also shows that in Punjab the microfinance programme is expanded only through the SHG-BLM and there are no MFI clients.

Penetration of Microfinance

The present study also analyses the progress of the microfinance programme in Punjab vis-à-vis India. For this purpose, a

Microfinance Penetration Index (MPI) and a Microfinance Poverty Penetration Index (MPPI) have been calculated. MPI measures the population outreach and MPPI measures the poverty outreach of microfinance in the state in comparison to the whole country. MPI is calculated by dividing the percentage share of the state in the total microfinance outreach in India with the percentage share of the state in the total population of India. MPPI is calculated by dividing the percentage share of the state in total microfinance outreach with the percentage share of the poor population. If the value of index is equal to 1, it indicates that the microfinance outreach is proportional to the population and poverty outreach in the country. But the score less than 1, shows the poorer performance of the state in the population and poverty outreach. Table-11 shows that the calculated values of MPI and MPPI for Punjab are 0.09 and 0.28 respectively. These low values show that in Punjab the penetration of microfinance programme is very less in terms of population outreach as well as poverty outreach as compared to the country as a whole.

Table 11
Calculation of MPI and MPPI for Punjab

Particulars	*India*	*Punjab*
Number of People Covered Under Microfinance up to March 2008	5,92,82,190	1,16,545
Percentage Share of Microfinance Coverage (I)	100	0.20
Total Population ('000)	11,01,318	25,839
Percentage Share of Population (II)	100	2.35
Number of Poor People (Lakh)	3,017	21.63
Percentage Share of Poor Population (III)	100	0.72
Value of MPI (I/II)	1	0.09
Value of MPPI (I/III)	1	0.28

Source: Calculated on the basis of secondary data up to March 2008.

Table 12 shows the ranking of some of the states on the basis of MPI and MPPI. The table shows that Andhra Pradesh, Tamil Nadu, Karnataka, Kerala, Orissa and Himachal Pradesh find a place among the top 5, while the states such as Jammu & Kashmir, Punjab, Haryana, Bihar, Gujarat, Madhya Pradesh and Jharkhand have very low penetration of microfinance with the index score being 0.35 or less. Therefore, there is a need for some innovative measures to be undertaken to enhance the coverage of microfinance programme in these states.

Table 12
Ranking of Select States Based on MPI and MPPI

Name of the State	*MPI*	*Name of the State*	*MPPI*
	Top 5		
Andhra Pradesh	3.03	Andhra Pradesh	5.27
Orissa	2.68	Himachal Pradesh	3.33
Tamilnadu	2.18	Tamilnadu	2.66
Karnataka	2.15	Karnataka	2.37
Kerala	1.29	Kerala	2.36
	Last 5		
Jammu & Kashmir	0.08	Bihar	0.20
Punjab	0.09	Haryana	0.26
Haryana	0.13	Madhya Pradesh	0.27
Bihar	0.30	Punjab	0.28
Gujarat	0.35	Jharkhand	0.29

Source: Calculated on the basis of secondary data up to March 2008.

Deserving Poor are Still not Reached

The microfinance delivery models are not exclusively focused on those who are below the poverty line or very poor. Though the programme is spreading rapidly yet there is slow progress in targeting the bottom poor households. According to Ghate (2008), approximately 75 million households in India are poor and only 22 per cent of these poor households (i.e. 16.5 million) are currently receiving microfinance services.

In 2007, a detailed survey of poor families was carried out in Punjab for the purpose of providing subsidised wheat and pulses to the poor families under *Atta-Dal* scheme. In this survey, poverty line was fixed at the household income of Rs. 30,000 per annum. This poverty line is equivalent to income of Rs. 500 per capita per month considering a family unit of five persons. This poverty line is slightly less than the World Bank defined poverty line of $1.25 per capita per day adjusted for PPP. According to this survey 38.9 per cent of the total households in Punjab live below poverty line.

On the basis of this poverty line the present study shows that 81 percent of programme participants were above poverty line (APL) and just 19 per cent of the participants were below poverty line (BPL) at the time of joining microfinance programme (Figure 1). Therefore, it can be said that substantial groups of poor population have been excluded from availing the benefits of the programme. It is also shown in the figure that 9 percent of the participants remained BPL even after getting the benefits of the programme.

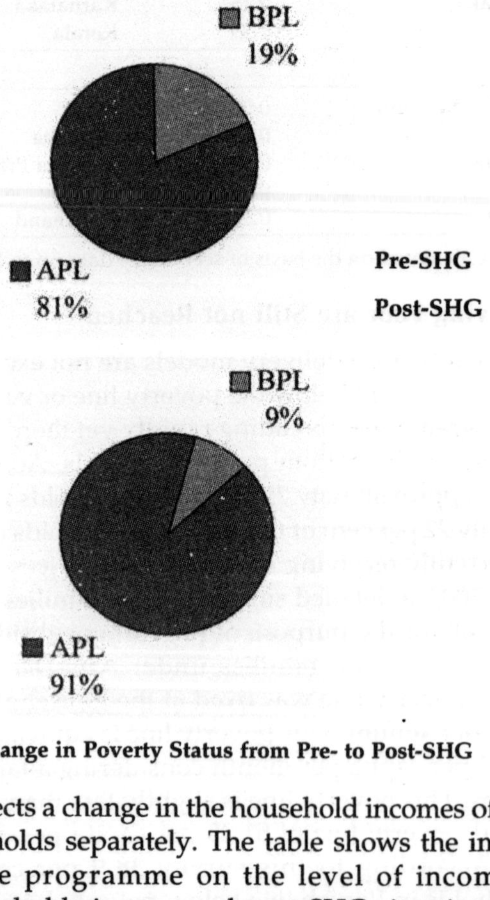

Figure 1: Change in Poverty Status from Pre- to Post-SHG

Table 13 reflects a change in the household incomes of BPL and APL households separately. The table shows the impact of microfinance programme on the level of income of participant households in pre- and post-SHG situation. It is found that nine per cent of the households surveyed which remained BPL even after getting the benefits of the microfinance programme were relatively poorer at the time of joining the programme and their household incomes was just Rs. 1,700 per month in their pre-SHG situation. These people who were extremely poor could not cross the poverty line. There was a minor increase in their income in the post-SHG.

Table 13
Impact of Microfinance Programme on BPL

Change in Poverty Status from Pre- to Post-SHG	*Number of Participants*	*Household Income in Pre-SHG*	*Household Income in Post-SHG*	*Difference in Income*	*Percentage Increase in Income*
BPL → BPL	17 (09)	1,700	1,918	218	13
BPL → APL	20 (10)	2,223	3,634	1,411	63
APL → APL	153 (81)	6,854	7,895	1,041	15
Total	190 (100)	5,905	6,912	1,007	17

Source: Field survey 2008.
Note: The figures given in parentheses indicate percentage of participants.

The table also reveals that ten percent of the BPL households crossed the poverty line in their post-SHG situation. The income level of these BPL households shows that they were close to the poverty line when they joined the programme. The income of these BPL households was Rs. 2,223 per month and microfinance programme led to a significant increase in their income and shifted them above the poverty line. The increase in their income is 63 per cent. These poor households are the largest beneficiaries of the microfinance programme.

Therefore, it is found that the programme is mainly benefiting the people who are either above the poverty line or are marginally below the poverty line.

Limited Depth of Outreach

Another problem faced by the microfinance programme is the depth of services provided. Though the outreach of the programme is expanding, large number of people are provided with microfinance services but the amount of loans is very small. The average loans per member in both MFIs and SHGs are between Rs. 3,500 and 5,000 (Srinivasan, 2009). Table 14 shows the average value of loans per SHG member for various years. This amount is not sufficient to fulfil the financial needs of the poor people. The duration of the loans is also short. The small loan size and short duration do not enable most borrowers to invest it for productive purposes. They, generally, utilise these small loans to ease their liquidity problems. Misra (2006) in a study of western and central part of India shows that small loans from the microfinance programme are mainly used for non-income generating activities such as consumption and other emergency needs.

Inflexibility in Programme

There are some fundamental requirements of the SHG-BLP, such as compulsory savings, group meetings, regular repayments etc. But these rigid conditions lead to the exclusion of the core poor from joining the microfinance programme. Poor people who generally do not have a regular source of income are required to save before getting a loan. These loans are to be repaid regularly in fixed installments. But due to their irregular and seasonal nature of jobs, poor people face difficulties while repaying the loans. It is found that the initial group loans are utilised for essential non-productive purposes rather than for generating incomes which leads to repayment difficulties. Weekly or fortnightly group meetings are made mandatory, so, the rural poor people who generally earn their livelihood through domestic labour and daily wage earning find it difficult to attend group meetings regularly. In this way the present structure of the programme is rigid and inflexible.

Limited Insurance Services

Poor people are vulnerable to financial shocks. A small change in their earning patterns due to natural calamities, health problems, death of earning member etc. can push them to destitute. So, a provision of insurance under the microfinance programme is very essential to help the poor to cross the poverty line. But, in reality, the current microfinance

Table 14

Average Loan Size per Member in SHGs

Particular	*Up to March 2003*	*Up to March 2004*	*Up to March 2005*	*Up to March 2006*	*Up to March 2007*	*Up to March 2008*
Total Amount of Loans (Rs. Million)	20,487	39,042	68,980	1,13,970	1,80,407	2,22,265
Number of SHGs	7,17,360	10,79,091	16,18,476	22,38,565	29,24,973	34,77,965
Average Loan Size per SHG (in Rs.)	28,558.88	36,180.45	42,620.34	50,912.08	61,678.18	63,906.62
Average Loan Size per member* (in Rs.)	2,039.92	2,584.31	3,044.31	3,636.57	4,405.58	4,564.76

Source: NABARD Data.

* Average size of an SHG in India is 14 members.

programme in India is just focused on regular saving and micro-credit. SHG-BLP developed by NABARD is also providing saving and credit services mainly and the provision of insurance is negligible. A research report by Invest India Market Solutions Pvt. Ltd. (IIMS, 2007) indicates that in India the penetration of life insurance is only 12 per cent among the rural poor and 19 per cent among the urban low-income population. So, the provision of insurance services is at the initial stage and this integral part of the microfinance programme is still neglected.

SECTION-IV

Conclusions

Microfinance has emerged as an innovative poverty eradicating and development programme. The analysis of primary data showed that microfinance programme has increased the income of the programme participants. Composite poverty index shows that the programme is benefiting the moderate poor people and they are shifted to the non poor categories. Impact of microfinance programme on employment shows that more number of programme participants are engaged in income generating activities as compared to the non-participants. Some participants have also started non-traditional income generating activities. The results of composite empowerment index shows that participant women are more empowered as compared to the non-participants.

The study also discusses some challenges and problems associated with this programme. It is found that the spread of the programme is regionally biased and it has flourished mainly in the states of southern India. The values of MPI and MPPI show that the spread of microfinance programme is very limited in Punjab. The study also shows that the programme is not specifically targeting the BPL households. The poor people marginally above the poverty line are the main entrants of the programme. It is found that just 19 per cent of the participants were BPL when they joined the SHGs. Besides this, current microfinance programme is just focused on regular savings and micro-credit. The provision of insurance service is very less.

These problems indicate that there are broader prospects for the expansion of programme by covering the un-reached regions; including the deserving poor people and making the programme more flexible.

Policy Implications

The study brings out that microfinance in Punjab is provided only through the SHG-bank linkage model, and there is no role of MFIs in delivering the microfinance. The MFIs may play an important role to reach the poor people especially in those areas where bank branch network has not reached. Therefore, government should provide a supportive environment to encourage MFIs to participate in delivering microfinance in Punjab.

The determinants of women empowerment show that the level of education of the programme participants influences their level of empowerment very significantly. Therefore, in addition to the financial assistance, education may also be provided to the women participants, under the microfinance programme.

The study further shows that loans used for productive purposes directly influence the level of income, employment and women empowerment. Therefore, the programme participants must be motivated and assisted to utilise the group loans for productive purposes only.

It is found that the maturity of the SHGs is quite significantly contributing to the reduction of poverty, generating employment and empowering the women participants. The mature group participants are availing the benefits of the programme continuously from the past many years. Therefore, keeping the long-term objectives in mind, efforts should be made for the stabilisation and sustainability of the group members. The problems faced by the members must be listened and resolved so that they can continue as group member for a longer period of time.

The low values of Microfinance Penetration Index and Microfinance Poverty Penetration Index for some states including Punjab show that the penetration of microfinance in these states is very low. These values are considerably less than those of some other south Indian states. So, efforts should be made to reduce the regional imbalance and some special measures should be taken to enhance the coverage of microfinance programme in the states with low microfinance outreach.

Microfinance programme is meant to reach the poor people, who actually are considered non-bankable by the formal financial institutions due to their irregular income and lack of collateral. But the study shows that just 19 per cent of the participants were below poverty line when they were selected for SHGs, and the remaining 81 per cent of the selected SHG participants were above poverty line. Composite poverty index also shows that only one per cent of the participants and non-participants are extremely poor. So, efforts must be made to reach the deserving poor people. There should be clear framework of guidelines to include people from BPL households at the time of forming SHGs. There is a need to eliminate the reasons which hinder the inclusion of bottom poor in the programme. In addition to this, poor people are vulnerable to financial exigencies. So, a provision of insurance under the microfinance programme is quite essential to help the poor to cross the poverty line.

References

Ghate, P. (2008), *Microfinance in India: A State of the Sector Report, 2007,* Microfinance India Publications, New Delhi.

IIMS (2007), 'Towards an inclusive financial system: Financial Services Demand and Utilisation by India's Low Income Workforce', Dataworks Research Report, Invest India Market Solutions Pvt. Ltd., New Delhi.

Misra, Alok (2006), 'Microfinance in India and Millennium Development Goals: Maximising Impact on Poverty', Discussion Paper for Workshop on World Bank, Singapore, 18 September.

Srinivasan, N. (2009), *Microfinance India State of the Sector Report 2008,* Sage Publications, New Delhi.

Appendix-I
Indicators of Poverty

Sl. No.	BPL Survey 2002 Indicators	Present Study Indicators	Comment	Classification	Score
1.	Size group of operational land holding	Value of land owned	Size of land holding is converted into values as the value of land varies from place to place	Nil	0
				Up to Rs. 2 Lakh	1
				Rs. 2 Lakh to 5 Lakh	2
				Rs. 5 Lakh to 10 Lakh	3
				Above Rs. 10 Lakh	4
2.	Type of house	Type of house	Same Indicator is used	Houseless	0
				On Rent	1
				Katcha	2
				Semi-pucca	3
				Pucca	4
3.	Food Security	Consumption expenditure (per capita per month)	As Punjab is relatively a prosperous state so per capita consumption expenditure is taken instead of food security	Less than or equal to Rs. 400	0
				Rs. 401 to 600	1
				Rs. 601 to 800	2
				Rs. 801 to 1000	3
				Above Rs. 1000	4
4.	Sanitation (toilet facility)	Sanitation (toilet and drainage)	'Drainage' is also considered along with 'toilet'	Drainage	1
				Toilet	2
				Drainage and Toilet both	4
5.	Ownership of consumer durables (group 1 and 2)*	Ownership of consumer durables (group 1 and 2)**	Group items have been slightly modified	1 item in group 1	1
				2 items in group 1	2
				3 items in group 1	3
				4 items in group 1/ any one item from group 2	4

Contd...

Sl. No.	BPL Survey 2002 Indicators	Present Study Indicators	Comment	Classification	Score
6.	Literacy status of the highest literate adult	Literacy status of the highest literate adult	Same Indicator is used	Illiterate	0
				Up to primary	1
				Up to High	2
				Up to Secondary	3
				Above Secondary	4
7.	Means of livelihood	Means of livelihood	Same Indicator is used	Dependent on others	0
				Casual Worker	1
				Own unskilled Business	2
				Own skilled Business	3
				Regular Job	4
8.	Status of the Household Labour Force	Household income (per capita per month)	Per capita household income is taken as proxy for the status of household labour force	Less than or equal to Rs. 500	0
				Rs. 501 to 750	1
				Rs. 751 to 1000	2
				Rs. 1001 to 1250	3
				Above Rs. 1250	4
9.	Indicators from 9 to 13 are omitted# and two other indicators are used	Cooking fuel used	Cooking fuel used is also an important indicator to reflect the condition of a household. This indicator is used by NSSO.	Firewood	0
				Dung-cakes	1
				Kerosene/Coal	2
				Kerosene/Coal and LPG	3
				LPG	4
10.		Source of drinking water	This indicator is also used by NSSO.	Well	1
				Street Tap	2
				Public Water Supply	3
				Own Hand Pump/Motor pump	4

* Group 1: B/W TV, Electric Fan, Pressure cooker, Radio
Group 2: Telephone, Fridge, Colour TV, Computer, 2/3 Wheeler, LMV, Tractor etc.
**Group 1: B/W TV, Electric fan, Pressure cooker, Radio, Table and chair, Almirah, Bicycle.
Group 2: Telephone/Mobile phone, Colour TV, Scooter/Motorcycle, Refrigerator, Tractor.
\# The omitted indicators are: Status of the children, Type of indebtedness, Reason for migration from household, Preference of assistance and Average availability of normal wear clothing.

Appendix-II
Indicators of Women Empowerment

Sl. No.	Particulars		Score
Indicators of Economic Empowerment		Unemployed	0
1.	Women's access to employment (Number of days per annum)	Up to 50	1
		50 - 100	2
		100 - 140	3
		140 – 180	4
		Above 180	5
2.	Woman's contribution to household income (Rs. per month)	No income	0
		Up to 1000	1
		1000 - 2000	2
		2000 - 3000	3
		3000 - 4000	4
		Above 4000	5
3.	Access to and control over resources	Owns house	1
		Owns house and land	2
		Owns house, land and jewellery	3
4.	Participation in household financial decision making	No participation	0
		Joint participation	1
		Independence in decision-making	2
5.	Saving in bank account	No deposit	0
		Irregular deposit	1
		Regular deposit	2
Indicators of Socio-cultural and Familial Empowerment			
6.	Women's freedom and Confidence of movement	Can't go outside	0
		Can visit another village	1
		Can visit other village and Nearest town	2
		Can visit other village, nearest town and city	3
7.	Visiting market for purchase of raw material and household goods	Not confident	0
		Less confident	1
		More confident	2
8.	Ability to Raise voice against social exploitation	Not confident	0
		Less confident	1
		More confident	2
9.	Positive attitude towards education of girls	No	0
		Yes	1
10.	Getting help of other family members	Never	0
		Occasionally	1
		Always	2
11.	Participation in general domestic matters	Never	0
		Occasionally	1
		Always	2

Contd...

Sl. No.	*Particulars*		*Score*
Indicators of Political Empowerment			
12.	Exercising the right to vote	No	0
		Yes	1
13.	Awareness of local, state level and national polity	No awareness	0
		Know the name of village *sarpanch* and resognise him	1
		Know the names and resognise *sarpanch* and Chief Minister	2
		Know and recognise *Sarpanch*, CM and PM	3
14.	Participation in *panchayat's* meetings	Never	0
		Occasionally	1
		Always	2
15.	Leadership Qualities	No	0
		Yes	1
Education, Skill and Training Empowerment			
16.	Education and ability to read and write	Illiterate, not able to read and write	0
		Illiterate, but able to read and write	1
		Education up to Primary level	2
		Up to Middle	3
		Up to High	4
		Above High	5
17.	Ability to do basic calculations	Not able	0
		Some difficulty	1
		No difficulty	2
18.	Maintaining records of financial transactions	Never	0
		Occasionally	1
		Regularly	2
19.	Ability to understand basic banking operations	Not able	0
		Some difficulty	1
		No difficulty	2
20.	Reading newspaper to have general awareness	Never	0
		Occasionally	1
		Regularly	2
21.	Training for the job	No	0
		Yes	1

12

Human Development in Punjab: Emerging Challenges

Reena Bhasin

Introduction

The larger human development paradigm stresses on human beings as ends in themselves and not so much as means of development. (Haq, 2003). Further the ends can be in multiple domains. It is in this context that Mahbub Ul Haq (the founder of Human Development Reports) considers one dimensionality as the most serious drawback of the income-based measures of economic development. This led to the birth of the Human Development Index (HDI), which identifies three basic capabilities as prerequisites to a life. They are, the capacity to lead long and healthy lives, access to the seeking mind, and the ability to ensure for one self a reasonably good standard of living. Without these resources, peoples' choices are restricted and life's opportunities are out of reach. Human Development is the process of building these capabilities to enable people to lead productive lives. Once these capabilities are assured, then other opportunities in life follow.

Difference between HD Approach and the Non-HD Approach

Issues	*HD approach*	*Non-HD approach*
Development for what?	Well-being, dignity, freedom, addressing inequalities, exclusion and poverty.	National Income, economic and social growth which trickles down.
Development for whom?	People	For people and things
Who is the agent of development?	People	People and things: Human capitaql+physical capital+natural resources
How?	No recipes but elements of good policies such as: Economic growth, pro-poor, pro-employment: Equity of choices: equitable distribution of assets: Good Social Policies: Interventions to serve needs of vulnerable sub-populations:Political democracy:Civil Participation:	Structural adjustment "recipes"Do not raise industrial wages. Hand out contraceptives: Sow improved seeds: Investment in Housing: Spend on basic needs: Send the right signals.

Source: UNDP, 2004. HDR.

Acknowledging the importance of HDI, almost all the countries and even the provinces of a country have prepared the Human Development Report (HDR) with an aim to supplement their policy decisions.

Human Development Index is computed every year by UNDP. This measures average achievements in basic human development and assigns ranking to countries. The HDI is a composite index, comprising longevity, educational attainment as well as command over resources. According to the Human Development Report 2010 published by UNDP, India is ranked at 119th position with HDI value 0.628 in 2009 and is grouped among the medium human development countries. HDI of India has increased from 0.439 in 1980 to 0.628 in 2009 yielding an almost 43% increase in human development.

The state of Punjab has always occupied an important place in India. It is known for its economic growth, high standard of living and hardworking people. But for human development it is still behind Kerala. National Human Development Report

(2001) places Punjab at the second rank with HDI value of 0.537, Kerala being at the top with HDI value 0.638. Moreover, its health and education compare poorly with those of countries like Vietnam and Sri Lanka. Within Punjab, level of human development varies from one district to another.

Of late, some recent development in the state present disturbing scenario. The state is witnessing a slowdown in its economic growth particularly since last one decade. It has lost its first place to fourth place in terms of per capita income. The state is passing through a phase of fiscal crisis. Incidence of income poverty may be low (8.4%) (in 2004-05) but income inequalities have increased in the state. These developments are also affecting the human development indicators. State is placed relativelys at a low level so far as Infant Mortality Rate, Child Mortality Rate and Maternal Mortality rates are concerned. Gender deficit is continuously increasing in the state. For education, it is placed at a low level, so far as primary education is concerned. According to a latest study (IFPRI, 2008), Punjab is facing a serious hunger situation, if not alarming. In the global context, state is placed even below some countries viz. Handuras and Nicaragua. Hence it becomes imperative to analyze the dynamics of human development in the state and the challenges being faced in this regard.

The present study is an attempt in this direction. The study is organized in the manner that Section II provides an overview of the nature of human development in the state vis-a-vis India It also highlights the degree of difference in the Human Development Index and Gender Development Index at the disaggregated level. The determinants/causative correlates of Human Development have been examined in Section III. Section IV throws light upon some challenges being faced by the state in improving the human development situation and overall quality of life of the people. It also discusses the current education status and health status in the state. Conclusions of the study are documented in Section V. The study is mainly based upon the secondary data taken from various govt. reports and govt. offices.

Overview of Human Development in Punjab

All over the world, advancement of science and technology, rising incomes and economic growth have led the people living longer and healthier lives. It is pertinent, however, at this juncture, to have a look at the overall human development in Punjab vis-à-vis India and the same across different districts of Punjab. Table 1 makes it evident that there are sharp variations in the HDI values across the states.

Table 1
HDI scores and Rank of the States (1981-2001)

States	*1981*	*Rank*	*1991*	*Rank*	*2001*	*Rank*
Andhra Pradesh	0.298	9	0.377	9	0.416	10
Assam	0.272	10	0.348	10	0.386	14
Bihar	0.237	15	0.308	15	0.367	15
Gujarat	0.360	4	0.431	6	0.479	6
Haryana	0.360	5	0.443	5	0.509	5
Karnataka	0.346	6	0.412	7	0.478	7
Kerala	0.500	1	0.591	1	0.638	1
Madhya Pradesh	0.245	14	0.328	13	0.394	12
Maharashtra	0.363	3	0.452	4	0.523	4
Orissa	0.267	11	0.345	12	0.404	11
Punjab	0.411	2	0.475	2	0.537	2
Rajasthan	0.256	12	0.347	11	0.424	9
Tamil Nadu	0.343	7	0.466	3	0.531	3
Uttar Pradesh	0.255	13	0.314	14	0.388	13
West Bengal	0.305	8	0.404	8	0.472	8
All India	0.302		0.381		0.472	
C.V.	21.80		18.37		15.75	

Source: Govt of India (2002) National Human Development Report 2001, Planning Commission, oxford university press, P 25.

However the dispersion of HDI (as measured by CV) across states is declining over the period. It may be noted that some of the states, having attained poor HDI score in 1980-81, have performed better over a period of 20 years. The table brings to the fore that states like Assam, Bihar, Orissa, UP and West Bengal have recorded fairly higher scores in 2000-01 over the initial period 1980-81. However, since the already developed states have maintained higher HDI score all through, the ranking of the states have not changed much, except for Tamil

Nadu, whose rank jumped to 3 by 2001 from 7 in 1981 and this could be attributed to its good performance in all the three dimensions of HDI over the years.

The various dimensions of HDI with regards to Punjab are presented in Table 2.

The data show that most developed district of Punjab is Ludhiana with HDI value 0.761 while Mansa with an index value 0.633 is languishing at the bottom. It can be seen from the table that the districts in south and south-western Punjab Viz. Muktsar, Bathinda, Sangrur etc. come lowest in the human development list.

So far as gender dimension of the HDI is concerned, a perusal of table 2 reveals that Rupnagar tops all districts in women development, followed by Kapurthala and Hoshiarpur. Fatehgarh Sahib and Gurdaspur which were third and fourth among the HDI districts slip down to 16th and 15th positions respectively in GDI. One point to be noticed here is that economically developed districts viz Ludhiana and Amritsar placed at 1st and 9th position in HDI status slip down to 9th and 17th position respectively showing miserable performance in GDI. This is an indication of the fact that in these areas probably the social structure and the system encourages preferential treatment towards the male. So these districts must be targetted to improve the social and economic status of the women. The very low "Income Index" component of the GDI essentially reflects the low workforce participation of women in Punjab, which is not commensurate with the high level of economic-development and education. In fact, "Punjab has the lowest female workforce participation rate in the country. The majority of women are included in the category of non-workers, conclusive evidence of the invisibility of women's work" (HDR 2004, Punjab)

Determinants of Human Development

Punjab, in fact, has followed the classical growth path, agricultural development first and then industrial development accompanied by the increasing urbanization. Of late, services sector has also started developing fast in the state. In order to

Table 2
Various Dimensions of HDI in Punjab

	Edu. Index		Health Index		Income Index						
Districts	HDI	GDI	HDI	GDI	HDI	GDI	HDI	Rank	GDI	Rank	HDI- GDI
Amritsar	0.681	0.655	0.784	0.784	0.636	0.182	0.700	9	0.544	17	-8
Bathinda	0.655	0.648	0.722	0.714	0.648	0.512	0.674	14	0.625	7	+7
FG Sahib	0.734	0.719	0.744	0.744	0.742	0.205	0.740	3	0.566	16	-13
Faridkot	0.669	0.665	0.752	0.746	0.673	0.518	0.698	10	0.643	4	6
Ferozepur	0.627	0.626	0.767	0.769	0.671	0.535	0.689	12	0.643	4	8
Gurdaspur	0.761	0.752	0.820	0.821	0.589	0.123	0.723	4	0.565	15	-11
Hoshiarpur	0.801	0.803	0.719	0.715	0.635	0.419	0.718	5	0.645	3	2
Jalandhar	0.765	0.760	0.685	0.708	0.674	0.427	0.708	6	0.632	6	0
Kapurthala	0.705	0.705	0.728	0.752	0.688	0.498	707	7	0.652	2	5
Ludhiana	0.692	0.702	0.863	0.864	0.728	0.291	0.761	1	0.619	9	-8
Mansa	0.567	0.567	0.722	0.714	0.602	0.477	0.633	17	0.582	13	4
Moga	0.647	0.649	0.753	0.749	0.648	0.423	0.683	13	0.607	10	3
Muktsar	0.618	0.612	0.753	0.749	0.582	0.458	0.651	16	0.606	11	5
Nawanshehar	0.738	0.749	0.695	0.710	0.686	0.410	0.707	7	0.623	8	-1
Patiala	0.680	0.676	0.741	0.732	0.670	0.393	0.697	11	0.600	12	-1
RupNagar	0.753	0.755	0.762	0.766	0.737	0.485	0.751	2	0.669	1	1
Sangrur	0.601	0.604	0.669	0.690	0.690	0.433	0.654	15	0.757	14	1

Source: Human Development Report 2004, Punjab.

examine the interdistrict variations, correlation coefficients of the HDI with the levels of urbanization and the shares of primary, secondary and tertiary sectors in the state domestic product are estimated in Table 3.

The results of the table reveal that the districts with higher shares of primary sector, that is, those which are predominantly rural, have low human development level. The level of human development is positively and significantly correlated with the share of secondary sector in the Gross District Domestic Product.

Table 3
Correlates of HDI with Structural Indicators of Development at the District level in Punjab

	HDI	*DPPi*	*DPSi*	*DPTi*	*URi*
HDI	1	-.775	.579*	.437	.438
DPPi		1	-.784**	-.514*	-.471
DPSi			1	-.130	.191
DPTi				1	1489*
URi					1

Note: ** Correlation is significant at the 0.01 level (2-tailed)
* Correlation is significant at the 0.05 level (2-tailed).

DPPi = Share of the primary sector in the total domestic product of the ith district.

DPSi = Share of the Secondary sector in the total domestic product of the ith district

DPTi = Share of the tertiary sector in the total domestic product of the ith district. URi is the level of urbanization in the ith district.

Source: Census of India 2001, Economic and Statistical organization, Punjab.

An achievement of the target of human development depends largely on the availability and functioning of accessible education and health institutions, and the income. Education develops basic skills and abilities and thereby boots productivity. It directly promotes human development because being educated allows people to have a better quality of life. From the economists like Theodore W. Schultz (1961) and Robert J. Barro (1991) to Amartya Sen (1998) have all emphasized the role of education in promoting human welfare in different perspective. Health is equally important input for human development, having immediate implications for the quality of life as well as for productive capacities and capabilities. So it is hypothesized in the present study that there is positive and close association between human development and education and health amenities. Income is meant to register the command over the resources to enjoy a decent standard of living. The estimated correlation coefficients of human development index with education and health and income are as follows.

Table 4
Correlation of HDI with Education, Health and Income

	HDI	*Edu. Index*	*Health Index*	*Income Index*
HDI	1	.779**	.505*	.630**
Edu. Index		1	.083	.275
Health Index			1	-.004
Income Index				1

Note: ** indicates correlation is significant at the 0.01level (2-tailed)
* indicates correlation is significant at the 0.05 level (2-tailed).

The estimated correlation coefficients are in accordance with the hypothesized signs. The relationship of human development index with education is significantly higher than both income and health.

A simple linear regression model is also built to highlight the causal relationship of human development index with explanatory Variables viz education and health and income. Table 5 shows the regression results.

Table 5
Results of the Regression Analysis

Included Variables	*Constant*	*Education Index*	*Health Index*	*Income Index*	R^2
Education Index	0.410	0.421** P<.001	-	-	.606
Edu and Health Index	0.183	0.401** P<.001	0.323** P<.001	-	.802
Edu., Health and income Index	-.001	.323** P<.001	0.332** P<.001	0.338** P<.001	1.000

** significant at 1% level

The regression results also support the hypothesized relationships. Human Development is highly and positively correlated with health, education and income. Education alone is explaining the 60% of variations in the levels of human development in the model 1. It infers that one percent increase in education index increases the HDI value by 0.421.

Another linear regression model has been fitted to the data where education is represented by female literacy (X_1). Female literacy is considered to be a better indicator of education because it is generally stated that as women become literate, fertility rate falls, infant and child health improves, children's education level increases and household nutritional and sanitary conditions improve. Then longevity is represented by life expectancy at birth which is clearly a valuable aspect of good life and is represented by (X_2). Gross District Domestic Product percapita is another variable which is included in the model which is required to lead a decent standard of life and is denoted by (X_3).

It is generally believed that urban areas have many education and health facilities, higher per capita income etc. which can enhance the human development level. So it is positively related with human development. So the level of urbanization in the district is also included in the model and is represented by (X_4). HDI is the dependent variable (Y). The results of this exercise are furnished below.

$$Y = 0.156+0.003X_1^{**}+0.005^{*}X_2+.0002X_3+.0004X_4$$

$$(5.73) \qquad (3.24) \qquad (0.55) \qquad (0.74)$$

$$R^2 = 0.852 \qquad F = 18.108$$

** Significant at 1% level.

* Significant at 5% level.

The results show that female literacy and life expectancy are found to be highly significant variables. A one percent increase in female literacy can increase the HDI value by 0.003. A one percent increase in life expectancy can increase HDI by 0.005 when other variables are kept constant. Variables X3 and X4 are found to be statistically insignificant meaning thereby that it is not always necessary that the districts having high level of urbanization and high GDDP per capita may be having high level of human development. This result is supported if we analyse the levels of GDP per capita and levels of urbanizations vis-à-vis human development at the state level. The result of this exercise does not get changed much if overall literary rate in the district is taken into account.

Challenges

Analysis in the previous section suggests that for the state as a whole, education and health are to be given the top priority in enhancing HDI. And here originates the importance of expenditure on social sectors such as education and health apart from taking measures for economic development in augmenting human development. For this high growth rate becomes essential so that adequate resources can be generated for social spending but economy of Punjab is growing at a relatively slower pace in the post liberalization period. Hence the state, not only in terms of per capita income, has lost its first place to fourth place, but is also lagging behind other states so far as the growth targets are concerned. Table 6 portrays the picture of the state regarding per capita income and growth rates of some comparable states.

Table 6
Per Capita Income and Growth Rates in GSDP in Punjab and Other States

States	*NSDP Per capita (2007-08) in Rs*	*Growth Rate 10th Plan (Actuals)*	*Growth Rate 11th Plan (Target)*
Punjab	31439	4.5	5.9
Kerala	32961	7.2	9.5
Haryana	39796	7.6	11.0
Gujarat	29798	10.6	11.2
Maharashtra	33302	7.9	9.1
Tamil Nadu	29445	6.6	8.5

Source: CSO (Base 1999-2000 constant prices) and Planning Commission.

Now, expenditure on social services is linked with human development index (HDI) directly. A fall in expenditure on social services becomes a hindrance in the way of promoting human development. Studies on social sector expenditure in India reveal that fiscal crisis of states in the post liberalization period had deleterious impact on the social sector expenditure including education and health (Tsujita, 2005). Revenue is a major determinant of social sector expenditure. Punjab is also experiencing fiscal crisis during this period and it is assuming large proportions since 2001. Fiscal deficit and revenue deficit is continuously growing and tax-GDP ratio is continuously declining. The picture becomes clear if we have a close look at the following diagram providing states comparison with some other states.

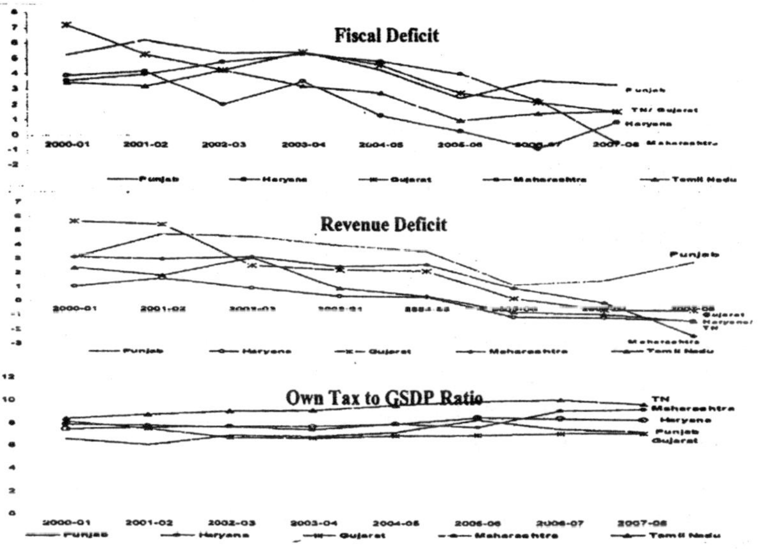

Source: Finance Department, Punjab and Planning Commission.

Diagram 1: Fiscal Indicators as Percentage of GSDP of selected States of India

And it is because of this fiscal crisis in the state that expenditure on social service sector is also declining continuously. Table 7 provides the trends in social sector expenditure/GDP ratio in Punjab with other comparable states.

Table 7
Social Sector Expenditure as % of GDP in Punjab.

State	*1980-85*	*85-90*	*90-95*	*95-2000*	*2001-05*	*2005-10*	*CAGR 1980-2010*
Punjab	4.8	5.7	4.7	4.3	4.3	4.4	13.1
Gujarat	5.3	7.1	6.0	5.7	6.5	5.1	14.6
Haryana	4.4	5.5	4.9	5.1	4.5	4.9	16.7
Karnataka	5.4	7.8	7.3	6.8	6.5	7.4	15.8
Kerala	7.6	9.2	7.9	7.8	6.7	5.8	12.8
Maharashtra	4.9	6.6	5.7	5.3	5.6	5.8	16.3
Tamil Nadu	6.4	7.8	7.8	6.7	6.4	6.7	14.9

Source: RBI. State Finances: A study of Budgets 2007-08.

The table makes it clear that allocation of resources to social sector has been considerably low which is having an adverse effect on the indicators of human development in Punjab particularly education and health.

Education Status in Punjab

Punjab has achieved much in the education. With literacy rate of 69.85%, Punjab stands at 5th position among the major states of India. Physical infrastructure in education is considered to be excellent in the state placing it at third position (Ahluwalia, 2010). But at the same time Gross Enrolment Ratio in Punjab (76.2) is quite low compared to all-India level (115.3). Moreover, Educational outcome Index places the state at 25th position among all states in India (Ibid).

So far as primary education is considered, taking the parameters such as literacy rate, proportion of 10+ children having completed primary education, ratio of girls to boys enrolled in primary and middle school, teacher-pupil ratio, total expenditure of education department on primary plus middle school population within the age group of 6-14 years, India Today conducted a study of the states of India and it was revealed that Punjab stood at 6th position during the year 2007, with kerala in the first place among the major states of India. The score and Rank of the states in India are given in the Table 8.

A close perusal of the table reveals that Punjab has slipped down to 6th position in 2007 from 5th place in 2006 so far as primary education is concerned. At the same time it is heartening to note that Sarva Shiksha Abhiyan (SSA) designed to fill the gaps in the Government agenda of education and launched with the support of govt of India, is operational in Punjab and it has made significant improvement in 2008-09 both in allocation patterns and utilization of funds.

Table 8
Primary Education Among States: Score and Rank (2006 and 2007)

		2006		2007	
SL. No.	*States*	*Score*	*Rank*	*Score*	*Rank*
1.	Himachal Pradesh	4.34	1	4.09	2
2.	Kerala	4.25	2	4.19	1
3.	Tamil Nadu	3.06	3	2.98	5
4.	Maharashtra	3.02	4	3.17	3
5.	Punjab	2.72	5	2.91	6
6.	Karnataka	2.61	6	2.77	7
7.	Assam	2.59	7	3.11	4
8.	Andhra Pradesh	2.42	8	2.29	10
9.	Haryana	2.34	9	2.34	9
10.	West Bengal	2.13	10	2.27	11
11.	Gujarat	1.94	11	2.45	8
12	Orissa	1.83	12	1.81	12
13.	Madhya Pradesh	1.72	13	1.72	14
14.	U. P	1.28	14	1.35	14
15.	Bihar	0.68	15	0.72	15

Source: India Today special issue, July, 2007.

Where, education scenario is somewhat satisfactory in Punjab, health outcomes are not commensurate with the high per capita income and extensive infrastructure of healthcare. The health scenario in Punjab is summarized in the Table 8.

A clear perusal of the table indicates the seriousness of the nutrition scenario of Punjab. It can be seen that anemia status of children is very poor and the state ranks low at the 12th position (NFHS-III) While poverty is generally considered to be a major contributing factor towards nutritional deficiencies, Punjab, with its legendary rivers of milk and abundance of food grains presents a paradoxical picture, where abundance combines with a high level of under nutrition among children.

Table 9
Indicators Related to Health and Nutrition Among States in India

States	*Per Capita Net State Domestic Product at Factor Cost (Rs.) (2005-06)*	*Infant Mortality Rate*	*Child Mortality Rate (<5 years)*	*Underweight Children (<5 years)*	*Maternal Mortality Rate*	*Anaemia Among Children*
Andhra Pradesh	21334	54	63	32.7	150	81
Assam	14419	66	85	36.4	492	78
Bihar	6719	61	84	56.1	300	87
Gujarat	25487	49	61	44.7	165	80
Haryana	32975	41	52	39.7	188	81
Karnataka	21913	43	54	37.6	210	83
Kerala	27220	15	16	22.7	110	57
Madhya Pradesh	12567	70	94	59.8	295	83
Maharashtra	28683	37	46	36.7	150	70
Orissa	13957	65	91	40.9	285	72
Punjab	28487	41	52	24.6	192	80
Rajasthan	15541	65	85	40.4	380	79
Tamil Nadu	25558	30	35	30.0	100	71
Uttar Pradesh	10758	73	96	42.3	425	85
West Bengal	20212	48	59	38.5	115	68

Source: CSO, NFHS-III (2005-06)

Another problem related with health and nutrition in Punjab is of Hunger. By taking into consideration three indicators viz. prevalence of calorie undernourishment, proportion of underweight among children less than five years and under-five mortality rate reported as deaths per hundred, India State Hunger Index[1] puts Punjab State in 'serious' category as in shown in the Table 9.

The three components of ISHI in case of Punjab are 11.1, 24.6 and 5.2. According to the report, "Sadly, despite being best performing state and known as India's bread basket, Punjab ranks at 34th place below Gabon, Honduras and Vietnam in the global context". So on one side where several people go to the bed hungry, wheat worth crores of rupees gets rotten while lying in the open in the state. Punjab faces the storage problem for storing the food grains. Lying in the open, it gets rotten and becomes unfit for human consumption. So it becomes the duty of the state to act in time so that not even a single grain of what is produced in Punjab goes wate.

The problem of nutritional inadequacies gets aggravated by the fact that gains of nutrition are also drained away by the diseases resulting from unsafe drinking water and the poor state of sanitation. Intensive use of pesticides, insecticides and synthetic and chemical fertilizers for obtaining bumper crops have consequently polluted the potable water in Punjab, particularly in the south western regions. Moreover, the pollutants of the industrial wastes are being thrown in the rivers etc. which is also playing havoc to the health status of the region. Further, presence of radio active minerals, celenity and alcholy content of the soil has further added health hazards in the state. Recently government of Punjab has initiated a project with the Nandi Foundation for providing safe drinking water at a nominal charge. One point to be noticed here is that the pace at which urbanization is taking place in the state along with growth in slum population may make the problem of potable water and sanitation more grim in the near future. This requires added attention of the state govt.

Hence the analysis given above emphasizes the need for the expansion of expenditure on social sector in the state particularly in education and health, but the latest available data in this regard presents a disturbing scenario. The ratio of education and health expenditure to aggregate expenditure in 2001 was 13.2% and 4.5% respectively and it has fallen down to 8.2% and 2.7% respectively in 2007. So far as share of GDP spent on education and health is concerned, it is quite disheartening that the progressive state of Punjab is spending only 2.23% of GDP on education in 2009-10. Though it is higher than that of Haryana (2.05) but lower than that of even the less developed states viz. U.P. (3.67%), Bihar (5.70), Rajasthan (3.57%) and Madhya Pradesh (3.38%). As regards to health expenditure, Punjab spends Rs. 4593 crs for upgrading health

Table 10
Severity of India State Hunger Index by State

< 4.9. (low)		*<5.0-9.9 (moderate)*		*10.0-19.9 (Serious)*		*20.0-29.9 (alarming)*		*>30.0 Extremely alarming*	
State	*ISHI*	*State*	*ISHI*	*State*	*ISHI*	*State*	*ISHI*	*State*	*ISHI*
				Punjab (1)	13.6	Haryana (5)	20.0		
				Kerala (2)	17.7	Uttar Pradesh(9)	20.9		
				Andhra Pradesh (3)	19.5	Tamil Nadu (6)	21.0		
				Assam (4)	19.8	Rajasthan (7)	21.0		
						West Bengal (8)	22.2		
						Karnataka (11)	22.8		
						Orrisa (12)	23.7		
						Maharashtra (10)	23.8		
						Gujarat (13)	24.7		
						Bihar (14)	27.3		
						M.P. (15)	30.9		

Source: IFPRI-Report on India State Hunger Index 2008.

care facilities against Rs. 3981crs of Haryana, Rs. 7711 crs of Madhya Pradesh and Rs. 4855 crs of Rajasthan (ASSOCHAM, 2010). Consequently per capita health expenditure in Punjab is only Rs. 360 which is much below the all-India level (Rs. 503), and places the state at 25th position among all the states (India current affairs, 2010).

Gender Deficits

Another dimension of the human development Index (HDI) which is of great concern is of declining sex ratio in general and child sex ratio in particular. Punjab is having the lowest sex ratio among all the states. The overall sex ratio in the state is 798 girls per thousand boys. Of the ten districts in India that have lowest child sex ratio, seven are in Punjab (UNDP, 2004). These districts are Amritsar (783), Bathinda (779), Mansa (779), Gurdaspur (775), Kapurthala (775), Patiala (770) and Fatehgarh Sahib (754). Female foeticide which is taking place at an alarming rate in Punjab, is contributing a lot to the warped sex ratios. A patriarchal social structure with a strong male preference predominating in certain communities is causing gender disparity and more skewed gender balance in this advanced state. This needs immediate stringent action on the part of the government.

Conclusions

The present study analyzed the dynamics of human development in the state of Punjab viz-a-vis other states and at the disaggregated level. The analysis reveals that the relative ranking of the states during 1981 2001 has remained almost same as far as HDI score is concerned. At the disaggregated level, it is found that the districts of south and south west Punjab are lowest in human development. This is supported by the correlation analysis of human development index with the relative share of primary, secondary and tertiary sectors in GDP at the district level. On the contrary, secondary sector is significantly correlated with human development. Hence in order to boost industrial development, government should promote a large number of agro based industries. Private sector should also come forward to undertake agro-processing activities.

Gender dimension of the HDI clearly reveals the existence of gender disparity in the state. The very low 'income index' component of the GDI reflects the low work participation rate of women which is not commensurate with the economic development and education levels. Another dimension of the gender disparity is the lowest sex ratio-in Punjab, particularly child sex ratio. The high rate of female infanticide and foeticide in a progressive and forward looking state like Punjab becomes unacceptable. So this disturbing social trend needs immediate attention and stringent action on the part of the government.

It has also been found that Punjab has witnessed a 'slowdown' in its economic growth. The rate of growth has been quite low (4.5%)in the state as compared to other states. This is a matter of great concern that the targeted growth rate for 11th plan has also been kept low. Consequently, the state has lost its first place to fourth place in terms of per capita income.

Then multivariate regression exercise clearly brings out the significant relationship of education and health with human development. So the deficiencies in both the sectors must be taken care of along with the overall growth concerns. The study finds that both the sectors are getting a meager share of GDP. As a result, the present status in both education and health is not very encouraging. There is lot of scope for improvement in both the sectors. Primary education needs more attention since many of the children till the age of 14 have still not come into the ambit of education.

Gross enrolment Ratio is very low as compared to all-India level. Since female literacy has turned out to be a significant variable in human development, it should be encouraged at all levels.

The health status also needs an improvement, particularly maternal health and child health. The state is lagging behind other states in the health indicators viz. IMR, CMR, MMR etc. Moreover it is facing serious hunger situation as per India State

Hunger Index. It is really discouraging that 24.6% of children (<5 years) in the state are underweight. Hence child malnutrition needs extra attention.

To sum up, both the sectors education and health need more budgetary allocations but if slow rate of economic growth continues and the share of both the sectors in the GDP declines further it may have an adverse effect on human development in the longrun.

Note

1. The India State Hunger Index represents the index calculated using a calorie undernomishment cut off of 1632 kcals per person per day to enable comparability of the India State Hunger Index with the Global Hunger Index 2008. The Index is computed by averaging the three component of Hunger Index.

References

Ahluwalia, I.J. (2010) : "Social Sector Development : A Perspective from Punjab" in, Shankar Acharya and Rakesh Mohan (eds) *India's Economy-Performance and challenges: Essays in Honour of Montek Singh Ahluwalia,* New Delhi: Oxford University Press.

ASSOCHAM. (2010), *Uttar Pradesh, Bihar Ahead on Education and Health* Allocations, *http://indiaeducationdiary.in/sholutest,usp?newsid=29hg*

Barro Robert J. (1991), 'Economic Growth in a Cross-Section of Countries', *Quarterly Journal of Economics, may.*

Govt of India (2007) , *National Accounts Statistics,* New Delhi, Central Statistical Organization.

———(2007-2012), *Eleventh Five Year Plan: Inclusive Growth,* Vol 1, Planning Commission, New Delhi.

———(2002), *National Human Development Report (2001),* Planning Commission, Oxford University Press.

———(2001) *Census of India; Final Population Totals, Part I,* office of the Registrar General, New Delhi.

Govt. of Kerala (2005), *Human Development Report,* (2005).

Govt of Punjab (2007),Statistical Abstract of Punjab (2007), Economic and Statistical Organisation, Punjab.

———(2004), Human Development Report, 2004.

Haq. Mhabub ul (2003): The Birth of the Human Development Index in Sakika Fukuda-Parr and A.K. Shiva Kumar (eds) *Readings in Human Development,* Oxford University Press, new York.

International Food Policy and Research Institution (2008), *Report on India State Hunger Index.*_(2008)

International Institute for Population Science (2007), *National Family Health Survey,* 3 (2005-06); Vol 1.

India Current Affairs (2010), *State Wise Per-Capita Expenditure on Health; http://indiacurrentaffairs.org/state-wise-per-capita-expenditure-on-health/*

T Sujita, Yuko (2005), *Economic Reforms and Social Sector expenditures; A study of fiftcen Indian States 1980/81 to 1999/2000,* Discussion Paper No. 31 Japan; Institute of Developing Economics (IDE).

UNDP (2004), *Human Development Report,* Oxford University Press, New York.

13

Development and Gender Inequality in North West India

Madhu Tandon

We choose Punjab and Haryana for our study as both the states are treated as most developed states in north India. Punjab is considered to have the best infrastructure in India; this includes road, rail and air links that are extensive throughout the region. Punjab also has the lowest poverty rate in India at 6.16% (1999-2000 figures), and has won the best state performance award, based on statistical data compiled by the Indian Government. Punjab (the five rivers region) is one of the most fertile regions. The region is ideal for wheat-growing. Rice, sugar cane, fruits and vegetables are also grown. Punjab is called the "Granary of India" or "India's bread-basket." Indian Punjab produces 2% of the world's cotton, 2% of its wheat and 1% of the world's rice. The state has essentially an agrarian economy with a lower industrial output as compared to other states of India. A prominent feature of the industrial scenario of the Punjab is its small sized industrial units. There are nearly 194,000 small scale industrial units in the state in addition to 586 large and medium units.

The economy of Haryana relies on manufacturing, business process outsourcing, agriculture and retail. Haryana is also considered one of the most industrialized states in India with many SEZs. The state has a developed banking system with over 4500 bank branches. The two financial hubs of Haryana, Gurgaon and Faridabad lie on the south east of the state. The contribution of primary, secondary and tertiary sectors for the Gross State Domestic Product (GSDP) in 2007-08 is Rs. 21,265.92 crore, Rs. 30,919.95 crore and Rs.49,133.55 crore respectively. Gurgaon has seen emergence of an active information technology industry in the recent years. Despite recent industrial development, Haryana is primarily an agricultural state.

The major contradiction facing this century relates to development sans equality, growth without equitable distribution, prosperity alongside rising gender inequalities, none of which are natural but are rather influenced by social and cultural factors. The need to broaden the concept of development to encompass the overall well-being of people rather than just denoting rising incomes has been clear ever since the weak links between economic growth and welfare have been established. (Preet Rustagi, 2010). Based on the three components - life expectancy, infant mortality and literacy, the first composite index was the Physical Quality of Life Index (PQLI) propounded by Morris. D. Morris in 1979. This composite index PQLI, was not a substitute for GNP, but served instead as a complement to measure of income.

The launch of Human Development Report (HDR)'90 denoted the beginning of a new era of measuring human development. This approach to development of enhancing capabilities is indeed, well conceived. It questions earlier assumptions of development as a gender-neutral process benefiting all income classes.

States in India are a geographical large area comprising of substantial diversities, hence there is a need to look at a particular state. The present study attempts to look into various facets of human development with a view to emphasis and highlight gender disparities in India and particular North-West India. This exercise limits itself to secondary data and draws out the profile of gender differences in North-West India (Punjab and Haryana).

Methodology and the Scope of Study

The study is an exercise to draw the backwardness towards the gender-bias based on individual indicators. Since the objective of the study is to assess the relative levels of backwardness or development in relation to one indicator at a time, no standardization of the variable is required. Through the identification of gender backwardness stage in the both states, this exercise will serve policy makers and enable focus intervention in the area of weakness to planned welfare programs in a systematic manner. Our hypothesis of the study is that Punjab and Haryana which are treated as relatively prosperous states of the North-West India are relatively gender backward or biased. It needs to be stated here that it is a one point study and no attempt has been made to look at transactions over time. A selected set of gender sensitive indicators consisting of sex ratio, female literacy, and health, work participation, social and cultural are taken for study. The study will utilize secondary source of data to identify the states (Punjab and Haryana) that are backward with regard to each of the specific indicators. The data sources used for this study are Census of India 1991, 2001, UNDP reports, NFHS data (1st, 2nd and 3rd and micro studies related to this issue.

The sex ratio is used as a demographic variable. The female literacy serves as a basic indicator of educational status. The health related variable is mortality rate. The socio-cultural variables employed are mean age at marriage and fertility rates. Female work participation along with the difference in male-female work participation rates is the economic indicator selected for the study.

Demographic Indicators

According to ILO, gender equality starts with equal valuing of girls and boys. This implies that women and men have equal condition for realizing their full potential and contributing to and benefitting from economic, social, cultural and political development.

UNESCO indicates that-

"Gender equality means equality between men and women: the freedom to develop and make choices unhindered by gender stereotypes roles and prejudices; that the different behaviors, aspiration and need of women and men are considered, valued and favored equally. It does not mean that women and men have to become the same, but their rights, responsibilities and opportunities do not depend on whether they are born male or female."

Therefore, gender inequality, is when women typically have less access to and control over facilities, opportunities and resources. The gender gap index report of World Economic Forum, 2007 place India at the 114th position out of 128 countries, which shows the extent of gender inequality in our country. The sex ratio (as females per 1000 males) is a composite indicator of women's health, nutrition and survival status. The imbalance in sex ratio observed in India is a very disturbing factor. This demographic imbalance is not due to problems of invisibility that is missing out of females while enumerating censuses, but a case of a 'missing women' (See Kundu and Sahu, 1991; Dreeze and Sen 1995 among others).There is a clear and sharp decline in the sex ratio since 1901 to 2001 from 972 to 933 for India as a whole.

Table 1
Sex Ratio in India

Year	*1951*	*1961*	*1971*	*1981*	*1991*	*2001*
Sex Ratio	946	941	930	933	927	933

Source: Census of India 2001.

Table 1 shows a clear picture of gender inequality as the sex ratio declined to 933 in 2001 from 946 in 1951. This downward fall of the sex ratio implies that the orthodox traditions of the past are still dominating the societies which view females as liabilities.

The state level sex ratio above 6 ranking reveals that the demographic imbalance is prominent in the north Indian states of Haryana, U.P., Punjab, Bihar and Rajasthan. Table 2 shows that while Punjab and Haryana have the sex ratio 876 and 861 respectively whereas the southern states are relatively better in their demographic gender balance. It is only the state of

Kerala which actually record higher female population-1058 females for every 1000 males.

Table 2
State-wise Distribution of Population and Sex Ratios

India/State/Union Territory	*Persons*	*Males*	*Females*	*Sex ratio*
India	1,028,610,328	532,156,772	496,453,556	933
Jammu & Kashmir	10,143,700	5,360,926	4,782,774	892
Himachal Pradesh	6,077,900	3,087,940	2,989,960	968
Punjab	24,358,999	12,985,045	11,373,954	876
Chandigarh	900,635	506,938	393,697	777
Uttaranchal	8,489,349	4,325,924	4,163,425	962
Haryana	21,144,564	11,363,953	9,780,611	861
Delhi	13,850,507	7,607,234	6,243,273	821
Rajasthan	56,507,188	29,420,011	27,087,177	921
Uttar Pradesh	166,197,921	87,565,369	78,632,552	898
Bihar	82,998,509	43,243,795	39,754,714	919
Sikkim	540,851	288,484	252,367	875
Arunachal Pradesh	1,097,968	579,941	518,027	893
Nagaland	1,990,036	1,047,141	942,895	900
Manipur	2,166,788	1,095,634	1,071,154	978
Mizoram	888,573	459,109	429,464	935
Orissa	36,804,660	18,660,570	18,144,090	972
Chhattisgarh	20,833,803	10,474,218	10,359,585	989
Madhya Pradesh	60,348,023	31,443,652	28,904,371	919
Gujarat	50,671,017	26,385,577	24,285,440	920
Daman & Diu	158,204	92,512	65,692	710
Dadra & Nagar Haveli	220,490	121,666	98,824	812
Maharashtra	96,878,627	50,400,596	46,478,031	922
Andhra Pradesh	76,210,007	38,527,413	37,682,594	978
Karnataka	52,850,562	26,898,918	25,951,644	965
Goa	1,347,668	687,248	660,420	961
Lakshadweep	60,650	31,131	29,519	948
Kerala	31,841,374	15,468,614	16,372,760	1058
Tamil Nadu	62,405,679	31,400,909	31,004,770	987
Pondicherry	974,345	486,961	487,384	1001
Andaman & Nicobar Islands	356,152	192,972	163,180	846

Source: Census Of India 2001.

For India as a whole, the female-male ratio of the population under age 6 has fallen from 94.5 girls for 100 boys in 1991 to

92.7 girls per 100 boys in 2001. Where there has been no such decline in some parts of the country (most notably Kerala), it has fallen very sharply in others, such as Punjab, Haryana, Gujarat and Maharashtra, which are among richer Indian states.

Taking together all the evidence that exists, it is clear that this change reflects not a rise in female child mortality, but a fall in female births, in comparison to male births, and is almost certainly connected with increased availability and use of gender determination of foetus. The practice of female foeticide and infanticide in prosperous states of Haryana, Punjab, and Delhi etc. creates a situation (Maira A., 2009) where girls have to be imported from the poor states to be used as domestic help and for sex. Several reports suggest that sex selective abortion became more common in the 1990s. Amartya Sen believes that the pattern of gender inequality shifted from 'mortality inequality' to what he calls 'natality inequality' due to female feticide after the facility for antenatal sex determination became available.

Amartya Sen took the female-male ratio for the 0-5 age group as 94.8 as the cut-off point below which he suspects anti-female intervention. The use of this dividing line (94.8) produces a remarkable geographical split of India. There are the states in the north and the west where the female-male ratio of children is consistently below the benchmark figure led by Punjab, Haryana, Delhi and Gujarat (with ratios between 79.3 and 87.8), and on the other side of the divide, the states in the east and the south tend to have female-male ratios that are above the benchmark line of 94.8 girls per hundred boys: with Kerala, Andhra Pradesh, West Bengal and Assam (each between 96.3 and 96.6). The north and the west have clear characteristics of anti-female bias in a way that is not present - or at least not yet visible - in most of the states of east and the south. This contrast does not have any immediate economic explanation. The states with anti-female bias include rich ones (Punjab and Haryana) as well as poor States (Madhya Pradesh and Uttar Pradesh), and fast-growing States (Gujarat and Maharashtra) as well as growth failures (Bihar and Uttar Pradesh). Also, the incidence of sex-specific abortions cannot be explained by the availability of medical resources for determining the sex of the foetus: Kerala and West Bengal in the non-deficit list, both with the ratio of 96.3 girls to 100 boys (comfortably higher than the benchmark cut-off of 94.8), have at least as much medical facilities as in such deficit states as Madhya Pradesh or Rajasthan. If commercial facilities for sex-selected abortion are infrequent in Kerala or West Bengal, it is because of a low demand for those specific services, rather than any great supply side barrier (Amartya Sen, 2001).

Educational Indicators

According to last census held in 2001, the percentage of female literacy in the country is 54.16%.The literacy rate in the country has increased from 18.33% in 1951 to 65.38% as per 2001 census. The female literacy rate has also increased from 8.86% in 1951 to 54.16%. It is noticed that the female literacy rate during the period 1991-2001 increased by 14.87% point whereas male literacy rate rose by 11.72% point. Hence the female literacy rate actually increased by 3.15% point more compared to male literacy rate.

Table 3
Gender Differentials in Literacy Rates in India (%)

Year	*Male*	*Female*	*Total*	*Gender Gap*
1951	27.16	8.86	18.33	18.3
1961	40.4	15.35	28.35	25.05
1971	45.96	21.97	34.45	23.98
1981	56.38	29.76	43.57	26.62
1991	64.13	39.29	52.21	24.84
2001	75.85	54.16	65.38	21.69

Source: Economic Survey 2003-04, Government of India Planning Commission.

Table 3 shows the gender gap in literacy rates, there is a declining trend in the gender gap since 1981 but it's not adequate and even the female literacy has gone up but there is still a wide range of disparity among both the sexes.

Table 4 and 5 shows the literacy rates in states in decreasing order. Kerala has the highest literacy rate of 87.86 percent, almost equal to developed countries and gender inequality is very low. In case of Punjab female literacy rate is 63.55 percent

Table 4

Literacy Rates in States Above National Average-in Decreasing Order (%)

State/UT	*Total*	*Male*	*Female*
1. Kerala	90.92	94.20	87.86
2. Mizoram	88.49	90.69	86.13
3. Lakshadweep	87.52	93.15	81.56
4. Goa	82.32	88.88	75.51
5. Delhi	81.82	87.37	75.00
6. Chandigarh	81.76	85.65	76.65
7. Pondicherry	81.49	88.89	74.13
8. A & N Islands	81.18	86.07	75.29
9. Daman & Diu	81.09	88.40	70.37
10. Maharashtra	77.27	86.27	67.51
11. Himachal Pradesh	77.13	86.02	68.08
12. Tripura	73.66	81.47	65.41
13. Tamil Nadu	73.47	82.33	64.55
14. Uttaranchal	72.28	84.01	60.26
15. Gujarat	69.97	80.50	58.60
16. Punjab	69.95	75.63	63.55
17. Sikkim	69.68	76.73	61.46
18. West Bengal	69.22	77.58	60.22
19. Manipur	68.87	77.87	59.70
20. Haryana	68.59	79.25	56.31
21. Nagaland	67.11	71.77	61.92
22. Karnataka	67.04	76.29	57.45

Source: Census of India 200.

Table 5

Literacy Rates in States Below National Average-in Decreasing Order (%)

State/UT	*Total*	*Male*	*Female*
1. Chhattisgarh	65.18	77.86	52.40
2. Assam	64.28	71.93	56.03
3. Madhya Pradesh	64.11	76.80	50.28
4. Orissa	63.61	75.95	50.97
5. Meghalaya	63.31	66.14	60.41
6. Andhra Pradesh	61.11	70.85	51.17
7. Rajasthan	61.03	76.46	44.34
8. Dadra & Nagar Haveli	60.03	73.32	42.99
9. Uttar Pradesh	57.36	70.23	42.98
10. Arunachal Pradesh	54.74	64.07	44.24
11. Jammu & Kashmir	54.46	65.75	41.82
12. Jharkhand	54.13	67.94	39.38
13. Bihar	47.53	60.32	33.57

and Haryana 56.31 percent, it is above national average but the gender biasness still exists, as it is very clear with the sex ratio. It seems that social and cultural factors are responsible for this biasness. The available sex determination techniques are used by and large, which are conveniently available and helps the parents, who prefer boys over girls. There is a custom of 'son preference' in the Punjabi society, which is reflected in low sex ratio in the state.

It is ironical that Punjab, a high female literacy rate state co exists with rampant female foeticide and infanticide (Kalpana, S. 2004). Punjab tops the list in number of female foeticide cases reported over the last three years with Rajasthan coming next. The country as a whole reported 294 cases during the same period. According to figures released by the National Crime Records Bureau, in Punjab, 81 cases were registered for female foeticide while for Rajasthan the corresponding number was 51. Madhya Pradesh registered 21 cases, Haryana 18 and Chhattisgarh 24.In Rajasthan, the number of cases registered has shown a steady decline since the last three years with 25, 16 and 10 cases being registered in 2006, 2007 and 2008, Minister of State for Health Dinesh Trivedi said in a written reply in the Rajya Sabha. (Reported by PTI).

Socio-Cultural Indicators

Female foeticide is a consequence of traditional gender bias and gender discrimination. Girls are seen as an economic liability and burden, partly because of the very expensive dowry that must accompany her future marriage. However, dowry is not the only cause for the selective abortion of girls; sons carry on the family name and often the business, usually inherit the property and perform the last rites." The poor eliminate their girls because of the poverty situation and for the rich; daughters are seen as less desirable. This is the deep rooted patriarchal society that we live in. In spite of the progress of India on the global stage, the mindset is still primitive", lamented Dr Manorama, laureate of the 2006 Right Livelihood Award (also known as the Alternative Nobel). This social evil is deep rooted in Indian ethos and the most shocking fact is that the innovative and high-end technologies are eliminating our girl-child. Attitudinal change is essential to put an end to this social malaise.

This tragedy is no secret in India – the real tragedy is that Indian society, and even stringent legislation — seem powerless to stop it. In April Prime Minister Manmohan Singh - who has three daughters—launched the "Save the Girl Child" campaign. He declared that no nation could claim to be part of a civilized world if it condoned female foeticide. An estimated 50 million girls have been sacrificed because of son preference. "Census figures illustrate that in some of the richer states the problem is most acute. These states include Punjab which had only 798 girls (per 1,000 boys), Haryana 819, Delhi 868 and Gujarat 883 girls in the 2001 Census. Growing economic prosperity and education levels have not led to a corresponding mitigation in this acute problem," he said.

Table 6
Child Mortality Rates in India (1981 -2000)*

	Rural			*Urban*		
Years	*Male*	*Female*	*Total*	*Male*	*Female*	*Total*
1981	43	48	46	20	21	20
1986	39	43	41	20	22	21
1991	28	30	29	15	17	16
1996	24	28	26	14	15	14
2000	21	23	22	11	12	12

**Source:* Office of the Registrar General of India, 1997 SRS Statistical Reports, 2000.

Table 6 tells us that in the rural area, female child mortality rates (CMR) have declined by 25 percentage points from 1981 to 2000, compared to the 9 percentage points in the urban area for the same period. Regarding the gender differentials, the difference is of not much significance in 2000 as male CMR stands at 21 percent and female CMR at 23 percent in rural areas, while in urban areas, female CMR stands at 12 percent and male CMR at 11 percent. Thus the difference in rural area is of 2 percentage points while, in urban areas, it is of 1 percentage point. However the declining CMR among rural females is higher than that of urban females and which may be due to the working of SHG's and NGO's working at the rural level.

According to the Government of India's first periodic report to the UN Committee on the rights of the Child, 2001, "every year, 12 million girls are born - three million of whom do not survive to see their 15th birthday. About one-third of these deaths occur in the first year of life and it is estimated that every sixth female death is directly due to gender discrimination". UN figures out that about 750,000 girls are aborted every year in India. Abortion rates are increasing in almost 80% of the India states, mainly Punjab and Haryana.

Despite a rapid economic transformation, Haryana lags far behind in the field of social change. The society is governed by a patriarchal structure that subjugates women in all possible ways. An abnormally large deficit of females in the population is a manifestation of this phenomenon. A general neglect of girl children and the resultant sex differentials in mortality along with a widespread practice of female foeticide in the wake of strong son-preference are indicators of persisting gender bias in the society. On the basis of correlates between the child sex ratio and select indicators, a study of Hassan indicates that gender bias does not necessarily decline with improvement even in the material well-being of women. It, therefore, argues for some more radical and rapid social progress that can effectively make inroads into the pernicious effects of patriarchy. (Mohammad Izhar Hassan, 2008.Sage Journal online).

This dismal story has recently been documented in yet another report, *Disappearing Daughters*, from Action Aid and Canada's International Development Research Centre reported. Their researchers looked at a representative sample of about 6,500 households in five districts in states already known to have especially skewed sex ratios: Punjab, Rajasthan, Haryana, Himachal Pradesh and Madhya Pradesh. Anjali Lewis, reported the sex ratio had dropped in four of the five districts, compared to 2001 census data. And worst of all, there were only 300 girls for every 1,000 boys among upper-caste Hindus in urban areas of Punjab's Fatehgarh Sahib District.

"There are only a third of the girls there should be in those communities. We're talking about whole villages where there are hardly any girls and we're talking about classrooms with no girls in them, and streets where only boys are playing." Ms Turquet said. A women's rights activist, Dr Ruth Manorama, told *Mercator Net*, "It is a misconception to think that this is a problem related to extreme poverty and as is revealed, female foeticide is very high in Punjab and Haryana – some of the best-off states in the country. . . "

Gender-discriminatory practices have also extended to the pre-natal stage so as to influence the sex composition of *births* as well as of surviving children. Amniocentesis and ultrasound screening technologies are increasingly used to detect the sex of the foetus and then the females are aborted. This is shown by a marked shift in sex ratios at birth in north and north-west India and urban areas of central India and supported by various smaller scale studies and reports.

The most important source of disempowerment faced by women are-

(i) Harassment through violence, both physical and sexual.

(ii) Severe disparities in access to assets, such as land and low share of 'paid' work and income.

Women face physical, mental, emotional and sexual abuse both within and outside their home. Table 7 shows the high incidence of violence against women in almost all parts of the country but especially in Bihar, M.P., Tripura, Rajasthan, Manipur, Tamil Nadu, West Bengal, U.P., Assam, Orissa and Arunachal Pradesh.

Punjab is a low risk state as compared to other states of India in terms of incidence and rate of crimes committed against women (Human Development Report, Punjab, 2004). It was ranked 28th in the extent of violence per perpetrated against women but many of the crimes and atrocities against the women go unreported. This include intimidation of wife, resorting to pressure tactics, or even depriving women if health, education employment and other opportunities. Low sex-ratio in Punjab state also indicates the prevalence of barbaric practice of female

Table 7
Percentage of Women, ages 15-49, who have Experienced Physical or Sexual Violence in India, 2005-06

State	*Physical and Sexual Violence*
Bihar	55.6
M.P.	46.8
Tripura	44.7
Rajasthan	44.6
Manipur	38.9
Tamil Nadu	38.7
West Bengal	38.3
U.P.	38.1
Assam	36.5
Orissa	36.2
Arunachal Pradesh	35.5
Jharkhand	34.8
Andhra Pradesh	33.8
Punjab	30.9
Chhattisgarh	30.1
Maharashtra	29.2
Haryana	29
Gujarat	27.8
Uttrakhand	26.8
Mizoram	25.5
Sikkim	20.9
Karnataka	19.9
Nagaland	19
Kerala	17.3
Delhi	16.5
Meghalaya	16
Goa	15
Jammu and Kashmir	12.9
Himachal Pradesh	5.6
India (total)	35.4

Source: NFHS-3

feticide and infanticide which are the most severe criminal act against the women. While rich countries are by no means free of violence against women the problems –which range from domestic violence to honour killing – are perceived to be more serious in developing countries. Attitudes in society need to change so that women can be more forthcoming in resolving their problems. Legislation also has a part to play as in the Domestic Violence Bill in India which came in to force in 2006.

Economic Indicators

Figures of female labour participate in India are still low. NorthWestern states (Haryana, Jammu & Kashmir, Punjab not only have lower female labour participation rates for a given level of development but also are the only states which do not play the increasing part of the U- shape relationship. That is, in these states, development is not easing female access to the formal labour market-these states are characterized by highly unequal gender relations(large literacy gap by gender, strictly restricted female property rights, strong boy preference, and neglect of female children(Berta Esteve-Volart,2009).In contrast, in South India, where gender relations are less patriarchal and for instance female education has spread relatively rapidly (Dreeze & Sen,1995),states are in the increasing part of the U-shaped relationship.

The success of Green Revolution of Punjab has pushed women, so far important contributors in production process, back into the private domain. They lost their economic independence and their higher status within their class, because, with increased income and consequent higher social status for the families, women were the first to be withdrawn from the work force as symbols of newly-acquired status (Human Development Report, Punjab, 2004).The activities in which women are engaged in Punjab are- dairy, bee-keeping, pappad/ badi and pickles. Besides these activities, poultry, basket/mat preparation, mushroom, vermi-composting are the other most popular agricultural activities in the region. Although Punjab is an economically developed state in the country but it has the lowest female work-force participation rate in the country. Sanjay Kumar found in his study of Punjab that Gurdaspur district has the lowest female work-participation rate among all the districts in the state. Most of the rural household in the state used to rear the cattle therefore the dairy is the main agro-based enterprise adopted by women in Punjab (Sanjay Kumar et al, 2004,).

Table 8
Major Indicators of Status of Women in Selected Districts of Punjab, 2001

	Districts		
Particulars	*Gurdaspur*	*Amritsar*	*Punjab (total)*
Proportion of females in total main workers and marginal workers	18.50	21.69	23.74
Female work participation rate	12.7	16.3	18.7
Female literacy rates	67.10	63.4	63.40
Sex ratio	840	876	876

Source: Statistical Abstracts of Punjab.

The Ministry of Statistics and Program Implementation conducted a Time Use Survey in 18,591 households spread over six selected states namely Haryana, M.P., Gujarat, Orissa, Tamil Nadu and Meghalaya. The percentage of time spent by females in unpaid activities was highest in Haryana (86%), followed by Meghalaya (76%) and Orissa (69%).The percentage was lowest for Tamil Nadu (32%). The report also states that, 'it was generally found that females spent about double the time as compared to males in activities relating to taking care of children, sick and elderly people'.

Gender Empowerment Measures (GEM) is intended to measure women's and men's ability to participate actively in economic and political life and their command over economic resources. It focuses on opportunities and captures gender inequality in key area of political participation and decision-making power. The 73rd and 74th Constitutional Amendments led to the resolution for women of one third seats in Panchayati Raj Institutions/Urban local bodies. Therefore, policy based affirmative action or positive discrimination has tried to empower women by ensuring their participation in decision making and domestic institution at the local level. Table 9 shows the huge gap between the percentage of seats held by women in Parliament and Gram Panchayats.

Himachal Pradesh has the highest representation of women in parliament with women holding 25 percent of seats. This is followed by Jammu and Kashmir with 17 percent, Punjab with

15 percent and Delhi with 14 percent. Only four other states have more than 10 percent of seats in Parliament held by women.

Table 9

Per cent Seats Held by Women in Parliament and Gram Panchayat in 2006

(States above 10 percent representation)

	Percent seats held by women in-	
State/ U.T.	*Parliament*	*Gram Panchayat*
Himachal Pradesh	25.0	39.13
Jammu and Kashmir	16.7	-
Punjab	15.4	35.03
Delhi	14.3	-
Haryana	10.0	36.65
Kerala	10.0	35.32
Maharashtra	10.4	33.33
Tamil Nadu	10.3	33.69

Source: Ministry of Panchayati Raj, 2008

Health Indicators

In many parts of the world, women receive less attention and health care than men do, and particularly girls often receive very much less support than boys. As a result of this gender bias, the mortality rates of females often exceed those of males in these countries.

Table 10

Marriage and Fertility Status of Women in Punjab and Haryana

	NFHS-3			*NFHS-2*	*NFHS-1*
Marriage and Fertility	*(2005-06)*	*Urban*	*Rural*	*(1998-99)*	*(1992-93)*
Women age 20-24	P* 19.7	18.1	20.6	11.6	41.5
married by age 18(%)	H** 41.2	33.3	44.8	14.9	57.3
Men age 25-29	P 27.2	30.1	24.8	NA	NA
married by age 21(%)	H 33.7	30.0	35.8	NA	NA
Total fertility rate	P 2.0	1.9	2.1	2.2	2.9
(children per women)	H 2.7	2.2	2.9	2.9	4.0

Source: NFHS-3, 2 and 1. (P*- Punjab, H**- Haryana) .

Table 10 shows increase in percentage of normal age of marriage in Punjab for women from 1992-93, while in Haryana percentage of such women is declining. It may be in the age of 18-20 years. Total fertility rate is declining in both the states but it is higher in Haryana. The rural women are married earlier and have higher fertility rate in comparison to their urban counterparts in both the states

In terms of nutrition, studies from rural Punjab in northern India generally reported that gender disparities in nutrition among children were greater among landowning than landless households. Excess levels of female mortality there also tended to be much greater for higher order female births. The fact that first-born daughters were more likely to survive suggested that parents used the 'lethal neglect' of daughters to achieve their preferred number and gender composition of children. Moreover, while *absolute* levels of mortality were lower among the propertied classes, excess levels of female mortality were higher. In addition, it was also higher among educated mothers.

Table 11
Nutritional Status of Women and Men in Punjab and Haryana

		NFHS-3			NFHS-2	NFHS-1
Nutritional status of Ever-married adults (age 15-49)		*(2005-06)*	*Urban*	*Rural*	*(1998-99)*	*(1992-93)*
Women whose body mass index is below normal (%)	P	13.5	11.8	14.5	16.9	NA
	H	27.8	16.9	32.5	25.9	NA
Men whose body mass index is below normal(%)	P	12.0	13.2	11.2	NA	NA
	H	26.8	19.3	30.0	NA	NA
Women who are overweight or obese (%)	P	37.5	45.4	32.9	30.2	NA
	H	21.0	34.8	15.0	16.6	NA
Men who are overweight or obese (%)	P	30.3	34.1	27.4	NA	NA
	H	14.4	26.5	9.3	NA	NA

Source: NFHS-3, 2 and 1.

Table 11 reflects improvement in health in comparison to 1998-99 in women of Punjab but at the same time obesity has increased. While male health is better in rural area, they are obese also in urban area. In urban area women are more obsessed than rural women and women are much obese than men. In Haryana women health shows decline in health in comparison to 1998-99 and condition in rural sector is worst than urban area. It applies for rural male, who are underweight in higher percentage than urban male. Obesity in women shows increase and higher in urban area than rural women. Males of urban area are comparatively higher in obesity than rural area. But obesity in male and female both is higher in Punjab in comparison to Haryana.

Being responsible as homemakers, nurtures, most of the women are unable to afford to take care of them. Anemia is the most common disease among women. It is a cause by a combination of poor nutrition, the burden of excessive childbearing and the heavy labour they perform .If we look the status of anemia in Punjab and Haryana state in children, married women and men ,we find the nutritional status is not so good in these states.

Table 12
Status of Anemia Among Children, Women and Men in Punjab and Haryana

	NFHS-3			NFHS-2	NFHS-1
Anemia among children and adults	*(2005-06)*	*Urban*	*Rural*	*(1998-99)*	*(1992-93)*
Children age 6-35 months who are	P 80.1	80.5	80.0	80.0	NA
anemic (%)	H 82.3	79.8	83.3	83.9	NA
Ever-married women	P 38.3	40.0	37.4	41.4	NA
age 15-49 years, who are anemic (%)	H 56.6	55.6	56.9	47.0	NA
Pregnant women age	P 41.6	42.6	41.0	37.1	NA
15-49years, who are anemic (%)	H 69.7	61.5	71.7	55.5	NA
Ever married men	P 12.6	11.1	13.8	NA	NA
age 15-49years, who are anemic (%)	H 17.6	17.0	17.8	NA	NA

Source: NFHS -3, 2 and 1.

Table 12 shows that anemia in children in both the states are cause of concern. Their conditions are same as in 1998-99.the married women in Punjab shows a little improvement over 1998-99 and rural women are slightly better in position than urban women. But it has increased in pregnant women but rural women have marginally lower anemia than urban women. Married male are more anemic in percentage in rural area. In Haryana, children anemia is little improved over the time but the percentage is too high still. The anemic position of Women of Haryana is get worse over 1998-99.The increase in percentage of 14.2 is cause of concern in pregnant women, who are anemic ,even it is worst in rural area. Married men are slightly better in urban area. Overall situation is astonishing, where people have better food in comparison to other parts of the country. Punjab and Haryana is treated as food provider to the nation, they are an agro based economy with dairy and poultry business. But health parameter of women and children is great cause of concern. They are anemic although obesity is on higher side (table 11). It shows they are getting high calorie but nutrition deficit food.

Table 13
Status of Women Empowerment in Punjab and Haryana

	NFHS-3			*NFHS-2*	*NFHS-1*
Women empowerment	*(2005-06)*	*Urban*	*Rural*	*(1998-99)*	*(1992-93)*
Currently married women who usually participate in household decision (%)	P 37.4	42.4	34.5	NA	NA
	H 41.7	49.5	38.4	NA	NA

Source: NFHS-3, 2 and 1.

Table 13 shows a reasonable good percentage of urban women in decision making while rural women are not that privileged in both the states Women are more empowered in both the states than other part of the country as they have better representation in Parliament by number of seats. A major parameter of women equality to their male counterpart is decision making in political and economic affairs and power over economic resources. The higher percentage of women in both the states in decision making is symbol of women empowerment. It is significant to note that they are more empowered for participation in household decision in comparison to other states, but gender inequity shows their involvement in making decisions for birth of male/female child.

Conclusion

Punjab is a prosperous state. Punjab (the five rivers region) is one of the most fertile regions. Punjab is called the "Granary of India" or "India's bread-basket. But its geographical situation has also affected by invasion of foreigners several times. As, history of India clarifies that most of the attacks in past and recent times were alone from Punjab border, even in post-independence period, Punjab faced three wars and later severe terrorism in late70'st and early 80's, safety and security of women in such situations became very difficult, moreover to counter such attacks male members in family were highly useful. Hence, a mindset for higher number of male members in family was prevailing since then, which continued for longtime, moreover to handle the legacy of land and business by son also remained a necessity, in such circumstances, their need for son became their social characteristic in Punjab and Haryana , which is still existing.

We took several indicators to judge the status of gender equity in both the states. The demographic indicator shows that sex ratio in both the states, Punjab and Haryana (876 and 861 respectively) is great cause of concern as this imbalance hinders the growth of these states and will affect social scenario in future. This imbalance in sex ratio is indicator that states are relatively gender biased.

The micro-studies show that with the availability of modern techniques to determine the sex of foetus, sex selective abortions have become common in both the states. It reconfirms the gender backwardness in both the states and confirms the hypothesis. Even special campaigns are organized by government and NGOs to save 'the girl child '.

The economic participation of women is quite low in both the states, although literacy rate is near to national average. The low participation in economic activities shows that women's economic involvement is quite less in the development of the states as they may play a crucial role in the development process of the states.

Through the health indicator, we found in our study that women fertility rate is 2.0 and 2.7 in Punjab and Haryana respectively and women receive less attention in health care than men do. We found that nutritional status is not satisfactory in these states. Though, women are obese, but they are anemic also.

Women between ages of 15-49 have experienced physical and sexual violence (30.9% and 29%) in these states. It shows the low regards towards women. Violence against women is a big social evil and it is one of the most brutal consequences of the economic, social, political and cultural inequality that exist between sexes.

As study shows, women empowerment regarding house hold decisions is high in these states. It is clear that they too prefer sons over daughters, which causes imbalance of sex ratio in both the states.To have gender equality, there should be a long term strategy at different levels and in different sectors. The first and foremost step should be started at the grass root level, i.e. from the households so that the parents realise their daughters as assets not a liability. As early feminist economist Ester Boserup, told about the status and standing of women may be enhanced by their economic independence. Measures to improve the status, role and participation of women are needed in the stream of development. It is clear from the micro studies that the result of women's participation is not merely to generate income for women, but also to provide many other social benefits that come from women's enhanced status and through law. It is only through the process of sensitizing various branches of the government and more importantly the members of the society to the rights and the concerns of women, than only gender justice can become a reality in these states.

Reference

Agnihotri, S.B. (1997), *Sex Ratio Imbalances in India - A Disaggregated Analysis*, Unpublished Ph.D. Thesis submitted to the School of Development Studies of the University of East Anglia, April.

Agnihotri, S.B. (1995), *"Missing Females- A Disaggregated Analysis"*, *Economic and Political Weekly*, August 19.

Bardhan, Kalpana (1985), *"Women's Work, Welfare and Status: Forces of Tradition and Change in India"*, *Economic and Political Weekly*, Vol. 20, No. 50, December 14 & 21-28.

Boserup, Ester, 1970, *"Women's Role in Economic Development"*, New York: St. Martin's Press.

CSWI (1975), *Towards Equality, Report of the Committee on Status of Women in India*, Ministry of Education and Social Welfare, Government of India, Delhi.

Dreeze; Jean and Amartya Sen (1995), *"India: Economic development and Social Opportunity"*, Oxford: Oxford University Press.

Esteve-Volart, Berta (2009), *"Gender Discrimination and Growth: Theory and Evidence from India"*, York University.

GEM estimates for India and the states (UTS: Results and Analysis).

"Gender Equality and Human Development Outcomes: Enhancing capabilities." (Online)

Government of Punjab, 2004: Punjab Human Development Report 2004, Chandigarh.

http//portal.unesco.org

Izhar Hassan, Mohd. ,*"Gender Bias and Economic Development in India: a casestudy of Haryana"*, SAGE Journal online.

Kumar, Sanjay; Jasdev Singh and G.S. Gill (2008), *" Agro-based Enterprises and Women in Punjab"*, in *"Gender Development in India-Dimensions and Strategies"*, edited by Himanshu Shekhar Pant and Prashant Kumar Panda. Century Publication, New Delhi.

Kundu, A. and M. Sahu (1991), *"Variations in Sex Ratio: Development Implications"*, *Economic and Political Weekly*, Vol., 26, Issue 41.

Lewis, Anjali, 2008,*" A Nation Without Women"*, Mercatornet.com

Maira, A. (2009), *"Lesser Children of God"*, The Economic Times, Lucknow (Ed.), 13-2-2009.

National Family Health Survey Reports 2005-06. (online)

Rustagi, Preet, 2010, *"Gender Development Indicator: Issues, Debates and Ranking of Districts" www.cwds.ac.in/OCPaper/GDIPreetRustagi.pdf*

Sen, A. (1992),*"Missing Women"*, find this article online.

Sen, Amartya," Many Faces of Gender Inequality", *Based on the text of an inauguration lecture for the new Radcliffe Institute at Harvard University, on April 24, 2001.* Frontline cover story (on line).

UNDP report-*"Innovative New Measurement Chart Impact of Poverty, Gender, Inequality."* UNDP, 4th Nov. 2010.

14

Post-Reform Economic Development in Punjab: A Comparative Perspective and Alternative Strategy

Lakhwinder Singh

Introduction

The economic development experience of the economy of Punjab state since the advent of green revolution remained quite dynamic. The prosperity ushered in Punjab in the late sixties allowed its economy to occupy first rank in terms of per capita income among the major states of the Indian Union. The dynamic economy of Punjab not only continued its leading position in terms of per capita income for more than three decades, but dramatically reduced population living below the poverty line[1] along with ensuring food security of the country as a whole. Legitimately, the development experience of the Punjab economy has been presented as a successful capitalist model of economic development worth emulating in other states of India in particular and the less developed countries in general. The serious scholars, working on the economy of Punjab state, had recognized the contribution of agrarian capitalist development in terms of generating the required surpluses for economic transformation of its economy but cautioned in the late nineteen eighties about the limits of such a model of economic growth (Johl 1986 and Gill 1988) to continue to provide sustained economic development. The suggested corrective measures by them could not receive the desired attention of the policy makers precisely because of the reason that the country was swayed in the early nineteen nineties by the policies of liberalization, privatization and globalization on the one hand and Punjab state was trapped in a political turmoil on the other hand. However, the policies of liberalization, privatization and globalization became quite handy to the state political leadership to pursue their self-interest and also allowed them to ignore the structural problems faced by the Punjab model of economic development, which were persisted over the decades. Consequently, the economic development process slowed down and turned the Punjab economy from the most dynamic and leading economy to a laggard one as compared with the overall economic performance of the Indian economy as well as with the fast growing states. Therefore, the process of turning a successful experience of economic development that went kaput needs thorough investigation. An attempt has been made in this paper to investigate the derailment of development process with a view to provide plausible alternative policy suggestions for rejuvenation of the economy of the Punjab state. The rest of the paper is organized into four sections. The empirical evidence on the Post-reform deceleration of economic growth in Punjab is presented in section two. The section three contains discussion on identification of the constraints related to economic growth process of Punjab economy. The relevant policy options for reforming the governance pattern of Punjab economy have been outlined in the section four. The concluding remarks are presented in the last section.

Post-Reform Deceleration of Economic Growth in Punjab: Evidence

In the post reform period, Punjab economy grew at a rate much slower than the overall rate of economic growth of the Indian economy[2]. However, according to per capita income estimates, the rank of Punjab state was number one towards the end of the 20th century, that is, 1999-2000. The per capita income of Punjab state in 1999-2000 was of the order of Rs. 25,631, which was higher than per capita income of the India's economy (Rs. 15881) of the order of Rs. 9750. This gap of Punjab state's per capita income declined substantially, during the early years of 21st century, which was just Rs. 7367 in the year 2007-08.

When we compare the ranking of per capita income across Indian states between the period 1999-2000 and 2007-08, it is important to note that fast growing major states of India over took Punjab state and reduced it from a leading state to number five in terms of per capita income level (Table 1). Haryana state has emerged number one with per capita income of the order of Rs. 39, 462, followed by Maharashtra, Kerala and Gujarat. The per capita income growth rates of major 15 states shown in Table 1 reveals that four states (Haryana, Andhra Pradesh, Kerala and Gujarat) have grown at a rate 6 per cent or higher. The per capita income of seven states, that is, Orissa, Tamil Nadu, Karnataka, Bihar, Himachal Pradesh, West Bengal and Maharashtra, was increased between 4 and 5 per cent per annum. It is pertinent to point out here that the per capita income of Punjab has grown at a rate 2.37 per cent per annum, which is just half the all India average and can be ranked number 13th among the major states of India according to compound growth rate of per capita income per annum during the period 1999-2000 to 2007-08. The four states (Haryana, Maharashtra, Kerala and Gujarat), which are having higher per capita income than Punjab state, have shown dynamism in economic development and have substantially increased the gap in per capita income over Punjab state. Himachal Pradesh is another state, which has reduced gap in per capita income at a fast rate and soon will over take Punjab. This is evidence enough to show that Punjab state has turned from 'a leading to a laggard state' during the post-reform period of economic growth.

To disentangle the slow pace of growth of per capita income during the post-reform period, the sectoral NSDP growth rates have been estimated and presented in Table 2. The perusal of the table 2 reveals that the performance of Punjab state is

Table 1
Per Capita Income across Major Indian States (1999-2000 and 2007-08)
(Figures at 1999-2000 prices)

State	*1999-2000*	*Rank*	*2007-2008*	*Rank*	*Compound Growth rate 1999-2000 to 2007-08*
Andhra Pradesh	15427	10	26195	9	6.06
Bihar	5786	15	8703	15	4.64
Gujarat	18864	7	31780	4	6.00
Haryana	23222	2	39462	1	6.07
Himachal Pradesh	20806	4	30856	6	4.48
Karnataka	17502	8	26418	8	4.68
Kerala	19461	5	32968	3	6.03
Madhya Pradesh	12384	12	13299	13	0.79
Maharashtra	23011	3	33302	2	4.19
Orissa	10567	13	16149	12	4.82
Punjab	25631	1	31662	5	2.37
Rajasthan	13619	11	18095	11	3.21
Tamil Nadu	19432	6	29445	7	4.72
Uttar Pradesh	9749	14	11939	14	2.28
West Bengal	15888	9	23229	10	4.31
All India	15881	-	24295	-	4.84

Table 2
Sectoral Net State Domestic Product Average Annual Growth Rates (1999-2000 to 2007-08) at 1999-2000 Prices

Sector/Year	*1990-91 to 2007-08*	*1990-91 to 1999-2000*	*2000-01 to 2007-08*
Agriculture	3.33	4.45	2.21
Manufacturing	4.73	4.43	5.03
Registered Manufacturing	4.59	5.35	3.84
Unregistered Manufacturing	5.68	4.71	6.66
Electricity	11.84	12.46	11.23
Construction	7.61	4.42	10.80
Trade	4.60	4.24	4.96
Transport	11.92	11.14	12.7
Banking	10.33	9.99	10.68
Real Estate	2.42	4.66	1.79
Public Administration	6.74	9.16	4.32
Other services	7.80	13.06	2.54
NSDP	5.26	5.73	4.79
PCI	3.32	3.7	2.9

deteriorating when we compare with its own past performance and achievements. There is a strong evidence of deceleration in economic growth of Punjab state's economy in terms of NSDP growth rates recorded during the period 2000-01 to 2007-08 compared with 1990-1991 to 1999-2000. The agriculture sector occupies prime place in the economy of Punjab. The relative share of agriculture sector in the NSDP product was 32.45 per cent in 2007-08. It has declined from 44 per cent in 1990-91 to 39 per cent in 1999-2000 and further to 32 per cent in 2007-08 (Government of Punjab 2009). This clearly brings out the fact that agriculture sector of the state of Punjab still constitutes the major contributing sector in the health of the state economy. The growth of agriculture sector as indicated from the post-reform period not only remained quite slow (3.33 per cent), but decelerated in the second sub-period, that is, 2000-01 to 2007-08. During the decade of 1990s, the agriculture sector of the state has grown at a rate 4.45 per cent and it was 2.21 per cent during the period 2000-01 to 2007-08. However, the agriculture sector has grown at a rate of 5.15 per cent per annum during the 1980s (Singh and Singh 2002). The foregoing discussion brings out the fact that the deceleration of rate of growth of agriculture sector has contributed substantially to the slow down in the growth of per capita income of the economy of Punjab state.

Industrial sector has been regarded as the most dynamic sector of an economy and provides desired economic transformation from low wage-low productivity economic activities to high wage-high productivity economic activities. However, in the case of Punjab, the industrial sector of Punjab economy in terms of its relative contribution to the NSDP remained quite small. The manufacturing sector of Punjab state contributed 15.1 per cent of NSDP in 1990-91 and declined to 13.6 per cent in 2007-08. The relative share of the registered manufacturing sector in NSDP was 8.8 per cent in 1990-91, which has declined to 7.4 per cent in 2007-08. The rate of growth of the registered manufacturing sector has decelerated during the period 2000-01 to 2007-08 compared with the 1990-91 to 1999-2000. The registered manufacturing sector has grown at rate of 5.35 per cent during 1990-91 to 1999-2000, which was much below the 1980s level. However, the growth rate for the period 2000-01 to 2007-08 was 3.84 per cent per annum. Contrary to this, unorganized manufacturing sector has recorded higher growth rate during the 2000-01 to 2007-08 compared with the growth experience of the 1990s (Table 2). That was precisely the reason that the manufacturing sector as a whole has shown marginal acceleration of rate of growth in the later period compared with the 1990s. The other sectors, which have recorded deceleration of economic growth during the 2000s compared with 1990s, are electricity, real estate, public administration and other services. It is worth mentioning here that the combined share of all the sectors of the Punjab economy, which have observed deceleration in growth during the 2000s, was 68.52 per cent in 1990-91. This share has declined to 57.74 per cent in 2007-08. Obviously, the slow growing sectors have contributed to the slow growth of per capita income and net state domestic product of the Punjab economy. Although, the fast growing sector failed to arrest the deceleration of economic growth in Punjab because of their relative share in the NSDP was less than 32 per cent in 1990-91, but have triggered the process of structural transformation in terms of changing the relative contribution of the sectors to the state's economy. From the foregoing analysis, it can be safely said that the engine of growth of Punjab economy still continued to be the 'agriculture sector'.

The agriculture sector of Punjab economy directly absorbs more than 39 per cent of the total work force. The cultivators constitute 22.96 per cent of the total work force of Punjab state and agricultural workers were of the order of 16.40 per cent (Gill and Singh 2006). It is significant to note that agriculture sector generates more than 32 per cent of the state income but employs more that 39 per cent of the work force. This empirical evidence brings out clearly that the structure of Punjab economy is not only imbalanced but highly agriculture sector dependent both for livelihood and employment. Therefore, the growth performance of this sector heavily impinges on the well being of the population living in the rural areas of Punjab. The performance of agriculture sector also affects the growth prospects of the other sectors of the Punjab economy directly and indirectly due to the interconnections between sectors.

Constraints on Economic Development in Punjab

Among the macroeconomic policies, fiscal policy has been widely recognized and acclaimed for its impact on economic development process. The impact of fiscal policy on economic growth is mainly dependent on the efficiency with which resource mobilization and expenditures are incurred. However, the fiscal policy of the Punjab state remained continuously in disarray since the mid eighties (Rajmal 2009 and Ahluwalia 2009). The fiscal deficit of the Punjab state remained 5.3 per cent during the period 1985-1990, which was highest among the 14 major states of India. Whereas the overall fiscal deficit of the 14 major state of India was 3.3 per cent and the fiscal deficit of Haryana and Maharashtra states were 2.7 and 3.1 per cent of gross state domestic product respectively (Rajmal 2009). One fundamental reason for running a high fiscal deficit of Punjab state was due to relatively low revenue receipts as a percentage of gross state domestic product and was bracketed with the state of West Bengal, Bihar and Uttar Pradesh. State tax to gross state domestic product (tax effort) was 6.86 per cent in 2007-08 (Government of Punjab 2010). Therefore, the fiscal deficit over the years has been financed through borrowings from the Union government and increasingly during the post-reform period through commercial borrowings. This has generated huge amount of debt stock over the years and consequently, the substantial proportion of the tax revenue goes as interest payments. The total amount of interest payments and services of debt was of the order of Rs. 4526.92 crore in 2007-08, which increased to Rs. 5348.64 crore in 2009-10. This comes out to be nearly 45 per cent of the state taxes in 2007-08. This has led to further deterioration of fiscal situation of the state and has crippled the capacity of the state government to involve itself in developmental economic activities. It is indicative from the fact that the developmental expenditure in gross state domestic product has declined from

10.8 per cent during 1990-95 to 8.4 per cent during 2000-2007 (Table 3). It is perturbing to note that Punjab state in terms of development expenditure is ranked number 13 among the major states of India. However, the proportion of non-developmental expenditure in gross state domestic product has increased from 5.9 per cent during 1990-95 to 9.8 per cent during 2000-2007 and occupies first rank among the major Indian states (Table 3). Similarly, the capital expenditure in the total expenditure of the state has been very low but marginally improved from 1990-95 to 2000-07 period. But compared with other major states, the capital expenditure has been one of the low priorities of the state government. The rising non-developmental expenditure and falling developmental

Table 3
Development, Non-Development and Capital Expenditure Across Major States

	Development Expenditure as % of GSDP		*Non-Development Expenditure as % of GSDP*		*Capital Expenditure as % of Total Expenditure*	
State	*1990-1995*	*2000-2007*	*1990-1995*	*2000-2007*	*1990-1995*	*2000-2005*
Andhra Pradesh	12.8	12.4	4.3	6.1	19.8	24.8
Bihar	11.8	14.9	5.9	8.7	13.0	21.3
Gujarat	12.8	11.9	4.0	5.5	18.5	22.9
Haryana	10.7	9.4	6.4	5.1	15.3	21.3
Karnataka	13.0	12.6	4.5	5.9	15.6	21.3
Kerala	10.9	9.1	5.5	7.4	14.0	14.2
Madhya Pradesh	11.5	13.8	3.9	6.1	13.0	21.4
Maharashtra	10.7	9.6	3.9	5.6	18.3	19.1
Orissa	14.8	11.7	5.8	9.2	18.2	23.0
Punjab	10.8	8.4	5.9	9.8	16.7	18.3
Rajasthan	13.6	12.8	5.4	7.7	22.5	21.9
Tamil Nadu	13.3	9.9	4.0	6.0	12.2	18.9
Uttar Pradesh	11.6	12.2	5.9	8.2	16.6	21.2
West Bengal	8.9	8.2	4.0	7.2	17.2	19.9
All India	11.8	11.1	4.7	6.8	16.7	20.9

Source: Derived from Rajmal (2009) *State Finances and Growth: A Study of Major States of India,* Unpublished Ph. D Thesis, Indian Institute of Technology Bombay, Mumbai.

expenditure has a capacity of crowding out investment that adversely affects economic growth. Obviously, the fiscal policy pursued by the state government during the post-reform period seems to have impacted in slowing down the process economic growth of the economy of the state.

The operation of monetary policy, although is not under the control of the state government, has substantial role in acceleration or derailment of the economic growth process. One of the most important indicators of the functioning of the monetary policy is the credit-deposit ratio, which shows the investment pattern of the state. The analysis of the credit-deposit ratio across states during the post-reform period presented in Table 4 shows that the credit-deposit ratio remained below the national average. This ratio was 48.04 in 1990 and accordingly Punjab among major 14 states was ranked number 14th. This ratio was much below the minimum level prescribed by the Reserve Bank of India. However, the credit-deposit ratios declined to 38.95 in 2000, but improved substantially in 2009 and its state rank. It is significant to note that the southern states, that is, Tamil Nadu, Andhra Pradesh,

Table 4
Credit-Deposit Ratio Across Indian States (1990-2009)

State	*1990*	*Rank*	*2000*	*Rank*	*2009*	*Rank*
Andhra Pradesh	88.28	3	67.27	3	102.39	2
Bihar	38.61	14	23.35	14	26.38	14
Gujarat	59.58	9	47.56	6	59.75	9
Haryana	57.49	10	39.44	11	72.13	6
Karnataka	89.15	2	62.03	4	77.39	5
Kerala	63.35	7	40.66	9	61.15	8
Madhya Pradesh	66.66	6	49.31	5	59.00	10
Maharashtra	79.40	4	88.72	1	89.67	3
Orissa	76.55	5	39.60	10	51.96	12
Punjab	44.08	13	38.95	12	67.43	7
Rajasthan	61.24	8	46.39	7	84.05	4
Tamil Nadu	101.24	1	83.56	2	108.41	1
Uttar Pradesh	46.96	12	28.41	13	41.23	13
West Bengal	50.05	11	44.55	8	58.59	11
All India	64.35	-	56.37	-	70.24	-

Source: Government of India (1991, 2001 and 2010) *Economic Survey*, New Delhi: Ministry of Finance.

Karnataka, and Maharashtra observed through out the period of analysis high credit-deposit ratios (Table 4). In comparison to above mentioned states, the credit-deposit ratio of Punjab remained quite low. This clearly brings out the fact that resources of the state due to operation of the banking sector transferred Punjab state's precious savings to other states of India, which otherwise could have been invested in the Punjab state. Punjab State recorded investment-gross state domestic product ratio 18.7 per cent, which was the lowest among 14 major states as against 35 per cent of the national average as measured in 1995-96 (Ahluwalia 2002). Due to this deficiency of investment, the growth process of the Punjab deteriorated over the years. Therefore, centralized monetary and fiscal policies have initiated the process of crowding out investment from Punjab, which has adversely affected the economic growth process of the economy of the Punjab state[3].

Apart from macroeconomic policies, the process of modern economic growth is highly constrained by the availability of superior human capital and institutional arrangements. The development process according to Sen (1999) enhances human capabilities, expands economic opportunities, freedom to make choices and change in institutional arrangements. He has also established a positive relationship between indicators of human capital and instruments of freedom. The indicators of human capital across states in comparison to per capita income are presented in Table 5. Punjab state has been ranked number two so far as the human development index is concerned. However, according to literacy and infant mortality rates, Punjab state is ranked 5th and is much behind other dynamic states such as Kerala, Maharashtra and Tamil Nadu. If we look at the functional aspect of literacy, that is, which provide threshold level to participate in labour markets, the current estimates of literacy are deceptive. However, the functioning of the educational institutions and imparting real literacy that matter for the participation in the organized sector economic activities begins from matric (that is 10th class) level education. A recent survey of 36 villages of Punjab revealed that the 68.85 per cent of the rural households do not have any member in

Table 5
Indicators of Human Capital Across States

State	*Literacy Rate2001*	*Life Expectancy 2002-2006*	*Per Capita Income 2007-2008*	*Infant Mortality Rate 2007*
Andhra Pradesh	60.47	64.4	26195	54
	(13)	(7)	(9)	(8)
Bihar	47.0	61.6	8703	58
	(16)	(10)	(15)	(10)
Gujarat	69.1	64.1	31780	52
	(6)	(8)	(4)	(7)
Haryana	67.91	66.2	39462	55
	(9)	(4)	(1)	(9)
Himachal Pradesh	76.48	NA	30856	NA
	(3)		(6)	
Karnataka	66.64	65.3	26418	47
	(10)	(5)	(8)	(6)
Kerala	90.86	74	32968	13
	(1)	(1)	(3)	(1)
Madhya Pradesh	63.74	58	13299	72
	(11)	(13)	(13)	(14)
Maharashtra	76.88	67.2	33302	34
	(2)	(3)	(2)	(2)
Orissa	63.08	59.6	16149	71
	(12)	(12)	(12)	(13)
Punjab	69.65	69.4	31662	43
	(5)	(2)	(5)	(5)
Rajasthan	60.41	62	18095	65
	(14)	(9)	(11)	(11)
Tamil Nadu	73.4	66.2	29445	35
	(4)	(4)	(7)	(3)
Uttar Pradesh	56.27	60	11939	69
	(15)	(11)	(14)	(12)
West Bengal	68.64	64.9	23229	37
	(7)	(6)	(10)	(4)
All India	64.84	63.5	24295	55

Source: Government of India (2010) *Economic Survey 2009-10*, New Delhi: Oxford University Press.

Note: Figures in parentheses are ranks.

the household possessing education up to matric level. The situation is worse when we consider non-landed rural households. Nearly 90 per cent of the rural non-landed households do have any member educated up to matric level (Ghuman, Singh and Singh 2007). This situation of Punjab state may be a reflection of poor state of the functioning of the educational institutions despite achieving higher level of per capita income. The matter of fact is that Punjab state has created primary school facilities almost in every village of the state. However, there are as many as 22.6 per cent of the primary schools of Punjab state, which are being run by a single teacher (Chakraborty 2009). There are even instances of a single teacher running two schools along with numerous data collection survey conducting type activities assigned by the state government from time to time and consequently primary school remains closed for many days. This impinges on the performance of students studying in such schools in terms of achieving educational capabilities. Somewhat similar is the situation in the health care system of Punjab (Singh and Aggarawal 2010). The public sector institutions have deteriorated over the years in terms of delivery of education and health related services, which has been acting as a constraint on the supply of high quality human capital and hence in the long run reduces chances of achieving high rate of economic growth.

The sustainability of growth of the agriculture sector of the economy of Punjab is under question mark. On the one side, the agriculture sector is turning less remunerative compared with early green revolution period and on the other, natural resource constraint such as degradation of soil health and dramatically falling underground water table is increasingly becoming more severe. The green revolution in Punjab dramatically altered the cropping pattern. During the seventies and eighties, the diversified rural economy of Punjab turned towards predominantly wheat-paddy rotation. The number of crops sown in Punjab was 21 in the year 1960-61 and declined to 9 in 1990-91 and remained so thereafter. The area sown under crops other than wheat declined from 62.74 in 1960-61 to 17.12

per cent in 2004-05. The area under rice increased from merely 6.05 per cent in 1960-61 to 63.02 per cent in 2004-05. Crop diversification index for the winter season declined from 0.79 in 1960-61 to 0.303 in 2004-05 and this index for summer crop season declined from 0.98 in 1960-61 to 0.58 in 2004-05 (Toor, Bhullar and Kaur, 2007). This indicates that there has occurred a clear "reversal" of diversification of the rural economy of Punjab. The rising cropping intensity has dramatically increased the input intensity especially water, fertilizers, pesticides, tractors and other various kinds of agricultural machinery (Singh and Aggarwal 2010). The biological and mechanical intensity of agriculture has substantially increased pressure on natural resources, which has lead to degradation of soil health and underground water table.

During the period of 1990s, the green revolution technology has shown signs of fatigue. Productivity growth stagnated along with near freeze of prices, which resulted into the decline of agriculture sector's contribution to the state income. Growth rate of income generated in the agriculture proper (income from crops) was less than 1 per cent during the nineties and early years of twenty first century. This has created imbalance in the structure of Punjab state's economy, whereas share of agriculture sector's (crops and dairying) income has sharply declined in the state domestic product from 54.27 per cent in 1970-71 to 33.70 per cent in 2005-06. But the proportion of workforce engaged in agriculture sector of Punjab continue to be very high, that is, 48 per cent in the year 2004-05. This comes out to 66.9 per cent of the total rural workforce of Punjab in the year 2004-05. It needs to be noted here that agricultural workforce was as high as 82.5 per cent of the total rural workforce of Punjab in the year 1983. The workforce engaged in the agricultural sector of Punjab has declined to 74.6 per cent of the total rural workforce in the year 1993-94 compared with 1983. It further declined to 66.9 per cent in the year 2004-05 (NCEUS, 2007). Furthermore, the 90.9 per cent of workforce in Punjab is engaged in the unorganized sector where the wage rate is very low. The workforce working in the agriculture sector, especially agriculture labour, small and marginal farmers, are earning below Rs 20.3 per capita per day[4], which is called vulnerable by the National Commission on Enterprises in the Unorganised Sector. The slow growth of agriculture sector and high dependence of workforce are expected to further worsen the working and living conditions of the rural workforce. This has led to rise in the burden of debt among the farming and non-farming households in Punjab (Shergill 2010). The interlinked agrarian markets have further perpetuated the debt cycle and generated circumstances, which have forced farmers and agricultural labourers to commit suicides (Gill, 2005).

The most dynamic sector in modern economic growth process considered is the industrial sector of an economy. The pertinent question that begs for an explanation here is why deceleration in industrial growth has occurred in the post-reform period. The comparative analysis of prerequisites across Indian states reveals that Punjab was the most suitable state for new industrial investment opportunities (Table 6). Punjab was ranked number one among the Indian states in terms of its competitive index at the beginning of new economic policy. This competitive index was computed on the basis of eleven socio-economic variables. The noteworthy feature of industrial growth here is that the high and low ranking states, in terms of competitive index, performed sluggishly in the post-reform period compared to some of the middle ranking states such as Maharashtra. Human development index is now considered in economic thinking as a more appropriate indicator of development compared to purely income based measures; here too Punjab state has shown quite higher level of human resource development. It was ranked number two just next to Kerala among the Indian states which clearly indicates that Punjab can legitimately expect to be a highly attractive place for new investment, both domestic and foreign, in the absence of 'license-quota raj'. Contrary to expectations, the investment, both domestic and foreign, tended to concentrate in few states in the post-reform period as it was during the license-quota raj. The perusal of the Table 6 clearly shows that Punjab was among the low priority states to attract direct foreign investment proposals as well as industrial investment of the private corporate sector of India. It was ranked number twelfth in the priority accorded by the foreign investors and eighth by

Table 6
State Wise Indicators of Competitiveness and Investment Proposals

States	*State Competitive Index*	*Human Development Index*	*FDI Approvals (Numbers) 1991-2007*	*FDI Approvals Amount Rs. crore 1991-2007*	*IIP nos. Aug. 1991-March 2004*	*IIP proposed investment Rs. crore*
Punjab	82.80	0.58	225	5740.50	183	4887
	(1)	(2)	(12)	(9)	(7)	(8)
Kerala	67.71	0.65	350	1859.00	67	2782
	(2)	(1)	(10)	(13)	(11)	(12)
Haryana	63.25	0.54	940	4094.13	233	4318
	(3)	(3)	(6)	(11)	(6)	(9)
Gujarat	60.63	0.50	1304	13033.45	438	14567
	(4)	(5)	(5)	(5)	(3)	(2)
Karnatka	56.19	0.48	2741	24934	233	9598
	(5)	(6)	(3)	(3)	(6)	(6)
Tamil Nadu	49.10	0.52	2826	25214.03	736	11273
	(6)	(4)	(2)	(2)	(1)	(3)
Maharashtra	48.77	0.48	5388	58152.85	558	21028
	(7)	(6)	(1)	(1)	(2)	(1)
Andhra Pradesh	46.69	0.43	1360	16067.74	434	10715
	(8)	(7)	(4)	(4)	(4)	(4)
Orissa	46.61	0.34	161	8428.30	37	5444
	(9)	(10)	(13)	(7)	(12)	(7)
Assam	46.41	0.43	28	37.40	12	2433
	(10)	(7)	(15)	(15)	(14)	(13)
Rajasthan	38.90	0.29	357	3129.78	97	1626
	(11)	(12)	(9)	(12)	(9)	(14)
Madhya Pradesh	36.80	0.31	252	9277.40	141	3160
	(12)	(11)	(11)	(6)	(8)	(11)
West Bengal	34.18	0.48	723	8154.67	90	4047
	(13)	(6)	(8)	(8)	(10)	(10)
Uttar Pradesh	25.27	0.36	842	4935.32	353	9752
	(14)	(8)	(7)	(10)	(5)	(5)
Bihar	22.36	0.35	50	739.70	33	1462
	(15)	(9)	(14)	(14)	(13)	(15)

Source: 1. Government of India (2010), and Singh (2005).
Note: 1. Figures in parentheses indicate the rank.

the Indian private corporate sector during the post reform period. It is clear from the analysis of Table 6 that Maharashtra, Tamil Nadu, Karnataka, Gujarat and Andhra Pradesh accounted for substantial amount of investment, both Indian private corporate and foreign direct investment. This has propelled industrial growth in these five states leaving the others as permanent laggards (Babu 2002). The rigorous scrutiny of the determinants that have accelerated growth in some of the states and retarded growth in majority of the states in general and Punjab state in particular are investment-GSDP ratio, plan expenditure, human resources and quality of infrastructure. Punjab continues to show highest index of infrastructure both in the pre and post-reform period, but the index declined from 193.4 in 1991-92 to 185.6 in 1996-97. However, quality of infrastructure and human resources are difficult to judge from the indicators, which are based on physical characteristics. Low level of investment, decline in the planned expenditure and lack of strategic human skills as well as infrastructure are the major factors, which do have a bearing on the slow down in the industrial growth in Punjab (Ahluwalia 2002, Singh and Singh 2002).

Apart from investment constraint, the industrial economy of Punjab has been suffering from the constraint on the demand side as well. The collapse of Soviet Union on the one side and changing preference patterns of the western consumers from woollen to cotton hosiery on the other have dampened the demand of Punjab industry. The changes in the freight equalization policy of the Union government and environmental regulation on woodcutting have severely affected the input supply and cost of inputs especially of light engineering and sports goods industries. Lack of industry-agriculture linkage in Punjab has adversely affected the sustainability of the growth process of the economy of the state. The information and communication technology (ICT) revolution have bypassed the economy of Punjab due to lack of matching scientific institutional arrangements and non-availability of the scientific manpower desired for such economic activities to take place firm roots.

On the top of it, Punjab state is politically very sensitive and inflammable on social and political matters. This kind of societal culture has high costs in terms of crowding out investment and putting a permanent constraint on the economic growth process of her economy. Along with this, the Punjab state shares international border with Pakistan and Indian relations with Pakistan usually does not remain cordial. Therefore, Indian Pakistan fragile political relations generate high risks for investors and therefore, Punjab state cannot realize its full potential of economic development. It is pertinent to point out here that the constraints on economic growth faced by the Punjab economy are partly under the purview and control of the state government and partly comes under the purview and control of Union government of India and thus needs joint efforts of both the governments for the removal of constraints in realizing the potential.

Policy Options and Alternatives

Keeping in view the constraints on Punjab economy the governance pattern of state of Punjab needs sweeping changes for rejuvenating the economy and reversal in the deceleration of economic growth. The government of Punjab has to seek cooperation of the Union government in dealing with the problems posed by the functioning of the macroeconomic policies, that is, monetary and fiscal policies. The government of Punjab needs to set its own house also in order specifically realizing the potential of tax revenue, while making suitable reforms in the tax collection machinery of the state. The existing tax structure has potentialities to raise the proportion of tax in GSDP to the level of dynamic states, while wiping out the current level of tax evasion taking place in Punjab. It is significant to note here that Punjab state has bifurcated the ministry of finance into revenue ministry and expenditure ministry (present ministry of Finance is doing the work of expenditure ministry only). Therefore, it is suggested that governance reform must begin with integrating the functions of the finance ministry for achieving the efficiency in conducting fiscal policy of the state government on the pattern of Union government. Monetary and fiscal policies should work in harmony to raise the level of investment-GSDP ratio at least to the national average. In this direction Union government and state government needs to work in tandem and close cooperation in realizing the objective of achieving investment-GSDP level equivalent to national average for making suitable amendments in revenue proceeds transfer system to the state government and operations of banking system. This can be achieved if governance pattern, both at the Union government and the state government, is decentralized to achieve the desired objective of reversal of deceleration in economic growth. Once the disarrayed macroeconomic policies along with institutional reforms at the state level put in place, there is some possibility in reversing the pattern of deceleration of economic growth in Punjab.

While altering the course of macroeconomic policies has a capacity to change the direction of economic growth, it does not have the capacity to resolve all the constraints on economic growth of the economy of Punjab. Therefore, long term measures also need to be initiated simultaneously for structural transformation of the economy unleashing the process of economic development that will improve the general well being of the people as outlined by Sen (1999). It is worth mentioning here that the ongoing reforms process both of the Union government and state government has failed to stimulate the economic growth of Punjab economy. This is precisely because of the reason that the economy of the state is already predominantly governed by the private sector and rules based on the market economy. Therefore, a further higher dose of market to the state economy will not give the desired outcomes in terms of stimulating economic growth process. An alternative course of economic transformation is desired to trigger the economic growth process against the TINA (there is no alternative) syndrome.

Agriculture sector of the state assumes central importance given the current level of global and national food shortage, which have spiraled the inflationary pressure on the Indian economy. The rejuvenation of the agriculture sector of the state is urgently required both in meeting the requirements of national food security as well as the population dependent on agriculture. The slowing down of agricultural rate of growth has been caused by rising input costs and stagnating productivity on the one hand and deterioration of soil health and exhaustion of natural resources on the other. This is a clear case of technological constraint resulting into diminishing returns to scale. On the technological plane solutions exist which have a capacity to raise productivity multiple times and reduce per unit costs of agricultural produce through harnessing the biotechnological revolution. This requires massive public investment in frontline technologies and strengthening institutional infrastructure, which can interact closely with the individual farmers because the small sized farmers do not have a capacity to spend resources on R&D and essential training of the manpower. However, the liberalization regime has left the farmers to fend for themselves or depend on the profit oriented agribusiness firms.

Keeping in view the evidently growing agricultural crisis, government of Punjab had shown early awareness and appointed an expert committee under the chairmanship of S. S. Johl in 1985 to diagnose the problem and suggest suitable remedial policy measures. Johl committee put forward the idea of diversification of agriculture from the existing wheat-paddy cropping pattern (Johl1986). Diversification aims at to transfer area from cereal production to remunerative crops such as fruits, vegetables and pulses not only to increase income of the farmers but also to reduce environmental degradation for long-term sustainability of Punjab agriculture. Agriculture diversification based rural industrialization growth strategy has been prodded from its successful experience in the early eighties in many Southeast Asian countries. Thus, emulating the success story of the diversification through rural industrialization and increasing rural income in several Southeast Asian countries seemed to be a fascinating policy option for the state of Punjab. However, the proposed agriculture diversification strategy of agriculture completely ignored the fundamental ingredients of the strategy which were the corner stone of success in Southeast Asia. Diversification strategy was based on the widely spread misinformation of the multilateral financial institutions and independent experts, those who have tied their knot with market, and success of diversification in Southeast Asia was essentially attributed to use of market forces (Jomo 2001, Wade 1990). Therefore, diversification strategy, which relied upon market responses and expected cold response from the Government of Punjab, however, received enthusiastic response from the individual farmers. The cruel response of the market soon dampened the enthusiastic response of the farmers and they had no other option left but to fall back on the well-known wheat-paddy cropping pattern. In a recent attempt, government of Punjab has taken the lead to promote diversification of agriculture while adopting the path of contract farming. Government of Punjab has been playing the role of an intermediary between the farmers and the agribusiness firms. However, the very design and implementation of contract farming scheme leaves small sized farmers at the mercy of the private firms, which have secured monopoly position in the market. Farmers who have opted contract farming with the private agribusiness firms, have filed complaints with the Punjab governments' agriculture department regarding the way agribusiness firms exploited them in terms of providing lower prices and charged for services without rendering any service. These complaints of the farmers were investigated by the governments' agriculture department and found correct. Contract based on purely private profit considerations and market orientation in the absence of enforcement agency acted against the farmers. Thus, farmers have no choice but for perpetuating the wheat-paddy cropping pattern (Gill 2004).

Diversification of agriculture of Punjab is a desired goal for transformation of agrarian economy to industrialized one. Transformation experience of the developed countries has shown that agriculture sector of the economy in the process of transformation provides surplus resources to the industrial sector and consequently, the agriculture sector marginalized in the economy. Thus, decline in the share of real incomes in the agriculture sector was a universal phenomenon and was experienced by the OECD countries and middle-income countries. As long as the processing activities of agriculture production is taking place away from the farm gates, agriculture sector will have the potential of exploitation and continue to face decline in the rural incomes (Timmer 1988). Contrary to this, the experience of diversification of agriculture and rural industrialization in the Southeast Asian countries in general and Taiwan in particular has not only integrated the agriculture with the industry but also generated substantial rise in rural income. Agricultural produce was processed on the farm gates and surplus was ploughed back to expand rural industrial activities as well as raising the level of living of the people living in the countryside. The fundamental factor of success of Taiwan's agricultural diversification experience was the farmers' associations. The farmers' association of Taiwan was nothing but the farmers' cooperatives which were responsible for controlling all the economic activities; from credit to production, processing and marketing (Moore 1993). Therefore, the value addition was done through processing activities and was realized through marketing activities and redeployed the surpluses for the welfare of the association/ cooperatives. This process very successfully eliminated the intermediary agency, which is the major source of exploitation and absorbing surpluses without looking after the interest of the fundamental producers. However, it is important to note here that state in the Southeast Asian countries played a crucial role to provide essential institutional infrastructure and investment in rapid technical change to raise agricultural output and rural incomes. Elimination of the high rents charged by the middleman and endogenous technological progress has the power to transform agriculture into an industry along with raising the rural income. This is possible if organization of production is changed from individual to cooperative. The cooperatives suggested here are not the bureaucratic-state controlled cooperatives, but modern cooperatives strictly based on membership and which adhere to market rules with accountability as an endogenous tool of organizational behaviour. There are many such examples of the cooperatives, which have succeeded in our own country. Amul is a remarkable success story of small rural milk producers' cooperative, which has now highly diversified into consumer products. The creative organization of Amul contributed to the generation of surpluses after the elimination of intermediary agency and these surpluses have been utilized for developing local infrastructure and investment in the technology to raise the productivity of the farmers' output (Patibandla and Sastry 2004). Another important example of farmer's cooperative is in Narayangao area in Junnar taluka in Maharashtra state for industrialization of grape cultivation, which was established in 1991. There are 45 members and they pooled 130 acres of vineyards to export table fresh grapes to the European markets. This cooperative has diversified both marketing and product related activities. It has succeeded in raising the level of rural income both of the farmers and the rural labour. Reduction of risk through collective action, elimination of middlemen and investment in technological progress were the central factors which contributed to the success story of the transformation of farmers as business enterprise (Rath 2003).

Punjab government and farmers organization, which are striving to transform farming through diversification of agriculture, have a strong need to learn lessons from the success story of the Southeast Asian countries as well as from well-known Indian examples. Farmers' organizations so far have successfully organized agitations to secure some concessions for survival but completely ignored their collective role in generating economic enterprises to reduce the role of middleman. Post-reform deceleration of industrial growth and shying away of both foreign and Indian private corporate investors to invest in Punjab's industrial economy are the other hard lessons which clearly point out that local investment efforts are direly needed to transform the economy. Local investment efforts have a capacity to crowd in investment, both foreign and Indian. Therefore, the strategy that needs to be adopted by the government of Punjab is not to offer purely private and market based solutions, but to lead farmers' organization to organize production, processing and marketing activities. This requires essential suitable institutional and infrastructural arrangements, which should encourage farmers to process their produce at the farm gates and eliminate mark up of the middleman. It needs to be suggested here that government of Punjab should enact suitable policy and provide exclusive industrial parks as agro-processing zones for farmers' cooperatives on similar pattern as have been provided and offered to foreign and domestic private industry.

Conclusions

Punjab economy has experienced deceleration of economic growth in the post-reform period contrary to acceleration of economic growth of the national economy as well as majority of the major states of the country. The process of divergence of economic growth performance of Punjab state vis a vis of national economy as well as of dynamic states has been examined with a view to identify the growth reducing sectors and constraints. The post-reform economic growth pattern of Punjab economy clearly brings out that the dominant sectors of Punjab economy like agriculture, registered manufacturing, electricity, real estate, public administration and others services, which contributed 68.52 per cent of the net state domestic product at beginning of reform period, have experienced deceleration in economic growth. The major constraints that have impinged upon the development process of the Punjab economy are structural rigidities, macroeconomic policies, human capital development, low investment-GSDP ratio, demand and supply factors and non economic factors such as social, political and an active international border. Keeping in view the grassroot realities, alternative policy measures are suggested to rejuvenate the economy of Punjab. The reforms related to governance pattern of both state and union government have been suggested with regard to the purview of both the stakeholders. To harness long term sustained and inclusive growth, an alternative structural transformation pattern of economic growth has been outlined. The alternative policy options devised keeping in view the specificities of the economy of Punjab state, if implemented have a capacity to restructure and rebuild the economy of state along with involving people as a partner of economic growth.

Notes

1. Punjab state has dramatically reduced population below the poverty line. The population living below the poverty line in Punjab, according to consumer expenditure survey conducted by the NSSO during 2004-05 was 8.4 per cent against the 27.5 per cent of all India (Chaudhuri and Gupta 2009). It is important to notice here that during peak period of green revolution (1973-74 to 1977-78), the population below poverty line declined at a rate over 2 percentage points per annum. However, the poverty reduction rate has slowed down during the period 1993-94 to 2004-05 and the rate of decline was just 0.3 percentage points per annum (Ahluwalia 2010).
2. Economic development experience, during the last two decades, in Punjab suffered a setback due partly to the impact of militant moment in the 1980s. But the end of militancy in the early period of 1990s and continued deterioration in the growth process thereafter has pointed out the failure of the government policies to stimulate economic growth in Punjab (Ahluwalia 2009).
3. To attract industrial investment in the states of Himachal Pradesh, Jammu and Kashmir and Uttaranchal-all neighbouring states of Punjab has been given package of fiscal concessions by the Union government in 2003 is one such example of the centralized fiscal policy. This has resulted into investment flight from Punjab (Ahluwalia 2009).
4. The wheat-paddy predominant cropping pattern gives on an average returns to a farmer owning one hectare of land over and above the variable costs is Rs. 35, 621 per annum. This turns out to be Rs. 19.52 per person per day in a five member farm household in Punjab (Ghuman and Romana 2010).

References

Ahluwalia, I. J. (2010), 'Social Sector Development: A Perspective From Punjab', in Shankar Acharya and Rakesh Mohan (eds.) *India's Economy-Performance and Challenges: Essays in Honour of Montek Singh Ahluwalia,* New Delhi: Oxford University Press: 286-327.

Ahluwalia, I. J. (2009), 'Challenges of Economic Development in Punjab' in Kaushik Basu and Ravi Kanbour (eds.) *Arguments for a Better World-Essays in Honor of Amartya Sen:* Vol. II Society, Institutions, and Development, New York: Oxford University Press, 303-326.

Ahluwalia, M. S. (2002), 'State-Level Performance under Economic Reforms in India' in Anne O. Krueger (ed.) *Economic Policy Reforms and the Indian Economy,* New Delhi: Oxford University Press, 91-122.

Babu, S. (2002), 'Competition and Competitiveness among States', *Economic and Political Weekly,* Vol. 37, No.13.

Chakraborty, Achin (2009), 'Some Normatively Relevant Aspects of Inter-State and Intra-State Disparities' *Economic and Political Weekly,* XLIV, Nos. 26&27, June 27:179-184.

Chaudhuri, S. and Nivedita Gupta (2009), 'Levels of Living and Poverty Patterns: A District- Wise Analysis for India', *Economic and Political Weekly,* Vol. XLIV, No. 9, February 28: 94-110.

Gill, Anita and Lakhwinder Singh (2006) 'Farmers' Suicides and Response of Public Policy: Evidence, Diagnosis and Alternatives', *Review of Agriculture-Economic and Political Weekly,* Vol.XLI, No. 26, June 30:2762-2768.

Gill, Sucha Singh (2005), 'Economic Distress and Suicides in Rural Punjab', *Journal of Punjab Studies,* Vol. 12, No.2: 219-237.

Gill, Sucha Singh, 2004. 'Contract Farming Hurts Farmers: Area under Wheat, Paddy Increases', ***The Tribune,*** Chandigarh, September 27.

Gill, Sucha Singh (1988) 'Contradictions of Punjab Model of Growth and Search for Alternative', *Economic and Political Weekly,* Vol. XXIII, No. 42:

Ghuman, R. S., Lakhwinder Singh, and Inderjeet Singh (2007), *Status of Local Agricultural Labour in Punjab,* Mohali: The Punjab State Farmers Commission.

Ghuman, R. S. and G. S. Romana (2010) 'Sustainability of the Existing and Alternative Cropping Systems in South-west Punjab' in Sucha Singh Gill, Lakhwinder Singh and Reena Marwah (eds.) *Economic and Environmental Sustainability of the Asian Region,* New Delhi: Routledge-Taylor and Francis Group: 317-336.

Government of India (2010), *Economic Survey 2009-10,* New Delhi: Oxford University Press.

Government of India (2010), *Hand Book of Industrial Policy and Statistics*, Ministry of Industry and Commerce, New Delhi: Government of India.

Johl, S. S. (1986), *Diversification of Agriculture in Punjab*, Report of Expert Committee, Chandigarh: Government of Punjab.

Jomo, K.S. (2001), 'Rethinking the Role of Government Policy in Southeast Asia', in Joseph E. Stiglitz and Shahid Yusuf (eds.) *The East Asian Miracle*, New York: Oxford University Press.

Moore, M. (1993), 'Economic Structure and the Politics of Sectoral Bias: East Asian and Other Cases', *Journal of Development Studies*, Vol. 29, No. 4.

NCEUS (2007) Report on Conditions of Work and Promotion of Livelihood in the Unorganised Sector, New Delhi: *National Commission on Enterprises in the Unorganised Sector, Government of India.*

Patibandla, M. and Trilochan Sastry (2004), 'Capitalism and Cooperation: Cooperative Institutions in a Developing Economy', *Economic and Political Weekly*, Vol. 39, No. 27.

Rajmal (2010), *State Finances and Growth: A Study of Major States of India*, Unpublished Ph. D Thesis, Indian Institute of Technology Bombay, Mumbai.

Rath, S. (2003), 'Grape Cultivation for Export: Impact on Vineyard Workers', *Economic and Political Weekly*, Vol. 38, No. 5.

Sen, Amartya (1999), *Development As Freedom*, New Delhi: Oxford University Press.

Shergill, H. S. (2010), *Growth of Farm Debt in Punjab1997 to 2008*, Chandigarh: Institute for Development and Communication.

Singh, Inderjeet and Parmod Kumar Aggarwal (2010), 'Ecological Implications of Agricultural Development in Punjab', in Sucha Singh Gill, Lakhwinder Singh and Reena Marwah (eds.) *Economic and Environmental Sustainability of the Asian Region*, New Delhi: Routledge-Taylor and Francis Group:183-200.

Singh, Lakhwinder (2005), 'Deceleration of Industrial Growth and Rural Industrialization Strategy for Rural Punjab', *Journal of Punjab Studies*, Vol. 12, No. 2, 271-284.

Singh, Lakhwinder and Sukhpal Singh (2002) 'Deceleration of Economic Growth in Punjab: Evidence, Explanation and a

Way-Out', *Economic and Political Weekly,* Vol.XXXVII, No. 6, February 9: 579-586.

Timmer, C.P. (1988), 'The Agriculture Transformation', in H. B. Chenery and T.N. Srinivasan (eds.) *Handbook of Development Economics,* Vol. 1, Amsterdam: Elsevier Science Publishers.

Toor, M.S., A. S. Bhullar and Inderpreet Kaur (2007) 'Agriculture-Led Diversification and Labour Use in Punjab: Potentials and Constraints', *Indian Journal of Labour Economics,* Vol. 50, No. 4.

Wade, R. (1990), *Governing the Market: Economic Theory and the Role of Government in East Asian Industrialization,* Princeton: Princeton University Press.

15

Utilization of Maternal and Child Health Care Services in North-West India: Observations from National Family Health Survey-3

Sukhwinder Singh & Shifali Jain

SECTION–I

Introduction

An examination of India's health situation points unequivocally to two larger population groups - pregnant women and newborns - that are vulnerable to the disease and death (Chatterjee, 1988). By nature, health problems of mother-child are linked with each other biologically and socio-economically. For instance, a child from the moment of conception to the weaning time is physically dependent on his/her mother. And, mother's health, particularly her nutrition, infectious and education levels directly affect the child's health and survival (Singh, 1991). Poor health conditions of mothers and newborns were highlighted even in the pre-independence studies (GOI, 1946; Gill, 1987 and Singh, 1991). To tackle their health problems, maternal and child health (MCH) services were made an integral part of overall planned development strategy since the early 1950s in India as envisioned in the Bhore Committee

Report (GOI, 1946) and Sokhey Committee Report (National Planning Committee, 1948).

Under this strategy, more public funds were spent to create an extensive network of public health system for enhancing basic capabilities women and children by keeping them healthy both physically and mentally (World Bank, 1993; Misra, et al., 2003; and Singh and Gill, 2008). And, this high public expenditure has certainly improved the child survival rate and helped to reduce population growth in India. Consequently, maternal and infant/child mortality rates are reduced to one-half what they were in the early 1950s. However, many research studies still point out the dismal picture of women and children health in India (Visaria, 1985; Jeffery, 1988; Tulasidhar and Sharma, 1993; and Misra, et al., 2003). Early marriages and conception, repeated pregnancies and unsafe abortions, gender bias in nutrition and health care, poor state of pre-natal and postnatal care, etc. only intensify women' health problems.

In India, MCH services were developed as the part of officially adopted family planning programme since 1950-51 and continued up to the Fourth Five Year Plan (1969-74). During the Fifth Five Year Plan (1974-79), nutrition services were made an integral part of MCH services. In subsequent years, child survival and safe motherhood were also added to this programme in 1992-93 (GOI, 1992). In October 1997, it was named as reproductive and child health (RCH) programme. The latest RCH, in its holistic approach, seeks to integrate the maternal health, child health, and fertility (reproductive health) aspects together. The most crucial aspects of RCH are: (a) provisions for antenatal care, including at least three antenatal visits, iron and folic acid tablets (IFA) for pregnant mothers, two doses of tetanus vaccine, detection and treatment of anemia in the mothers, and management and referral of high-risk pregnancies; (b) promotion of institutional deliveries or home deliveries assisted by the skilled health personnel; (c) provisions for postnatal care, including at least three postnatal visits; and (d) identification and management of reproductive tract and sexually transmitted infections (GOI, 1997). Recently, National Rural Health Mission (NRHM) stresses upon safe motherhood and enhancing child survival rates, particularly in rural areas across the states (GOI, 2005). It means that MCH/RCH services have become the most important programme in India to enhance health status of mothers and children, particularly belonged to the weaker sections of society.

This paper examines the utilization pattern and determinants of MCH services in North-Western Indian states, i.e., Punjab, Haryana and Himachal Pradesh (HP). The study utilizes the information generated on women's health related variables by two National Health Family Surveys (NFHS-3 and NFHS-2) conducted in India during 2005-06 and 1998-99 respectively. The data were collected from nationally representative sample of 109,041 households and 124,385 ever-married women (including never-married) aged 15-49 years during the NFHS-3 (IIPS, 2007) compared to 92,486 households and 90,303 ever-married women aged 15-49 years during the NFHS-2 (IIPS, 2000). Both surveys collected comparable data on various aspects of women's health like fertility, family planning practices, nutritional level, maternal and child health, HIV prevalence, etc. (Roy, et al., 2004) The study examines critically the various factors behind utilization of MCH services, particularly antenatal care (ANC), child delivery and postnatal care across three neighbouring states.

The paper is divided into 5 sections. Section I, besides introducing problem, portrays the significance of MCH services in India. Section II deals with the utilization patterns of various types of antenatal care. Section III features the postnatal care across three neighbouring states. Section IV analyses other important determinants of utilizing maternal care services (fertility, mother's age at marriage/first childbirth, birth order, education, caste, etc.). Section V wraps the summary of main conclusions and public policy issues.

SECTION–II

Antenatal Care

In medical parlance, antenatal care (ANC) refers to pregnancy-related health care, which is usually provided by a qualified doctor or an auxiliary nurse midwife (ANM), or any other health professional trained for such a care. Under the ANC, any of them monitors the signs of complications, if any; detects and treats pre-existing or concurrent problems of pregnancy; and provides counselling regarding the diet, preventive care, delivery, and other pregnancy related issues. ANC visits begin with the confirmation of pregnancy; continue at four-week intervals during first seven-months of gestation; and then every two weeks until actual delivery (MacDonald and Pritchard, 1980). In practice, it is very difficult for women with limited income or residing in remote areas to follow recommended schedules of ANC visits. Under these circumstances, a minimum of four ANC visits - in the third, sixth, eighth and ninth months of pregnancy - has been advised for pregnant women (Park and Park, 1989 and WHO, 2006). In India, however, a minimum of three ANC check-ups has been considered as a more achievable goal under the latest RCH guidelines (GOI, 1992). During each ANC check-ups, a skilled health worker must ensure body weight and blood pressure check-up, abdominal examination, immunization against tetanus (two doses of TT), consumption of iron and folic acid tablets (at least 100 IFA tablets per pregnancy), and managing anemia (GOI, 2005). After registration of each pregnancy, RCH guidelines state that first ANC check-up should take place before the start of second trimester of pregnancy (GOI, 1997).

An assessment of data (Table 1) shows that, in totality, more than three-quarter of pregnant women (77.2 per cent) in India received ANC visit/s during the NFHS-3, whereas just 65.9 per cent of pregnant women utilized ANC services during the NFHS-2. However, the data did not show much variation in utilization of ANC services across three neighbouring states (Punjab, Haryana and HP) during the NFHS-3. For instance, about 90 per cent of pregnant women in these states received at least one ANC visit during the NFHS-3. Further, Punjab and Haryana have made noticeable improvements in utilizing the ANC during the NFHS-3 over the NFHS-2. For instance, 90.3 per cent of pregnant women in Punjab received ANC during the NFHS-3, which was improved upon 74.1 per cent of pregnant women during the NFHS-2. Similar improvements were made in Haryana and HP, whereas 89.8 per cent and 89.5 per cent of pregnant women received ANC during the NFHS-3 compared to 58.1 per cent and 86.8 per cent during the NFHS-2 respectively.

Regarding the ANC providers, 56.1 per cent of pregnant women in Punjab preferred qualified doctors, 26.6 per cent skilled health providers (ANM/Nurse/ Midwife/LHV/ Anganwadi/ICDS Worker, etc.) and 7.6 per cent Dai/ TBA during the NFHS-3. On the other hand, pregnant women who preferred doctors for ANC during the NFHS-3 were more in the HP (66.0 per cent) compared to that of Punjab (56.1 per cent) and Haryana (42.1 per cent). Further, the pregnant women who approached skilled health providers for ANC were more in Haryana (36.6 per cent) compared to Punjab (26.6 per cent) and HP (18.5 per cent) during the NFHS-3. In the case of pregnant women seeking ANC from unskilled health workers (Traditional Dai/ TBA), 11.1 per cent, 7.6 per cent and 5.0 per cent mothers in Haryana, Punjab and HP respectively preferred them, whereas All-India average was just 1.4 per cent. Surprisingly, across all the three states, almost one out of every tenth pregnant women did not receive any sort of ANC instead relied upon family members during the NFHS-3, but it showed vast improvement over the NFHS-2.

Further, an analysis of data showed (in Table 2) that utilization pattern of ANC by visit/s of health persons differs greatly across the three neighbouring states. For instance, 88.9 per cent of pregnant women in Punjab received at least one ANC visit during the NFHS-3, whereas 74.0 per cent of pregnant women received such care during the NFHS-2. Likewise, Haryana too showed an improvement where the proportion of pregnant women received at least one ANC visit rose from 58.1 per cent during the NFHS-2 to 88.3 per cent during the NFHS-3. However, the pregnant women who received at least one ANC visit in the HP showed a negligible downfall from 86.8 per cent during the NFHS-2 to 86.4 per cent during the NFHS-3.

In the case of pregnant women received 3 or more ANC visits, 74.8 per cent of pregnant women in Punjab utilized this

Table 1

Percentage Distribution of Pregnant Women Received ANC by Type of Provider

			Type of Provider							
	Pregnant Women Received ANC		*Doctor*		*Skilled Health**		*Unskilled Health***		*No one*	
State	*NFHS-3*	*NFHS-2*	*NFHS-3*	*NFHS-2*	*NFHS-3*	*NFHS-2*	*NFHS-3*	*NFHS-2*	*NFHS-3*	*NFHS-2*
Punjab	90.3	74.1	56.1	41.3	26.6	32.8	7.6	na	9.7	26.0
Haryana	89.8	58.1	42.1	34.9	36.6	23.1	11.1	0.1	10.1	41.9
HP	89.5	86.3	66.0	58.1	18.5	28.7	5.0	na	10.4	13.2
India	77.2	65.9	50.2	48.6	25.6	16.5	1.4	0.8	22.8	34.0

Note: *Skilled Health Provider includes Auxiliary Nurse Midwife (ANM)/Nurse/Midwife/Lady Health Visitor (LHV)/Anganwadi or ICDS worker/some other health personnel.

**Unskilled Health Provider includes Dai or Traditional Birth Attendant (TBA).

Source: IIPS, 2007.

Table 2
Percentage of Pregnant Women Receiving Maternity Care by Type of ANC

State	*At Least One ANC Visit*		*Three or More ANC Visits*		*ANC visit during First Trimester*		*Two or More TT Injections*		*IFA Tablets*	
	NFHS-3	*NFHS-2*	*NFHS-3*	*NFHS-2*	*NFHS-3*	*NFHS-2*	*NFHS-3*	*NFHS-2*	*NFHS-3*	*NFHS-2*
Punjab	88.9	74.0	74.8	57.0	60.4	42.6	83.8	89.9	65.5	79.6
Haryana	88.3	58.1	59.2	37.4	51.4	32.8	83.4	79.7	61.3	67.0
HP	86.4	86.8	62.6	60.9	56.8	48.2	72.1	66.2	84.2	85.6
India	76.4	65.4	52.0	43.8	43.9	33.0	76.3	66.8	65.1	57.6

Source: IIPS, 2007 and IIPS, 2000.

facility during the NFHS-3 compared to 57.0 per cent women during the NFHS-2; a considerable improvement. Likewise, in Haryana and HP, 59.2 per cent and 62.6 per cent of pregnant women received 3 or more ANC visits during the NFHS-3, whereas this proportion was 37.4 per cent and 60.9 per cent respectively during the NFHS-2. Regarding an ANC visit during the first trimester of pregnancy, the data pointed out that 60.4 per cent of pregnant women in Punjab got this facility in the NFHS-3 compared to 42.6 per cent of women enjoyed such facility in the NFHS-2. A similar improvement had been observed among the pregnant women of Haryana and HP; showing an incremental ratio from 32.8 per cent during the NFHS-2 to 51.4 per cent during the NFHS-3 in Haryana and from 48.2 per cent during the NFHS-2 to 56.8 per cent during the NFHS-3 in HP.

Another significant aspect of childbearing women is the immunization against tetanus disease. In fact, in order to prevent nearly all tetanus infections in the mother and yet to born baby, two doses of tetanus toxoid (TT) vaccine, one month apart, are usually recommended during pregnancy. The data revealed that proportion of mothers who received two or more TT injections were slightly more in Punjab (83.8 per cent) than its adjoining states (83.4 per cent in Haryana and 72.1 per cent in HP) during the NFHS-3. In Punjab, this proportion was decreased from 89.9 per cent of mothers who got at least two TT injections during the NFHS-2. On the other hand, childbearing mothers in Haryana and HP who got two or more dozes of TT injections showed an increasing trend; jumped up from 79.7 per cent and 66.2 per cent during the NFHS-2 to 83.4 per cent and 72.1 per cent during the NFHS-3 respectively.

In India, a greater majority of women belonged to weaker sections of society are subject to the hunger, malnutrition (thin body) and anemia. The provision of iron and folic acid (IFA) tablets to pregnant women are of great importance in India for safe motherhood and prevention of nutritional anaemia. It is, therefore, recommended under the RCH that a woman must consume 100 IFA tablets during her pregnancy (IIPS, 2007). In all three states, contrary to all-India trend, proportion of pregnant women consuming IFA tablets for 90 days or more had dropped drastically. For instance, 65.5 per cent, 61.3 per cent and 84.2 per cent of mothers in Punjab, Haryana and HP respectively got IFA tablets during the NFHS-3, whereas these proportions were 79.6 per cent, 67.0 per cent and 85.6 per cent during the NHFS-2 respectively. It is a matter of concern and demands policy attention.

Further, utilization pattern of ANC revealed an urban bias in these states, i.e. the pregnant women living in urban areas of these states enjoyed ANC in a better way during the NFHS-3 (Table 3). For instance, 80.9 per cent of pregnant women residing in urban Punjab received at least three ANC visits compared to 71.2 per cent of women residing in rural Punjab. In HP, 75.1 per cent of pregnant women residing in urban areas utilized at least three ANC visits compared to 61.1 per cent of pregnant women living in rural areas. In Haryana, urban-rural gap was wider (18.8 percentage points), whereas 72.9 per cent pregnant women of urban areas received at least three ANC visits compared to 54.1 per cent in rural areas during the NHFS-3.

For expectant mothers who received two or more TT injections, urban-rural differences were not as sharp as were found in the case of at least three ANC visits. An interesting point was observed in the case of Punjab, whereas 83.8 per cent (82.8 per cent for rural areas and 85.4 per cent in urban areas) of mothers got two or more TT injections during the NFHS-3 compared to 89.9 per cent (88.0 per cent for rural areas and 96.2 per cent in urban areas) during the NFHS-2. However, in Haryana and HP, it was the other way around, where percentage of mothers who got two or more TT injections had shown improvement both in the rural and urban areas during the NFHS-3 as against the NFHS-2 (Table 3).

Regarding the proportion of mothers given or purchased IFA tablets or syrup, rural-urban differences were not pronounced across these neighbouring states during the NFHS-3. But, there was a sharp rural-urban difference especially in the case of Haryana during the NFHS-3. Surprisingly, utilization of IFA tablets showed a downward trend in these neighbouring states. In Punjab, 65.5 per cent of mothers

Table 3

Percentage of Pregnant Women Receiving Maternity Care by Type of ANC and Location

Indicator (%age of Mothers Received)	Survey	Punjab			Haryana			HP		
		T	*U*	*R*	*T*	*U*	*R*	*T*	*U*	*R*
At least 3 ANC Visits	NFHS-3	74.8	80.9	71.2	59.2	72.9	54.1	62.6	75.1	61.1
	NFHS-2	57.0	na	na	37.4	na	na	60.9	na	na
Two or More TT Injections	NFHS-3	83.8	85.4	82.8	83.4	88.9	81.4	72.1	79.8	71.2
	NFHS-2	89.9	96.2	88.0	79.7	86.9	77.5	66.2	75.3	65.4
IFA Tablets or Syrup	NFHS-3	65.5	67.8	64.1	61.3	68.6	58.6	84.2	87.5	83.8
	NFHS-2	79.6	86.9	77.4	67.0	74.3	64.8	85.6	94.8	84.9

Source: IIPS, 2007 and IIPS, 2000.

(64.1 per cent for rural areas and 67.8 per cent in urban areas) given or purchased IFA tablets during the NFHS-3 compared to 79.6 per cent (77.4 per cent for rural and 86.9 per cent in urban areas) during the NFHS-2. Similarly, in Haryana and HP, where percentage of mothers who were given or purchased IFA tablets or syrup had shown downward trend both in rural and urban areas during the NFHS-3 as against the NFHS-2.

SECTION–III

Childbirth and Postnatal Care

The health of mothers/newborns depends not only upon utilization of ANC during pregnancy, but also during the childbirth and postnatal care within first few hours/weeks of childbirth. Indeed, a large proportion of maternal and neonatal deaths occurred in India during the first 48 hours after delivery (IIPS, 2007). Although childbirth is a normal physiological process, yet complications of various types like prolonged labour, obstructions, septicemia, ante-partum hemorrhage, convulsions, cord prolepsis, etc. may occur (Singh, 1991). The latest RCH guidelines recommend that all childbirths must be institutionalized and the mothers/new babies should get three postnatal visits of trained health person (GOI, 1997). Further, all mothers must receive at least a medical check-up within two days of delivery. Postnatal check-ups are more important for non-institutional deliveries (GOI, 2002).

The data on childbirths pointed out (Table 4) that a little more than one-half of childbirths (51.4 per cent) took place in health institutions in Punjab compared to all-India average of 38.6 per cent childbirths. Clearly, 37.9 per cent childbirths in Punjab took place in private owned institutions, 12.3 per cent in the public owned and just 1.2 per cent in the NGO/Trust owned institutions during the NFHS-3. Further, a little less than two-fifth childbirths (38.8 per cent) took place at own premises and 9.6 per cent at the mother's parental homes and 0.2 per cent at other's homes. On the other hand, only 37.4 per cent of childbirths took place in health institutions (29.6 per cent in the private, 7.6 per cent in the public, and 0.2 per cent in the

NGO/Trust owned institutions), 55.5 per cent of at own home and 7.1 per cent at mothers' parental home during the NFHS-2. Comparing to its adjoining states, institutional deliveries were more in Punjab (51.4 per cent) than that of Haryana (35.7 per cent) and HP (43.0 per cent). And, even the childbirths that took place at own premises were lesser in Punjab (38.8 per cent) than that of Haryana (59.7 per cent) and HP (51.3 per cent) during the NFHS-3. During the NFHS-2, Punjab also performed better than its counter parts in the case of institutional deliveries. For instance, 37.4 per cent of childbirths took place in health institutions in Punjab compared to 28.9 per cent childbirths in HP and 22.4 per cent in Haryana during NFHS-2.

Further, Punjab and Haryana lagged behind in the usage of public health institutions for child delivery purposes. As per the NFHS-3, only 12.3 per cent and 13.9 per cent of childbirths in Punjab and Haryana took place in public health institutions compared to 37.0 per cent childbirths in HP. Naturally, dominance of private health institutions for deliveries was more pronounced in Punjab (37.9 per cent) than that of Haryana (21.8 per cent) and HP (5.4 per cent) during the NFHS-3. Further, when institutional and non-institutional deliveries compared across the two surveys (NFHS-2 and NFHS-3), the analysis revealed an appreciable increase in institutional deliveries and reduction in deliveries that took place at home. The scale of improvements in Punjab was at par with Haryana and HP; that being 14 per cent, 13.3 per cent and 14.1 per cent respectively, but still Punjab is far ahead its neighbouring states (Table 4).

Regarding urban-rural differences by place of childbirths (Table 5), the data supported that urban mothers in these states were better placed in terms of institutional deliveries than that of the rural mothers during the NFHS-3. In comparison, 75.9 per cent of child deliveries in urban HP were reported at the institutional level, followed by the urban areas of Haryana (64.0 per cent) and Punjab (57.9 per cent). On the other hand, rural Punjab placed better in attracted institutional deliveries as 47.6 per cent childbirths were at institutional level, followed by HP (39.8 per cent) and Haryana (26.7 per cent) during the NFHS-3. Among the childbirths assisted by skilled health persons, 77.5

Table 4
Percentage Distribution of Childbirths by Source of Facility

State	Health Facility/ Institution								Home							
	Public Sector		*NGO/ Trust*		*Private Sector*		*Total*		*Own Home*		*Parent's Home*		*Other Home*		*Missing Cases*	
	NFHS-3	NFHS-2	NFHS-3	NFHS-2	NFHS-3	NFHS-2	NFHS-3	NFHS-2	NFHS-3	NFHS-2	NFHS-3	NFHS-2	NFHS-3	NFHS-2	NFHS-3	NFHS-2
Punjab	12.3	7.6	1.2	0.2	37.9	29.6	51.4	37.4	38.3	55.5	9.6	7.1	0.2	na	0.1	na
Haryana	13.9	6.0	na	0.1	21.8	16.3	35.7	22.4	59.7	73.3	4.2	4.2	0.2	na	na	0.1
HP	37.0	23.2	0.6	na	5.4	5.7	43.0	28.9	51.3	60.7	4.6	9.8	0.6	na	0.4	0.6
India	18.0	16.2	0.4	0.7	20.2	16.7	38.6	33.6	51.3	53.2	9.2	12.2	0.5	na	0.3	1.0

Source: IIPS, 2007 and IIPS, 2000.

Table 5
Percentage Distribution of Childbirths by Type of Care/ Assistance

		Punjab			*Haryana*			*HP*		
Type of Care for Childbirths	*Survey*	*T*	*U*	*R*	*T*	*U*	*R*	*T*	*U*	*R*
Institutional	NFHS-3	51.4	57.9	47.6	35.7	64.0	26.7	43.0	75.9	39.8
	NFHS-2	37.4	56.1	31.9	22.4	47.1	14.9	28.9	72.0	25.4
Assisted by (Doctor/Nurse/ LHV/ ANM/ etc.)	NFHS-3	68.2	70.3	67.1	48.9	73.5	41.1	47.8	77.5	44.9
	NFHS-2	62.6	77.8	58.1	42.0	66.1	34.7	40.2	78.2	37.1

Source: IIPS, 2007 and IIPS, 2000.

per cent of deliveries in urban HP were assisted by skilled health persons, followed by the urban Haryana (73.5 per cent) and urban Punjab (70.3 per cent). In the case of rural areas, 67.1 per cent childbirths in Punjab were assisted by skilled health persons, followed by HP (44.9 per cent) and Haryana (41.1 per cent) during the NFHS-3.

Seeking qualified doctor is always better course for woman's pregnancy and childbirth. The next best alternative is the supervision of skilled health personnel (ANM/Nurse/Midwife/LHV, etc). The data revealed (Table 6) that 46.6 per cent of childbirths in India were assisted by skilled health personnel (35.2 per cent by a qualified doctor, 10.3 per cent by an ANM/Nurse/Midwife/LHV and just 1.1 per cent by any other trained health personnel) and 53.4 per cent by unskilled personnel (36.5 per cent by TBA/Dai, 16.2 per cent and 0.7 per cent by others) during the NFHS-3. Contrary to this, 68.2 per cent of childbirths in Punjab were assisted by the skilled health personnel (44.9 per cent by a qualified doctor, 22.1 per cent by an ANM/Nurse/Midwife/LHV and just 1.2 per cent by any other trained health personnel) and 31.9 per cent by unskilled persons (30.5 per cent by a TBA/Dai, 1.3 per cent by friends/relatives, and 0.1 per cent by others. However, during the NFHS-2 in Punjab, 62.5 per cent childbirths were assisted by skilled health personnel (35.1 per cent by a qualified doctor, 27.0 per cent by an ANM/Nurse/Midwife/LHV and 0.4 per cent by any other trained personnel) and 37.2 per cent childbirths were assisted by TBA/Dai. Across Haryana and HP, 48.9 per cent and 47.9 per cent childbirths respectively got assistance of any skilled health personnel. Further, number of childbirths assisted by qualified doctor was 44.9 per cent in Punjab and the corresponding figures were 33.8 per cent and 37.9 per cent for the Haryana and HP respectively. Again, in the case of seeking assistance from TBA/Dai during the childbirth, Punjab placed better as only 30.5 per cent childbirths preferred to seek services of TBA/Dai, whereas this proportion was 45.3 per cent and 49.5 per cent in HP and Haryana respectively. In nutshell, childbirths attended by skilled health personnel improved during the NFHS-3 over the NFHS-2 in these states.

Table 6
Percentage Distribution of Childbirths by Type of Health Personal

	Punjab		*Haryana*		*HP*		*India*	
Type of Health Personal	*NFHS-3*	*NFHS-2*	*NFHS-3*	*NFHS-2*	*NFHS-3*	*NFHS-2*	*NFHS-3*	*NFHS-2*
Doctor	44.9	35.1	33.8	27.9	37.9	30.9	35.2	30.3
ANM/ Nurse/Mid-wife/LHV	22.1	27.0	13.6	14.0	10.0	9.0	10.3	11.4
Other Health Provider	1.2	0.4	1.5	0.2	na	0.3	1.1	0.6
Skilled (Sub-Total)	68.2	62.5	48.9	42.1	47.9	40.2	46.6	42.3
Dai/TBA	30.5	37.2	49.5	57.8	45.3	56.6	36.5	35.0
Friends/ Relatives	1.3	na	1.2	na	6.5	na	16.2	Na
Other*	0.1	0.2	0.3	0.2	0.3	3.2	0.7	22.7
Unskilled (Sub-Total)	31.9	37.4	51.0	58.0	52.1	59.8	53.4	57.7

*It includes no one.

Source: IIPS, 2007 and IIPS, 2000

Regarding the postnatal care, the data elucidated (Table 7) that more than three-fifth mothers (63.7 per cent) got a postnatal check-up in Punjab during NFHS-3. Of them, 35.3 per cent of mothers approached a qualified doctor, 18.9 per cent from any skilled health provider and 9.7 per cent followed the traditional rules. The corresponding results of mothers having postnatal care for Haryana and HP were as under: 57.6 per cent and 50.6 per cent mothers got it from either qualified doctor or skilled health provider or TBA/dai. Out of these, 25.3 per cent mothers in Haryana and 31.8 per cent in HP preferred qualified doctor for their first postnatal check-up. Further, 17.3 per cent mothers in Haryana and 10.1 per cent in HP sought Dai/TBA instructions for postnatal check-up during the NFHS-3. Further, a substantial proportion of mothers in these states did not seek postnatal check-up. In India, too it showed a dismal result (57.6 per cent mothers were without a postnatal check-up). Intriguingly, 34.9 per cent of mothers in Punjab compared 41.6 per cent Haryana and 47.6 per cent HP did not get any kind of postnatal check-up.

Table 7
Percentage of Mothers Received Postnatal Check-up by Type of Provider

	Type of Provider					
State	*Doctor*	*Skilled Health Worker*	*Dai/ TBA*	*Total*	*No Postnatal Check-up*	*Missing/ Other Response*
Punjab	35.3	18.9	9.7	63.7	34.9	1.4
Haryana	25.3	15.0	17.3	57.6	41.6	0.8
HP	31.8	8.6	10.1	50.6	47.6	1.7
India	29.5	8.6	3.1	41.2	57.6	1.2

Source: IIPS, 2007.

Moreover, urban-rural variations in the utilization pattern of postnatal care of mothers are pointed out clearly (Table 8) that, contrary to 37.3 per cent of mothers in India, 62.0 per cent of mothers in Punjab got their first check-up within specified time period during the NFHS-3. However, the corresponding figures for Haryana and HP were 55.9 per cent and 43.2 per cent respectively. The data elucidated that 69.3 per cent mothers received postnatal care in urban Punjab compared to 57.7 per cent women living in rural Punjab. On the other side, 68.1 per cent and 51.4 per cent of urban mothers living in Haryana and HP respectively received postnatal care within prescribed time period compared to 51.4 per cent and 42.3 per cent of rural mothers in Haryana and HP respectively. Further, the relative position of both urban and rural Punjab was found to be better than that of urban and rural Haryana as well as HP during the NFHS-3.

Table 8
Percentage of Mothers Received Postnatal Check-up by Location

		NFHS-3	
State	*Total*	*Urban*	*Rural*
Punjab	62.0	69.3	57.7
Haryana	55.9	68.1	51.4
HP	43.2	51.4	42.3
India	37.3	61.0	28.6

Source: IIPS, 2007.

SECTION–IV

Dominant and Explanatory Variables: ANC Services

Many factors such as fertility level, age of marriage, education level, income level, availability of health facilities, etc. determine the health conditions of a pregnant woman/ mother. In demographic theory, total fertility rate (TFR), i.e. average number children borne to a woman not only determines pattern and pace of population growth, but also health of mothers and infants in a country. Actually, women who get motherhood at the age of 15-19 years, in the absence of contraceptive use, result in the high fertility, and the high fertility, in turn, adversely affects health status of both the mother and child (Singh, 2008). The data highlights that TFR in Punjab was 1.99 children per woman, whereas it was 2.69 children in Haryana and 1.94 children in HP as per the NFHS-3. Moreover, urban women in these states had low TFR than that of rural women. In these states, TFR during the NFHS-3 had shown a slight positive improvement compared to the TFR of NFHS-2.

Table 9
Percentage of Married Women by Materna Health Care Indicators

		Punjab			Haryana			HP		
Indicator	*Survey*	*T*	*U*	*R*	*T*	*U*	*R*	*T*	*U*	*R*
Total Fertility Rate	NFHS-3	1.99	1.88	2.06	2.69	2.17	2.92	1.94	1.57	1.98
(Children per Women)	NFHS-2	2.21	1.79	2.42	2.88	2.24	3.13	2.14	1.74	2.18
Median Age at First	NFHS-3	21.4	21.8	21.1	20.3	20.9	20.0	21.2	22.7	21.1
Childbirth for Women	NFHS-2	21.5	22.3	21.0	20.1	21.2	19.7	20.5	22.1	20.4
Aged 25-49 Years										
Percentage of Women	NFHS-3	19.7	18.1	20.6	41.2	33.3	44.8	12.3	13.6	12.2
Aged 20-24 Years Married	NFHS-2	11.6	na	na	41.5	na	na	10.7	na	na
before 18 Years										
Percentage of Women	NFHS-3	21.6	19.4	22.9	41.4	32.9	45.2	14.4	13.7	14.4
Aged 18-29 Years	NFHS-2	na	na	na	na	na	na	na	na	Na
married by exact age 18										

Source: IIPS, 2007 and IIPS, 2000.

Further, median age of women aged 25-49 years at their first childbirth was 21.4 years in Punjab, 20.3 years in Haryana and 21.2 years in HP as per the NFHS-3 which was almost same as the previous survey. The urban areas of these states are modestly better than that of the rural areas so far as median age of mothers aged 25-49 years at their first childbirth was concerned. The data also revealed that, during the NFHS-3, more than two-fifth of women (41.2 per cent) aged 20-24 years were married in Haryana at the age of 18 years, whereas about one-fifth of women (19.7 per cent) in Punjab and comparatively much lesser proportion of such women (12.3 per cent) in HP got married by age of 18 years. Further, urban women aged 20-24 years married at age of 18 years in Punjab and Haryana constituted low proportion than the women living in rural areas of these states, but the proportion of such women (aged 20-24 years) in urban HP who got married at the age 18 years (13.6 per cent) was more than the ones living in rural HP (12.2 per cent).

Another significant aspect of woman's age at marriage is that, in Punjab, more than one-fifth of women aged 18-29 years (21.6 per cent) at the time of survey (NFHS-3) got married before reaching the minimum legal age of marriage (i.e.18 years), whereas the proportion of such women in Haryana was 41.4 per cent and in HP just 14.4 per cent. As said before, proportion of women aged 18-29 years who got married by 18 years was lesser in urban areas than in the rural areas across all these states. But, married women aged between 18-29 years of age category in Haryana during the NFHS-3 are far behind than that of Punjab and HP and needs to make many efforts.

About utilization of different types of ANC by the mothers during their most recent live birth, the data highlighted two interesting points (Table 10). *First,* age of pregnant woman is an important predictor for using ANC services. By treating it as a control variable, it was found that proportion of mothers aged below 20 years getting 3 or more ANC visits during their last childbirth was lesser than that of mothers aged 20-34 years across all these states. It was more pronounced in the case of pregnant women consuming of at least IFA tablets for 90 days or more. *Second,* it is generally believed that utilization of ANC services would be higher for first order births and is expected to decline as the birth order increased. The data lent support to this conclusion. For instance, a high proportion of mothers in Punjab (83.6 per cent), followed by HP (73.4 per cent) and Haryana (72.9 per cent) utilized at least three ANC visits during the first order births, whereas this proportion decreased as the birth order increased across all these states. The same was true in the case of getting two or more TT injections and consumption of IFA tablets at least for 90 days or more by the mothers of these states.

Further, antenatal check-ups are expected to be more common among more literate and educated mothers compared to uneducated mothers because they know the advantages of preventive health check-ups. The data on pregnant women' health seeking behaviour by education level revealed (Table 11) that more than one-half of illiterate women (52.4 per cent) in Punjab, almost two-fifth of illiterate women (39.9 per cent) in Haryana and HP (38.5 per cent) reportedly received 3 or more ANC visits during the NFHS-3. In contrast, a very high proportion of pregnant women with matriculation or above level of education in Punjab (92.4 per cent), Haryana (78.8 per cent) and HP (78.4 per cent) reportedly received 3 or more ANC check-ups.

It was also true in the case of utilizing TT injections and IFA tablets. For instance, 72 per cent, 69.9 per cent and 66.5 per cent illiterate pregnant women in Punjab, Haryana and HP respectively received two or more TT injections during pregnancy during the NFHS-3. In contrast, a very high proportion of pregnant women of Punjab (91.8 per cent), Haryana (93.4 per cent) and HP (79.2 per cent) with matriculation or higher level of education received two or more TT injections during their pregnancy. Similarly, more than two-fifth pregnant women in Punjab (42.9 per cent) and Haryana (44.4 per cent) and nearly one-half in HP (48.6 per cent) having matriculation or higher education level consumed IFA tablets or syrup for 90 days during the NFHS-3. In contrast, a little more than one-tenth illiterate women both in Punjab (11.8 per cent) and Haryana (12.5 per cent) and about one-fourth such

Table 10
Utilization of ANC by Background Characteristics, NFHS-3

Characteristics	Percentage of Mothers Utilizing Different Types of ANC								
	Punjab			Haryana			HP		
	3 or more ANC Visits	2 or more TT Injections	At least IFA for at least 90 Days	3 or more ANC Visits	2 or more TT Injections	At least IFA for at least 90 Days	3 or more ANC Visits	2 or more TT Injections	At least IFA for at least 90 Days
Mother's Age at Childbirth									
< 20	72.7	75.7	18.6	56.5	87.2	22.2	43.6	83.0	31.4
20-34	75.6	84.7	29.3	61.7	85.0	28.1	64.2	71.6	38.7
35-49	-	-	-	22.6	46.1	15.2	-	-	-
Birth Order									
1	83.6	87.6	36.5	72.9	90.1	35.5	73.4	87.2	45.8
2-3	74.7	82.8	25.2	63.3	87.7	27.2	62.1	66.4	35.0
4+	51.9	77.5	15.9	32.9	65.2	14.8	38.1	63.3	32.6
Education Level									
Illiterate	52.4	72.0	11.8	39.9	69.9	12.5	38.5	66.5	23.8
Primary	64.0	75.1	19.9	65.4	76.3	15.4	na	na	na
Middle	76.2	85.5	25.4	62.8	88.7	27.8	54.1	66.1	30.9
Matric or +	92.4	91.8	42.9	78.8	93.4	44.4	78.4	79.2	48.6
Caste/Tribe									
SCs	63.1	75.7	17.0	57.9	86.8	21.5	48.3	65.0	28.3
STs	na	na	na	na	na	na	60.0	80.0	56.0
OBCs	72.3	85.1	27.9	57.0	78.0	26.1	65.0	68.8	34.1
Other*	82.1	83.2	34.4	61.0	83.9	30.0	68.4	75.4	41.8

Contd...

	Percentage of Mothers Utilizing Different Types of ANC								
	Punjab			*Haryana*			*HP*		
Characteristics	*3 or more ANC Visits*	*2 or more TT Injections*	*At least IFA for at least 90 Days*	*3 or more ANC Visits*	*2 or more TT Injections*	*At least IFA for at least 90 Days*	*3 or more ANC Visits*	*2 or more TT Injections*	*At least IFA for at least 90 Days*
Wealth Index									
Lowest	na	na	na	(31.1)	(51.1)	(8.9)	na	na	na
Second	34.6	62.3	13.1	34.5	73.6	15.7	(41.0)	(68.6)	(25.3)
Middle	54.0	68.3	7.1	48.0	78.1	13.6	45.2	64.3	35.5
Fourth	70.6	84.1	22.3	64.2	87.8	23.7	62.4	69.4	36.2
Highest	92.2	92.6	41.1	78.7	93.2	47.6	81.9	82.2	45.0
Total	74.8	83.8	27.9	59.2	83.4	26.7	62.6	72.1	37.9

* means not-belonging to the SCs, STs, and OBCs. (...) based upon 25-49 un-weighted cases.
-Percentage not shown; based on fewer than 25 un-weighted cases.

Source: IIPS, 2007.

Table 11
Utilization of Postnatal Care and Childbirth Assistance by Background Characteristics, NFHS-3

	Punjab			*Haryana*			*HP*		
	Percentage of Childbirth			*Percentage of Childbirth*			*Percentage of Childbirth*		
Background Characteristics	*Health Institution*	*Assisted by Health Personnel **	*Women having Postnatal Check-up #*	*Health Institution*	*Assisted by Health Personnel**	*Women having Postnatal Check-up #*	*Health Institution*	*Assisted by Health Personnel **	*Women having Postnatal Check-up #*
Mother's Age at Birth									
< 20	43.4	59.9	56.9	37.3	52.5	53.2	30.2	31.0	(39.1)
20-34	53.3	70.4	62.5	36.6	49.3	57.3	44.4	49.7	43.3
35-49	(21.0)	(31.4)	na	12.2	29.1	(38.7)	na	na	na
Birth Order									
1	64.8	73.9	74.1	51.8	64.7	68.1	56.8	62.7	54.8
2-3	46.5	65.1	58.9	34.2	49.0	57.5	37.1	41.4	41.2
4+	26.7	45.0	42.7	13.4	23.6	37.4	21.1	24.6	25.0
Education									
Illiterate	28.3	45.9	45.3	12.8	26.9	37.4	19.2	22.0	19.9
Primary	(47.6)	(62.4)	(44.3)	(34.3)	(44.2)	(58.8)	(13.1)	(19.6)	na
Middle	46.9	67.8	57.3	38.8	52.5	56.3	32.7	36.4	37.7
Matric or +	77.3	89.5	79.7	66.4	78.1	78.3	60.7	66.8	55.9
Caste/Tribe									
SCs	34.0	55.4	46.6	28.6	43.6	52.8	32.7	37.8	36.8
STs	na	na	na	na	na	na	(44.1)	(47.1)	(48.0)
OBCs	52.8	63.8	54.8	33.2	45.3	55.3	33.1	38.1	40.4
Other*	62.5	75.6	71.7	40.7	53.5	58.3	50.5	55.2	46.5

Contd...

Background Characteristics	Punjab			Haryana			HP		
	Percentage of Childbirth			Percentage of Childbirth			Percentage of Childbirth		
	Health Institution	*Assisted by Health Personnel **	*Women having Postnatal Check-up #*	*Health Institution*	*Assisted by Health Personnel**	*Women having Postnatal Check-up #*	*Health Institution*	*Assisted by Health Personnel **	*Women having Postnatal Check-up #*
Wealth Index									
Lowest	(14.3)	(31.3)	na	3.9	18.4	(26.7)	na	na	na
Second	21.2	39.5	32.9	12.7	22.1	35.4	20.8	19.4	(16.4)
Middle	29.9	50.1	50.4	21.0	38.5	48.0	27.5	32.6	32.4
Fourth	40.8	65.0	54.2	35.2	49.3	53.2	39.2	45.1	42.7
Highest	74.9	84.9	76.8	68.4	78.6	78.3	66.9	71.6	58.2
Total	51.3	68.2	62.0	35.7	48.9	55.9	43.0	47.8	43.2

means within 2 days of birth. () based on 25-49 un-weighted cases.

Source: IIPS, 2007.

women (23.8 per cent) in HP took IFA tablets or syrup for at least 90 days as reported in the NFHS-3. In nutshell, it is proved that proportion of pregnant women receiving ANC increases as their education level increases.

Caste of expectant mothers is also an important factor in explaining differentials in utilizing ANC services. The data pointed out that pregnant women who did not belong to either of the SC/ST or OBC were utilizing more ANC visits. Further, pregnant women belonged to the OBCs both in Punjab and HP utilized better than ones living in Haryana, whereas the women belonged to the SCs in Haryana did comparatively better than the ones in Punjab and HP.

Further, likelihood of receiving any ANC service is strongly related to household's standard of living. Among pregnant women living in households having lowest standard of living, about one-third pregnant women in Haryana (34.5) and Punjab (34.6) and two-fifth in HP (41.0 per cent) received three or more ANC check-ups. In contrast, more than nine-tenth women in Punjab (92.2 per cent) and nearly eight-tenth in HP (81.9 per cent) and Haryana (78.7 per cent) having high standard of living received three or more ANC visits during the NFHS-3. A similar pattern has been observed in the case of two or more TT injections and even in the consumption of IFA tablets. In nutshell, there was a sharp increase in utilizing ANC services with increasing level of household's standard of living.

Dominant and Explanatory Variables: Childbirths and Postnatal Care Services

Like the ANC, many factors like demographic (mother's age, birth order, etc.) and socio-economic (household income, mother's education, caste, etc.) influence preferences for institutional delivery and postnatal care of mothers/infants. The date on mother's age at birth revealed (Table 11) that proportion of institutional deliveries were lesser for mothers aged below 20 years in Punjab (43.4 per cent) and HP (30.2 per cent) than that of mothers aged 20-34 years (53.3 per cent in Punjab and 44.4 per cent in HP), whereas Haryana showed the results in a slight reverse manner. Across birth orders, proportion of institutional deliveries was the highest for the first order birth and it reduced as the birth order increased. For instance, 64.8 per cent pregnant women in Punjab, 51.8 per cent in Haryana and 56.8 per cent in HP preferred institutional delivery for their first child, whereas only 26.7 per cent women in Punjab, 21.1 per cent in HP and 13.4 per cent in Haryana used a health institution for their fourth or more childbirth.

Further, literate mothers went for more institutional deliveries than the illiterate ones. For instance, proportion of institutional deliveries among mothers with no education was very less in Punjab (28.3 per cent), followed by HP (19.2 per cent) and Haryana (12.8 per cent) compared to the mothers with matriculation or more education in Punjab (77.3 per cent), followed by Haryana (66.4 per cent) and HP (60.7 per cent). As expected, a greater proportion of mothers belonging to 'other castes' had gone for institutional deliveries than that of mothers belonging to SC/ST or OBC counterparts. And, mothers from lower economic strata went for lesser institutional deliveries (14.3 per cent in Punjab, 3.9 per cent in Haryana) compared with the mothers from higher economic strata (74.9 per cent in Punjab, 68.4 per cent in Haryana and 66.9 per cent in HP).

In the case of assisted deliveries by health personnel, proportion of such deliveries was lower for mothers aged 35-49 years than that of younger mothers aged less than 20 years and 20-34 years in all states, and moreover, percentage of deliveries assisted by health personnel decreased sharply as the birth order increased. For example, the proportion of mothers assisted for delivery of their first child were more (78.9 per cent in Punjab, 64.7 per cent in Haryana and 62.7 per cent in HP) compared to the mothers assisted for delivery of their fourth or more child (46.0 per cent in Punjab, 23.6 per cent in Haryana and 24.6 per cent in HP).

Similarly, proportion of childbirths assisted by health personnel increased sharply with the mother's education and the household wealth index. 89.5 per cent mothers in Punjab, 78.1 per cent in Haryana and 66.8 per cent in HP with matriculation or above education level preferred assisted delivery compared with 46.9 per cent of mothers in Punjab,

26.9 per cent in Haryana and 22.0 per cent in HP with no education. Similarly, less proportion of mothers in the lowest wealth quintile households got assistance from any health personnel compared to those mothers who belonged to the highest wealth quintile. Among the caste groups, 56.4 per cent of mothers in Punjab, 43.6 per cent in Haryana and 37.8 per cent in HP who belonged to SCs were assisted by health personnel compared to 76.6 per cent, 53.5 per cent and 55.2 per cent in these states respectively who belonged to other castes.

The data also highlighted that percentage of mothers who got postnatal check-up within 2 days of delivery was lower for younger mothers aged less than 20 years than for mothers aged 20-34 years in all states, and the percentage of mothers who got postnatal check-up within two days of delivery decreased sharply as the birth order increased. For instance, proportion of mothers who got postnatal check-up for their first child were higher (74.1 per cent in Punjab, 68.1 per cent in Haryana and 54.8 per cent in HP) compared to the ones who got postnatal check-up for their fourth or more child (42.7 per cent in Punjab, 37.4 per cent in Haryana and 25.0 per cent in HP).

Education level of mothers and household wealth index seems to be determined postnatal check-ups within 2 days of delivery. For example, 79.7 per cent (Punjab), 78.3 per cent (Haryana) and 55.9 per cent (HP) mothers having matriculation or more education level got postnatal care compared to 45.3 per cent (Punjab), 37.4 per cent (Haryana) and 19.9 per cent (HP) mothers with no education. Similarly, mothers in the lowest wealth quintile households were likely to get less postnatal check-up within 2 days of delivery compared to the ones belonging to the highest wealth quintile. Among the cast groups, 46.6 per cent in Punjab, 52.8 per cent in Haryana and 36.8 per cent in HP mothers belonging to the SCs/STs got a postnatal check-up compared to 71.7 per cent, 58.3 per cent and 46.5 per cent mothers respectively who belonged to 'other castes'.

SECTION–V

This section presents summary of main conclusions and emerging public policy issues. In India, pregnant women and infants especially belonged to the poor households, in the absence of state support base, are highly vulnerable to the disease/death/ both. Despite rapid economic progress made by India and her states, achieving goal of lowering infant mortality to 25 per thousand live births and maternal mortality to less than 100 per lakh live births by 2015 (GOI, 2010) is still far away. Recognizing its seriousness, public health services in the form MCH/RCH programmes were started and improved upon from time to time in India. Although significant improvements in per capita income, quality of life and population control have been achieved in these states (Punjab, Haryana and HP), but still they lagged behind than many other states like Kerala and Tamil Nadu on several health counts such as IMR, birth rate, death rate, low utilization of MCH services, etc.

Receiving ANC by pregnant women across three states seems to be at par, but Punjab and Haryana had made noticeable improvements in utilizing ANC services during the NFHS-3 over the NFHS-2. In Punjab, 74.8 per cent of mothers during the NFHS-3 had at least 3 ANC visits; an improvement upon 57 per cent mothers during the NFHS-2. It showed that mothers in Punjab are ahead of those in Haryana (59.2 per cent) and HP (62.6 per cent) in receiving at least 3 ANC visits as per the NFHS-3. However, proportion of pregnant women who received two other types of ANC (TT injections and IFA) in all these states has dropped down compared to the previous NFHS-2.

Further, 51.4 per cent childbirths were delivered in a health institution in Punjab as per the NFHS-3; up from 37.4 per cent of the NFHS-2. Whereas these percentages in Haryana and HP were 35.7 per cent and 43.0 per cent respectively during the NFHS-3 compared to 22.4 per cent and 28.9 per cent respectively during the NFHS-2. On the question of childbirths assisted by any health personnel, the analysis pointed out that in Punjab, 68.2 per cent childbirths were assisted by any trained health personnel; this proportion was only 48.9 per cent in Haryana and 47.8 per cent in HP. Moreover, proportion of institutional deliveries was lower in the rural areas than in urban areas across all these states. Truly, less than one-half pregnant woman in

Punjab, three-tenth in Haryana and two-fifth in HP living in rural areas preferred for institutional delivery. More childbirth was found to be assisted by skilled medical personnel in the rural Punjab (67.1 per cent) compared to HP (44.9 per cent) and Haryana (41.1 per cent).

On account of postnatal care, a majority of mothers in Punjab (62 per cent) had got recommended postnatal check-up within two days of birth compared to 55.9 per cent in Haryana and 43.2 per cent in HP. On the other side, more than one-third of women (34.9 per cent) received no postnatal care during their last child birth during the NFHS-3. Further, at current fertility levels, a woman in Punjab and HP is expected to have an average of 2.0 children in her lifetime compared to an average of 3 children in Haryana. Moreover, fertility rate was found to be declined marginally by 0.2 children between the NFHS-3 and NFHS-2 in all the states. Though the state governments have passed strict rules, but still practice of marrying girls (before 18 years) and childbirths at an early age has not been curbed fully in these states.

The proportion of women receiving ANC and for institutional delivery was higher in urban areas compared to those living in rural areas, higher income quintile compared to lower income quintile, educated mothers compared to illiterate mothers. Moreover, percentage of mothers receiving ANC was more for the first order childbirth and it gradually decreased as the birth order increased. Caste of mothers too played an important factor in explaining utilization MCH services in these states. Pregnant women belonging to SC/ST/ OBC categories were found to be lagged behind in utilizing health facilities than the ones not belonging to them.

In the light of these findings, it is suggested that state must take bold initiatives in raising the demand of better ANC, institutional deliveries and postnatal care of mothers/new born babies. For this, there should be universal registration all pregnant women for ANC visits by doctors or other trained health personals in these states. The institutional deliveries should be encouraged. Moreover, health care agencies should come up with new programmes informing women about the importance of antenatal and postnatal cares from a skilled health professional. And, women should also be guided about the significance of delayed childbirths and assisted deliveries either by doctor or trained health personnel. In these areas, Punjab although lagged behind Kerala but better than its adjoining states of Haryana and HP.

Further, public awareness must be launched to guide the gullible public about the benefits of institutional childbirths, not marrying daughters before legal marriageable age (18 years) and having greater birth intervals for better health of both mother and child. Mass or electronic media can be of great use in spreading the safe motherhood. More state organizations and the NGOs/Charitable Trusts should be involved in the success of latest RCH programmes so as to ensure that rural women should utilize more health services for safe pregnancy outcomes. Rural areas should be given top priority in various policies and programmes to bridge the gap between rural and urban facilities. The commendable work of some NRI promoted trusts providing quality health care and education to the poor masses need to be extended and encouraged in these states.

References

Chatterjee, M. (1988), *Implementing Health Policy,* New Delhi: Manohar Publications.

Gill, S. (1987), *Health Status of the Indian People,* Bombay: The Foundation for Research in Community Health.

GOI (1946), *Report of Health Survey and Development Committee,* (Bhore Committee), Delhi: Manager of Publications.

GOI (1992), *Family Welfare Programme in India Year Book: 1990-91.* New Delhi: Ministry of Health and Family Welfare (MOHFW).

GOI (1997), *Reproductive and Child Health Programme: Schemes for Implementation.* New Delhi: Ministry of Health and Family Welfare (MOHFW).

GOI (2002), *National Health Policy 2002,* New Delhi: Ministry of Health and Family Welfare (MOHFW).

GOI (2005), *Annual Report 2004-2005,* New Delhi: Ministry of Health and Family Welfare (MOHFW).

GOI (2010), *Millennium Development Goals – India Country Report 2009*, New Delhi: Central Statistical Organization, Ministry of Statistics and Programme Implementation.

IIPS (2000), *National Family Health Survey (NFHS–2), 1998-99*, Mumbai (India) and Maryland (USA): International Institute for Population Sciences, October.

IIPS (2007), *National Family Health Survey (NFHS–3), 2005-06*, Mumbai (India) and Macro International 2007: International Institute for Population Sciences, September.

Jeffery, R. (1988), *The Politics of Health in India*, Berkeley and London: University of California Press.

MacDonald, P. C. & Pritchard, J. A. (1980), *William's Obstetrics*, Sixteenth edition.

New York: Appleton-Century-Crofts.

Misra, R., Chatterjee, R. & Rao, S. (2003), *India Health Report*, New Delhi: Oxford University Press.

National Planning Committee (1948), Report of Sub-Committee on National Health (Sokhey Committee Report), Bombay: Vora and Company Publishers Ltd.

Park, J.E. and Park, K. (1989), *Text Book of Preventive and Social Medicine*, 12th Edition, Jabalpur: Banarsidas Bhanot Publishers.

Roy, T.K., Kulkarni, S. and Vaidehi, Y. (2004), "Social Inequalities in Health and Nutrition in Selected States", *Economic and Political Weekly*, Vol. 39 (7), February 14-20.

Singh, S. (1991), Development and Use of Health Care Services in Rural Areas: A Case Study of Punjab, *Unpublished Ph.D. Thesis*, Department of Economics, Punjabi University, Patiala.

Singh, S. and Gill, S.S. (2008), "Health Services in Punjab: A Rural Perspective", in Dhesi, A.S. and Singh, G. (eds.), *Rural Development in Punjab: A Success Story Gone Astray*, New Delhi: Routledge.

Tulasidhar, V. B. and Sharma, J. V. M. (1993), "Public Expenditure, Medical Care at Birth and Infant Mortality: A Comparative Study of States in India", in Berman, P. and Khan, M.E. (eds.), *Paying for India's Health Care*, New Delhi: Sage Publications.

Visaria, L. (1985), "Infant Mortality in India: Level, Trends and Determinants", *Economic and Political Weekly*, Vol. 20 (32, 33 & 34).

World Bank (1993), ***World Development Report, 1993,*** New York: Oxford University Press.

WHO (2006), "Provision of Effective Antenatal Care", ***Standards for Maternal and Neonatal Care,*** Geneva, Switzerland: WHO Integrated Management of Pregnancy and Childbirth Care (IMPAC), WHO.

16

Out Migration: Causes and Impact on Rural Households in Punjab

Baljinder Kaur, J. M. Singh, Jasdev Singh & B. R. Garg

Introduction

Punjab is one of the most developed states of India. Punjab State is predominantly an agricultural state with two-third of its population directly or indirectly dependent on agriculture. Since mid-sixties, with the evolution of high-yielding varieties of crops and the adoption of modern and improved farm practices, the agriculture in state has witnessed an unprecedented growth. Punjab is now considered as food bowl of the country. The tremendous increase in production has made possibly by the increase in productivity as well as increase in area especially under wheat and rice crop. Thus, presently this small state with only 1.5% of total geographical area of India contributes about 50-60% of total food grains to central pool since last two decades.

The level of technology, agricultural development and efficiency as well as pattern of employment of available labour force are closely related which also led to a process of change in rural society of Punjab. Since early eighties, the mechanization of farm operations which at early stage were considered complementary to bio-chemical component of green revolution started competing with labour force. The level of mechanization is already higher in Punjab, where man days employed in production of crops are low as compared to other parts of the country and negative growth in agricultural employment was experienced against a positive growth rate of real agricultural out put in the nineties (Haque and Sharma, 2004). The mechanization of farm operations are of no concern if off farm income and non farm employment opportunities goes simultaneously with it to absorb the displaced labour. But unfortunately, this has not been happening. A high workforce concentration in agriculture sector of state has not only given rise to high work participation ratio, but also shorter duration of work. The result is that man power dependent on agriculture is idle and underutilized either during part of day or year. This resulted into unemployment or underemployment of a large number of farm household members. Under such situation, along with several other factors like fragmentation of holdings, small uneconomical farm size, relative lack of capital and infrastructure facilities, lack of rural industry to absorb the surplus labour, the people are bound to look for other avenues of employment and earnings. Growing landlessness among small and marginal farmers and increased social conflicts are also resulting into breakdown of socio-economic relations and even social unrest among rural households under which many people are leaving their traditional work in rural economy and migrating to more prosperous areas in search of better employment and income opportunities. Along with these push factors, the pull factors like better educational facilities, medical facilities, more entertainment, enhanced status and many other facilities that are not available in villages are equally important in encouraging the rural out migration (Kaur, 2003).

Migration is a shift from the place of residence to other place for some length of time or permanently. It includes different types of voluntary as well as involuntary movement having great impact on economic, social, cultural and psychological life of people, both at place of migration as well as of emigration. In search of better opportunities the rural people are migrating to other areas or cities of state, to other states and countries. Many of them send or use part of their earnings from emigration place to help their families back at home which is being used for production, consumption or savings. This way the migrants are having significant impact in rural areas through encouraging technological changes by inducing productive investments in land, other agricultural or non agricultural activities along with changes in pattern and level of consumption. The demonstration effect of out migrants is very strong which further encourage the rural people to take steps some times even highly risky for migration of themselves or their wards. In light of the above, the present study has been taken to examine the factors behind the out migration and its impact on households in rice-wheat dominated rural economy of Punjab.

Methodology

The present study was conducted in central zone of Punjab where predominantly paddy-wheat crop rotation is followed. In order to make the sample more representative six tehsils were randomly selected in the first instance and out of these tehsils six villages were randomly selected. Out of each selected village a sample of twelve rural households were randomly selected. The selected sample in each village included two households from landless, four each from small (0-2.0 ha) and medium (2.0-5.0 ha) and two from large (> 5.0 ha) farm size category. Therefore, there were 12 landless, 24 small, 24 medium and 12 large rural households thereby making a sample of 72 households. The households selected in each category were not same due to less number of respondents in landless and large size category in the selected villages. Hence more respondents were selected from small and medium size category.

The requisite information for the year 2009-10 was collected on a specially designed schedule by personal interview method for this study. The data were collected regarding age, education status, nature of employment, income, reasons of migration and improvement in social and economic status of the respondents. Simple tabular analysis was carried out to arrive at the results.

Results and Discussion

The results of the study have been presented under various sub heads as under:

Age and Education

The age wise distribution of family members of selected rural households has been depicted in Table 1. It can be observed from the table that family members migrated from landless category were 30.77 per cent followed by 19.84 per cent from small, 13.16 from medium and 11.36 per cent from large size category. This shows that with increase in farm size the migration percentage declined. As far as per cent of family members migrated is concerned, it was highest between 25-50 years age group. In case of landless category 25 per cent members migrated were in the 25-50 years age group followed by 16.03 per cent from small, 9.65 from medium and 7.95 per cent from large farm size category. The per cent of family members migrated in 18-25 age group were 3.85 per cent from landless, 1.53 per cent from small and 3.41 per cent from large farm households.

Table 1
Age wise Distribution of Family Members Migrated Out

(Number)

	Landless		*Small*		*Medium*		*Large*	
Age group (years)	*Total*	*Migrated out*	*Total*	*Migrated out*	*Total*	*Migrated out*	*Total*	*Migrated out*
0-18	15	-	33	1 (0.76)	29	0	13	0
18-25	8	2 (3.85)	13	2 (1.53)	12	0	17	3 (3.41)
25-50	25	13 (25.00)	53	21 (16.03)	42	11 (9.65)	39	7 (7.95)
50 & above	4	1 (1.92)	32	2 (1.52)	31	4 (3.51)	19	0
total	52	16 (30.77)	131	26 (19.84)	114	15 (13.16)	88	10 (11.36)

The figures in the parentheses are percentages to the total family members.

The education wise distribution of the sample households has been shown in Table 2. It can be seen that majority of the family members migrated in each category were educated up to secondary level except in case of medium category where it was post secondary level. In relative terms 15.38 per cent family members were educated up to secondary level in landless category, 12.97 per cent in small, 4.39 per cent in medium and 5.68 per cent in large category. In case of medium category 5.26 per cent members migrated were educated above post secondary level.

Table 2
Education Level of Family Members Migrated Out

(Number)

	Landless		*Small*		*Medium*		*Large*	
Age group (years)	*Total*	*Migrated out*	*Total*	*Migrated out*	*Total*	*Migrated out*	*Total*	*Migrated out*
Illiterate	10	2 (3.85)	29	0	23	0	15	0
Upto Primary	15	5 (9.62)	32	2 (1.53)	23	1 (0.88)	8	0
Upto Secondary	24	8 (15.38)	45	17 (12.97)	33	5 (4.39)	34	5 (5.68)
Secondary	1	0	15	3 (2.29)	18	3 (2.63)	25	4 (4.54)
Post secondary	2	1 (1.92)	10	4 (3.05)	17	6 (5.26)	6	1 (1.14)
Total	52	16 (30.77)	131	26 (19.84)	114	15 (13.16)	88	10 (11.36)

The figures in the parentheses are percentages to the total family members.

Social Characters

The improvement in the social status of respondents due to out migration of family members has been depicted in table 3. In an overall situation out of the total migrated family members, 64.18 per cent reported improvement in social status of the family in the village, 55.22 per cent in terms of improvement in social relations with relatives, and 50.74 per cent reported improvement in education of children and 10.45 per cent benefited in terms of guidance in farming. Thus improvement in the social status in the village, relations with relatives and education of children were the major impacts of out migration of the family members.

Table 3
Improvement in Social Status After Out-migration

(Multiple response)

Particulars	*Effect on social life*
Education of Children	34 (50.74)
Social status in the village	43 (64.18)
Social relations with relatives	37 (55.22)
Guidance in farming	7 (10.45)
Special training etc.	3 (4.48)

The figures in the parentheses are percentages to the total migrated out.

Reasons of Out Migration

The reasons of out migration have been depicted in Table 4. The major reason for out migration was unemployment as reported by 37.31 per cent of the migrated family members and 23.88 per cent revealed as small holding size. There were other reasons such as to get higher studies, custom hiring in agriculture and better employment opportunities as reasons of migration as reported by 20.89 per cent respondents. Indebtedness was reported as reason of migration by 17.91 per cent of the respondents.Therefore, unemployment and small holding size were the major reasons of out migration of the family members of sample households.

Table 4
Reasons of Out-migration of Sample Households

Reasons	*Response*
Small land holding	16 (23.88)
Indebtedness	12 (17.91)
Unemployment	25 (37.31)
Others (for studies, custom hiring in agriculture, for better employment opportunity, factory training, to enhance income etc.)	14 (20.89)

The figures in the parentheses are percentages to the total migrated out.

Impact on Investment Pattern of Out-migrants

The impact on investment pattern of sample households due to out migration of family members has been depicted in Table 5. There were 29.85 per cent of the respondents which reported investment in home construction, repayment of loan revealed by 22.38 per cent, investment on farm building by 14.92 per cent, leasing in of land by 11.94 per cent, investment in purchase of land by 8.95 per cent, while 4.47 per cent reported investment on purchase of farm machinery. Hence, the impact in terms of investment on house construction, repayment of loan, farm building and leasing in land was observed on the sample households.

Table 5
Impact on Investment Pattern of Out-migrants

Particulars	*Investment items*
Dairying	5 (7.46)
Repayment of loan	15 (22.38)
Farm building construction	10 (14.92)
House construction	20 (29.85)
Purchase of land	6 (8.95)
Leasing in of Land	8 (11.94)
Farm machinery	3 (4.47)

The figures in the parentheses are percentages to the total migrated out.

Nature of Employment and Income of Out-migrants

The Nature of employment and income of out-migrants has been depicted in Table 6. In as overall situation it was seen that nature of employment in out migrants was 46.26 per cent as commuters, 40.30 per cent as permanent and 13.43 per cent as seasonal. The education level of permanent settlers was up to secondary level while that of seasonal and commuters was matric. Overall for the sample as a whole the increase in family income was enormous i.e. 288.02 per cent in case of permanent settlers abroad while it was 117.5 per cent in case of commuters and just 54.98 per cent in seasonal migrants. Category wise employment shows that maximum increase in family income was seen in case of permanent settlers belonging to medium category (378.74%) followed by small (334.11%), landless (315.93%) and large size category (155.22%). The increase in income was less in case of large category due to fewer remittances sent by them to their family. In case of commuters the increase in income was more in small size category i.e.

Table 6
Nature of Employment and Income of the Out-migrants

Out-migrants	*No.*	*Average age (years)*	*Average education*	*Income before migration*	*Income After migration*	*%age change in income*
			Landless			
Seasonal	3 (4.47)	26	Primary	21667	36667	69.23
Permanent	3 (4.47)	41	Middle	37667	156667	315.93
Commuter	10 (14.92)	41	Middle	24111	47333	96.31
			Small			
Seasonal	-	-	-	-	-	-
Permanent	11 (16.42)	35	Middle	44900	194917	334.11
Commuter	15 (22.38)	37	Matric	59530	133816	124.79
			Medium			
Seasonal	2 (2.98)	31	Middle	34000	80000	135.29
Permanent	7 (10.45)	38	Secondary	96086	460000	378.74
Commuter	6 (8.95)	39	Secondary	104800	208000	98.47
			Large			
Seasonal	4 (5.97)	35	Upto secondary	226667	330000	45.59
Permanent	6 (8.95)	25	Matric	111667	285000	155.22
Commuter	-	-	-	-	-	-
			Overall			
Seasonal	9 (13.43)	31	Middle	101625	157500	54.98
Permanent	27 (40.30)	34	Upto secondary	71229	276393	288.02
Commuter	31 (47.26)	38	Matric	56229	122325	117.54

The figures in the parentheses are percentages to the total migrated out

Table 7
Places of Migration of the Out-migrants

Out-migrants	*No.*	*Average age (years)*	*Average education*	*Income before migration*	*Income After migration*	*%age change in income*
			Landless			
Foreign country	2 (2.98)	42	Matric	32500	190000	484.62
Other states	1 (1.50)	19	Middle	0	0	0
Other cities within the state	2 (2.98)	38	Middle	30000	54000	80.00
Other rural areas	11 (16.42)	39	Middle	26182	50727	93.75
			Small			
Foreign country	9 (13.43)	36	Matric	51978	213778	311.29
Other states	1 (1.50)	34	Matric	15000	40000	166.67
Other cities within the state	2 (2.98)	40	Matric	12500	50000	300.00
Other rural areas	14 (20.90)	34	Middle	56815	144030	153.51
			Medium			
Foreign country	7 (10.45)	37	Upto secondary	96086	460000	378.74
Other states	-	-	-	-	-	-
Other cities within the state	3 (4.47)	33	Post secondary	104667	240000	129.30
Other rural areas	5 (7.46)	38	Upto secondary	82333	172667	109.72
			Large			
Foreign country	7 (10.44)	29	Matric	102857	251429	144.45
Other states	-	-	-	-	-	-
Other cities within the state	1 (1.50)	20	Secondary	200000	300000	50.00
Other rural areas	2 (2.98)	31	Upto secondary	215000	320000	48.84
			Overall			
Foreign country	25 (37.31)	35	Secondary	77016	291360	278.31
Other states	2 (2.98)	27	Middle	7500	20000	166.67
Other cities within the state	8 (11.94)	34	Matric	74875	153500	105
Other rural areas	32 (47.76)	34	Middle	60831	128801	111.73

The figures in the parentheses are percentages to the total migrated out

124.79 per cent followed by 98.47 per cent in medium and 96.31 per cent in landless size category. In case of seasonal employment increase in income was more i.e. 135.29 per cent in medium size category, 69.23 per cent in landless and 45.59 per cent in large farm size category.

Places of Migration of Out Migrants

The places of migration of out migrants have been shown in Table 7. The out migrants who migrated to other rural areas in the country were 47.76 per cent followed by 37.31 per cent to foreign country, 11.94 per cent to other cities in the state and 2.98 per cent migrated to other states. Increase in income was maximum for out migration to foreign countries i.e. 278.31 per cent followed by to other states (166.67 %), to other rural areas (111.73 %) and to other cities with in the state (105 %). The category wise places of migration and increase in income of households of migrants who visited some foreign country was maximum i.e.484.62 per cent in landless category, followed by 378.74 per cent in medium, 311.29 per cent in small and lowest i.e. 144.45 per cent in large size category. Therefore, remittances from the family members migrated to some foreign country resulted in maximum increase in the income of the sample households in all the categories.

Conclusion

The migration by human beings for better life and opportunities with in other areas in the country and world is continuing since ages. It results in improving the social and economic status of the family whose members have migrated out. From the present study it was seen that among the sample households the majority of the family members migrated were in 25-50 years age group with education up to secondary level and reason of migration was less employment opportunities in the rural areas, small size of holding and indebtedness. The improvement in the social status of family in the village, relations with relatives and better education of children were the major effects of out migration of the family members. The impact in terms of investment on house construction, repayment of loan, farm building and leasing in land was observed on the sample households. The increase in income of households of permanent settlers was maximum in all the categories and remittances from the family members migrated to some foreign country resulted in maximum increase in the income of the sample households in all the categories.

References

Haque T. and Sharma Shailja (2004), *Trends in Crop Output and Employment in India*, vol. 61(5), pp. 273-280.

Kaur Amandeep (2003), *Pattern of Utilization of Remittances of NRI's in Doaba villageofPunjab*. M. Phil thesis, Deptt. of Economics, Punjabi University, Patiala.

17

Performance of National Rural Employment Guarantee Scheme in Punjab: A Case Study of Hoshiarpur District

Parvinder Kaur & Ranjit Singh Ghuman

Introduction

Though there were many schemes such as National Rural Employment Programme (NREP), Rural Landless Employment Guarantee Programme (RLEGP), Jawahar Rojgar Yojana (JRY), Sampoorna Grameen Rojgar Yojana (SGRY) etc, yet the National Rural Employment Guarantee Schemes (NREGS) under MGNREGA is significantly different from the earlier employment schemes. The Mahatma Gandhi National Rural Employment Guarantee Act (MGNREGA), enacted by the Indian Parliament in August 2005, mandates 100 days of guaranteed employment to any rural household, who demands, in India. MGNREGA is right- based, community centered bottom to top approach in which the State is legally bound to fulfill the demand of the employment seekers

The scheme was first implemented on February 2, 2006 in 200 districts of the country on pilot basis. The government announced the addition of another 130 districts in the financial year 2007-08. In April 2008, NREGA expanded its cover to all the districts of India. The work guarantee can also serve other objectives like generating productive assets, protecting environment, empowering rural women, reducing rural to urban migration and providing social equity, etc. It also empowers local citizens to play an active role in the implementation of employment guarantee schemes through Panchayats, social audits, participatory planning and other means. The act is towards realizing of the right to work and also to enable people to enhance their livelihoods on a sustained basis by developing economic and social infrastructure in rural areas. The choice of activity aims to address causes of chronic poverty such as droughts, deforestation and soil erosion. If implemented effectively it can transform the geography of poverty prove to be an historic land mark in the economic history of the Indian Republic.

The present paper is an attempt to evaluate the implementation and effectiveness of the Act. The paper is also an attempt to study the socio economic background of the job seeker households and those who have got employment under the Act. The study is based both on secondary and primary data. The primary data and information have been collected through a questionnaire from 20 randomly selected villages, two from each of the 10 development blocks of Hoshiarpur District. The study pertains to 300 households, 15 from each of the sampled villages. The present paper has been organized into VIII sections. Section 1 gives a brief introduction of MGNREGA. Section II presents brief literature review. Generation of employment under the scheme in Punjab has been discussed in section III. A brief profile of Hoshiarpur District is given in section IV. The employment generation under MGNREGA in district Hoshiarpur has been examined in section V .The socio economic status of the sampled job card holders in Hoshiarpur District is presented in section VI. Profile of the Panchayat heads and members is given in section VII. The concluding observations are given in the last section.

Literature Review

Though the implementation of NREGS started only four years ago, yet a good number of studies have been conducted regarding its implementation. Pratima Yadav's study (2008) about Uttar Pradesh says that there are significant differences between the job cards issued to the job seekers and the actual job supplied. Also in overall NREGS employment, Scheduled castes have drawn fairly substantial share. Almost half of the NREGS fund goes to the wages given to the unskilled manual workers.

The position of West Bengal in terms of NREGS performance indicators has also not been impressive. However, average number of days of work per job card (or per household demanded employment) shows a clear negative relation with the incidence of poverty (Mukherjee, 2008). According to another study (Dey, 2008) of Purulia district of West Bengal, the average days of employment per family was nearly the thirty days in a years in the study area. Inadequate arrangement for the historic programme has been reflected in official data.

The study of Hoshiarpur (Ghuman and Parvinder, 2008) reveals that the achievement of the Act in terms of annual average days of employment per household has been nearly $1/4^{th}$ of the minimum statutory 100 days employment.

Jacob (2006) highlighted the socio-economic conditions which had a great influence on the successful implementation of NREGS in Kerala. The higher participation by women in the scheme and minimal corruption levels are important features in his study, the practicality of the unemployment allowance is questioned, as no serious steps are being taken.

Narayana (2008) says that the absence of individual employee- employer relation has also encouraged the women from the upper caste to take up employment under the scheme. They could escape from the shame of working under some individual. The payment of wages after completion of the piece of work, that too into the bank account of woman, adds to her economic empowerment.

The Tamil Nadu study highlights that the crèche facility at the work place was grossly insufficient (Narayanan, 2008). Almost 85 per cent of the mothers who left their children at home said that if a crèche was provided at the worksite, they would certainly bring their children particularly the young ones. So the provision of effective childcare facilities at NREGS worksite is an important issue that calls for creative thinking and action. Nevertheless the Act has removed the sense of insecurity in the minds of the workers to a large extent as they are entitled to get work for 100 days. Thus this Act is aimed at ensuring food security to poor rural household (Goswami, 2008).

Unemployment in general and rural unemployment in particular has become a serious phenomenon in Punjab in view of the shrinking employment opportunities in agriculture in particular and rural economy in general Out of the total workers in Punjab nearly 70 per cent are engaged in rural sector. Further out of the total rural workers, 31.5 per cent are cultivators, 22.0 per cent are agricultural labourers, 3.1 per cent are engaged in households industry and 43.4 per cent are other workers. The proportion of agricultural workers in Punjab has declined from 55.2 per cent in 1991 to 39.4 per cent in 2001 (Government of India, 2002a).

As regards rural workers, working partially in agriculture and partially in non-agricultural sectors, the average wage earnings were Rs. 77 per day during 2006-07. In fact, the agricultural labourers are also committing suicides in Punjab, mainly due to their poor economic conditions and outstanding loan (AFDR, 2000; Iyer, 2000). The average amount of outstanding loan of the deceased agricultural labourers is Rs. 57121 per household (Singh, Gurpreet, 2008). Despite the countless efforts by the central and the state governments, the agrarian distress and disparities across the states continue to haunt the policy makers (Bhalla and Singh,1997.The ever rising rural unemployment, declining employment elasticity in agriculture, slow growth rate of over all employment (Bhalla, 1987 and 1989; Gill, 2002) , high growth rate of labour force, predominantly capitalist agriculture (Gill and Ghuman,2001) and decelerating per hectare net return (Ghuman, 2005) have further accentuated the agricultural and rural distress.

Generation of Employment under NREGA in Punjab

The Mahatma Gandhi National Employment Guarantee Scheme (MGNREGA) became operative in only one district

(Hoshiarpur) of the Punjab on February 2, 2006. It was extended to Amritsar, Jalandhar and Nawanshahr districts on April 1, 2007 and to the remaining 16 districts on April 1, 2008.

As such, the district-wise employment scenario under the NREGS has been examined for only two years, i.e., 2008-09 and 2009-10. In 2008-09, in all the 20 districts of Punjab, 524,928 households were issued job cards and out of them 72.98 per cent were scheduled caste (SC) households (Table 1). But in district like Moga, 96.30 per cent of the job card holders were SC households. Out of the total job card holder households, 28.56 per cent were also given employment. Again, out of the total employment provided (4017 thousand person days), the share of SCs was 74.17 per cent. The SCs constituted 28.85 per cent of the total and 33.04 per cent of the rural population in Punjab (Govt. of Punjab, 2008). Across the districts, the proportion of SCs in rural population varied between 26.15 per cent (Gurdaspur) and 45.78 per cent (Jalandhar). Women's share in total person-days of employment under the scheme was only one-fourth of the total (24.61 per cent). Thus, the demand for the government sponsored guaranteed wage employment in the rural Punjab is largely confined to the SCs and women.

It is significant to note that Punjab has the highest proportion of SC population amongst the major states in India. During the British period, all the non-tillers were not allowed to own/purchase agricultural land. Hence the SCs in Punjab have historically been non-owners of land. Of late, they, however, have been having some operational holdings and their share in the total operational holdings and in total operated area is only 4.67 per cent and 2.14 per cent, respectively. The average size of their operational holdings is 1.77 hectares (Govt. of India, 2003).

The overall level of demand for the government sponsored wage employment in the State is low, which further varied across districts. The number of job card holder households was only 9237 in Kapurthala, but 72543 in Ferozepur. The share of SC households varied between 52.33 per cent in SAS Nagar and 96.30 per cent in Moga. Similarly, the number of households who were provided with employment varied between 996 in

Ludhiana and 35512 in Hoshiarpur. The proportion of such households in the total number of job-card holder households varied between 5.16 per cent in Tarn Taran and 78.68 per cent in Hoshiarpur (Table 1).

The number of households provided employment as a ratio to the job card holders is low in most of the districts. Out of the total 20 districts, the proportion of households with employment to the job-card holder households was only up to 25 per cent in 11 districts. In another seven districts, this proportion was between 25 per cent and 50 per cent. Only in two districts, the proportion of such households was above 50 per cent, but below 80 per cent.

The amount of employment generation during 2008-09 varied between 37,000 person days (Faridkot) and 12.06 lakh person days (Hoshiarpur). The share of SCs in the total person-days is quite sizeable and varied between 28.68 per cent in Sangrur and 99.41 per cent in Bathinda. In 14 districts, more than 80 per cent of the person days of employment was availed by the SC households. The proportion was between 50 per cent and 80 per cent in another five districts. Only in one district, this was 28.68 per cent. It is to be noted that the share of SCs in the total job card holder households was also very high in all the districts of Punjab.

The proportion of women in the person days employment was, however, not very high, except in some of the districts (Table 1). Their share was less than 50 per cent in 17 of the 20 districts. In two districts, the share of women was nil. This means women in Punjab are either not participating in the work or are not encouraged to undertaking work under NREGA.

The mean days of employment per households varied between 5 days (Ferozepur) and 43 days (Fatehgarh Sahib) across the districts of Punjab during 2008-09 (Table 2). The districts of Ludhiana and Barnala, with 184 days and 71 days, respectively, were an exception. In the case of Ludhiana the number of households who demanded work was very small. Almost similar was the case in Barnala district.

The number of households completing 100 days of employment is quite low and almost negligible in most of the

Table 1
Employment Status Under NREGS Across the Districts in Punjab During 2008-09

	Commutative no. of HHs issued job cards			*HHs provided employment*		*Employment generated (lakh person days)*		
Districts	*Total*	*SC*	*3 as % of 2*	*Total Col. 2*	*% of*	*Total*	*SC (%)*	*Women (%)*
(1)	(2)	(3)	(4)	(5)	(6)	(7)	(8)	(9)
Hoshiarpur	45135	27590	61.13	35512	78.68	12.06	59.45	26.04
Amritsar	36163	32751	90.56	14913	41.24	6.17	89.95	0.49
Jalandhar	16566	14086	85.03	4234	25.56	1.08	97.22	36.11
Nawanshahr	16373	12176	74.37	4154	25.37	1.46	86.99	52.74
Barnala	17385	12385	71.24	1268	7.29	0.90	96.67	48.89
Bathinda	23532	22208	94.37	17036	72.40	3.40	99.41	1.76
Faridkot	11899	8946	75.18	5319	44.70	0.37	86.49	10.81
Fategarh Sahib	15830	12568	79.39	1955	12.35	0.85	80.00	29.41
Firozepur	72543	49392	68.09	9943	13.71	0.50	86.00	100.00
Gurdspur	51378	28445	55.36	7036	13.69	1.93	60.10	0.00
Kapurthala	9237	7813	84.58	2566	27.78	0.38	68.42	23.68
Ludhiana	11450	9786	85.47	996	8.70	1.83	82.51	4.35
Mansa	25134	21403	85.16	7241	28.81	0.95	91.58	22.11
Moga	18137	17466	96.30	1703	9.39	0.52	86.54	1.92
Muktsar	25038	23488	93.81	11259	44.97	1.74	95.40	100.00

Contd...

	Commutative no. of HHs issued job cards			HHs provided employment		Employment generated (lakh person days)		
Districts	Total	SC	3 as % of 2	Total Col. 2	% of	Total	SC (%)	Women (%)
(1)	(2)	(3)	(4)	(5)	(6)	(7)	(8)	(9)
Patiala	22748	15572	68.45	4398	19.33	1.47	80.95	29.25
Rupnagar	14233	7915	55.61	1046	7.35	0.29	55.17	17.24
Sangrur	43082	22600	52.46	11652	27.46	2.55	28.68	19.62
SAS Nagar	12101	6333	52.33	5763	47.62	1.24	59.68	94.35
Taran Taran	36964	29832	80.71	1908	5.16	0.48	81.25	0.00
Pb: Total	524928	383115	72.98	149902	28.56	40.27	74.17	24.61

Source: *www.nrega.nic.in*, dated 13th May, 2010.

Note:

1. Hoshiarpur was covered under First Phase of NREGA and the three districts – Amritsar, Jalandhar and Nawanshahr were covered under second phase. The remaining 16 districts were covered in the third phase.
2. The number of job card holder households who demanded employment under NREGA and the number of households who were provided employment is exactly the same, as per the official record.
3. 10 lakh = one million.

Table 2

Generation of Employment Under NREGS Across the Districts and Employment Gap in Punjab during 2008-09

	Emp. generated (lakh person days)		*HHs employed for 100 days*		*Required emp. (lakh person days) to provide 100 days emp.*		*Emp. gap (lakh person days)*	
Districts	*Total*	*Mean days per HH*	*No.*	*%*	*for HHs demanding work*	*For HHs with job cards*	*Col. 6 – Col. 2*	*Col. 7 – Col. 2*
(1)	*(2)*	*(3)*	*(4)*	*(5)*	*(6)*	*(7)*	*(8)*	*(9)*
Hoshiarpur	12.06	33.96	3534	9.96	35.51	45.14	23.45	33.08
Amritsar	6.17	41.37	78	0.52	14.91	36.16	8.74	29.99
Jalandhar	1.08	25.51	00	0.00	4.23	16.57	3.15	15.19
Nawanshahr	1.46	35.15	172	4.14	4.15	16.37	2.69	14.91
Barnala	0.90	70.78	01	0.08	1.27	17.38	0.37	16.48
Bathinda	3.40	19.96	00	0.00	17.04	23.53	13.64	20.13
Faridkot	0.37	6.96	00	0.00	5.32	11.90	4.95	11.53
Fategarh Sahib	0.85	43.48	33	1.69	1.95	15.83	1.10	14.98
Firozepur	0.50	5.03	00	0.00	9.94	72.54	9.44	72.04
Gurdspur	1.93	27.43	00	0.00	7.04	51.38	5.11	49.48
Kapurthala	0.38	14.81	00	0.00	2.57	9.24	2.19	8.86
Ludhiana	1.83	183.73	23	2.31	0.99	11.45	0.84	9.62
Mansa	0.95	13.12	18	0.25	7.24	25.13	6.29	24.18

Contd...

Districts	Emp. generated (lakh person days)		HHs employed for 100 days		Required emp. (lakh person days) to provide 100 days emp.		Emp. gap (lakh person days)	
	Total	Mean days per HH	No.	%	for HHs demanding work	For HHs with job cards	Col. 6 – Col. 2	Col. 7 – Col. 2
(1)	(2)	(3)	(4)	(5)	(6)	(7)	(8)	(9)
Moga	0.52	30.53	00	0.00	1.70	18.14	1.18	17.62
Muktsar	1.74	15.45	12	0.11	11.26	25.04	9.52	23.3
Patiala	1.47	33.42	98	2.23	4.40	22.75	2.93	21.28
Rupnagar	0.29	27.72	01	0.09	1.05	14.23	0.76	13.94
Sangrur	2.55	22.74	00	0.00	11.65	43.08	9.00	40.43
SAS Nagar	1.24	21.15	00	0.00	5.76	12.10	4.52	10.86
Taran Taran	0.48	25.16	00	0.00	1.91	36.96	1.43	36.48
Pb: Total	40.27	26.86	3970	2.65	149.90	524.93	109.63	484.66

Source: Same as Table 1.

Note: Column 6 has been computed by multiplying column 5 of table 1 by 100; column 7 has been computed by multiplying column 2 of table 1 by 100.

districts. In 10 out of 20 districts, not a single household completed 100 days of employment (Table 2). In another two districts, only one household completed 100 days of employment. However, in Hoshiarpur, about 10 per cent of the households could complete 100 days of employment. In five districts, the proportion of such households was less than one per cent. In another four districts, the proportion of such households varied between 1.69 per cent and 4.14 per cent.

Based on the presumption that all those households who are demanding employment would work for 100 days, the State should have generated 14.99 million person days of employment in 2008-09. As against this only 4.02 million person-days of employment were generated, thereby leaving a gap of 10.97 million person days in 2008-09. The required extent of employment, across the districts, varied between 99 thousand person days (Ludhiana) and 3.55 million person days (Hoshiarpur). The employment gap across the districts ranged from 76 thousand person days (Rupnagar) to 2.34 million person days (Hoshiarpur). If all the job card holder households were to be provided with 100 days employment during 2008-09, the required employment generation would have been 52.49 million person days. Accordingly the employment gap would have been 48.47 million person days (table 2) in Punjab. The employment gap across the districts varied between 0.87 million person days (Kapurthala) and 7.20 million person days (Firozepur).

There is an overall increase in the employment demanded and provided in 2009-10 (Table 3). The number of job card holder households increased from 524,928 in 2008-09 to 709,186 in 2009-10. Out of them 77.61 per cent were SCs. An increase of 184,258 (35.10 per cent) job card households in one year indicates the increasing level of demand for the Scheme in the State.

The total number of households who were provided with employment increased to 270,713 in 2009-10 from 149,902 in 2008-09. The percentage of such households to the total job card households increased from 28.56 per cent in 2008-09 to 38.17 per cent in 2009-10. Across the districts, this percentage varied mainly between 6.34 per cent (Moga) to 43.94 per cent (Jalandhar) in majority of the districts. In three districts this proportion was around 67 per cent, with Sangrur (93.21 per cent) as an exception.

The employment generation during 2009-10 (Table 3) was 7.66 million person days. Out of this 79.90 per cent were availed by the SCs and 26.35 per cent by women. Across the districts, the proportion of SCs varied from 52.03 per cent in Gurdaspur to 97.90 per cent in Bathinda. The proportion of women, across the districts was between 2.44 per cent in Moga and 73.38 per cent in Sangrur. The number of woman workers was nil in Faridkot district.

The average days of employment per household was 28.30 days in 2009-10. Across the various districts, it varied between 8.79 days (Sangrur) and 57.21 days (Mansa). District Rupnagar, with 70.35 days of average employment, was an exception (Table 4).

In terms of 100 days of employment, only 7657 households (2.83 per cent) with employment completed 100 days in 2009-10 (Table 4). In two districts no household got employment for 100 days. In another seven districts the proportion of households who got employment for 100 days was less than one per cent. In eleven districts, this proportion varied between 1.38 per cent and 10.60 per cent of the households. Presuming that all those households who were provided employment would like to work for 100 days, the State was required to generate 27.07 million person days as against 7.66 million person-days generated in 2009-10. This required an additional employment generation of 19.41 million person-days. The requirement for additional employment generation would have gone up to 63.26 million person days in order to provide 100 days employment to all the existing job card holder households.

Thus, the level of implementation across districts reflects wide variations in the demand for employment under the NREGA and employment provided. However, the level of demand has to be understood in the context of employment available in the agriculture and non-agriculture sectors. It is significant to note that 63.43 per cent of labourers in Punjab

Table 3
Employment Status Under NREGS Across the Districts in Punjab During 2009-10

	Commutative no. of HHs issued job cards			No. of HHs provided emp.		Emp. generated (lakh person days)		
Districts	*Total*	*SC*	*3 as % of 2*	*Total*	*% of 2*	*Total*	*SC (%)*	*Women (%)*
(1)	(2)	(3)	(4)	(5)	(6)	(7)	(8)	(9)
Hoshiarpur	66025	39242	59.43	44581	67.52	12.86	62.36	25.19
Amritsar	55126	47224	85.67	37425	67.89	15.24	85.70	3.08
Jalandhar	29612	27437	92.66	13012	43.94	4.05	94.07	53.09
Nawanshahr	20026	14969	74.75	7835	39.12	2.93	77.13	54.27
Barnala	19552	14449	73.90	7100	36.31	0.98	89.80	50.00
Bathinda	36425	34506	94.73	14942	41.02	7.63	97.90	12.32
Faridkot	14731	11784	79.99	4647	31.55	1.09	80.73	0.00
Fategarh Sahib	22208	17615	79.93	3133	14.11	0.75	86.67	50.67
Firozepur	81953	65789	80.28	18564	22.76	3.13	79.87	22.68
Gurdspur	57049	30162	52.87	23602	41.37	5.42	52.03	4.43
Kapurthala	15690	14038	89.47	3270	20.84	0.8	82.50	18.75
Ludhiana	40390	32032	79.31	7188	17.80	2.19	82.65	32.42
Mansa	40425	36382	90.00	6135	15.18	3.51	80.06	33.33
Moga	26665	23119	86.74	1690	06.34	0.41	92.68	2.44
Muktsar	40996	38156	93.07	27594	67.31	6.04	92.22	59.27
Patiala	29606	20554	69.43	9378	31.68	3.33	76.88	50.45
Rupnagar	16964	9213	54.31	3090	18.27	2.18	60.55	17.89
Sangrur	33942	25688	75.68	31638	93.21	2.78	71.58	73.38
SAS Nagar	17509	12691	72.48	3094	17.67	0.57	82.46	24.56
Taran Taran	44292	35317	79.74	2786	31.04	0.73	86.30	15.07
Pb: Total	709186	550367	77.61	270713	38.17	76.62	79.90	26.35

Source: Same as Table 1.

Table 4

Generation of Employment Across Districts Under NREGS and Employment Gap in Punjab during 2009-10

	Emp. generated (lakh person days)		*HHs employed for 100 days*		*Required emp. (lakh person days) to provide 100 days emp.*		*Emp. gap (lakh person days)*	
Districts	*Total*	*Mean days per HH*	*No.*	*%*	*for HHs demanding work*	*For HHs with job cards*	*Col. 6 – Col. 2*	*Col. 7 – Col. 2*
(1)	*(2)*	*(3)*	*(4)*	*(5)*	*(6)*	*(7)*	*(8)*	*(9)*
Hoshiarpur	12.86	28.85	614	1.38	44.58	66.03	31.72	53.17
Amritsar	15.24	40.72	3966	10.60	37.43	55.13	22.19	39.89
Jalandhar	4.05	31.13	359	2.76	13.01	29.61	8.96	25.56
Nawanshahr	2.93	37.40	502	6.41	7.84	20.03	4.91	17.10
Barnala	0.98	13.80	11	0.15	7.10	19.55	6.12	18.57
Bathinda	7.63	51.06	787	5.27	14.94	36.43	7.31	28.80
Faridkot	1.09	23.46	34	0.73	4.65	14.73	3.56	13.64
Fategarh Sahib	0.75	23.94	52	1.66	3.13	22.21	2.38	21.46
Firozepur	3.13	16.86	00	0.00	18.56	81.95	15.43	78.82
Gurdspur	5.42	22.96	75	0.32	23.60	57.05	18.18	51.63
Kapurthala	0.80	24.46	19	0.58	3.27	15.69	2.47	14.89
Ludhiana	2.19	30.47	244	3.39	7.19	40.39	5.00	38.20

Contd...

	Emp. generated (lakh person days)		*HHs employed for 100 days*		*Required emp. (lakh person days) to provide 100 days emp.*		*Emp. gap (lakh person days)*	
Districts	*Total*	*Mean days per HH*	*No.*	*%*	*for HHs demanding work*	*For HHs with job cards*	*Col. 6 – Col. 2*	*Col. 7 – Col. 2*
(1)	*(2)*	*(3)*	*(4)*	*(5)*	*(6)*	*(7)*	*(8)*	*(9)*
Mansa	3.51	57.21	130	2.12	6.14	40.41	2.63	36.90
Moga	0.41	24.26	03	0.18	1.69	26.67	1.28	26.26
Muktsar	6.04	21.88	418	1.51	27.59	41.00	21.55	34.96
Patiala	3.33	35.51	141	1.50	9.38	29.61	6.05	26.28
Rupnagar	2.18	70.35	234	7.55	3.10	16.96	0.92	14.48
Sangrur	2.78	8.79	65	0.21	31.64	33.94	28.86	31.16
SAS Nagar	0.57	18.42	00	0.00	3.09	17.51	2.52	16.94
Taran Taran	0.73	26.20	03	0.11	2.79	44.29	2.06	43.56
Pb: Total	76.62	28.30	7657	2.83	270.71	709.14	194.09	632.57

Source: Same as of Table 1.

Note: Column 6 has been computed by multiplying column 5 of table 3 by 100; column 7 has been computed by multiplying column 2 of table 3 by 100.

get employment in agriculture between 96 days and 120 days in a year (Ghuman, et al, 2007; p.40). For them, there is demand for employment under the Scheme. However, 79 per cent of the labourers get employment between 120 days and 240 days in year, both in agriculture and non-agricultural activities (Ghuman et al, 2007, p. 41). This inter-alia may be one of the reasons for a low demand for employment under NREGA.

But the number of households who demanded job and that of households that were given employment has been recorded as exactly the same in the official data, which has to be viewed with a note of caution. The job provided is not based on the demand placed through application. Contrarily, the head of the Gram Panchayat calls people for work as and when required. There was no other mechanism to inform the potential job-seekers about the availability of work. It is significant to note that under the NREGA the public announcement about the availability of work is mandatory.

Also, the demand for the NREGA employment is confined mostly to the SC households who constituted 77.61 per cent of the job card holders and accounted for 79.90 per cent of the employment days provided in 2009-10. The share of SCs in employment varied across districts. However, in most of the districts, SCs constitute the largest proportion of the job card holder households and largest share in the total person days of employment generated under NREGA.

The low participation of women in most of the districts indicates that women are yet to come forward to avail employment opportunities under the Scheme in large number. In most of the districts, the percentage share of women in total person days is less than the national average and less than the stipulated minimum of 33 per cent. In district like Amritsar, Gurdaspur (known as Majha region) the participation of women was very low in 2009-10.

This needs to be understood in the context that the female work participation rate has always been low in Punjab. The female work participation rate in Punjab in 2001 was 18.7 per cent (26th rank, among the states and UTs in India, in the descending order). It was only 16.3 per cent in Amritsar and

12.7 per cent in Gurdaspur. Compared to it, the male work participation rate in Punjab has been above 53 per cent during 1961 to 2001. It is significant to note that the female work participation rate in Punjab was merely 2.3 per cent in 1981 and 4.4 per cent in 1991 (Govt. of India, 2002a, P. 54). In the districts of Amritsar and Gurdaspur it was 2.7 per cent and 2.4 per cent, respectively in 1991.

The low women work participation rate in Punjab, particularly in the rural area, may be mainly attributed to social reasons. Women are normally not encouraged to go in for out of home work. Nevertheless, the women in rural Punjab are largely engaged in unpaid household work.

It is significant to note that the average female work participation rate in India was 25.6 per cent in 2001, whereas in the rural India, the female work participation rate was 30.8 per cent (Govt. of India, 2008, P. 12).

The supply side constraint is also visible. For, the number of households seeking job cards has increased from 524,928 in 2008-09 to 709,186 households in 2009-10, an increase of nearly 35 per cent. Further, the average person days of employment provided was only 27 days in 2008-09 and 28-30 days in 2009-10, which was only a little less than the national average for the two years.

One fundamental reason for low level of employment generation under NREGA is the provision of employment generation through eight types of work which are practically applicable more in the case of dry areas. Because of the high percentage of irrigated area, in almost of all the districts, the scope of work of water conservation and harvesting has almost saturated. In view of this, Punjab would have to devise new ways and means to conserve and harvest water, particularly rain water. A large part of the Punjab is plain (except Hoshiarpur district), the scope of taking land development work is also limited. Further, most of the villages are connected with all weather pucca roads that also limits the scope for road construction under the scheme.

It is significant to note that, being a success story of green revolution, Punjab is beset with specific limitations in regard to NREGA. The peak season work in agriculture is confined to a maximum of three months. The market wage rate (earnings by the labourers) is almost three times higher than the wage rate under NREGA during these months. So, during the peak season hardly any worker is available for work under the rural employment guarantee scheme. During the remaining period of the year, the work is mainly available in the urban and semi-urban areas in construction related activities and in other seasonal activities. The market wage rate earnings in such activities are also higher (say by 25 to 50 per cent) than the wage rate under NREGA. In many seasonal activities the earnings are almost double than the stipulated minimum wage rate.

The availability of work under NREGA in other states (particularly in Bihar and U.P., the main supplier of migrant labourers to Punjab) has further tightened the supply side. Recently, the Punjab Government has launched an interest-free loan (ranging form Rs. 2500 to Rs. 15,000) scheme for daily wage-earners (The Tribune, 2010). The scheme is mainly a strategy to attract migrant workers who are known as the backbone of the rural economy of Punjab. It is pertinent to note that the number of migrant laboures in Punjab in 2001 was 1.75 million out of which 0.95 million were in urban area (Govt. of India, 2002). According to a recent study (Ghuman, et al, 2007) the estimated number of migrant labourers in Punjab in 2007 was 0.82 million. In view of the shortage of labour, mainly, due to declining supply of migrant labour, the government of Punjab has offered heavy subsidy on paddy transplantation machines (The Tribune, 2010a). The extent of subsidy is to the tune of Rs. 75,000 on each transplanting machine and in addition, the farmers who will help the fellow farmers will be given an additional subsidy of Rs. 5000 per acre.

In view of the above, Punjab would have to plan its employment generation under NREGA during the non-peak season. Also, the minimum wage rate would have to be raised so as to make this scheme attractive to the workers. In addition to that the scope and coverage of works under the scheme shall have to be widened keeping in view the requirements of the developed states like Punjab.

A Brief Profile of Hoshiarpur District

Hoshiarpur is predominantly a rural district with 80.33 per cent rural population and 81.94 per cent rural workers. According to the Census 2001, the district has a total population of 14.78 lakh and the sex-ratio is quite high: 935 females for 1000 males.

Compared to it, the sex ratio in Punjab is 874. It is interesting to note that nearly 80 per cent male population and about 90 per cent of female population in district Hoshiarpur lives in rural area. Similarly, the proportion of rural workers in district Hoshiarpur is nearly 82 per cent. The corresponding proportion of females is approximately 89 per cent.

About 79 per cent main workers and 94 per cent marginal workers in district Hoshiarpur are rural workers. The corresponding proportion of male and female marginal workers is 92 per cent and 96 per cent, respectively. The share of rural marginal workers in the total rural workers in the district is also higher than the average of Punjab. Such a high proportion of marginal rural workers in the district are expected to be benefited by NREGA. The cultivators with very tiny operational holdings and the agricultural labourers would also get benefit under NREGA in view of the ever shrinking employment opportunities in the agricultural sector. The proportion of marginal operational holdings in Hoshiarpur is more than double (26.72 per cent) than that in Punjab (12.31 per cent). The proportion of small operational holdings in the district is 23.49 per cent whereas in Punjab their proportion is 17.35 per cent (GOP 2006).

Though the district has highest literacy rate in the state yet it is economically backward. Its economic backwardness is mainly due to its topography. The Shivalik Hills, from North-East and South-East alignment, run throughout the length of the district. The foothill plains and flood plains of the river Beas constitute the remaining part of the district. The hill track known as 'KANDI' area cover roughly one-half of the district. In fact, the variant topography has been the main cause for the economic backwardness of the district.

The district consists of 10 development blocks. Out of 1426 villages 1396 are inhabited villages which have 1317 gram panchayats. The total number of households is 2.35 lacs in the district. The number of panchayats per block varies from 82 to 168 across the blocks.

Employment Generation under NREGS in Hoshiarpur District

Table 5 represents the employment scenario under NREGS in Hoshiarpur district during 2009-10.It is significant to note that 68861 households were issued job cards till Nov 25, 2010. Out of them 39878 were scheduled castes. Across the blocks, the cumulative number of job card holders varied between 4676(Hoshiarpur II) and 8748 (Bhunga).The cumulative no. of households who were provided with employment was 20762 and cumulative no. of households who demanded employment was 20771. It is to be noted that the difference between the households demanded employment and households provided with the employment was very small i.e. 9. Across the blocks the cumulative no. of households provided with the employment varied between 1046 (Garshankar) and 4288 (Dasuya).The cumulative no. of households who completed 100 days was 264(2010-11), in which Dasuya block was on the top most (77) and in Hajipur block was at last i.e. only 2 households completed 100 days of work.

Table 6 presents that in 2006-07, 11,331 person days work was completed by 300 households. Across the villages, the person-days work varied between 92 (Manjpur) and 1583 (Khun Khun Sarki). In 2007-08, 7 villages did not generate any employment under NREGS. In Badowal village, 45 person days work was completed by 15 households and 329 person days work was completed by same no of households in village Takri. In 2008-09, 6 villages could not generate any employment under the scheme. The generation of employment varied between 61 days in Jassowal and 693 days in Haveli villages .In the financial year 2009-10, 3065 person- days work was completed by 300 households. Thus in the last four financial years, total of 19802 person days work was completed by 300 households.

Table 5
Employment Status under NREGS Across the Blocks in Hoshiarpur District 2009-10

Block	*Cumulative No. of HH issued Job Card*						
	SC	*ST*	*Others*	*Total*	*Cumulative No of HH demanded employment*	*Cumulative No. of HH provided employment*	*Cumulative No of HH completed 100 days*
Bhunga	6598	1	2149	8748	3429	3429	68
Dasuya	4660	9	3721	8390	4228	4228	77
Garshankar	4878	2	2350	7230	1046	1046	6
Hajipur	1967	8	4075	6050	1502	1502	2
Hoshiarpur-1	8164	2	408	8574	2389	2389	7
Hoshiarpur-2	1698	0	2978	4676	1231	1231	25
Mahalpur	4898	3	1861	6762	2439	2439	4
Mukerian	2264	0	3351	5615	1195	1193	10
Talwara	335	0	6640	6975	2019	2012	18
Tanda	4416	8	1417	5841	1293	1293	47
Total	39878	33	28950	68861	20771	20762	264

Source: www.nrega.nic.in dated 25-11-2010

Table 6
Person-Days Employment Completed by Sampled Households During 2006-10

Villages	*2006-07*	*2007-08*	*2008-09*	*2009-10*	*Total*	*Average*
Kotli Khurd	216	0	179	0	395	98.75
Khun Khun Sarki	1583	0	179	155	1917	479.25
Dhakki	272	258	0	167	697	174.25
Nangal Ishar	607	166	196	629	1598	399.50
Saroa	687	252	0	73	1012	253.00
Singhpur	219	0	0	303	522	130.50
Burey Jattan	502	120	137	83	842	210.50
Hardo Khanpur	802	120	107	72	1101	275.25
Badowal	1248	45	145	287	1725	431.25
Manan	409	0	159	98	666	166.50
Beh Chuhar	874	194	90	274	1432	358.00
Dohar	499	132	341	214	1186	296.50
Simbli	442	0	0	0	442	110.50
Jassowal	297	0	61	57	415	103.75
Bhagtupur	366	148	164	47	725	181.25
Haveli	465	89	693	73	1320	330.00
Mehatpur	520	0	0	245	765	191.25
Manjpur	92	245	156	219	712	178.00
Takri	818	329	454	0	1601	400.25
Kaloa	413	247	0	69	729	182.50
Total	11331	2345	3061	3065	19802	4950.50

Source: Field Survey

Table 7 represents the generation of employment under NREGS in the 20 sampled villages in the four financial years. During 2006-07, only 16 households, who were called for work, could complete 100 days employment. No household could complete 100 days employment during 2007-08, 2008-09 and 2009-10. Only 35 households could get employment between 80-120 days during the last 4 years. As many as121 households could get work between 40-80 days. Further, 528 households could get employment between 1-40 days during the last 4 financial years. Most of the work done was in the financial year 2006-07. The employment generation during the financial year 2007- 08 was very minimal.

Table 7

Number of Work Days Completed by the Households Under NREGS in Sampled Villages in District Hoshiarpur During 2006-10

	Work days completed: Number of households											
	1-40 Days				*40-80 Days*				*80-120 Days*			
Name of the Village	*2006-07*	*2007-08*	*2008-09*	*2009-10*	*2006-07*	*2007-08*	*2008-09*	*2009-10*	*2006-07*	*2007-08*	*2008-09*	*2009-10*
Kotli Khurd	15	0	7	-	-	-	1	-	-	-	-	-
Khun Khun Sarki	-	-	10	8	2	-	-	-	13	-	-	-
Dhakki	13	12	-	9	-	-	-	-	-	-	-	-
Nangal Ishar	4	9	9	4	10	-	-	9	-	-	-	-
Saroa	3	8	-	13	10	-	-	-	-	-	-	-
Singhpur	6	-	-	11	2	-	-	3	-	-	-	-
Burey Jattan	4	13	13	8	10	-		-	-	-	-	-
Hardo Khanpur	4	9	11	5	8	-		-	1	-	-	-
Badowal	2	3	8	3	2	-	1	2	11	-	-	1
Manan	15	-	13	9		-	-	-	-	-	-	-
Beh Chuhar	5	7	4	5	6	1	-	3	4	-	-	-
Dohar	4	6	10	4	2	2	2	3	1	-	-	-
Simbli	13	-	-	-	2	-	-	-	-	-	-	-
Jassowal	15	-	8	4	-	-	-	-	-	-	-	-
Bhagtupur	15	10	13	6	-	-	-	-	-	-	-	-
Haveli	10	11	3	9	5	-	9	-	-	-	-	-
Mehatpur	7	-	-	7	8	-	-	3	-	-	-	-
Manjpur	13	11	10	10	-	1	-	-	-	-	-	-
Takri	4	9	11	-	3	3	4	-	4	-	-	-
Kaloa	12	7	-	7	3	1	-	-	-	-	-	-
Total	162	115	129	122	73	8	17	23	34	0	0	1

Source: Field Survey

Table 8
Caste and Educational Status of the Job Card Holders and Family Size of their Households

	Jab Card holder				*Caste*			*Education Level*			
	Sex		*Age years*								
Name of the Village	*M*	*F*	*18-35*	*36-70*	*GC*	*BC*	*SC*	*Illiterate*	*<8th*	*<10th*	*Family size*
Kotli Khurd	7	8	7	8	1	1	13	11	2	1	4.5
Khun Khun Sarki	15	0	8	6	8	1	6	4	8	2	4.5
Dhakki	10	5	0	15	2	0	13	6	4	4	4.5
Nangal Ishar	15	0	1	14	2	0	13	6	6	3	4.7
Saroa	6	9	2	13	0	0	15	8	6	1	4.6
Singhpur	13	2	4	11	2	1	12	5	6	4	5.6
Burey Jattan	11	4	7	8	0	0	15	5	6	4	4.9
Hardo Khanpur	12	3	1	14	0	0	15	7	6	1	4.9
Badowal	15	0	1	14	0	1	14	6	4	5	4.3
Manan	4	11	6	9	0	1	14	7	8	0	5.2
Beh Chuhar	15	0	3	12	15	0	0	1	11	4	4.9
Dohar	13	2	9	6	13	1	1	6	5	3	4.9
Simbli	13	2	4	9	1	1	13	6	9	0	5.1
Jassowal	14	1	5	10	3	2	10	4	8	1	4.0
Bhagtupur	15	0	5	10	0	0	15	8	5	2	5.2
Haveli	13	2	1	14	2	2	11	8	5	3	4.9
Mehatpur	15	0	6	9	0	2	13	8	3	4	4.4
Manjpur	13	2	5	10	3	3	9	9	5	1	4.8
Takri	15	0	6	9	6	2	7	5	9	0	3.9
Kaloa	11	4	0	15	0	0	15	5	6	3	3.9
Total	24581.5	5518.4	8127	21973	5819	186	22475	12542	12240	4615	93.7
	%	%	%	%	%	%	%	%	%	%	4.7

Source: Field Survey *Note:* Six job card holders are 12th. One job card holder is MA.

Table 9

Profile of the Panchayat Head and Panchayat Members in the Sampled Villages in Various Block of Hoshiarpur District (Punjab)

		Panchayat Head			Panchayat Members				
					Sex		Caste		
Name of the Block	*Name of the Village*	*Sex*	*Caste*	*Education Level*	*M*	*F*	*GC*	*SC*	*BC*
Dasuya	Kotli Khurd	M	BC	12th	4	2	4	2	0
	KhunKhun Sarki	M	SC	Middle	2	2	2	2	0
Bhunga	Dhakki	F	SC	Middle	3	1	2	2	0
	Nangal Ishar	M	GC	Matric	2	2	2	2	0
Hajipur	Saroa	F	SC	Matric	3	1	3	1	0
	Singhpur	M	SC	Middle	2	2	3	0	1
Hoshiarpur-1	Burey Jattan	F	SC	B A	2	2	1	3	0
	Hardo Khanpur	F	SC	Illiterate	4	4	2	5	1
Hoshiarpur-2	Badowal	M	SC	BA	2	2	0	4	0
	Manan	M	GC	Matric	4	2	2	4	0
Talwara	Beh Chuhar	M	GC	Matric	2	2	4	0	0
	Dohar	M	GC	Matric	2	4	2	1	3

Contd...

Name of the Block	*Name of the Village*	*Panchayat Head*			*Panchayat Members*				
					Sex		*Caste*		
		Sex	*Caste*	*Education Level*	*M*	*F*	*GC*	*SC*	*BC*
Garshankar	Simbli	M	SC	Matric	4	2	4	2	0
	Jassoval	F	SC	Matric	5	1	2	3	1
Mahalpur	Bhagtupur	F	SC	Matric	3	1	1	3	0
	Haveli	F	GC	Matric	4	2	3	2	1
Mukerian	Mehatpur	M	GC	BA	2	2	2	2	0
	Manipur	M	GC	12th	4	2	5	0	1
Tanda	Takri	F	BC	BA	2	2	0	1	3
	Kaloa	M	SC	12th	3	3	2	2	2
TOTAL		M-12 F-08	GC-7 SC-11 BC-02	Middle-3 Matric-9 Twelveth-3 B.A.- 4 Illiterate-1	59	41	46	41	13

Source: Field Survey

Socio-Economic Status of Sampled Job Card Holders

It is clear from table 8 that most of the job card holders are males. In terms of sex ratio, 81.6 per cent job card holders were male and 18.4 per cent were female .With regard to age only 27 per cent were in the age group of 18-35 years and 73 per cent were in the age group of 36-65 years. Table 8 also reveals that 75 per cent of job card holders belonged to scheduled caste where as 19 per cent and 6 per cent belonged to general caste and backward caste, respectively. Amongst 5 sampled villages, 100 per cent card holders belonged to scheduled castes and in one village 100 per cent card holders were from general caste. It is worth mentioning that 42 per cent of the job card holders were illiterate. As regards educational qualification, 40 per cent and 15 per cent job card holders were up to middle and matric level, respectively. The average size of the family was 4.7 persons.

Profile of the Panchayat Head and Panchayat Members

Table 9 presents the social profile of the Panchayat heads and members in all the 20 sampled villages. Out of 20 Panchayat heads (Sarpanches), 12 were males and 8 were females. Further 7,11and 2 were general, scheduled caste and backward caste, respectively. It is significant to note that all the Panchayat heads were educated except 1. 3of them were middle pass, 9 Panchayat heads were qualified up to matric level and 3 Panchayat heads had qualification of 12th standard. It is interesting to note that 4 panchayat heads were having the B.A. degree. In terms of sex ratio, the 59 per cent Panchayat members were male and 41 per cents were females. About 41 per cent Panchayat members were from scheduled caste where as 46 per cent were from general caste. The remaining13 per cent belonged to backward caste.

Summing Up

The study reveals that the performance of NREGS in Punjab has not been very satisfactory. The study also highlights that the performance of NREGS in district Hoshiarpur has not been very encouraging during the last 4 years of its implementation.

Though the Act is an historical intervention by the State, yet much needs to be done beyond that.

Out of the 300 sampled households, who were called for work, only 16 could complete 100 days norms of employment in the district during the last 4 years period. The unemployment allowance was not paid in a single village. Regarding possession of job cards, only 45 per cent households were having their job cards with them whereas 45 per cent job cards were still under the possession of Gram Pradhans Again there was no public notice for availability of employment. The job card holders are called for work by the panchayat head as and when there is work. There was no system to inform the job-card holders for employment. It was pick and choose. Problems concerning opening of account for payment of wages of workers were also found. The other facilities at work place were also missing. There was hardly any social auditing. The commitment on the part of the official machinery was also missing.

The average age of the beneficiaries is 45.5 years. Out of the 300 job card holders 81.6 per cent are males and remaining 18.4 per cent are females. Caste composition of the job card holders shows that 19 per cent belong to general category, 6 per cent to backward caste and 75 per cent to scheduled caste. Further, 87 per cent households are nuclear families, while 13 per cent joint families. An overwhelming proportion of sampled households are landless and small proportions are marginal farmers.

Nevertheless, the programme can be a great agent for socio-economic upliftment and providing livelihood security to the poorest of the poor in rural India, if implemented earnestly. The employment and earnings under NREGA should be treated as additional avenues for such households. The existing rural employment should not be transferred under NREGA. The executing machinery and the beneficiaries under NREGA need to be sensitized about the fundamental objectives of NREGA. The state government must appoint whole time programme officers who must be dedicated, committed and honest persons. There is a need to adopt a holistic approach to fully implement the NREGS.

References

AFDR, Punjab (2000), "Suicides in Rural Punjab: A Report", *Patiala unit of AFDR* is an NGO, namely. Association for Democratic Rights, Punjab.

Bhalla, G.S. and Gurmail Singh (1997), "Recent Developments in Indian Agriculture: A State Level Analysis", *Economic and Political Weekly*, Vol. 32, No. 13, pp. A2-A18.

Bhalla, Sheila (1987), "Trends in Employment in Indian Agriculture, Land and Asset Distribution", *Indian Journal of Agricultural Economics*, Vol. 42, No. 4, October-December, pp. 537-60.

——— (1989), "Employment in Indian Agriculture; Retrospect and Prospect", *Social Scientist*, Vol. 17, No. 5-6, pp. 3-21.

Dey K Debatra "NREGA : A study of West Bengal paper presented in the *Conference on Employment opportunities and Public Employment policy in Globalising India*, Organized by on Employment opportunities CDS during April 3-5,2008.

Ghuman Ranjit Singh and Parvinder kaur "NREGA and Rural Employment in Punjab" Paper presented in the *Conference on Employment opportunities and Public Employment policy in Globalising, India*. Organized by CDS during April 3-5, 2008.

Ghuman, Ranjit Singh (2005), "Rural Non-farm Employment Scenario: Reflections from Recent Data in Punjab", *Economic and Political Weekly*, Vol. 41, No. 41, October 8.

Ghuman, Ranjit Singh, et. al. (2007), Status of Local Agricultural Labour in Punjab, *The Punjab State Farmers Commission*, Government of Punjab, SAS Nagar, Mohali.

Gill, Sucha Singh (2002), "Agriculture, Crop Technology and Employment Generation in Punjab", in S.S. Johl and S.K. Ray (eds.), *Future of Agriculture in Punjab*, CRRID, Chandigarh, pp. 56-68.

Gill, Sucha Singh and Ranjit Singh Ghuman (2001), "Changing Agrarian Relations in India: Some Reflections from Recent Data", *The Indian Journal of Labour Economics*, Vol. 44, No. 4, pp. 809-26.

Goswami Chandrima "A critical analysis of the effectiveness of employment policies in Assam" paper presented in the *Conference on Employment opportunities and Public Employment policy in Globalising India*, Organized by CDS during April 3-5,2008.

Government of India (2002a), *Census of India 2001*, Series 4, Punjab, paper 3 of 2001, *Distribution of Workers and Non-workers*, New Delhi.

Government of India, Ministry of Agriculture (2003), *Agricultural Census: 1995-96*, New Delhi.

Government of India (2008), *Census of India 2001: Workers and Non-Workers*, New Delhi, P. 12.

Jacob Arun (2006)-NREGA "Implementation-1 Reasonable beginning in Palakkad (Kerala)", *Economic & Political Weekly*, 2nd December, Vol. 41, No. 48, pp 4943-4947.

Mukherjee Subrata and Ghost Saswata "What determines the success of 100 days work at Panchyat Level? A study of Birbhum District in West Bengal" paper presented in the *Conference on Employment opportunities and Public Employment policy in Globalising India* Organized by CDS during April 3-5, 2008.

Narayana D et al " Do those who need Employment get it A study of NREGA in a Gram Panchyat in Wayanand Kerala", paper presented in the *Conference on Employment opportunities and Public Employment policy in Globalising India* Organized by CDS during April 3-5,2008.

Narayanan Sudha "Employment Guarantee Women's work and childcare", *Economic and Political Weekly*, March 1 2008,Vol. 43,No. 9, pp. 10-13

Singh, Gurpreet (2008), Farmers Suicides in Punjab: A Socio-Economic Analysis, M.Phil. Dissertation (unpublished), Punjabi University, Patiala.

Yadav Pratima, "Natioinal Rural Employment Guarantee Schemce-2005 An overview of situation in Uttar Pradesh", paper presented in the *Conference on Employment opportunities and Public Employment policy in Globalising India*, Organized by CDS during April 3-5, 2008.

Index

F